Needle

Needle

Craig Jordan Goodman

Printed in the United States of America

Cover art and design by Vince Joy

For David Minter—without whom I would have never thought
this worthy, Theron Raines—without whom I would have never
thought this possible, and Emily—without whom this would
have never been written…or, it would have been written a hell
of a lot faster than it was.

Mostly though, it's for the dogs.

Needle

The events depicted here are **true**. Sometimes, I wish they weren't. That said, certain identifying names, characteristics, dates and places have been changed to protect anonymity. A few individuals are composites, some timelines have been expanded or compressed, and some of the dialogue has been recreated or reconstructed to help support the narrative, and to clarify and illuminate critical aspects of the story.

Needle

Needle

Needle

One

"I don't think this is such a good idea."
"*What's* not such a good idea?"
"It's a lot, Craig."
"Don't worry about it," I told him.
"No way—this is too much."
"That's ridiculous."
"You're gonna be sorry," he said.
"Don't worry about it."
"No, seriously—"
"DON'T WORRY ABOUT IT."
So he didn't…and then I must have vomited on myself.

###

The last thing I recall before the warm, momentary tightness lost its grip on my heart and began creeping upward, was telling Perry to keep his filthy hands away from me. Suddenly, and without provocation, he had lunged at me and my temper flared. After all, I was wearing my nicest shirt. It was silk or black or satin or something, and as he clawed at my finest garment with an outstretched hand I could hear the seams begin to give way. I then remember slapping at his dirty paw until I was finally free to meet fate, headfirst, at the bottom of a staircase.

For exactly how long I lay there, unconscious, on the 17th floor of a Harlem housing project remains a mystery. What I do know is that when I awoke my head had a couple of bumps, my right shoulder was swollen, and my fancy shirt was covered with semidry puke. Perry, however, was nowhere to be found and in his place were a concerned

EMT, a relieved/amused firefighter, a disgusted cop and a few residents who were quite disenchanted by the junky white boy with the nerve to have overdosed in *their* stairwell.

As I gradually came to, the fear of being incarcerated pierced my consciousness along with a dawning awareness as to what had just happened. I already had an outstanding warrant for my arrest, so the last thing I needed right now was to get locked up…*again.*

The old warrant had been issued back in 1995 after I elected not to appear in court. I was supposed to contest a flimsy trespassing charge filed by a cop with a sneaking suspicion that I might not actually be looking for "maintenance work" in the abandoned Harlem brownstone he found me in. In fact, he was so sure that I was up to no good that he also tacked on an *intent to purchase narcotics* charge to better justify an arrest, even though there wasn't a stitch evidence to support the added allegation. The officer was—*of course*—entirely correct in his suspicions, but it was clear to me that he wasn't playing by the rules and so—*neither did I.* Hence, after the court date was ignored, the resulting warrant along with the initial charges would go unaddressed for eight months, as I imposed my own brand of self-serving justice upon a legal system I saw as clearly corrupt.

Upon emerging from the overdose and regaining consciousness in the staircase I made a snap decision. I would use valium as a defense strategy to hopefully avoid arrest, as well as the warrant-driven fallout sure to follow. Valium is a much more socially acceptable drug to abuse, and Perry had already removed any evidence that might expose heroin as the true culprit. I was also fortunate enough to be in the presence of not only a police officer but other municipal employees as well, so as long as I avoided dropping the H-bomb I thought I'd survive without going to jail.

Although the logic behind the valium-defense was sound—its execution was a bit shoddy, and as the cop maneuvered himself to get a better look at me I lost some composure.

"IT WAS THE VALIUM, IT WAS THE VALIUM, IT WAS THE VALIUM!!!" I screamed before anyone even said a *word* to me. **"I SWEAR TO GOD, BROTHA! IT WAS THE FUCKING VALIUM!!!"**

Of course, all parties present—including the cop—knew that nausea is a common side effect of shooting dope, and the vomit-laden shirt and condition they found me in certainly didn't help bolster the defense strategy. In fact, had the firefighter and paramedic *not* been first to arrive, things would have ended up quite differently. Typically, whether in possession of drugs or not, an overly medicated white boy covered in puke and lying in a Harlem stairwell would have been just too much for any blue-blooded New York City police officer to resist. And certainly, unconscious and sprawled out on the stairway floor, it would've been difficult to argue what *now* should be the most rock solid trespassing charge in city history. I was extremely lucky. The worried EMT and relieved firefighter proved to be my saviors as the cop was simply outnumbered by his truly concerned, fellow civil servants.

Score one for the junky.

They sat me atop a gurney, wheeled me to an elevator, and then rolled me out of the building to an ambulance on 124th Street amidst a throng of smiling black faces that seemed to take gleeful satisfaction in the proceedings. Some of the little kids were *actually* dancing.

When I arrived at Metropolitan Hospital the EMT transported me to an emergency room hallway and said, "Whatever you do, promise me you won't leave."

"OK."

That day, about a half-hour after I overdosed, Perry and I were scheduled to meet with Bob Donnelly, music lawyer extraordinaire. Donnelly's list of clients included the Dave Matthews Band, Aerosmith and Def Leppard—just to name a few. Here was a man who could help transform ordinary potential into extraordinary success, and if our band was half as talented, beautiful, and skinny as we thought it was—the sky was absolutely the limit.

Did I mention that our egos were utterly enormous? An egomaniac with a penchant for shooting dope can take that false sense of well being and really run with it. Once addicted to heroin, junkies are bestowed magical, dissociative powers as we see life deteriorate before our very eyes and remain truly unaffected. However, a heroin addict with some sort of talent surrounded by people extolling that virtue is a ticking time bomb. Even without stores of cash and hordes of devoted worshippers, a few sincere words noting unproven greatness is enough to cushion even the most rapid descent to rock-bottom.

Due to the unscheduled overdose, I missed the big meeting with Mr. Donnelly. As a result, I was especially determined not to waste what was left of the day sitting in a hospital just because I insisted on

3

doing a little too much dope. Now able to walk, more or less, I left the medical facility to enjoy what was left of my nod in Central Park and half-consciously thought about nothing for several hours. Life was good again and things were finally back on track, as the setting sun and emerging lights reflected against the metallic mountains and I was gently nudged from my peaceful inner space.

2

Now, the backstory:

In September of 1973 my father died from lung cancer. Later that year, my mother learned that he *and* I had been cheating on her with his secretary, Phyllis. I was only four years old at the time of the infidelity, but as far as Mother was concerned we were partners in crime and the illicit affair was a father/son conspiracy.

I can very clearly recall the moment I had first learned of his passing. It occurred while returning home to Queens after an extended visit with my grandparents in the Bronx. My younger sister, Nicole, and I had been spending a good deal of time there while my mother inconspicuously made funeral arrangements, and as we headed home the question came out of nowhere.

"Mommy…Did Daddy die?"

To this day I have no idea what provoked it, but as I asked the question I remember desperately hoping yet truly expecting her to say, *"Of course not, you silly goose!!! Your Daddy isn't dead—he's just at the office,"* or *"in a meeting,"* or *"on a business trip."* Instead, she simply turned her head and looked back at me for a moment. Then, after pulling the car to the side of the road, in a very calm and all too collected voice she said, "Yes, Craig. Your dad died…but he really, really, loved you a lot."

I hadn't seen him in quite some time, but the possibility that he had died only occurred to me half seriously and literally as I posed the question. Hence, the affirmative answer I received should have elicited *some* outpouring of emotion; however, there wasn't a teardrop in sight or even a follow-up question. Mother just laid it out there as she turned herself around, put the car back in drive, and continued home to Queens.

I didn't attend my father's funeral. I have never visited his gravesite. In fact, *I don't even know where it is.* He was tucked away before I ever knew he was missing.

Without question I was the apple of Daddy's eye, and almost every evening he brought me a gift home from work. From my bedroom I would listen for the bell, and then in a snap—like one of Pavlov's drooling dogs—I'd be at the door to collect my prize. Of course, every so often he'd come home empty handed and I'd be traumatized with disappointment. Although on these rare occasions I'd be smart enough not to publicly display any signs of grief, I clearly recall skulking back to my room and flinging my body across the bed in very dramatic though truly uncontrollable fits of weeping hysteria.

Spoiled-rotten, crybaby-bitch.

Now and then, after considerable begging, he would take me with him to work in Manhattan. His offices were located near the Flatiron Building in a Helmsley property that housed showrooms for the world's leading toy manufacturers. My father was president of a company called Intoport, where after years of fruitless business efforts he'd finally struck it rich manufacturing transistor radios that bore the likenesses of Mickey Mouse and Donald Duck.

My father was one of the first to truly realize the merchandising potential of Disney, and *I* soon realized that going off to work with Daddy could be almost as lucrative, as my four-year-old demeanor and a head full of curly red hair would tug at the heartstrings of young secretaries and toy reps from every corner of the building. The moment we arrived, pretty young women—perhaps trying to quell the steady ticking of maternal clocks—began filing into his office with gifts of product samples for none other than yours truly. I got tremendous mileage out of those curls and apparently, in terms of ass, my father did equally as well.

An afternoon of ice skating at Rockefeller Center with Daddy and Phyllis eventually led to my life-altering confession. Though it resulted in years of retribution, I can only recall this one instance of my father's—I mean *our* infidelity. It stood out not because of where we were or who we were with, but because I clearly remembered his advice:

"Don't tell mommy…It's a *surprise!*"

A surprise? Brilliant!!! A *surprise* would surely guarantee I'd shut my mouth and not ruin all the careful work and thoughtful planning that went into my father fucking his secretary.

Much to his advantage, my father died before my mother became aware of the marital transgression, leaving me alone to carry the brutal baggage for both of us. Then again, I was the one who let the cat out of the bag, so perhaps in some strange way I got just what I deserved.

I made the big disclosure on Christmas Day at the Queens residence of my Aunt Rosie and her family, about three months after my father's death. That fateful evening, as I sat on the kitchen floor with the dog while Aunt Rosie quietly washed the dishes, I suddenly remembered the previous holiday spent with Daddy and Phyllis beneath the gigantic Christmas tree. Then, out of nowhere it all came rushing back:

Oh my gosh…The Surprise! What about the big surprise for Mommy?!?

I was suddenly overcome by the horrible feeling that I might be missing out on something. Everyone knows that "a surprise" calls for cake, candy, and of course—wrapping paper and presents. Now granted, the surprise wasn't for me, but past experience indicated that I would certainly be a beneficiary, and there was just no way in hell I was going to let something as trivial as a dead father stand between me and a good time.

"Aunt Rosie! Aunt Rosie!!!" I shouted with all the passion and excitement the not-so-late-breaking news seemed to warrant. "Guess what!"

"What's that, Craig?" she asked with a big grin.

"Daddy took me ice skating at Rockefeller Center with Phyllis!" I gleefully shouted. "But don't tell Mommy because **IT'S A SURPRISE!!!**"

Aunt Rosie stopped doing the dishes.

"It certainly is," my *mother's* sister agreed.

I don't quite remember the immediate fallout—but there definitely wasn't any cake. Soon afterwards, however, it became clear that due to the confession I'd been branded a co-conspirator and sentenced to a childhood of physical punishment for Daddy's adultery. The notion that given my age, I might not be responsible for my actions—never factored into the equation. As far as Mother was concerned, I knew what was going on and did nothing to prevent it.

3

I would like nothing better than to blame my mother for the drug problems I experienced as a young adult. It would be incredibly easy to manufacture a connection between the daily, physical and emotional abuse she doled out and the poor choices I made later on. Though there definitely were external forces that contributed to my undoing, I would have to say that I *don't* include my mother with that group of factors. If she is a factor in some way, I would consider her to be a subconscious influence—if there even is such a thing.

Ironically, my tendency to categorically reject a dysfunctional childhood as cause for adult dysfunction stems from my mother's attempt to use it to justify her own abhorrent behavior. Years later, she gave me a half-assed apology along with the standard excuses: *it was an inherited cycle; she was slapped around as a child at the hands of her old-school, Italian father (as was he); and the times and norms were different back then.* Her rationalizations sickened me, as I would relive endless nighttime beatings followed by early-morning rehearsals of explanations for the new laceration or bruise.

I remember some nights underestimating her endurance and falling asleep, only to be ripped back into consciousness with a burning smash to the face. Then dazed, I'd run wildly down dark, endless hallways desperately looking for a way out and yet always knowing there wasn't anywhere to go. Mother had conditioned Nicole and me into believing that the moment we tried to escape, she would call the police and we'd be hunted down and cast off to reform school. What exactly "reform school" was nobody seemed to know, but if Mother was threatening us with it then surely it must have been a fate worse than life with her.

Although anywhere from two to five times a week Mother found a reason to beat the crap out of us, the fact that I cheated on her seemed to be the underlying cause—at least as far as *I* was concerned. Her fury might be triggered by a footprint left on the freshly-mopped kitchen floor, or perhaps a few overlooked cookie crumbs; but somewhere in between disciplinary kicks and retributory punches she would usually let me know that she hadn't forgotten The Grand Deception.

Early on, as a survival mechanism designed to deflect

accountability for my father's affair, I told Mother that he had given me a beating to scare me into keeping my mouth shut. It was a complete fabrication, but to some degree it worked. I informed her of the preventative measure he had taken to secure my silence, and in a moment of hilarious hypocrisy she berated and cursed his memory for being not only an adulterer—but a *child abuser* as well. Though the beatings continued on at the same steady pace, my mother never again referred to the past or my previous infidelity. Unfortunately, the real damage was already done. From the moment I accidentally trumpeted our adulterous behavior she destroyed most of his photographs and did everything she could to dissuade me from reflecting on and appreciating the loss. Instead, the only emotion encouraged or openly permitted was born from fatherly resentment, and through a regimen of physical abuse and psychological conditioning she effectively brainwashed me into despising a man who did nothing other than put me on a pedestal.

By 1980 my mother learned she had breast cancer and though she ultimately survived the disease, at the time of her diagnosis she began drinking heavier than usual. This only further escalated her aggressive and dangerous behavior, and since she generally refused to cook we'd usually spend the evening in an expensive restaurant—followed by a drunk and death-defying drive home that occasionally resulted in a collision with someone or something. And on those occasions when she ordered dinner in, or the scant few when she attempted to prepare something, we usually ate in separate rooms with Nicole and me in the kitchen and Mother in the living room. Incidentally, right up until around the time I graduated from high school, Nicole and I weren't even *permitted* in the living room unless it was a major holiday or special occasion. Indeed, living in that apartment was like living in a museum. It was very cold, very tiled, and very beautiful to look at, but you couldn't touch anything and you certainly didn't sit on the couch.

As I entered adolescence, though my father's bigamy became a dot on the horizon of his memory, I finally realized that my mother was completely absurd in blaming me for his affair. However, I also resented my father—not because of my mother's indoctrinations, but for leaving me with this incredible mountain of emotionally charged bullshit to deal with. Sadly, while growing up, I don't think I ever said or thought a nice thing about a man who cherished me beyond words. The posh apartment I lived in, my unrivaled collection of toys, winters in Puerto Rico, summers in Disney World, and for everything else that was good in my life I had my father to thank for his business acumen and the clever investments he made before his death. But in an effort to hijack that appreciation my mother would constantly belittle him and drone on about how *she* selflessly forfeited her own career so he could succeed and ultimately provide us with such lavish surroundings. And though she did little in terms of managing the family's investments even *after* he died, as far as she was concerned we had *her* to thank for everything—not him.

That's really what it all came down to. She thought *she* should get the credit and the moment someone dared acknowledge my father as a thoughtful posthumous provider, she would launch into a self-serving tribute, partially shrouded in the martyrdom of single motherhood, but mostly centered on the limitless generosity she showered her children with. She would go on at length about how she dressed us in the finest clothes and sent us to the most exclusive summer camps. She would commend herself for providing extravagant Christmases and birthdays, and was quick to point out how we almost always got what we wanted which was mostly true. But of course, her generosity only came in the form of bandying my father's money about as this was the sole means by which she measured the depth of her parental commitment, because if it didn't have a price tag—Mother didn't seem to know about it: Though she would gladly pay for little league, she'd rarely drive me to the games and never stay to watch. Though she would bring in fabulous fare from fantastic restaurants, we almost always dined alone. Though we'd usually have our cake, we'd never really get a chance to eat it. And when she did shower us with the fruits of my father's labors it seemed as though she was logging it in a child-rearing ledger of sorts. In fact, sometimes it seemed like our relationship was part of a business agreement, as if she was fulfilling her end of a financial obligation. Even college had been discussed in similar terms several years before I would attend, when I once blurted out that I had no intention of actually going.

"Oh, don't worry about it, Craig—*you're going*," she said in a way that left little room for dissension.

"But I don't want to go to school any longer than I have to."

"It doesn't matter, you're definitely going…and then I'll finally be through with it all."

*Apparently, there'd be no empty-nest syndrome for **my** mama.*

"Well what if I drop out?" I asked with just a hint of indignation.

"You *won't* drop out. But honestly, Craig—what you do when

you get there is *your* business," she said as if sending me to school would signal the fulfillment of her commitment.

It wasn't until junior high school that I met Troy Holst and saw evidence of the family dynamic. Troy and I had hit it off immediately, and for the next several years I'd spend more waking hours in his home than anywhere else. It was there where I witnessed the manifestation of family. It was there where I saw people of the same bloodline watching television together in the living room with their feet on the couch and as if they were all actually there by choice. Of course, it was completely foreign to me—*but I liked it.* There was no drama, no drunks, no wronged and angry widows. There were only home-cooked meals at dinnertime that *everyone* was expected to attend, and holidays when the whole clan would sit around and bask in each other's glow—*while in my family we only went through the motions.*

Troy introduced me to his older brother, Eric, when I was twelve and over the years he'd often play a similar role for me, which, given my particular set of circumstances was an invaluable asset. Although Troy's entire household treated me like extended family, Eric's gestures were especially meaningful and ranged from assisting me with technical school projects to driving me to a few of the little league games my mother chose to sleep through. Although I doubt Eric was ever aware of the impact he had on my life, he would later affect me in ways that I cannot yet begin to describe.

4

I hold no one, besides myself, responsible for my dark and seemingly endless descent into the abyss of heroin addiction. But just for the sake of argument: Let us consider for a moment that I was suffering through a painful bout of retrospection, desperately seeking a way out of accepting accountability for my own poor judgment and the consequences that have followed. If that was, in fact, the case then maybe—just maybe I might point an accusatory finger at...Nancy Reagan.

During the 1980's, the First Lady and wife of our 40th President built her legacy on nothing if not a battle cry as **"JUST SAY NO"** was passionately preached throughout the New York City school system. Three ordinary words—yet with the help of school administrators they were given new life as brightly colored, **JUST SAY NO** posters were plastered in classrooms and cafeterias as if the phrase itself was running for school office. Of course, there were no other candidates to vote for and the posters were never removed, for this was the start of a grueling campaign dedicated to helping us elect a way...*to be*.

Our conditioning was thorough, and its blanketed simplicity left little room for questions as we ate, slept, and **just said no** across the board: *No is good; yes is bad. Negative is positive; positive is negative. In is out; up is down. Don't ask questions, stupid—just say no. Don't try to think for yourself because you'll probably fuck up and say yes, so* **JUST SAY NO**. *All drugs are bad except for the ones that aren't—but take a hit off a joint, man, and you'll definitely go crazy and kill somebody you love. Just like in 'Reefer Madness' dude! It's a true story, you know. Ever see it? No? Well, **you will!!** They'll sit you down in the auditorium and you'll watch people smoke pot, jump out of windows and kill each other. They'll show it to you at the beginning of the semester...in September...**every** September.*

For a while it worked. As a teenager I was firmly against smoking pot or any other drug use for that matter, with the one exception being that of alcohol which I would only occasionally indulge in. Though often unsaid, as long as I didn't overdo it, a little booze every now and again seemed perfectly acceptable to almost everyone around me. In fact, on at least one occasion, even my crazy mother was aware of the fact that I had come home a little drunk but chose to overlook it with a lighthearted chuckle as though it was a rite of passage. But there would be no *real* drugs for me or any of my friends, by God—else they would suffer the lecture. I simply drew the line.

Year after year JUST SAY NO remained the maxim, and though it has assumed a variety of different appearances since its inception, the country's drug education is still riddled with some of the same shortcomings, inconsistencies and misinformation—as well as a lethal lack of understanding when it comes to adolescent psychology. And if there *was* an external factor that contributed to my heroin addiction, it was this very, *ask no questions and just say no* curriculum.

I don't blame marijuana for my troubles with heroin. I don't believe that pot—*in and of itself*—is a "gateway" to harder, more lethal drug use. From an informed perspective, there really is no reasonable segue between taking a few hits off a joint and sticking a needle in your arm, and for me personally—a little honesty and clarification would have gone a lot further than simply being conditioned to JUST SAY NO.

Once I noticed that murdering those nearest and dearest was just about last on my *Things To Do While Stoned* list I began to question the experts. And when I realized that pot was less expensive than alcohol, didn't make me sick or suffer from any hangover-related symptoms, and didn't generate a physical or psychological craving for more I concluded that federal legislation was at least partially driven by special interests. At that point the conspiracy theory was officially set in motion as I decided that JUST SAY NO TO DRUGS, actually meant JUST SAY NO TO *ILLLEGAL* DRUGS. But by exclusion, it apparently also meant JUST SAY YES to alcohol, cigarettes and pharmaceuticals.

During my freshman year at Bethany College in West Virginia I smoked a lot of pot and can honestly say that the only damage I ever did was to a box of Bugles. I never drove into a school bus or got into a barroom brawl when I was stoned. In fact, I recall experiencing nothing other than enjoyable and enlightening moments, except when I was once convinced that my feet were too big for my body.

This period marks a pivotal, yet dangerous point in the formulation of my own, personal, drug policy. It was a policy anchored in unrestricted experimentation, born from an incomplete education, and one which I would mistakenly attempt to share with others. Thankfully, none of those whom I shared my revelations with are still using and again, a little bit of honesty might have made a big difference.

Of course, I now realize it isn't as black and white as I'd originally thought and there are many shades of gray that I completely missed—*but so did Nancy and I feel that hers was the graver transgression.* Had the JUST SAY NO campaign been a little more detailed and informative, and drawn a distinction between marijuana and other drugs like heroin and cocaine—I might not have ended up so determined to uncover the truth for myself.

5

After graduating from Binghamton University in June of 1990, I immediately moved into Manhattan with Helmer. Troy and I had first met Helmer Pelaez in 1983 when his older sister, Virginia, began dating Eric. Eric and Virginia were eventually married, while their siblings and I remained virtually inseparable until we each went off to college in August of 1986.

After a brief, post-collegiate reunion, Troy relocated to Paris and Helmer and I decided to share a small studio apartment on East 80th Street between Central Park and Madison Avenue, literally a stone's throw from the Metropolitan Museum. From there with a degree in hand, I focused on getting my foot in the door of an advertising agency as I thought it might be a good outlet for me. In retrospect, I can see the desire was largely a passionless one. I would eventually secure a position at an agency as a glorified receptionist, but in the meantime I was bartending at Oscar's Chop House on Third Avenue while Helmer was managing The Chess Shop in the West Village.

Oscar's was my first exposure to the strange drama and turbulence that exists within so many New York City restaurants, and where I first met Perry. He was employed there as a waiter at the time, and one evening while I was making a round of drinks he posed a question:

"So what do *you* do?"

"I'm trying to get into advertising," I answered in between Martinis.

"Yeah, sure…but what do you *do*?"

At that time in New York City, especially Manhattan, I would estimate that approximately 90% of all restaurant staffs were comprised of struggling artists schlepping food to pay the bills. They were actors, writers, and musicians mostly—so what he really meant was, *"What would you **like** to do?"*

Professing a desire for a future in advertising was a bit on the sacrilegious side, and yuppie wannabees were often frowned upon by Manhattan waiters, waitresses and bartenders—as the yearning to work for a monolithic corporate entity was somehow offensive to the sensibilities of an artist. Of course, such aspirations were relatively rare in Manhattan restaurants, as the bearers of these less sensational ambitions usually suffered through limited service-industry stints. In fact, aspiring yuppies would often achieve their career goals rapidly and in stark contrast to more artistically inclined co-workers, who would continue doling out burgers until that big break finally arrived—or they got too old, too tired, or were simply beaten down by rejection. But regardless, Perry didn't seem to believe my answer, or it was insufficient in some other way.

"Well I mean, do you write or sing or anything?" he pressed.

I could have, and probably should have said "No" and it might very well have ended there. But in college I *had*, in fact, written quite a few songs with a fellow student named Matthew Anson, and tentative plans had been made to record a demo tape. I say "tentative" because for quite a while I harbored an incredible reluctance to include myself in the legions of starving artists that saturated the city. Although I actually defined myself through the songs I was writing and felt that Matt was about the greatest guitarist I'd ever heard, at least in the beginning I simply refused to cater to any unrealistic aspirations of fame and fortune. As far as I was concerned, I was bartending because I couldn't pound out 60 words-per-minute and hadn't yet come up with a way to cheat on the typing test. At this juncture music was only something that I *might* dabble in on the side, just to see what *might* happen.

"Well actually," I said, "I wrote a bunch of songs with a guy at school. Eventually we might try to record them."

That was all I needed to say. From that point on, without hearing any of the music, Perry continued to push the matter until he somehow got me to take it and him seriously.

Perry Ward was an interesting fellow. In fact, "Perry" is actually short for Paris, and for some reason I've always found that vaguely obnoxious. Already once married and divorced, he had first relocated to Ohio after fleeing his childhood home in Florida. It was in Florida where his mother, Felicia, was able to leave him with his grandparents—but only on the condition that she waive her parental rights and allow him to be adopted by them. This permitted Felicia to relocate to New York and pursue her dream of becoming an actress, while still being able to maintain some semblance of a relationship, albeit a distant one, with her son. And then, like his mother, Paris Ward eventually made his way to the big city to become a star.

6

Using heroin for the first time that summer was a complete accident. I swear. It was ultimately fated one evening when Perry's girlfriend, Shannon Whirry—the now, well known erotic movie maven—decided not to go grocery shopping and instead order dinner in. Had she gone shopping and been absent during the critical communication I might never have tried heroin. But she didn't, she wasn't, and I did. It was all pure chance, right from the very beginning.

That same day Troy was back in town and to commemorate his return, I was bound and determined to score a bag of weed. At the time, however, this was easier said than done as Washington Square Park had been overrun by a crew of morally bankrupt drug dealers peddling oregano and I no longer had a reliable source. Fortunately, I thought Perry would be able to help with the search even though, perhaps ironically, Shannon was a tad on the puritanical side. Even *cigarette* smoking was frowned upon and Perry had abandoned both habits to ensure unfettered booby access. *The man did have his priorities.* Regardless, I picked up the phone and called to ask if he knew where I could get my hands on a bag of dope.

"A bag of what?!?" he replied, sounding more than a bit surprised by my question.

"Dope!" I responded impatiently. "Can you get any?"

"Wait a minute... What do you mean?"

I tried to be more specific:

"Hey moron, I wanna get high!"

"Yeah, Craig. I *know*... but I'm not sure what you mean. Say it again."

At that point I realized my friend was apparently unable to speak freely. Shannon would obviously disapprove of Perry being involved in a drug transaction, and based on the way he was behaving I assumed she was in close proximity. What I didn't understand was why my friend should have suddenly become stupid. My question was a fairly pointed one, requiring nothing more than a yea or a nay.

"Listen. I don't know what your problem is, but Troy's in town and I wanna get fucked up. Pick up a bag of dope if you can find one and come over. Goodbye."

A few hours later he showed up.

Though my open-minded attitude and opinions regarding illegal drug use should have quelled any shock to my system, seeing heroin for the first time made a significant impact. Even I'd considered that this might be the one drug to avoid, and my renegade experimentalism and impenetrable cockiness couldn't prevent me from stepping back for a moment.

"ARE YOU FUCKING CRAZY?!?" I shouted as he presented me with a tiny, folded, glassine envelope. "You know, Perry, I ask you to do a simple thing and you fuck it all up! All I wanted was some dope!!"

"Heroin *is* dope," he pointed out.

(Oh)

Alas, my real-life drug education was finally afoot.

"Don't worry about it. I knew you were a little confused, so I also picked up a bag of weed—*just in case,*" he added, impressed with himself for covering all the bases.

Ignoring his resourcefulness I went on a mini-tirade:

"WHAT THE FUCK WERE YOU THINKING!!!? THIS SHIT IS DEADLY, MAN, DEADLY! WHADDAYA THINK ALL THE STREET URCHINS ARE STRUNG OUT ON?!! CHRIST, PERRY!! I CAN'T EVEN **BELIEVE** YOU BROUGHT THIS SHIT INTO MY APARTMENT!!! ISN'T MY LIFE FUCKED UP ENOUGH ALREADY???! WELL??!! ISN'T IT?!!!... OK, give me some."

Don't get me wrong. I was totally shocked and even a little horrified at the sight of a bag of heroin sitting on my coffee table. That's the truth. In fact, my first impulse was to throw it away and light up a joint. But then, somewhere in the back of my mind I was thinking, *When the fuck am I ever gonna see **this** shit again?*

Perry emptied the contents of the little bag on to a notebook. It seemed paltry. He then divided the powder into two lines. Before I had a chance to ask him how to smoke it he rolled-up a dollar bill and snorted a line. I later learned that this was hardly Perry's maiden voyage down heroin alley. Although I didn't know it at the time, Perry—almost three years my senior—had dabbled with the drug before in California, though supposedly not for any significant length of time.

After he finished his line it was my turn. I had never snorted anything before, but I lowered my head and inhaled deeply. The heroin burned my nasal passages and tasted like shit, and at first I didn't feel anything other than a craving for nicotine. The closest place to buy cigarettes at that hour was from a machine at the Madison Pub, so we left my apartment and made our way to the little bar near the corner of 80th Street. Literally, as I opened the door to the establishment I began to feel the effects of the heroin.

Ah yes, here it comes now—that false sense of well being I've heard so much about.

A euphoric transformation came over me that began in my head and crept downward to the very tips of my toes. I liked it. I liked it *a lot*. Of course, this was only the tip of the iceberg as the metamorphosis would eventually prove itself to be much more consuming and enduring than I had at first realized.

7

I met Matthew Anson during my freshman year at Bethany College. He was from the Bronx and had been dating my friend, Maggie, whom I had a crush on. Of course, Maggie did have eleven toes—but that wasn't the only reason I loved her. Regardless, my feelings went unrequited; however, I did eventually spark-up a friendship with Matt and we continued to stay in touch even after I transferred to Binghamton.

Matt was an incredibly gifted guitarist. His riffs and chord progressions were infectious, and I credit his greatness as the catalyst for helping me discover my own talent. Although my guitar playing remained limited, I realized it could completely stagnate as long as Matt continued to crank out the grooves. As a result, I mainly restricted myself to lyrics and lyrical melodies which were areas I seemed to excel in.

Giving in to Perry's unbridled enthusiasm and to a certain degree, allowing him to infect *me* with it, I finally arranged for the three of us to meet at my apartment during the middle of August. After Matt and I ran through a few of our old songs, Perry's enthusiasm became greater than ever and the three of us decided to make a go of it. From that moment on, Perry's reaction to the music and belief that he was in on something truly special remained the driving force in the band. He was sure he'd hitched his wagon to a galactic train, bound for places that neither he—nor even his mother had ever dreamed of. In a way he was right.

This moment also marked Matt's virgin experience with heroin. Matt, however, was hardly a novice to the world of illicit drugs, and asking him if he'd be interested in a snort of dope was like asking Popeye about a spoonful of spinach. He showed no hesitation whatsoever, snorting not only his allotted line but *accidentally* inhaling most of what was left for us. It never mattered what the drug was; if it was going to fuck him up, Matt wanted as much as he could get his hands on without getting his ass kicked.

Prior to this point, shared drug experiences with Matt were limited to beer and pot. But in reality Matt was a multi-drug abuser, even as a teen living under the despotic rule of his father—Detective Ernie Anson—who had been a member of the NYPD for close to 30 years. As a result, a significant portion of his life had revolved around doing drugs, getting caught by his father, and then getting the shit beaten out of him…over and over again, and it never really changed until he finally left for Bethany. Until then, no matter how many times the man pounded him, Matt would always live another day to do another drug. It was a standoff: Matt wouldn't stop doing drugs, and The Good Detective wouldn't stop kicking his ass. So yeah, Matt was OK with giving dope a shot, especially with his father safely tucked away in the Bronx.

Though I am less certain of Matt, at this juncture neither Perry nor I was addicted to anything. Heroin was still, at best, only a once-a-month diversion. But from almost the very beginning I found myself rationalizing it's occasional, *controlled* use in what is sometimes known as the "honeymoon period." During this preliminary stage of my addiction, a psychological component of the dependency began to take root as the opiate seemed to market itself as—like alcohol—just another drug and perhaps even a victim of bad press. As a matter of fact, in *comparison* to alcohol, a dope-fueled inebriation actually seemed preferable. It was certainly cheaper. For ten bucks I was good to go all night with no hangover and nothing to complain about beyond a little bit of nausea. Ultimately though, even this discomfort would dissipate as my body became more accustomed to the heroin.

I'd finally found my drug of choice and the only drawback I

noticed was sleep deprivation. However, it wasn't a miserable, cocaine or acid-like alertness where one remains wired and awake solely due to the subsiding effects of the drug. Instead, a sleepless slumber seemed almost self-inflicted as a necessary component to fully enjoying the high, regardless of the phase of intoxication. Of course, to the casual observer, an addict under the influence of heroin may—in fact—appear to be asleep, passed-out, or dead. But in reality, he is likely lingering somewhere between consciousness and unconsciousness in what junkies refer to as a "nod." There, while his ears halfheartedly monitor the land of the living—his mind, body and spirit have already embarked upon a journey to another side.

8

As I've already mentioned, during the early days while I was still living with Helmer on 80th Street—no one was addicted to anything. *Real* heroin addiction doesn't come that easily, and it's far too sneaky and seductive to pinpoint when dependency actually begins. As a matter of fact, you're never totally sure about it until your addiction has gone full throttle and certain body fluids begin flowing from completely unauthorized areas.

Personally, it took at least a year of increasing abuse before I realized I might be in trouble. During that first year, however, as far as I was concerned we were all just Weekend Warriors, perhaps of a more extreme variety. But after trying and welcoming heroin into my life there was really nothing left to be shocked by. As a result cocaine, marijuana, PCP, acid, mescaline, mushrooms and pharmaceuticals would all eventually be in play and potential catalysts for a good time. In fact, I would end up trying most of those drugs for the first time in September of 1990, and one afternoon that reckless month of experimentation ventured in yet another direction as Perry and Matt appeared at my apartment with not only heroin, but *crack*-cocaine as well.

Thinking ahead, Perry suggested that we first snort the dope in order to fend off the inevitable coke crash and I couldn't have agreed more. This would be my second exposure to cocaine as Matt had recently introduced me to the powdered variety, and though I was mostly ambivalent about that first experience I definitely hated the crash. Along with a sleepless night, I could recall a vague sense of depression that engulfed me as the drug exited my bloodstream, and obsessively grinding and clenching my teeth in response to what felt like a billion nicotine fits at once. As a result, I immediately decided that if I was ever to indulge in cocaine again, the sedating effects of a bag of heroin would also be required to offset its less appealing aspects. Of course, to truly appreciate the combined effects of the drugs, one must administer them simultaneously *and* intravenously; however, I was years away from this revelation and the thought of using a needle was still out of the question. I simply drew the line.

Incidentally, I have simply drawn the line on several occasions:

June, 1986: "Well, maybe I drink, but at least I don't smoke pot."
In November of 1986 I took a hit off a joint during a freshmen mixer at Bethany.

December, 1987: "OK. So I drink and smoke pot…but that's it."
In March of 1988 while studying in London, I smoked hash with a guy from Iowa.

November, 1988: "I party a little bit here and there, but I'll never touch anything like acid, mushrooms or mescaline.
Touched acid, mushrooms and mescaline in September of 1990.

May, 1989: "Don't worry about pot-smoking. Trust me. It's those fucking cigarettes that'll kill you."
Developed a taste for Camel Lights by July of 1990.

June, 1989: "You know… It's all a bunch of crap. Pot, hash, and even some of the hallucinogens are OK as long as you know the source. But you should definitely avoid cocaine and heroin."
Consistently failed to avoid cocaine and heroin throughout most of the 1990's.

February, 1998: "All right, **FINE**! I completely fucked up my life and wasted a lot of time. But at least I never got anyone pregnant."

Savannah Nicole, born November 27th, 1998.

Matt was the first to smoke crack that evening. Perry, who had evidently torched a few rocks in the past, loaded a tubular glass crackpipe—known as a "stem"—with a soft, almost soapy-white substance. Then, after a few directions Matt went at it. With Perry controlling the lighter, he took a long, patient drag. *The stem crackled.* Then, as Matt withdrew slowly and exhaled, his eyes lit up and his bottom jaw dropped as though he was suddenly aboard a roller coaster in the midst of its final, climactic, descent.

"Oh boy, oh boy, oh boy, oh boy, oh boy!" he uttered in rapid-fire repetition. Then, after about 30 seconds he slumped down on the futon.

It was my turn. With some hesitation I grabbed a freshly loaded stem and again, Perry manipulated the flame. I inhaled, held my smoke, and immediately knew I was putting my body through some really awful shit. The very next moment I felt as though I'd been pushed out of an airplane.

I was immediately addicted.

A minute after the pipe left my lips I wanted another blast, and the intense yearning continued until well after I finished my share. Even with the heroin racing through my system and battling against the wretched craving, I wanted more crack and would've sucked a dick to get it had the dope not fully begun to settle into my brain. Once again, I realized the importance of having a bag of heroin at the ready before delighting in any cocaine-related products.

That month of September in 1990 was rife with several examples of poor decision making which would only worsen in time. In fact, the next would occur only three days after my introduction to crack cocaine, while Perry, Matt, and I were working on a crude demo tape at the apartment. With the intoxicating assistance of some weed and whiskey, work progressed at a fair pace until Helmer returned from The Chess Shop. Somehow, a conversation then erupted about angel dust—the street name for PCP—and that was all it took. Without hesitation we jumped into Helmer's jeep and headed to Harlem on a blind quest for the drug without the assistance of Perry, who suddenly felt a stiff penis and the need to convene with Shannon.

As darkness fell, we combed the avenues looking for angel dust and were eventually directed to the corner of 122nd Street and Third

Avenue, where Helmer was certain a group of black guys would only be too happy to help us exploit their shithole-neighborhood for drugs. However, he no sooner stepped out of the jeep, from across the avenue the oldest of the bunch shouted, "Whatchoo white boys want?!" in not exactly the most hospitable tone, and failing to notice Helmer's deep tan and South American lineage.

Without wanting to openly expose the true nature of our mission, Helmer acknowledged the man's inquiry with a subtle wave and continued silently in his direction.

"Hey bro," he said as he got within a few feet. "You wouldn't happen to know where I could find some PCP?"

"You muthafuckin white boys!" the black man shouted with pointed agitation while once again ignoring the fairly obvious. "You got some fuckin' nerve comin' all up in here with your nice car and shit askin' niggas for drugs. I don't know nothin' about no fuckin' PCP! You muthafuckin crackas better go back downtown before somebody fucks ya'll up."

From the very beginning this seemed like an ill-advised method by which a "white boy" should go about procuring drugs in Harlem, and I was seriously wishing that Perry could've ignored his raging hard-on long enough to have handled things differently. But to my amazement, in no time at all a black kid in a denim jacket appeared with a piece of folded tinfoil in his hand. Helmer gave him $40 in exchange for the packet and then returned to the car.

After repositioning himself in the driver's seat, Helmer opened the foil and exposed a little pocket of crushed green leaves.

"What the fuck is this shit!" he bellowed.

Although none of us had any idea what angel dust looked like—Helmer was certain that this wasn't it. Without saying a word to anyone, he jumped out of the jeep and proceeded to strike fear in the hearts of its passengers. But first, a little bit about Helmer:

Hands down and no question about it, Helmer was and still is the single greatest bullshitter I've ever known. In fact, I've seen him talk his way in and out of situations with the greatest of ease, on far too many occasions to mention here. However, at about 5 foot 8 Helmer was never an aggressive bullshitter and always knew his limitations. So I don't know whether it was his Colombian heritage that made him think he had street creds, or the enormous penis he dragged around that made him feel somehow in league with the brothas, but whatever it was—when he jumped out of the jeep and started screaming,

"WHERE'S THE LITTLE BITCH THAT SOLD ME THE FUCKING BULLSHIT!!!" I thought we were dead already.

Matt and I sat there in the jeep watching in horror and disbelief. No one moved. *No one even breathed.* Yes, Helmer may have been King Of All Bullshitters—but this here was *Russian Roulette* bullshitting.

"You gotta muthafuckin problem there, *whitey*?!" the old black man bellowed at Helmer, though by now I was beginning to think that the racial misnomer was intended.

Helmer regained his composure, displayed an exaggerated grin, and after taking a few steps toward the street corner where the infraction occurred, went on to loudly disclose his recent findings with the community at large:

"You know…you can never trust a filthy fucking nigger."

That time I actually wet my pants.

"Especially not in the middle of fucking, stink-ass Harlem," he actually went on.

"Whatchoo say, cracka muthafucka?!" asked one of the other brothas as he menacingly walked toward the jeep with a brick in his hand.

*Yes, Helmer!!! What **did** you say? What the fuck did you just say!?!?!!*

We knew better than *that.* We'd been weaned on the civil rights era and the sanctity of Martin Luther King, spoon-fed the horrors of slavery as well as a distant sense of accountability, and didn't even use the "N-Word" in *private*, let alone in the midst of a drug deal gone haywire in Harlem.

"Time to go, Helmer!!!" I pointed out while inconspicuously taking the driver's seat.

With trembling limbs I managed to release the brake and engage the clutch as Helmer headed back to the jeep where now—two, terrified, teenage girls desperately awaited his return.

"Where's my fucking gun?!" he suddenly shouted while holding out his hand as if we were supposed to play along.

"I don't know!" Matt wept.

Without another word Helmer suddenly dove into the backseat, and though I think I had the tires squealing before he even landed, I noticed a brick come sailing past the windshield.

As the jeep began fishtailing up Third Avenue all three of us remained silent, and with the exception of pounding hearts and a groaning engine not a sound was heard. At 125th Street we then made a left turn and eventually headed south on Park Avenue as I slowly came to terms with what had just happened.

While replaying the incident in my mind I peered into the rearview mirror and noticed Matt with his head in his hands, though I think the sobbing had finally subsided. Helmer, however, seemed to be captured by the exhilaration of the moment, and as he sat there panting with an almost euphorically-relieved expression on his face, he reminded me of a man who'd just cheated death.

9

"What sort of people live about here?"

"In that direction," the cat said waving its right paw around, "lives a Hatter; and in that direction," waving the other paw, "lives a March Hare. Visit either one you want: they're both mad."

"But I don't want to go among mad people."

"Oh, you can't help that," said the cat. "We're all mad here. I'm mad. You're mad."

"How do you know I'm mad?"

"You must be," said the cat, "or you wouldn't have come here."

We were Weekend Warriors to say the least, especially during that month of September.

Helmer's enormous dick and apparently, balls to match, had somehow gotten us through the PCP fiasco in Harlem without getting killed. Interestingly enough, the next day Perry's description of angel dust more or less resembled what we ended up with that night, but thinking it was bogus Helmer had thrown it out of the jeep somewhere along Park Avenue.

On literally the following weekend, Alan Grier, a good friend of mine from as far back as junior high school, decided to take the train into Manhattan and surprise me with a visit. I hadn't seen Alan for some time and learned that he'd become a social worker in Nassau County. For about an hour he filled me in on the gory career details and I could sense he was less than thrilled with how his post-collegiate career was shaping up.

"This black fucking bitch actually spit in my face," he told me.

"What the fuck for?!"

"She thought I was cheating her out of money."

"That's totally fucked up."

"I need something else," he lamented. "I'm only 22 and I feel like life is passing me by."

"Well, we're looking for a drummer," I said with a chuckle.

"Hey! I've played the drums before," he informed me, somewhat offended by my laughter.

"Really?" I asked as he eagerly nodded. "Cool. Then let's get you a kit."

Alan was a great guy and had I known he played the drums, I would have asked him to join the band months ago. He'd never mentioned his drumming before, so I assumed he wasn't going to blow anyone away; however, I've always believed that the basic skills required to play most instruments were grossly exaggerated. I'd become a passable guitarist in about a week and was of the opinion that if you could dance—or at least keep a beat—you could learn to play almost anything. So, with Helmer, Perry, and Matt in tow we headed to Sam Ash and Alan purchased a basic drum kit to get started.

When we returned to the apartment and assembled the drums, there were problems. Apparently, Alan couldn't dance...*or keep a beat to save his life.* So we wrapped things up, smoked a joint, and decided to spend what was left of the day in Central Park.

The afternoon wore on and eventually, Perry and Matt disappeared. A few minutes later, as I helped Alan come to terms with the death of his music career, Helmer nudged my shoulder.

"That guy said he has mescaline," he told me while gesturing to a portly Hispanic male wearing red shorts, a white shirt, and standing by the rollerbladers.

"Right," I said doubtfully.

Buying drugs here was risky, but not necessarily from a law enforcement standpoint as Central Park—like 42nd Street—had always been a haven for drug dealers peddling fake drugs.

"He's not straight," I said dismissively.

"Uhhh, I beg to differ with you on that," Helmer responded.

After several minutes I saw his point. One trait common to all bogus drug dealers is that they're constantly on the move. You'll seldom see them lingering in any one location for more than a few seconds, else they risk a serious beating from a victimized buyer, not to mention a legitimate dealer. This guy, however, was stationary...*and* smiling. Helmer went over to where he was standing and within a minute or two, money was changing hands. He then returned, sat down, and displayed a plastic cigarette-pack wrapper containing three orange pills. Helmer swallowed his and then handed me one of the others. Alan was offered the remaining pill but declined, and as he was bombarded with vaginal references for not participating, I placed mine under my tongue. Slowly, it became the consistency of wet bread and then dissolved completely as we waited to feel the effects.

Within a half-hour, I wasn't quite tripping but had noticed the clouds above the skyline seemed richer and thicker. The grass beneath me seemed greener. In fact, everything seemed infinitely more beautiful than it was previously—including the drug dealer, who remained in virtually the same position he was when Helmer made the purchase. However, he was now not only smiling—but looking directly at me. As I stared back I could hear him thinking:

*"I know you're fucked up. I know **you** know you're fucked up. And I know you know **I** know you're fucked up. "*

We returned to the apartment while we still had some idea of what was going on. Alan sat on the bed and amused himself while Helmer and I became transfixed by nothing. Although I had never tried mescaline before, it was already my preferred brand of hallucinogen. Everything around me appeared more vivid, and my thoughts were much less chaotic than what I remembered experiencing with similar drugs.

As the apartment grew darker with the setting sun, we continued to remain within ourselves. Then at some point the phone rang:

It was Troy calling from Paris.

He and Helmer spoke for a moment or two as I suddenly felt the need to be alone. Given the dimensions of the studio apartment I was left with no option other than to retire to my closet.

I entered the closet and sat atop a dirty pile of laundry in almost complete darkness. With the door shut, the little alcove was restricted to only residual light emanating from the kitchen, and the dull glow made my winter jacket barely perceptible as it hung ten inches from my nose.

I stared at the sleeve of the jacket and heard Helmer drone on in the background. As he continued his conversation with Troy, a metamorphosis began to take place in the tiny closet. The jacket's left sleeve was rather quickly transforming itself into what appeared to be the profile of a cow. She was a beautiful cow, perhaps the most beautiful I'd ever seen. She had a sad little eye that looked around as if she was confused, suddenly finding herself alone in the closet with me.

The beautiful bovine then turned into something vaguely sinister, as her head became a platform of eyes that were each independently searching for something. For what seemed like hours the eyes scanned the darkness in angry desperation, and then slowly dissolved into the black background until just two remained. Suddenly, the greater part of a face began to materialize around the two intense eyes until it finally formed the countenance of a crazed monkey. It stared at me, angrily snapping its jaws in mechanical repetition like one of those symbol-clanging, toy simians.

As this appeared to be the onset of a bad trip, I left the closet. I then grabbed Helmer, interrupted his conversation with Troy and whispered, "Enter the closet, brother...*and become truly enlightened.*"

I knew there'd be no way he could refuse an invitation like that. He immediately dropped the phone and entered the closet seeking divine truth and understanding amidst my dirty socks and underwear.

I carried on the conversation with Troy for some time discussing the monkey, until Helmer finally exited the closet mentioning something about The Cheshire Cat. Meanwhile, Alan was growing a bit restless and suggested that we head out for some munchies. I had absolutely no interest in eating, but decided to accompany him since Helmer was determined to remain indoors and wax philosophical about the cat.

We ended up at a bodega on 79th Street and Lexington Avenue. Once inside, Alan stumbled upon a large bag of Cool Ranch Doritos but reacted as if he'd just uncovered the Dead Sea Scrolls.

"Dude! They've got Cool Ranch! **CHECK THIS SHIT OUT!!!**" he bellowed.

Now, by nature Alan was a little odd, but then again—we all were. However, his reaction to the bag of chips was a bit troubling, especially since he was supposed to be the one who *wasn't* tripping.

"I can't **believe** they have Cool Ranch," he continued.

"Cool-Fucking-Ranch! Unbelievable! There-is-only-one-true-chip-and-its-name-is-Cool Ranch. All praises be to the Cool Ranch."

The store's Asian proprietor was clearly becoming uncomfortable, and I once again saw all the signs of a bad trip developing. Then, as Alan stood in the middle of the store looking for Cool Ranch disciples to lead to the Promised Land, I noticed the blue bag of Doritos was beginning to undulate. Unfortunately, Alan seemed not to notice and instead went on extolling the virtues of this noble snack chip.

"Craig—you know Cool Ranch rules, right?!?"

I couldn't answer him. I was transfixed by the bag of chips which continued to bend with successive waves in alternate patterns and directions. However, as Alan patiently awaited my response, I realized that the bag of Doritos was now not only undulating—but also growing in dimension. Suddenly, the printed words, "Cool Ranch" sprung toward me in a menacing, holographic fashion—and then completely detached themselves from the bag. They lingered in the air for a moment and soon began encircling Alan, almost as if they were laying claim to him.

"Yo dude, what's wrong with you?" he asked.

"I can't talk right now."

The bag of Doritos was clearly attempting to exploit my friend's complete and utter devotion to it by stealing away his very life force to accomplish its own evil agenda. Yes...that sounded about right, but it was just too much for me to deal with. I dropped my juice box and ran out into the street.

I headed back in the direction of the apartment, and as a calm began to settle over me I thought it might be nice to finish up the trip in Central Park. Within minutes I arrived at the park and sat myself down on one of the benches that lined its perimeter. It was close to 11 p.m., so foot traffic was limited. I stared out into the darkness for a moment and could tell my trip was winding down.

After a few minutes passed, a well dressed older man approached me and introduced himself. Without much delay, and after about 30 seconds of small talk he said, "Hey, buddy—my wife's on a business trip. Not for nothin', but uhhh...You wouldn't be interested in giving me a blowjob—would ya?"

Not for nothin'? What the fuck does *that* mean?! And what an incredible buzz-kill.

28

Personally, I have nothing against homosexuals. People have no control over their sexual orientations and I am a steadfast supporter of the 'live and let live' sentiment. I truly believe what goes on amongst two consenting adults is nobody else's business, and I have many gay friends that are near and dear to me. In fact, with the notable exceptions of sucking dick and getting fucked in the ass, I find that I generally have a great deal more in common with gay men than straight. Nonetheless, the idea of putting a penis in my own mouth is a bit difficult to swallow, and when confronted with the question I simply raised a hand and looked away as if to shield myself from the very notion. He must have sensed my discomfort:

"You know," he said. "I *am* married and I do love my wife. But every now and then I need a little something else. Trust me, in the long run—it's makes for a healthier relationship."

This kept getting better. He now seemed to think that my disgust with his request stemmed solely from the adulterous nature of his yearnings. Apparently, the whole part about his dick being in my mouth was a nonissue. The important thing to understand was that by sucking him off, *I'd be helping his marriage.*

I thought I was going to retch. Again, I'm not gay, but that's beside the point. I was still feeling the mescaline and if ever there was a surefire recipe for a bad trip, this was it. Without saying a word, I stood up and started back in the direction of my apartment, disappointed that the experience had to end on such a disturbing note. Then, as I left the park I heard in the distance, "Hey!!! My wife cheats on me too, you know!!"

10

I would say that between 1990 and 1996, I worked for no less than twelve New York City employers. Among those twelve fortunate employers, ten were restaurants and about half of them would ultimately end our respective relationships. Regarding the other half, I would be the one to sever ties. Either way, this is obviously not a very good track record; however, contrary to the most popular and educated guess—my inability to remain employed by a single restaurant for any length of time *rarely* had anything to do with drugs.

Generally speaking, no one ever knew I was a junky unless I decided to share that information and I rarely did. Of course, my policy of nondisclosure absolutely included the workplace as I didn't discuss my extracurricular activities with co-workers, nor did I ever list them as hobbies or interests on any job application. Therefore, although I really hate to disappoint the JUST SAY NO contingent, the cause of my employment woes had less to do with drugs, and more to do with a unique dynamic that exists within New York City restaurants:

> Manhattan restaurant managers play a vital role in a system that reciprocally and simultaneously supports the city's hospitality *and* entertainment industries. In such a capacity, management can not only impact their employees' job performance, but also their ability to pursue more passionate and artistic aspirations. This is significant because many of these same, Manhattan restaurant managers are *the biggest bunch of motherfucking assholes one could ever have the unfortunate experience of working for.*

There…I said it.

Some of the wretched are even former actor/waiters who, no longer able to endure the seemingly endless parade of bitter disappointments, have decided to give up on their dreams. However, rather than seek out a new and perhaps more attainable career path, they remain stationary—languishing over what *could* have been. And, if they languish long enough, they'll get a chance to sell their souls to the devil in exchange for a management position, a few benefits, and a bit of authority. At this point a downward spiral ensues as they begin to observe life on the periphery. Eventually, with the taunting assistance of schedule requests that prioritize auditions and callbacks over hotdogs and hamburgers these souls can become lost and embittered, and after realizing they're stuck in a dead-end job earning less than the waiters they've been terrorizing they're almost unsalvageable.

On October 5th I uncovered a plot hatched by Oscar's evening manager, Eli Stanton, to do away with me at his earliest convenience. I was informed of this tidbit by Robert, a waiter, who had become aware of Stanton's intentions earlier that day.

"Oooh, baby. Better watch out! Eli's gettin' ready to fire your ass," he said to me as I clocked-in.

"Where'd you hear that?"

"Where you think? From that ugly bitch's mouth."

Robert was black and gay and as such, the ugly bitch to whom he was referring was none other than Eli himself.

Eli wasn't due for an hour, which left me time to mull over exactly how I wanted to handle the situation. I was the only bartender scheduled that night, so I knew that my termination would have to wait at least until the shift concluded. One thing I was certain of, however, was that my departure from Oscar's would hardly be inconspicuous. I hated the restaurant, hated the job, and most of all—hated Eli Stanton.

A casual observer might deduce that Eli's job was two-fold. First of all, he was to closely monitor the status of each and every glass on or around the bar. Then, the moment he noticed that one of them was empty he'd snap into action. *"Get that fucking glass off the bar,"* he would bark. Sometimes, just as a customer was finishing off a drink, Eli's uncanny ability to detect its ever-changing state of fullness would kick-in and he'd immediately point out the offending glass.

Beyond that annoyance, Eli sickened me on a daily basis as he would sit at the bar for hours scratching his dirty head. His scalp was apparently so dry that you could actually *hear* his fingernails raking up the crusty matter that lay hidden beneath his hairline. With each passing itch and irritation came a scratch, and then a little blizzard of dandruff would fall from his head and cascade down to the surface of my bar. At first, mortified with every passing squall, I would use a rag to clear away the accumulation. I thought that by continuously removing the biological debris he would eventually get the hint, and either take the hygienic steps necessary to correct the problem—or at least get the fuck away from me. But neither happened and I soon realized that it would be wiser to resist shoveling until the rancid weather system had completely moved out of the area.

My last shift at Oscar's ended up being the busiest of all. At one point, Eli must have felt a greater sense of purpose than ever before as not one, not two, but three empty martini glasses rested on the bar. Of course, he immediately made me aware of them, but being inundated with drink orders and a bar full of drunken assholes made it impossible to correct the situation.

31

Often, during times of volume-driven crisis, many restaurant managers are notorious for retiring to their peaceful back offices—rather than assisting their overwhelmed employees. But Eli was not one to be intimidated by hordes of thirsty customers, and when he detected an unprecedented fourth empty glass sitting on the bar—he met the challenge head on.

"Hey asshole!" he yelled at me. "I thought I told you to get those fucking glasses off the bar!"

"You got it," I said, and then slapped the empty glasses onto the floor before walking out of the restaurant forever. Obviously, I knew I wouldn't be able to cope with that type of environment and would have to find another way to chase the buck. Besides, I was supposed to be a *professional*.

11

Regardless of the excitement and anticipation for rock & roll glory, I was still extremely reluctant to embrace eventual success as a forgone conclusion. Fortunately, less than a week after fleeing Oscar's I'd landed a job as a secretary/receptionist for Archer Advertising and believe it or not, The Good Detective secured Matt a position as a special education teacher in the Bronx. Honestly though, it happened to be the only teaching position Matt was qualified for as he would be instructing a group of students whose educational expectation was actually *less* than he was equipped to deliver.

After getting hired at Archer I met Gail Garcia. Gail was vacating the position for which I had just been hired, and would be acquainting me with the daily tasks I'd now be responsible for completing. The job was absolutely dismal, but I liked Gail and we soon began dating. Though originally from Cuba, Gail was raised in Miami and had moved to New York in 1990 after graduating from the University of Florida. She wasn't incredibly beautiful, but she was tall and had sexy legs as well as an uncanny ability to make me laugh. Most importantly, however, it was because of Gail that we settled on "Sections" as the band's permanent name.

Within a night or two of learning that "Pray for Rain" was already taken by a band that was credited for work on the *Sid and Nancy* soundtrack, I noticed a training manual on a desk in Gail's apartment. As I thumbed through it my eyes landed on the top of a page with a highlighted heading that read, "These are the Sections to Remember:" Although I can't recall the manual's subject matter, for some reason the "Sections to Remember" part stuck with me. We officially adopted the name, and eventually people started referring to us as simply, "Sections."

October was apparently the month for love or something like it as not only I, but Helmer and Matt became involved in intimate relationships. Helmer met a very attractive French lady named Emmanuelle, I met Gail, and Matt began dating a girl he had first met at Bethany. Her name was Cynthia and it quickly became apparent that she was a bit too sheltered and proper for Matt, who was forced to maintain a facade of complete sobriety whenever around her. Evident to most, the relationship was doomed from the very beginning. Cynthia was deeply religious, didn't drink or do drugs, and while at Bethany she rarely left the library. In fact, she was so pious that Matt was convinced she was still a virgin, even though Cynthia claimed to have had her first and only intimacy just prior to meeting him at school. Even so, according to Matt, this first love was an invention of Cynthia's intended to reel him in, as she secretly felt that someone with his level of sophistication would never be interested in a 23 year-old virgin. "She even gave him a name....*Josh McGregor*!" he'd blurt out, in a way that made you want to punch him.

Throughout the rest of the month and on into November, Perry remained in the midst of helping Shannon relocate to Los Angeles, as she had finally landed a small but significant role in Steven Segal's, *Out for Justice*. For Shannon, the exposure meant a viable, future career in the film industry. For Perry, it meant packing up her shit and carting it out west; however, before departing he assured us that he'd be back within a month or so. Apparently even now, after he'd been politely dumped, it was still worth driving 3,000 miles just to touch the booby.

God love him...really.

12

At first, I really loved the 80th Street apartment. Located in the heart of New York City, it was only a half-a-block away from Central Park which has always been my favorite place in the world. Eventually though, I realized our building was in an area that we really didn't have any business being in. It was the wealthiest part of the wealthiest part of New York and wholly disconnected from everything adjacent. Without a need for fences or barriers, it was and still is neatly sequestered from the rest of the city.

The area makes up a large part of the 10021 zip code, one of the most affluent in the country and completely sanitized for your protection. It is here where the New York City aristocracy lives lavish lifestyles, with overbred dogs and an underbred sense of compassion in a zone exclusively reserved for the ruling class.

In this neighborhood brimming with untold riches to spare, you seldom see a panhandler, a homeless person, or any other member of New York's forsaken underbelly as the city can effectively shelter the privileged away from the homeless, but can't always shelter the homeless away from the winter. I soon became affected by it all; how those who ask so little have even less, while those who have so much want even more. We didn't belong in that part of town. We were disaffected, disenfranchised, and disappointed kids who had much more in common with those on the *outside*.

One evening in late November, we decided to celebrate Perry's return from California with an impromptu jam session. Unfortunately, an irritated neighbor—apparently unmoved by the infectious grooves emanating from our apartment—abruptly ended the drunken jam by filing a noise complaint with the doorman. As considerate tenants and rather than risk any additional complaints, we decided that a game of touch-football might be a more appropriate end to the evening's festivities.

Initially, we headed towards the park but quickly realized that darkness would soon become a factor. So, instead, we situated ourselves in front of the Metropolitan Museum which provided us with a huge, extremely well-lit area. Unfortunately, positioned across the street and almost directly on the 50-yard line lived the editor of the *New York Times*, who would soon become our *second* noise complainant of the evening. After only ten minutes of the first quarter the game was postponed due to police.

By January of 1991, Helmer and I seriously considered departing the stuffy Upper East Side location. It made no sense to remain there, sharing a tiny studio apartment in an area we were growing to despise, when for the same price we could afford something spacious in a more appealing part of Manhattan. A breaking point of sorts occurred one evening later that month while we were listening to music and a very angry man started bellowing outside our apartment and pounding on the front door. As I lowered the volume we were able to catch the tail end of his message:

"...*you fucking assholes!*"

I had a feeling this was going to be another noise complaint. I opened the door and cautiously stuck my head outside to see which particular neighbor we offended, only to get a glimpse of his departure through a fire exit.

"I think it was the guy from downstairs again," I informed my roommate.

"Yeah, probably," Helmer agreed looking up from a magazine. "He hates us."

Actually, *everyone* there hated us. We clearly didn't belong, and made no effort to ingratiate ourselves.

Before long we officially decided to vacate the premises. Helmer found an apartment in the Village with his French lady, while Perry and I agreed to share a place on East 74th Street in order to better manage the band. Then, on February 1st, Eric and Virginia drove their van into Manhattan to help us move.

Eric and Virginia Holst were two of my favorite people of all time, and though I've never been much for mementos, a prized and cherished possession was a photograph taken of them at their engagement party a few years prior. They were now married and Eric had just received his degree in dentistry. Though, of course, my relationship with Eric stemmed from childhood when he and Troy would often play the role of family surrogates, I was also extremely fond of his new wife. Virginia had a sense of humor that complimented her husband's perfectly, and a general concern for others that was palpable.

"Hey Craig," she said to me as I loaded their van with my last box of belongings. "I've been there before and I know things can be crazy, and sometimes it seems like it really doesn't matter, but it can get out of hand before you know it. Be really, really, careful because it's totally not worth it."

I'm not exactly sure how she got the inkling, but I believe this was Virginia's indirect way of suggesting that I **not** become a heroin addict. But by this point I was hardly an *addict* and the possibility of becoming one was beyond conception. I was still only a Weekend Warrior, though I must admit—I now found myself waiting like hell for the weekends to arrive. Even so, I'd completely stopped drinking alcohol as it only teased me with an unfulfilled euphoria that heroin delivered almost immediately—and much more cost effectively. In fact, friends who dabbled with nothing beyond liquor were spending almost three times as much on their vice than the 30 or 40 bucks I'd set aside each week for my own. Of course, in time that ratio would be dramatically reversed.

13

Perry and I had moved into a fairly reasonable, one-bedroom apartment on 74th Street between First Avenue and York. It was situated on the ground floor of a building that certainly wasn't as grand as the previous, but compared to some of the dwellings I would later inhabit it was nothing short of palatial. Although initially, Perry seemed to favor the bedroom, more often than not we would fall asleep on the living room couches. As a result, the apartment's only bedroom was treated like a walk-in closet and devoted to clothes, instruments, amplifiers and recording equipment.

As far as Sections was concerned, this was an important place. It was here where we'd begin to assemble the rest of the band and struggle to find our musical footing. It was also where I accepted the fact that, for better or for worse, I was meant to be a musician. Of course, getting fired from Archer helped facilitate that decision.

With two weeks severance pay I was let go at the end April and alas, my romance with the exciting world of advertising lasted a mere six months. Getting fired from a position that had previously been considered a foot in the door to my industry of choice was a bit disheartening. I would be lying, however, if I said it was a complete surprise. I found the job to be completely uninspiring and can only assume my performance reflected that. Furthermore, for months now I could sense a bitter dislike emanating from Judy who was Archer's CFO and who, ironically, had remained a close friend of Gail's even after she left the agency.

Judy had apparently considered herself an older sister-figure to Gail. They were both single women that had come to the big city to launch their respective careers, and I suppose they felt a kinship of sorts. As a result, Judy took great interest in Gail and would attempt to mentor her in a variety of areas. In fact, during the months leading up to my arrival at Archer she'd been delving into Gail's personal life, cautioning her not to be too selective when it came to men. Judy said that if Gail wasn't careful, she'd end up a spinster by the time she was 30. Judy herself—now *over* 30, single, and already sharing an apartment with 16 cats—was just about the last person on earth who should have been dispensing relationship advice. Nonetheless, when she first heard of our budding romance her response to Gail was a totally disgusted, "That's not what I meant by *lowering your expectations.*"

Nice.

Hence, an obvious lack of job interest combined with Judy's animosity contributed to not only my dismissal from the agency, but also the dissolution of my relationship with Gail which I was made aware of the very same day. As a result, I suddenly found myself jobless *and* single on an afternoon in April that officially marked the end of my advertising career, and the beginning of a serious commitment to the band. And though I was mostly indifferent about getting dumped, I was still a bit unsettled by the notion of embarking on such a shameless and conspicuous quest for glory. I realized, however, that if we were ever going to be truly successful, I would now have to bravely align myself with the legions of city dwellers that were there solely to become famous. Actually, the mere thought of it made me a little sick. On a more positive note, I decided that since my experience within the ad industry turned out to be dismal, I was now completely free to fuck up my life without having to feel as though I sacrificed anything of value to do it.

On the evening of my dismissal from Archer, Perry and I got high together and as far as he was concerned—the demise of my professional career was cause for celebration.

"None of this matters," he said matter-of-factly after preparing the dope. "Advertising jobs, restaurant jobs…none of it's real."

With that he handed me a rolled-up dollar bill, offering the first snort as though in recognition of some sort of achievement. I accepted the tribute, snorted deeply, and exhaled slowly.

"Someday you're gonna be famous, Craigie," he went on.

The heroin was beginning to help me see his point.

Since I'd suddenly found myself with a little extra time on my hands, that night we decided to begin to focus less on song-writing and more on performing. Of course, in order to commence with this next step it was first necessary to round out the band by securing a rhythm section.

Clearly, here would be a perfect segue for me to mention the original lineup. Unfortunately, though not surprisingly, much of the decade is a blur and I remember few details regarding this very early and extremely brief period of the band's development. In fact, as far as the first Sections drummer is concerned, I can recall nothing beyond the fact that he was overweight and had difficulty remembering the songs. I do remember a bit more about our first bassist, however. His name was Simon Coulter, he was 22, and though he played a variety of different instruments he sucked the same at every one.

Our very first performance was at Kenny's Castaways in Greenwich Village on Wednesday, May 22nd at 7 p.m. The gig was a disaster. Regarding the band's reputation, the poor showing wasn't that big of an issue. We were playing the beginner's slot at one of the city's less prestigious venues, in front of an audience of mostly friends. It was still, nonetheless, an extremely discouraging experience.

I wish I could blame excessive drug use for the shoddy performance; however, none of us were high that evening except for Matt. But by this point Matt was almost always high, especially when he was playing guitar. Though it would soon become a problem, on this evening his chemically induced stupor played only second fiddle to Simon's sober ineptitude. Ironically it was Matt, slurring with eyes half-open, who continuously stumbled across the stage to correct Simon's miscues, all while looking as though he was about to puke and pass out himself. It was the blind leading the irretrievably retarded, and from the very first note it was clear that a different rhythm section would be required before we attempted another performance.

Sections didn't truly begin to take shape until I ran into Danny at Ricochet which occurred, conveniently enough, on the Monday evening after our ill-fated first performance. Ricochet was a southwestern restaurant that Perry and I had been frequenting because he was obsessed with the bartender.

Although Perry rarely had a problem getting laid, I recall the two women he most doggedly pursued remained completely disinterested in him...at least sexually. Amy, the bartender at Ricochet, was the first. She was very beautiful and smart, and like many beautiful and smart women she wasn't the least bit interested in Perry. Of course, Perry wasn't easily discouraged and this time he had a plan. Each afternoon at 4 p.m. for most of that month of May, he would leave Oscar's and jump in a cab heading directly to Ricochet, where he'd execute a meticulous strategy intended to win Amy's affections. That is, he would attach himself to a stool, gaze at her, and order drink after drink. Unfortunately, he failed to consider one major flaw in the plan that would prove his undoing:

Perry's tolerance for alcohol was roughly that of a little girl.

Although he seemed unable to appreciate the profundity of his inebriation, after only three or four rounds Perry was *completely* finished. Then usually, after making a minor spectacle of himself, he would immediately leave Ricochet and head back to the apartment. But on more than one occasion he would end up totally trashed and passed-out on the subway. This was troubling. There was absolutely no reason for Perry to be on the subway in that condition...especially during rush hour...and especially when we lived about a block away from the restaurant.

After a few weeks and a few subterranean tours of the city, Perry finally realized his love for Amy would remain unrequited. Reality came crashing down around him on that fateful Monday evening when Helmer met us at Ricochet for drinks, about an hour before Danny happened to wander into the restaurant.

As I previously mentioned Helmer was not at all a large man. In fact, he was kind of *frail*. At first glance, Helmer's appeal to women lay mostly in his charm and charisma as you could literally watch him talk a girl right out of her panties. Besides his gift of gab, however, Helmer had one other asset which I've also already mentioned: **Helmer Pelaez had a penis that was gargantuan.** Although I swear I never went looking for it, we first ran into each other during our stay at the 80th Street apartment.

It happened one evening while I was watching television and Helmer stepped out of the bathroom with a towel wrapped around his waist. As he headed toward the kitchen and passed directly in front of me, the towel suddenly got snagged on the jagged edge of a wooden desk and broke free from his waist. As it fell to the floor I gasped out loud.

Although the television rambled on, an unnatural silence seemed to smother everything and you could have cut the tension in the room with a knife. There we were…all alone…just the *three* of us: I sat there dumfounded, Helmer was both terrified and embarrassed, and his shaft just sort of hung there in a contented way, like a once-exiled king at last returning to the throne.

After a moment, I tried to come up with just the right thing to say in order to delicately break the icy and uncomfortable silence.

"Helmer!!! Your dick is fucking huge!!!" I roared.

Not only was it massive, its girth somehow seemed to provide it with its own identity. In fact, its presence was so profound that one might be confused as to *who* was Helmer and who was the penis.

I stared with fear and amazement as I was both terrified and intrigued at the same time. It was like suddenly stumbling upon a very large, previously unknown species which had somehow managed to survive for years, undiscovered—*right in your very own bedroom*. At first it might seem tame enough, but you didn't dare touch it or get too close because you knew it could probably hurt you if it wanted.

If there was anyone even more consumed by the notion of Helmer's penis—it was Perry, and when Helmer strolled into Ricochet that evening and introduced himself to Amy he knew the game was over.

Of course, Perry had been intimidated by Helmer's penis ever since they first caught sight of each other in—of all places—an extremely busy pizza shop on 57th Street. At the time, I'd been discussing the size of Helmer's shaft on a regular basis but Perry would have none of it, as I suppose my estimation seemed a bit too outlandish for him to accept. That was until he actually saw the beast for himself.

We'd finished eating our pizza, and just as we were clearing the table it happened. Why exactly Helmer chose this moment and setting to unsheathe I will probably never know, for he still has yet to provide a satisfactory answer. Perhaps somewhere he sensed a subtle challenge to his position as the dominant male in the pizza place, or maybe he was just sick and tired of hearing Perry dismiss my account of his member's immensity. Whatever it was, in a flash Helmer not only whipped the fucker out—but slammed it against the top of the rickety old table. As it came crashing down its image was burned into my retina, and the thunderous sound it made still echoes in my head to this day.

The impact rang out, reverberated down the legs of the metal table, lingered in the air for several moments and then strangely made me sick to my stomach. In an effort to locate the cause of the mysterious sound, startled customers scanned the dining area as the ringing slowly faded away. Its source, fortunately for them, remained a mystery.

Perry's initial reaction to Helmer's penis was a mixture of both awe and dismay, but he eventually grew to accept and appreciate it along with the other mysteries of the universe. Regardless, that evening when Helmer stepped into Ricochet, Perry quietly ended his courtship of Amy as failure now seemed inevitable. Amy was at once smitten with Helmer and though he would have nothing to do with her, the mere thought of her atop that monstrous penis was enough to help Perry come to terms with the loss. However, most pivotal that evening was not the plight of Perry but rather, accidentally bumping into Danny.

Danny Lapidus was a short, very talented, and rapidly balding saxophone player who hailed from Brooklyn, though I'd first met him at Binghamton. We were both English majors and had crossed paths once or twice in classes. Oddly, that night at Ricochet I'd gotten to know him better than I had during the years we'd spent together at school. After a few drinks he came back to our apartment to hear some material and by the end of the evening it was unanimous: Danny would be our sax player and whenever needed, help out on vocals.

Although it went unsaid, we knew that we really didn't need a saxophone player in the band, but we also knew that we had absolutely no discipline as musicians. Danny was a technically solid player, and we felt his involvement would not only help improve the band as a whole—but also enhance our credibility as performing musicians. But ultimately, Danny's greatest asset was his charisma, which, though difficult to describe, would translate into a tremendous stage presence. Eventually, I realized that part of the secret to his success revolved around the fact that Danny was always smiling, regardless of the occasion. He would later tell me that Matt had more talent in the tip of his little finger than I did in my entire body—but as always, behind every venomous word was a warm and wonderful smile.

14

Not long after getting canned at Archer, I'd picked up a newspaper and scoured the classifieds for something that I stood a chance at being able to endure. Though it had been seven months since I'd ended my torment at Oscar's, the awful memories still lingered and I was determined to avoid another restaurant job. This was quite a challenge because the field of viable opportunities was smaller than you might expect. Although I had received a BA in literature the year before, it would not factor into my present search for employment as any career-oriented position would likely interfere with the musical commitments I now made to myself and those around me.

After about a month of job hunting, a Sunday edition of the New York Times yielded a vacancy at Barry's Bagels. They had several locations and the one for which they were recruiting was located on Second Avenue, approximately eight blocks from our apartment.

I made my way to the hiring location and was met by Gina Turner, the store manager. Gina was black, a little older than I, and very attractive. She hired me almost immediately and I was to report to work on the following Monday morning at 8 a.m.

The evening after I was hired at Barry's I had the first of what would become a long series of nightmares which have, periodically, plagued me to this day. In the dream, I am a senior again at Binghamton revisiting commencement, or some other event signifying the end of my college career. Then suddenly, I learn that I don't quite have the requirements to graduate.

This very first rendition of the dream took place during graduation ceremonies. While at Binghamton, Dr. William Spanos was not only my academic advisor but also a highly respected scholar. In the dream he stood on a stage conducting the ceremony, and at some point began announcing the name of each graduating student. As the students heard their names, they each took the stage and accepted a symbolic scroll noting their achievement. When my name was called I also went to receive the credential; however, rather than bestowing it to me the professor gently placed his hand on my shoulder like a disappointed father.

With very serious eyes and in the most distinguished way, he addressed me personally but before the entire commencement hall:

"Binghamton University strives to provide its students with a comprehensive view of the world. Hopefully, it is one that results in professional success and personal enrichment, as our graduating class will soon be faced with important decisions likely to affect them for the rest of their lives. In order to continue this longstanding tradition of excellence, it is of the utmost importance that all graduates possess attributes that subscribe to our cherished, educational standard. These attributes, mind you, are developed through one means and one means alone: The successful completion of all coursework mandated by the declared concentration, as well as the required disciplines."

"Didn't I successfully complete the requirements, sir?" I sheepishly asked.

"Much to the disappointment of myself, my fellow academics, and *your* fellow graduates I'm afraid to say that no, shithead, you did not."

Although the personalities would swap roles from dream to dream, the moral of the story remains the same: I don't graduate.

When I first received my degree I was very much ambivalent about it. However, I soon decided that it provided me with the symbolic blank check I needed to passionately pursue a dream, and not suffer any detrimental consequences because of it. I always believed that regardless of how badly I screwed up my life, I still ultimately had the safety of an education to fall back on that couldn't be compromised.

As my life would eventually spin further and further out of control, these nightmares would seem more real and represent another reality which I would do everything in my power to ignore.

15

I arrived early for my first day of work and was immediately greeted by Megan Cabrini. Megan had been working at Barry's for several years. She was in her forties and was one of the few lesbians I've ever *truly* gotten to know.

Having grown up in New York my entire life, I've always prided myself on having a very acute sense of GAYDAR. But in relation to Megan, any technique designed to detect latent homosexual traits was a wasted one. Megan was the stereotypical, stoutly built, butch-variety of lesbian and this was evident to even the most casual of observers. Her daily attire rarely deviated from that of corduroys and a plaid shirt, just as our daily chats rarely deviated from that of women and *sex* with women.

As far as the store's management was concerned, Gina was easy to get along with and after my first week at Barry's I realized I wouldn't completely despise working there. At no point was I expected to produce an original thought, and there was no dandruff-ridden dickhead telling me what to do. I spent my days slicing bagels and spreading cream cheese and that was all there was to it. I was in at eight and out by four, with no *real* work in between and no ass-kissing for tips. What more could I ask for? My nights were completely free and I would finally be able to focus on the music without suffering too badly in the process.

When I met Colin Emerson, another co-worker who had been at Barry's for almost two years, I knew I had it made in the shade. Not only was he a musician with a background and goals that were similar to my own, but he was also a really nasty asshole. It was hard to believe, but as long as Colin Emerson remained employed at Barry's I felt I had a fair degree of job security.

On Friday, my first week as bagel-boy was officially coming to an end. As I left the store and started toward my apartment, from across the street I noticed what surely had to be one of the city's sadder stories hobbling in my direction. Hunched slightly forward, which made his ass appear to stick out unnaturally, a shabby old man took bow-legged strides that were each no more than a foot in length. His unnatural gait seemed to indicate a recently suffered stroke and he struggled to keep pace with sidewalk traffic. He was just another forsaken member of society wading in a sea of abject indifference. I don't know what exactly came over me, but my heart went out to the guy because he really did appear to be suffering. I decided to cross the street to see if I could be of some assistance. Then I realized it was Matt and attempted to run in the opposite direction.

Unfortunately, he was on his way to Barry's and had seen me coming. As he desperately began to scream my name, I felt sympathy slowly transform itself into humiliation-by-association.

To be honest, Matt was a difficult person to feel sorry for because he was always the source of his own misery. Whatever his suffering, rest assured, it was typically the result of something stupid he did, thought, or said; so rather than compassion I usually felt he got just what he deserved.

Matt had no concept of moderation and was fast becoming a heroin addict—which ran afoul of my renegade drug policy. Under the pretext of jamming, almost every evening he would drop by the apartment only to get fucked up away from the Bronx and the prying eyes of his father. And if he got fucked up, I usually got fucked up. Well before physical dependency sets in, one of the first signs of addiction is an inability to, ironically, *just say no.*

Now thoroughly disgusted and with nowhere to run, I walked over to him. Up close he seemed even more pathetic and hunched over than I previously thought.

"What the fuck happened now?" I asked, much more annoyed than concerned.

"Craig, I really need some dope," he said ignoring my question.

Matt had yet to be officially introduced to the daytime dope dealers and as a result, they refused to serve him. This was clearly the reason for his surprise visit and I knew it the moment I realized it was him.

"Why are you walking like that?" I asked

"I was just at the clinic," he said a little reluctantly. "I had to have a minor surgical procedure taken care of. No big deal."

It didn't look minor.

"Where?" I asked.

"Don't worry about it," he answered though in obvious pain.

"I'm not worried," I assured him. "I just wanna know where you had the surgery."

"Please get me some dope," Matt said trying to change the subject. "I'm hurtin' real bad."

"OK—sounds great. But first tell me where you had it."

"On my fucking ass, all right!" he shouted in a whisper.

Unfortunately, that wasn't the "where" to which I was referring. Actually, I was curious to know what medical facility would perform such a debilitating procedure—and then allow the disturbing post-operative result to hobble right the fuck out the front door. Of course, now armed with this new bit of information I couldn't help but pursue a different line of questioning.

"Why?"

"Listen, man—I'm in a lot of pain. Let's get some fuckin' dope," he said, ignoring my question once again.

Now typically, there's nothing I liked better than using someone else's medical condition to justify my own drug use. However, by this point I wasn't quite the ravenous junky I'd soon become and I just couldn't let him get off that easy.

"WHY DID YOU HAVE ASS-SURGERY, MATTHEW?" I asked firmly.

"Craig, I'm really not in the mood right now. I'm in a lot of fucking pain here. Come on!" he begged.

"No problem, brother. Just tell me why you had ass-surgery and we'll hook it all up,"

"I caught anal warts and had to get them removed, all right?" he quietly confessed.

This was getting better by the second.

"Where'd you get 'em?"

"I fucking told you already, dickface!" he openly bellowed at me. "On my ass!!! Where the fuck else would I get them?!?!"

"Yeah, I know. But where exactly did you—"

"OK, YOU FUCK!!!" he roared. **"RIGHT UNDER MY ASSHOLE AND ABOUT TWO INCHES ABOVE MY BALLS!!! ARE YOU HAPPY?!?!"**

"I am," I said—though once again he was answering the wrong question. "But I wanted to know where you *contracted* the warts, not where they erupted on your ass. And incidentally, I believe the area to which you are now referring is known as the taint."

"Great, can we go now?!"

"So then you actually had *taint* warts removed—not anal," I confirmed.

"Yeah, fine, taint warts. Can we go?" he begged once more.

"Did they put you in stirrups like a lady?"

"No," he said a little on the patronizing side but I think he was lying. "Can we *please* get some dope?"

"Yeah, but where'd you catch'em?" I pressed. "Who was the dirty little slut that gave'em to you?"

"Cynthia," he said sheepishly, clearly embarrassed by the implication.

"CYNTHIA?!?!" I bellowed.

"Yeah." Matt quietly admitted.

I couldn't believe it was true. I had to make sure we were talking about the same girl.

"YOU MEAN TO TELL ME THAT CYNTHIA, PURE AS THE DRIVEN SNOW—CYNTHIA, YOUR GIRLFRIEND—CYNTHIA, GAVE YOU TAINT WARTS???"

"**Yes**," he reconfirmed.

"The bitch cheated on you?"

"No. She caught them from that guy at Bethany."

For a moment I had to digest the news because up until now, Matt had always insisted that "that guy at Bethany," also known as Josh McGregor, was merely a figment of Cynthia's imagination. Apparently though, Josh was a real person—with *very* real warts.

"You're telling me that the ex-boyfriend you previously denied the existence of not only took Cynthia's virginity, but also gave her anal warts which she has now transmitted to your taint. Is that correct, Matthew?"

Matt said nothing but his silence was confirmation enough. I was rendered speechless by the poetry of the moment.

I dropped the subject and followed Matt to his car, which The Good Detective had just purchased for him the previous day. It was a Ford Taurus, only three years old and in great shape. For a totally psychotic and physically abusive asshole, Ernie Anson wasn't a bad guy. He secured his son the cushiest of teaching jobs, provided him with free room and board, and now purchased him a car to go to work in and buy drugs with.

We hopped in the car and headed to Hell's Kitchen, aptly named and located in midtown on Manhattan's west side. At the time, to our knowledge, it was the only dope spot in the city. Of course, we would soon find other locations because as far as heroin was concerned—Hell's Kitchen was for suckers. There, a bag of dope sold for $15 as opposed to ten, which was the going rate.

Matt parked the car on 53rd Street facing Tenth Avenue. As always, the same slippery-looking Colombian with bad skin manned the appointed building stoop awaiting visits from a burgeoning list of clientele.

"Do you wanna come with me so you can meet him for yourself and stop busting my balls?" I asked though knew better.

"No," he said. "That's all right."

Of course it was all right, as long as someone else was willing to risk a trip to jail.

I grabbed $30, left the car, and made my way to the spot. As I walked toward the middle of the block I met the gaze of an incredibly beautiful girl. When we made eye contact she tried to maintain it—and she was so attractive that quite frankly, I found the moment unsettling and even a bit suspicious.

Why the fuck is she looking at me?

This was the type of girl who, typically, wouldn't stop to give me the time of day—let alone a come-hither look. But there she was like an angel in white with green eyes, blonde hair and alabaster skin—offering the sweetest and most tender smile—***and it was really beginning to piss me off.***

The dealer must have darted back inside the building to re-up, so I decided to circle the block and assess this new development that was now disturbing me more with every step.

Why was she looking at me like that? Is she a narc? Is that why the dealer took off?

No, I didn't think so. She had a kind of elegance and sophistication about her that would be impossible for a cop to mimic. I rounded the block and as I approached her once more, I could see she was *still* gazing at me.

Christ, she is really hot! So why the fuck is she looking at me?! For God's sake, who the fuck is she? Just then, as I came within a few feet of her I figured it out.

"Excuse me, miss?" I said, trying to get her attention as politely as the moment permitted.

"Yes?" she replied much like an angel, while a glowing luminescence seemed to engulf her as she spoke.

"Are you a prostitute?"

As it turned out she was **not** a prostitute, which I was able to determine from the middle finger she answered my question with before she reached into her purse and handed me a scrap of paper with her name and number scrawled upon it. Then Venus walked away, and clearly her parents were right.

The dealer was nowhere to be found, so I returned to the car to wait. Matt could barely contain himself.

"Did you get it? Huh, did you get it?!?" he asked in desperation.

"Not yet."

"FUCK!!! THIS IS SUCH FUCKING BULLSHIT! WHAT THE FUCK IS GOING ON?!" he wailed. "These motherfucking dealers don't give a shit. They know you'll wait! They know you'll come back!"

"Relax!" I said, "He probably ran out and went inside to re-up. I'm sure he'll be back in a few minutes—so calm the fuck down."

"Then what took so long?"

"There was this really beautiful girl staring at me," I told him a little reluctantly.

"Awesome. Did you say anything to her?"

"Yeah…I asked her if she was a hooker."

Within about 20 minutes the dealer returned. I again left the car, made the exchange, and returned to Matt who was by now almost completely covered in drool. The sun was setting, so I turned on the car's dome light and emptied both bags on to one of Matt's textbooks. As I arranged the lines, I was startled by the unmistakable sound of a police baton tapping against the window beside me. I couldn't believe it. The cops didn't even see the deal go down, but just happened by the car as I prepared the dope.

At this point in my fledgling junky career I was relatively fearless when faced with the prospect of arrest. In fact, the only thing I was feeling was resentfulness because I now knew I wouldn't be getting high but of course—I had yet to be acquainted with the world of hurt inflicted on those similarly stumbled upon by the NYPD.

I could tell that the cop with the baton wanted to drag me out of the car by my curly hair but thankfully—the door was locked which gave me a moment to assess the situation. As I slowly unlocked the passenger door, I had a feeling that at some point Matt would try to mention the fact that his father was "Detective Ernie Anson," but I wasn't sure how. I found out in less than a second as the now unlocked door was suddenly ripped open and Matt started squealing, "DETECTIVE ERNIE ANSON!!! DETECTIVE ERNIE ANSON!!! DETECTIVE ERNIE ANSON!!!"

There were two cops present and for a moment, both seemed

confused as they stood by looking at Matt and then back at each other. They had no idea of what in the world he was talking about, and I had no idea of what an incredible pussy he was.

The cop with the baton then grabbed the book with the dope and emptied it into the street. As the powder floated off into the twilight I could see a tear well up in Matt's eye, though I was unsure if it was due to the wasted dope or the thought of being arrested. Either way, I offered him a Kleenex to underscore the pussy theme. As I handed him the tissue, the cop with the baton pulled me out of the car and onto the sidewalk. Then, rather than collect Matt at the driver's side he instead chose the scenic route, dragging him across both seats and through the passenger's side as well.

"Detective Ernie Anson! Detective Ernie Anson! Detective Ernie Anson!" Matt wailed again and again as they threw him onto the pavement. It was all terribly undignified.

"Who the fuck is Detective Ernie Anson?!" asked the cop with the baton.

"He's my dad," said the poorest excuse that anyone had ever seen for a 24 year-old man.

"*Your* father's in the department?" asked the other officer in semi-disbelief.

"Yes sir," Matt said as he then cleared his throat to continue. "He works out of the 45th Precinct in the Bronx and was—"

"SHUT THE FUCK UP YOU MOTHERFUCKING PIECE OF PISS!!! YOU'RE A FUCKING DISGRACE!! DOES YOUR FATHER KNOW YOU'RE A FUCKED UP JUNKY?!?"

"And a pussy?" I added.

"No," he answered both of us.

"Where'd you get that shit?" the cop with the club asked me.

"Over there," I said, vaguely pointing toward Tenth Avenue.

"Who gave it to you?"

"The Spanish guy over there," I said, gesturing toward a street teeming with nothing other than "Spanish" guys.

Of course, I was being less than cooperative and the cops knew it. But these two were donut-dunkers and weren't the least bit interested in launching a drug investigation. Of course, they could have arrested us anyway, but I had a feeling that Matt's relationship to the Big Blue Wall of Silence would save us.

The cops took a few steps away, reconvened, and then the one with the baton pointed it in Matt's face and said, "The only reason

I'm not locking you assholes up is because your father's a cop, and I feel sorry that he has a piece-of-shit-junky for a son. But if I see either of you fucks again you're going to jail."

We got back in the car and I told Matt to wait until the police left the area. Initially, I thought we might try to score again as I was now consumed with the thought of getting high. Obviously, my very first run-in with New York's Finest didn't quite affect me in the way that it should have. But then again, by this point I looked at the whole experience as if it was just a game—the object of which was to not get busted. As far as I was concerned it was much more *James Bond* than *Law and Order,* and I didn't acknowledge the seriousness of it all. I simply thought of it as *us* versus *them* and nothing more. No hard feelings, really, because to me this wasn't about crime, it was about my right to do what I wanted—and what I wanted to do was drugs.

Though I still had heroin on the brain, Matt was overcome by the thought of incarceration. Apparently, the close call and potential implications involving his father were just too much for him to handle and he decided to call it a night. He then put the car in drive, and took me back to the east side saying not a word along the way.

16

I had been at Barry's for about four months. I'd settled nicely into my new routine, and was beginning to wear my starving artist label like a badge of honor. I'd also been dating Venus, and though I carelessly misplaced her phone number the same day she gave it to me, in a strange twist of fate she lived only a few blocks away from Barry's. As a result, good fortune suddenly smiled upon me during a sweltering afternoon in July when she strolled into the store for an iced tea and to punch me in the face. Fortunately, at the last minute she decided to cut me some slack and resist resorting to violence, but only because the chance encounter made her reluctant to risk altering what she thought might be some sort of a mystical, predetermined destiny.

Venus Bellini was unlike anyone I'd ever met. She was beautiful, bold and sometimes brash, and though she occasionally came across an unwilling but necessary component to getting what she wanted, her extreme confidence and flawless beauty were usually enough to overcome any obstacle or objection to her having her way. Venus had grown up in Forrest Hills, and after recently graduating from Princeton University with a degree in biology, she immediately landed a job as a sales rep for a medical equipment manufacturer.

As far as the band was concerned, most of that summer was spent searching long and hard for a rhythm section. We first looked for a drummer by placing ads in the Village Voice and The Daily News but initially came up empty. Of course, there were auditions, but the applicants were either short on chops or just a bit too drunk and stoned to be taken seriously—even by *our* standards. Then, at the very end of September, Danny Lapidus scheduled an audition for a drummer by the name of Pat Sullivan at a rehearsal studio on 23rd Street.

With each passing month Danny played an increasingly greater role in the band's development, as he was fairly well-connected throughout the city's independent music scene and that was a *major* asset. However, his musical contributions to Sections were mostly limited to a few notes on the sax, some backing vocals, a tap or two on the tambourine and a technically discerning ear.

Danny was also a guitarist and songwriter, but there was simply no room for another guitar player in the band, and though his songs were worthy—they were never quite right for Sections. These were hardly my own arbitrary rulings, however, and though I could be tyrannical during rehearsals, decisions with regard to songs and set lists were always made on a consensus basis. As things turned out, I was responsible for 80% of the material, but everyone had the same opportunity to contribute. In fact, Matt wrote two songs and even Perry co-wrote a few, but Danny's material never quite made the grade and though he had yet to mention it, I could tell the limited role was beginning to frustrate him. Unfortunately, the truth of the matter was that musically—Sections didn't really need a saxophone player and ultimately, Sections wouldn't need Danny. But I knew that if we could find a place for him, even if it was just temporary, it would only be to our benefit.

On September 30th at 7:45, Perry and I arrived at the studio for the drummer's audition. Danny appeared shortly thereafter along with the hopeful candidate. We introduced ourselves to Pat and discovered that he considered himself mainly a jazz musician, though he claimed to

be equally proficient in all styles of music. He was also from
Nebraska and about as green as they come.

Incidentally, the last thing I wanted to hear from a potential
drummer was a fondness for jazz because—quite frankly—I've never
been a fan. Although I can certainly appreciate the technical virtuosity
behind much of the music, the music itself never fails to leave me
feeling completely uninspired. *I'd rather listen to country.*

Frank Cotto stood in on bass to help facilitate the audition. He was
an extremely skillful player on loan from The Authority, perhaps best
known for being mentioned in the liner notes of the Spin Doctors'
Pocket Full of Kryptonite album. They were a funk band with a
hard-rock edge that I found only slightly more alluring than jazz, but
like the Spin Doctors they were being represented by David Graham's
management company. David, incidentally, was the son Bill
Graham—the iconic music promoter—and had also helped launch the
career of Blues Traveler. According to those in the know, The
Authority was to be the next big thing. As things turned out, however,
those in the know knew not—but at the time they were a pretty big
deal locally. Each weekend they would sell out The Wetlands, and
even Ice Cube was rumored to have been interested in taking them on
as his band.

As expected, I was less than thrilled with Pat's drumming but
decided to shut my mouth because things were moving slowly enough
as it was. Danny and Perry offered Pat the slot and without too much
fanfare, he accepted and then immediately left the studio.

While gathering his equipment together, Frank invited us to see
The Authority play later that evening at the Nightingale Lounge, as he
had several times throughout the summer. He and Danny had been
childhood friends, and I usually felt compelled to attend the gigs out
of politeness, if not politics. Tonight, however, would be different. I
had a big date planned with a hot bag of dope that would wait for no
one. I politely declined Frank's invitation as did Perry, but we
promised to be in attendance three weeks from Friday as The
Authority was being given a showcase at Limelight. Just then, Matt
showed up.

He walked in with his guitar as if he *wasn't* two hours late. To be
honest, I had completely forgotten that he was coming at all. His
attendance at even important sessions was becoming iffy at best,
especially if he didn't need help scoring. But regardless of the motive,
if he did make an appearance he would usually be wasted and worth

little. Today was no exception.

"Hey guys…Guess what?" Matt slurred as he made his grand entrance.

Nobody hazarded a guess.

With a big, ridiculous, grin that reeked of someone trying to convince himself of something, he made the joyous announcement.

"Cynthia and I just got engaged!"

"Hey, that's great," Danny congratulated. "When's the big day?"

"Oh, we're not sure yet. Probably sometime next summer."

"You should try not to be two hours late for the ceremony," I pointed out as I left the studio.

I hopped in a cab and headed over to Hell's Kitchen. The same slippery looking Colombian with bad skin was stationed at the same building stoop and we made the same exchange. I immediately tore into the bag, inserted a rolled-up dollar bill, and inhaled deeply. As I slowly exhaled and started on a northeasterly trek towards home, I was certain that even with all of our shortcomings the band would soon be well on its way.

17

By October Pat had settled in as our regular drummer, but we were still unable to close the deal on a bassist. We simply couldn't find anyone that sounded right, at least to the degree to which they'd be offered a permanent spot in the band. A bassist and drummer must work within a dynamic that is almost entirely their own, and neither can get too clever without the other musically reacting. This special relationship never developed during any of the auditions, and as far as I was concerned it was all Pat's fault—but I wasn't about to pick *that* fight. Danny loved Pat, and even Perry seemed to like him. Actually, he *was* a really nice guy. So at least for the short term, rather than make a fuss I decided to let things continue on as they were.

In the meantime, we decided to use Casey the Cop on bass. Casey the Cop was a friend of Pat's—and Lord knows if he wasn't a cop he would've been a criminal. He was an impulsive, 28 year-old,

Asian-American kickboxing champion with an untamable wild streak and though he wasn't a thug, he was a reckless and renowned alcoholic who for the past ten years had continuously transitioned his focus between martial arts and crime fighting arenas. As far as his bass playing was concerned, he was no more in sync with Pat than any of the others, but he was temporary and he knew it. We could use Casey to rehearse and perhaps for a gig or two, but eventually the search for a more permanent replacement would have to be resumed.

By the middle of the month, Danny managed to land us a gig at The Speakeasy on Bleecker Street. This was easier said than done, especially since we were still without a decent demo, but Danny happened to have been friends with a black guy named Big Al who operated the club's sound system. The gig was on a Monday night and considering the fact that it was only our second as a band, and first with the existing lineup, it went well. It went so well that the club's manager offered us 200 bucks to play the 11 o'clock slot a week from Saturday. Believe it or not, this wasn't a bad arrangement because Saturday night shows were coveted, and 200 bucks was exactly $200 more than he was presently paying us.

Although most of the city's venues do pay something, there's such a continuous influx of new bands that it's not uncommon to find bars and clubs that compensate with nothing beyond draft beer, but still manage to stay flush with reasonably decent talent. As a matter of fact, after purchasing its legendary sound system in the late eighties, CBGB's actually made local acts *pay* to play on their hallowed stage. By providing bands with a recording of their performance in exchange for a mandatory fee of $60, the club found a state-of-the-art way to pay off its state-of-the-art sound system.

By the time we made it to CB's, they'd done away with the controversial practice and I had heard two distinctly different stories regarding the change in policy. The first was that the city's local bands—realizing they were responsible for at least 80% of the club's shows—organized themselves and boycotted CBGB's in protest. The second and more plausible version was that at the end of a particular show, when the sound engineer presented the band with a recording of their performance and a bill for services rendered, the band presented the sound engineer with a trip to the hospital and a recording of him getting his ass kicked.

We scheduled two rehearsals during the week prior to the big Speakeasy gig. Matt completely missed the first, but made it to the second with his brains barely intact. Once again he was worthless. While everyone else worked tirelessly to make the songs tighter, Matt, with his mouth opened and eyes closed, only *pretended* to play his guitar—which given the alternative of him fucking-up was certainly the lesser of two evils. As usual, I was annoyed with him, but everything else was going quite well and at this point he simply wasn't worth interrupting progress over. Everyone seemed to know the set, and the band had worked out a funky rap/rock hybrid that erupted out of nowhere. Then, for no reason at all, Matt attempted to play something. What it was exactly we'll never know, as his guitar was so far out of tune that everyone immediately stopped what they were doing—dead in their tracks. I finally decided to lose control.

"What the fuck is wrong with you?!!" I screamed at him. "Don't answer! If you're too fucked up to actually play—just keep pretending, or leave, or do whatever the fuck you want but stop screwing everybody up!"

"Craig, relax!" said Danny as he put in his two cents.

"Fuck that!" I said and continued. "You're a fucking disaster, Matt, and if you can't hold it together for a couple of hours a week, then why even bother to show up at all? In fact, why don't you just get the fuck out right now?!"

With that and much to my pleasure, Matt gathered his things and left the studio. Unfortunately, Danny seemed unable to appreciate the moment.

"You shouldn't have done that," he said, pointedly. "You were way out of line."

"Fuck you!" I shot back. "I'm getting sick and tired of being a babysitter, and who the fuck are you to tell me what to do anyway?"

"Well," Danny said matter-of-factly, "all I know is that Matt has more talent in the tip of his little finger than you do in your entire body."

A dark hush fell over the room, time stood still, and nobody said a word as that little bastard threw down the gauntlet.

"Oh really?" I asked "In the tip of his little finger?"

"Yep," he confirmed.

"First of all, Danny—yes—Matt can be the most talented guitarist in the world…when he's not fucked up. But since he's always fucked up, he's not much use now is he?"

Having Matthew Anson perform as your lead guitarist was tantamount to having Rainman function as your bookkeeper: Every now and then he might pull off a remarkable feat of technical wizardry—but most of the time he acted like a fucking retard.

"And secondly," I continued, "if my contribution to the band can be measured against Matt's little finger, then how should we measure yours, Danny? I mean, what exactly do you do here besides toot your horn and run your fucking mouth?"

As Danny fell silent I desperately wanted to continue with the verbal onslaught, but couldn't quite remember a pivotal word that had stubbornly anchored itself to the tip of my tongue. It would have perfectly defined the little fucker's role in the band, but I just couldn't summon it forth and it was upsetting me. I decided to let it go. I knew I would eventually recall it and that Danny would eventually give me an opportunity to use it. It was becoming increasingly apparent that he was dissatisfied with his scope of contribution to the band, and I could tell he held me personally responsible. I so wanted him to accuse me of it directly. That would have given me an opportunity to provide him with a couple of other reasons for his limited capacity; however, that would have also implicated members of the band. Rather than throwing Sections into further turmoil, I decided to shut my mouth and with that—Elvis left the building.

I met Perry at the apartment later that evening. It was the night of The Authority's big showcase at Limelight which we had promised to attend. Although we were tempted to blow-off the performance, we didn't want to jeopardize our relationship with the band. Not only had Frank Cotto been helping us with auditions, but The Authority's road manager seemed interested in working with us. They were obviously well positioned with David Graham, so it would do us no good to ruffle any important feathers. With that in mind we got dressed, headed to Hell's Kitchen, and secured enough heroin to be able to endure The Authority. From there, we made our way downtown to Limelight.

18

At about 8:30 p.m. on the following Saturday, Perry and I left the apartment and headed over to The Speakeasy for our 11 o'clock performance. Even though I felt Pat and Casey were still missing the point musically, and the tension with Danny was mounting, it seemed as though things were generally moving in the right direction.

After the first Speakeasy show, I realized that my relationship with Danny had become very complex. For the first time I had been exposed to his stage presence and charisma which, I must admit, were very impressive. However, given the traditional constraints under which a supporting player typically performs, he would've never had the chance to affect the audience so significantly had he been with any other band, or at the side of any other singer. Fortunately for Danny, I was an incredibly reluctant front man. Especially in the beginning, I wasn't good at the chit chat part of the game and quite frankly, saw no reason why I should be. *What more could they possibly want from me?* Wasn't it enough for me to share my illicit thoughts and felonious feelings with a dark and smoky room full of drunken strangers...*in song?* Didn't that make me the committed artist without having to engage the audience in mindless banter, in between gut-wrenching musical testimonials to the misery and torture that was... *my life?*

When on stage, I receded to my own private place and just wanted to be left alone. Danny permitted me this luxury by picking up the slack and doing the other things that were expected of a singer, and of course, he savored every minute of it. In fact, he enjoyed it so much that while on stage it may have seemed as though Sections was actually *his* band.

As far as our stage performance was concerned and at least for the moment, Sections was an unusual configuration of disparate talents and personalities, intermittently coming to the fore and then stepping back again as the musical dynamic shifted and swayed. The formula seemed to work perfectly, and this was never more evident than during the second Speakeasy gig.

After we finished up with "The Wish," which was mid-tempo and on the softer side, the band broke into the funky rap that had erupted during rehearsal. Danny worked the audience into a frenzy, and though we had time for another song or two we decided to put the evening to bed on a high note. We promptly bid the audience adieu and left the stage.

For the first time in my life I really felt like a rocker. We all felt that way and Perry passed around a mailing list as it seemed as good a time as any to begin the arduous task of building a following.

After we left the stage and congratulated ourselves on an outstanding performance, Casey scolded me for introducing him to the audience as "Casey the Cop" because it apparently hindered his chances at getting laid.

"Come on, man!" he pleaded with me. "It makes everybody think I'm gonna take away their drugs!"

*Take them and **use them**, maybe.*

Actually, though, besides alcohol—*Casey didn't do drugs.* Interestingly enough, he was an unexpected byproduct of the JUST SAY NO generation, who bought in to the evils of *illegal* drugs wholesale and came out a raging alcoholic.

Casey's distress aside, however, it was clearly one of our greatest shows ever. The Speakeasy was packed and everyone was there. Cynthia, Venus, Helmer and everyone from Barry's was in attendance. Even Danny invited two of his childhood friends, Louie and Drew, but our personal guest list made up only a small fraction of the audience. We left everyone screaming for more from an unknown band that seemed to have literally come out of nowhere, *which we had.* Unfortunately though, the warmth and appreciation we received from the audience was not to be matched by the club's manager, Herbert Weismueller, an old German who had immigrated to the U.S. after World War II.

Weismueller already had a reputation for being a bit unreliable on payday, so within minutes after leaving the stage Danny decided to strike while the iron was sizzling.

"Hey Mr. Weismueller," Danny said as he tapped the old German on his shoulder.

"Danny! Good show. Tell the other boys, will you? Same time next week? OK?" Weismueller asked.

"I'll talk about it with the guys. But right now we kinda wanna get outta here, so can we settle up?" Danny asked, obviously referring to the $200 we were due.

"Of course," Weismueller said.

He unfolded an ancient wallet and produced a crisp, hundred

dollar bill. Unfortunately, there wasn't another forthcoming.

"Oh... Al said you offered us 200," Danny said.

"What the fuck is that stupid bastard talking about!!" he bellowed. "He's fucking crazy! I never said it."

He was very clearly telling a fib, as not only Al—but Danny, Perry and Pat also heard him make the offer.

"That's fine," Danny responded. But all would certainly not be fine.

Personally speaking, the $17 differential per person wasn't the biggest deal. After all, at this point we were hardly in it for the money, and as far as I was concerned it didn't seem to warrant that much of a scene. But of course, I'm from Queens. I mention this only because Danny, Drew, Louie and Casey the Cop—all grew up in Brooklyn and this may have had an impact.

I watched Danny weave through the crowd, intermittently shaking hands and shoving drunks aside until he came to a table where the Brooklyn contingent was seated. Within a moment, the four of them inconspicuously took the stage and quietly began dismantling the club's microphones, including the expensive drum-mikes which took some tinkering.

By this point the entire band, and a good portion of the audience, had already heard about Herbert's treachery as well as the Brooklyn-bred method of retribution that Danny and the others were attempting to exact upon the club.

Once the mikes were disconnected, Danny had Pat stash them in a drum bag and then casually strolled over to the bar where I was nursing a Dewars.

"That dirty fucker isn't paying us the full 200," he told me.

"I heard."

He then politely addressed a gothic-looking bartender:

"Excuse me, miss. We're gonna be taking the tequila," he said.

The bartender turned to gather up the bottles of liquid compensation. "Here. Take it…I hate that motherfucker," she said, apparently referring to Herbert. She then continued onward, lining up approximately 20 bottles of rum, gin, and vodka to further reward us for a job well done.

At some point it became a free-for-all. Realizing that all subsequent performances that night would have to be cancelled since we now owned much of the club's sound equipment, the other bands slated to perform began helping themselves to the remaining liquor.

Even some of the drunker audience members got involved. Within five minutes both bars were empty wooden shells.

As the free liquor continued to flow, Perry and I decided to head home to get high, and to avoid any possible police encounters in the near future. We arrived at the apartment by 2 a.m., and as soon as we walked in the phone started ringing. It was Big Al.

"Hey man, I'm really sorry about all the crazy bullshit," I told him immediately.

"No worries. Everyone knows that Herbert's a motherfucker. But the microphones are *mine*, bro," he informed me.

"Oh shit! I don't think Danny realized that. I'll take care of it," I told him.

I then left a message on Danny's answering machine making him aware of the situation and assuming that all would be taken care of by morning.

At some point during the early morning hours, my heroin-induced nod actually transformed itself into sleep. Unfortunately, after what seemed to be just a few minutes of slumber, the phone behind my head again started ringing as the sun simultaneously blasted through the living room window. It was only 7 a.m., and Big Al was already back at The Speakeasy and on the hunt for his microphones.

"Hey man, I'm sorry to call so early, but I gotta do a gig tonight and I just wanna make sure you guys know where my shit is at," he explained.

I disengaged with Al and called Danny again. This time he answered the phone and informed me that he had, in fact, gotten my message and relayed it to Pat, who, to his knowledge was still in possession of the equipment. More than that he couldn't say, but he promised to call Pat again and then get back to me.

I waited a few minutes, and just as I was beginning to fall asleep the phone rang once more. It was Big Al, who seemed to be growing more concerned with every passing phone call.

"What's the word, brother?" he immediately asked.

"Danny said Pat has your stuff and he's trying to get a hold of him. Relax, Al. I'm sure every little thing is gonna be all right," I tried to reassure him. "I'll call you the second I hear anything."

Just then I heard a call-waiting.

"Hang on a second, Al. I think that might be Danny," I told him.

I clicked over to the incoming call and it was none other than Pat himself.

"Hey Craig," he greeted me sounding as cool as a cucumber. "Don't worry, man. After I got home last night I spoke to Danny and brought the stuff right back to The Speakeasy," he said.

I was about to get seriously worried.

"You brought it back last night?" I asked.

"Yeah," he confirmed.

"Who'd you give it to?"

"I didn't get back until after it closed. There was nobody there, so I left it right in front."

Now I was definitely, seriously-worried.

"Right in front of *what*?" I asked, terrified at the prospect of what *might* be coming next.

"In front of the club. You can't miss it," he said, incredibly.

"On the fucking street?!" I asked without really believing anyone could be so stupid.

"No!" he said. "Are you crazy? Why would I leave it on the street? It could get run over by a cab or something. No, I left all the microphones in a paper bag on the sidewalk right in front of the club. You can't miss it," he said again.

"Pat. Are you kidding? Al needs his microphones **today.** What's he gonna do? What the fuck are *we* gonna do?" I asked, assuming the expensive equipment had already been stumbled upon and was now sitting in a pawn shop.

"Craig! It's right outside the front door of The Speakeasy in a brown paper bag. Right in front, man! Come on, you can't miss it."

I decided that if he said "you can't miss it" one more time, I was going to stick my hand through the phone and punch him in the face. I clicked back over to break the news to Big Al. Apparently, the duration on hold did him no good.

"Craig, talk to me—man—talk to me! I ain't shit without my mikes, man—**I ain't shit muthafuckaaaa!!!**"

Given his state, I thought it best not to jump to the obvious conclusion and decided to hope for the best.

"Hey Al," I said. "Good news!!! I just got off the phone with Pat. He said he left the mikes in a brown paper bag, right in front of the club...on the sidewalk...so why don't you go take a look...all right??? Al???"

For about ten seconds I heard nothing but complete silence and what sounded like a hyperventilated attempt to breathe. This was followed by a barely coherent and almost dreamlike,

"He...whaaaaa???"

Then the phone went dead.

Amazingly, as things turned out, at about 7:30 in the morning Al found his stuff sitting on the sidewalk—right where Pat said it would be. Apparently, the fear and revulsion of what may lay hidden in a crumpled paper bag left on a New York City sidewalk overcame even the most ardent sense of adventure.

Unfortunately, I didn't learn of the equipment's recovery until much later that day, and for a while was forced to wrestle with a mixture of guilt, regret, and anger over how empty-headed Pat could be—especially when he knew the band's stupid-quota had already been filled by Matt.

I was lying in bed feeling awful about everything when the dope in my bloodstream clashed with a continued lack of sleep, and the effect was finally overpowering. I allowed myself to drift off while clinging to the hope that somehow Al's stuff would be recovered. Just as I was about to fall asleep, the phone rang yet again and I think I saw a pattern developing.

As if things weren't bad enough already, Matt called to tell me that he'd left one of our guitars—a $600 Ibanez Artist—behind at The Speakeasy. He then suggested that I head down there straight away before somebody steals it. As it turned out, somebody already had.

19

I have never been one to flaunt the greatness of the city from which I am native. However, when it comes to pizza, bagels, and Halloween—there's no place like New York.

Each year the Halloween Parade travels along Sixth Avenue in Greenwich Village. The costumes are lavish, the colors are mesmerizing and accordingly—the majority of the participants are extraordinarily gay.

By this point Venus and I had been dating for about four months, and I wanted to take her to the parade as she'd never before witnessed the spectacle. Unfortunately, on Halloween morning she called to inform me that she wasn't going to be able to attend, as an old friend from college was in town and had invited her to see the ballet at Lincoln Center.

"Oh," I said upon hearing the news.

"Honey, it'll be over by ten o'clock. Would you mind? I promise, I won't be home late and we can do something afterwards. I just can't blow this off. We were really close."

And just who did the love of my life share this incredibly close bond with?

Well, I don't quite recall the name. All I do remember is that he was a former lineman for the Princeton University football team. Of course, they were *just friends*, and though I maintained my composure I found the news to be a little unsettling. Nonetheless, we agreed to scrap the parade and meet at her apartment by 11 p.m.

At about 3:30 that afternoon, Karen Rubio—a friend of mine from Binghamton—had called to inquire about my plans for the evening as she and a friend were coming into the city from Westchester to see the parade. I liked Karen. We were good platonic friends for almost three years, and with the exception of a few drunken moments during my junior year had remained as such. I agreed to meet her and her friend at 6:30 on the corner of 14th Street and Sixth Avenue.

At around 5 p.m. Venus called again to confirm our eleven o'clock rendezvous. "And don't stay home waiting for me," she said. "Go out with Perry or something."

"Perry has to work, but Karen's gonna go to the parade with me," I told her, trying to imply nothing as I could see my choice of guest might in some way be interpreted as retaliatory.

"Who's *Karen*?" she asked.

"A friend from school."

"You know, today *both* our horoscopes actually said that we should remain committed to established relationships."

"No kidding?" I said, surprised by the coincidence—but still unable to disguise my own utter lack of interest.

"Nope…no kidding," she said. "OK, then—so I'll see you at eleven. Bring over a pumpkin to carve!"

At 6:30 I ran into Karen and her friend, Ann, outside The Gap on Sixth Avenue. We smoked a joint but didn't need to because as usual, the parade was extremely entertaining. The highlight came as three gentlemen dressed as road workers passed by. Suddenly and from out of nowhere the first two pulled out foldable stools, sat down, and began eating sandwiches in the middle of the parade route. As they did, the third worker produced two lit flares and began redirecting the rest of the procession around his dining cohorts to ensure their mealtime went undisturbed. After a few moments they would stand and pack their "equipment" only to repeat the performance again, as those lining the parade route couldn't help but relive the daily commute. Art imitated life, as the impromptu moments of street theater and "work" stoppages caused traffic jams, delays, and collisions as confused paraders slammed into the backs of one another. Periodically, a mixture of flowers, feathers, and sequins could be seen exploding into the air as collisions reverberated down the route.

As the parade wound down, the girls and I headed to Peculiar Pub for a round of beers. Afterwards, we said goodbye and went our separate ways, though I still had a couple of hours to kill before Venus was due back from the ballet. I purchased the pumpkin she requested and as a surprise—filled a plastic jack-o-lantern with twelve orange and black roses anchored in mounds of candy corns. I then headed uptown to Venus' apartment.

It was only 10:30, so I decided to sit and wait on the steps of an elementary school located directly across the street from her building. After a few minutes, the sound of a very familiar giggle grabbed my attention. I looked toward Second Avenue and immediately recognized a thoroughly intoxicated Venus, hanging on the shoulder of her gigantic, football player friend. As they stumbled toward her apartment, however, their demeanor seemed to belie the platonic portrayal of their relationship.

I couldn't decide how to handle the situation:

Should I make my presence known before anything really fucked up happens, just in case something really fucked up is about to happen? Or, should I just sit tight and wait to exploit the situation as an opportunity to measure her loyalty—especially since she just stressed the importance of remaining faithful.

They made it across Second Avenue and I could tell that Venus was completely wasted as the football player was practically carrying her down the street. I so much wanted to jump up and prevent what might become my own undoing, but couldn't. The opportunity to see the *real* Venus, uninhibited by my presence, was simply too much for me to resist. I decided to remain seated and silent on the other side of the street.

Just after they reached the stairs of her building they began to kiss. With the candy and flower arrangement on my lap, a pumpkin at my feet, and the word "D-I-C-K" stamped across my forehead I watched the passion unfold.

Now in order to appreciate the ringside seat I had for my own humiliation, it's important to understand how narrow Manhattan streets are. Unlike the avenues, many of which support four lanes of traffic and two lanes of parked cars, the streets often provide barely enough room for one of each. That said, if I were any closer to the action it would have been a threesome.

For what seemed like an eternity they continued to kiss, and as the football player leaned her against the front door of her building they started grinding hips. It was like I was suddenly stuck in a John Hughes film. I sat there on the 50-yard line lost in a fog of anger, hurt, and resentment until Venus finally broke away from his grasp and ran upstairs to her apartment.

I didn't quite know how to deal with the situation. As the football player dejectedly walked away, my initial instinct was to do the same and save the confrontation for the following day. At first, after throwing the pumpkins in a trash can I did just that. Unfortunately, the need to respond had overwhelmed me as I turned around and headed back to her building.

She buzzed me upstairs, and when she came to the door she was even drunker than I had at first suspected.

"Hey baby!" she said with what seemed like feigned excitement. "I missed the shit out of you."

"I bet," I said, half smiling and desperately trying not to freak out.

"Did you have fun with *Karen?* You better not have kissed her."

"Venus, I saw you and your friend fucking around outside."

"You saw *what?*" she asked in a voice that sounded genuinely confused.

I lost my patience:

"Don't play stupid with me, you silly bitch! I saw you and the gorilla. I was sitting right there while you were making-out with it."

Then she said it. It was something so amazing and unbelievable that I've taken great pains to recall it precisely—word for word:

"I was not."

Perhaps she didn't understand what I was saying.

"Asshole! Don't you get it?!? I was sitting there…*watching*!! I

66

could have reached out and touched you with my fucking tongue! Please, save the bullshit for another time when I'm not actually there to witness the humiliation."

I then stormed out of her apartment and headed home.

As I stepped into my own apartment I could hear Venus leaving the first of what would be a series of drunken and contradictory phone messages, some of which begged my forgiveness while others berated me for overreacting. Stranger still, a few even reiterated her original denial.

The following afternoon I thought it best to I end my relationship with Venus Bellini and did so.

20

After prolonged substance abuse, most addicts—regardless of their poison—begin to show signs of it. The medical community does note visible symptoms of crack smoking; however, they're mostly concerned with singed eyelashes and burnt fingertips that become scarred after years of clutching on to that pesky crack pipe. But much like the gin blossoms that plague alcoholics and the raccoon-like rings that often surround the eyes of junkies, veteran crackheads show similar signs of their addiction—though they may be less recognizable to the casual observer.

It seems to me that after a while, the face of a serious crack smoker begins to appear—for lack of a better term—*waxy*. But it's more than just that. Looking back, I can recall many crackhead faces that slowly seemed to almost wash away and become less defined as the years passed and the addictions intensified.

From the very beginning we had a *feeling* that Jim was a crackhead, and with his long, dirty, hair and clothes that were always covered in grime, he did little to tarnish the impression. He was only in his mid-twenties but already wore a face that began to betray him, and though I'd seen him lingering outside our building for months, it wasn't until we actually met that I realized he was a crackhead *for sure*. Of course, it was obvious to me that Jim was fucked up on something long before we were officially introduced and I was forced to shake that burnt, crackhead hand. On almost a daily basis I saw him pacing the streets, strung-out, and accosting strangers with requests for food, money, companionship, or whatever he felt he was most in need of at the time.

As soon as we moved into the 74th Street apartment I found Crackhead Jim's lingering presence to be unsettling, and each day upon setting out or returning home from work I would find myself crossing streets to avoid crossing paths. Unfortunately, this was a bit of a challenge because he was always stationed within a hundred feet of my building's entrance. Perhaps he was attracted to motion, or maybe it was the shiny, spinning, doors—but whatever it was, the moment he saw me he would always come running.

At one point I actually suggested to the building's Mexican doorman—Eduardo—that he kindly ask Jim to find another place to loiter.

"I would, papi," Eduardo told me. *"But de junky is you fooking neighbor."*

I was vaguely offended when Eduardo referred to Jim as a "junky," a term almost exclusively reserved for heroin addicts. From what I could tell, *he* wasn't a junky—he was a crackhead and as far as I was concerned, crackheads were the lowest of the low. They were deceptive, often dangerous, and would stop at nothing to continuously fuel their habit. However, I have to consider that the indignity I felt from the doorman's remark was somehow related to a subconscious admission, or perhaps, denial of my own emerging problem.

Regardless of how quaint it was to have the friendly neighborhood crackhead living in your building—none of the tenants wanted him around and quite frankly, it was a strange place for him to be. Crackhead Jim would have been right at home in Hell's Kitchen, the East Village, or perhaps even Madame Tussaud's—but the Upper East Side was definitely the wrong location for a very obvious reason:

There are no crack dealers in the area.

For a crackhead, proximity to a continuous supply of crack is a fundamental consideration that must be factored into any decision regarding a permanent residence. It's simply the nature of the addiction. You never have enough, and the second you run out—you want more. But of course, you *still* never have enough.

On a November evening upon returning home from work, I was shocked to find Crackhead Jim standing in my living room with Perry, and smoking the biggest rock I've ever seen in my life. Though we still had yet to be officially introduced, apparently the size of the rock was reason enough to skip formalities.

"Dude!" Crackhead Jim shouted at me, as Perry looked on with an expression that revealed just how fucked up this little get-together was. "Look at this fat motherfucker!!! It's a fucking gram-and-a-half!"

For a moment or two I just stared in silence, as Jim's expression transformed itself from hopeful acceptance—to that of a basset hound caught sitting on the couch.

"You wanna hit the pipe, dude?" he asked, trying to sound as if it wasn't a fucked up thing for him to be standing there and asking me that question.

"Craig, this is Jim...*he's our neighbor,*" Perry interjected, as if this was a topic we *hadn't* discussed.

"You wanna hit it?" Jim asked again.

I hadn't dabbled with any form of cocaine in several months, and was far too fearful of its less savory side effects to do so without a bag of heroin at the ready.

"Come on dude, take a fuckin' hit," Jim urged me.

I politely declined.

"I have a bag of dope for you," Perry said.

I politely accepted.

"Where the fuck did you guys get *crack*?"

"WE MADE IT!" Perry said with a big smile and a bit more satisfaction than the moment deserved. "Jim showed me how to cook it up."

"Yeah, dude. We had crack-cookin' class!!!!" Jim said as he suddenly pulled a plastic ashtray out from under his dirty sweatshirt and lit one of Perry's Camel Lights.

"Why'd you bring an ashtray over here?" I asked, as there were no less than five scattered around the apartment.

"I take it with me wherever I go."

"What the fuck for?!?"

"I never leave my DNA anywhere because that's how they getcha, and *believe* me—they **will** getcha."

The three of us then smoked that enormous rock for about an hour while Perry explained how we had come to this sad moment in our lives. He had apparently returned home from work and of course, was approached by Jim at the entrance to the building. On any other day

Needle

the interaction would have gone no further; however, Perry had finally quit Oscar's and already snorted a bag of dope to celebrate his departure. That's pretty much it; he got himself all fucked up and thought it might be a good idea to invite Jim and his cocaine over for a visit.

I learned that Jim actually lived four doors down with his girlfriend, Jenny, whose family owned the apartment—which explained why the crackhead lived in this part of town to begin with. Apparently, the lure of free rent was enough to compensate Jim for the inconvenience of having to cook-up his own stash or travel uptown to score. Beyond that, I discovered that Eduardo was correct in his assessment, for in addition to Jim's crack-smoking he sported a nasty dope habit as well.

While sitting there in the middle of our living room, sharing a crackpipe with the area's leading crackhead, it's interesting to note that not for a second did I think I was a screw-up. Of course, Crackhead Jim certainly was, and though having him over to cook-up rocks the size of testicles was a tad unconventional, as far as Perry and I were concerned we were just living on the edge. We didn't have a daily drug habit or a physical addiction to contend with and that was all there was to it. Of course, my fondness for heroin was already laying the psychological groundwork for those things to develop.

Soon, the rock was completely spent and in a flash, Jim was again slaving over a hot stove in the kitchen. Then, within moments I started to crash.

"Hey. Give me that bag of dope," I told Perry and he immediately handed it over.

I then unfolded a little envelope stamped with the word TERMINATOR, and rolled-up a dollar bill.

"Dude, you should boot that," came a recommendation from Crackhead Jim. "I've got plenty of works," he added, gesturing to a bag of syringes sitting on the kitchen table.

"Only one demoralizing experience per evening, thank you," I said and then inhaled deeply.

Within seconds the heroin once again asserted itself as King of all Drugs, and the horrid crack craving subsided.

I made my way over to the kitchen and there was Jim, working diligently at the stove. I watched as he slowly added cocaine to a heated mixture of baking soda and water and within a few seconds, gelatinous-looking blobs appeared suspended within it. Jim corralled them together with a spoon forming a single entity, and then carefully removed it from the water to dry. He then added more coke and baking soda to the mixture and repeated steps two and three.

21

I hated to admit it, but I really enjoyed cocaine under the right circumstance, which simply meant having an ample supply of heroin on hand as well. Although I'd indulged in neither since the session with Crackhead Jim several weeks earlier, I thought about both drugs continuously which was probably a sign that my brain chemistry was beginning to change.

Working with Megan at Barry's was hardly a deterrent to my drug-related thought patterns. Our daily conversations now gravitated less toward the subject of women, and more toward that of cocaine and heroin. Megan was a fairly regular cocaine user and although I now seemed to have developed an appreciation for the drug, I was still firmly committed to heroin as my drug of choice. Furthermore, I failed to understand how anyone could enjoy coke—much less crack—without being overcome by the crash. From my own experience there was nothing other than heroin that could completely offset the horrible side effects, and I found it inconceivable how most cocaine users preferred to ride out the misery, or perhaps make a feeble attempt to drink it away.

"The blow I get is super clean and I don't really notice the crash," she told me.

"No such thing," I said.

"No, really—I'm *serious*. I get this primo shit from a nurse on 83rd Street. You should go over and pick some up."

Although I'd done my dabbling, to this point I'd never personally purchased cocaine and under normal circumstances the suggestion would have gone ignored. However, about an hour earlier Perry called to inform me that he'd landed a great job at Dabney's—a somewhat chic, Chelsea restaurant—and that he'd be bringing heroin home to celebrate. Even though dope purchases were still limited to weekends only, during the last two weeks of Perry's unemployment we addressed the shortage of cash by completely abstaining—so now it was apparently time to cut loose.

"Would you call her for me?" I asked Megan, thinking we might as well *really* cut loose.

After work, I walked over to Nurse Feelgood's building and she buzzed me in. When I got to her apartment she was at the doorway in a nurse's uniform, with one hand on her hip and the other wrapped around a big bag of cocaine. Yes, it *was* weird, but it would hardly be my first run-in with a member of the healthcare community that was secretly living the life of a drug dealer or abuser.

The coke was $120, but it seemed like a large amount for the price.

"This is a special price *only* for Megan, OK?" she had to point out.

"Yeah, whatever," I answered, and then hastily left her standing there in front of her apartment.

Though I lived only nine blocks away, the thought of getting high had gotten the better of me and I jumped in a cab heading south. Within a minute, I arrived at my building and was greeted by none other than Crackhead Jim, who seemed to sense my excitement—or perhaps he just smelled the cocaine in my pocket.

"Hey dude, you wanna hang out," he actually asked.

Without answering I rushed passed him and into the building. When I opened the door to the apartment I was confronted by a forlorn and dejected Perry. I knew something was terribly amiss.

"What happened?" I asked.

"I got beat."

"What do you mean?!"

"I think I bought baking soda from a fucking junky," he said.

This was the first instance in which either of us had ever been victimized by a dope fiend and we'd soon learn that—in general—you can never *really* trust a junky.

"That's great, Perry. Now what the fuck are we gonna do with this shit?" I said as I tossed the coke onto one of the couches.

"What do you think we're gonna do with it?" he rhetorically asked and then immediately pounced.

For three hours, Perry and I snorted lines as I tried to convince myself that the crash wouldn't be so bad because, after all—*Megan said so.* Then, at the three hour and one minute mark I wanted to kill myself. This was clearly the most cocaine I'd ever consumed and all without the sedating effects of a bag of dope to go with it. It was the worst and last coke crash that I would ever allow myself to suffer.

A half-hour after the last line was snorted I couldn't believe how badly I felt. A bag of dope was all I needed, but Hell's Kitchen was already closed for the evening. Then I thought about trying to hook-up with some more coke, but we couldn't afford it and I knew that doing so would only delay and intensify the inevitable misery to come.

I left Perry in the living room to wrestle with his own demons while I hid in the bathroom and began grinding my teeth. I then looked in the mirror and was disgusted by my own reflection, which further intensified the horrible depression. I chastised myself for wasting money on drugs, and then all reasonable thought was thrown out the window as I again began to devise a way to get more cocaine. This was probably the point at which most addicts either cry or resort to criminal activity. I chose to weep for about an hour.

*My life sucks, my job sucks, my band sucks... My drummer **really** sucks.*

I decided to take a bath which is something I've always found incredibly soothing. Even as a child, I'd often find myself jumping into a hot tub during moments of severe stress or discomfort. There was something primordial about it as perhaps, some deep recess of my subconscious found comfort in what it deemed to be the relative safety of water. Then, I thought about how easy it would be to drown myself in it.

Relax... It's the coke.

Deep in my heart I knew this to be true. But with the same conviction I also knew that had this overwhelming depression engulfed me without a traceable cause or foreseeable end to the misery, I definitely *would* have killed myself.

22

As far as Sections was concerned, there wasn't a great deal of activity during the month of December as Christmas came bearing down upon us and family commitments took center stage. As a matter of fact, Pat actually returned home to Nebraska for the entire month, which I thought provided us with the perfect opportunity to replace his ass. Unfortunately, no one else seemed to share that opinion.

On Christmas Day I made the obligatory appearance at my mother's condo in Bayside as we were *still* going through the motions. Later that evening upon returning home, I opened the front door and noticed that all of the lights were on as I was struck by a stream of cold air whistling through the apartment.

"Fucking asshole-Perry!" I yelled out loud. Not only was the door left opened but the apartment was even messier than usual. Several CD's and my own personal items were carelessly tossed about, clothes were strewn everywhere, and there was a trail of muddy footprints leading to the bedroom. I was really getting sick of Perry's bullshit and inability to clean up after himself. Then I realized what had happened:

Somebody broke in and ripped us off!

In fact, I may have actually walked in while the crime was still in progress as a stack of stereo components sat by the opened patio door, seemingly the next items to be heisted from our ground-floor apartment.

I stood there for a moment as it all sunk in. I was suddenly overcome by the fact that after 24 years of living in New York, I'd finally become a statistic and it took some time to come to terms with as I'd never before been the victim of a crime. But acceptance gave way to rage spurred on by the violation of my own private space, as I noticed pieces of my life scattered haphazardly on the floor along with the photograph of Eric and Virginia, now crumpled and creased as if cast aside and stepped upon. I wasn't one to carry around pictures of girlfriends or family members but for some reason that photo felt sacred—and its desecration only heightened my fury.

The entire apartment was a disaster. At some point I came to my senses and after calling the police, I attempted to take stock of what had been stolen. The list grew by the minute and included my college ring, about a hundred CD's, a CD player, a camera, a turntable, a television, $300 in cash and some very valuable baseball cards. They managed to grab Matt's bass guitar as well, but with the exception of that one item—almost everything taken was mine.

About ten minutes later, Perry returned from Brooklyn where he'd been spending the day with his mother, celebrating Peace on Earth and Goodwill Towards Men.

"Merry Christmas, asshole—*WE GOT ROBBED!!!*" I said as he entered the crime scene.

"What?!?" he responded while frantically scanning the living room. "Holy Shit!!"

He then darted back to the bedroom to discover that his most cherished possession—a twelve-string Rickenbacker—still lay hidden under a pile of his own dirty laundry. Apparently, being the biggest slob on earth had its advantages.

At some point Matt called and Perry informed him of the burglary, mentioning his bass as one of the stolen items. Matt then reacted much worse than expected.

"Oh, man—I need that bass!" he wailed.

"Dude, why don't you forget about the fucking bass and worry about getting it together on guitar?" Perry asked, but the question went ignored.

"Perry—that's a $200 bass," he went on. "I left it there thinking it would be safe. Someone's gonna have to help me replace it, man—*come on!*"

"Don't worry about it." Perry replied. "I'll take care of it."

"Seriously?"

"Yeah," Perry confirmed. "As soon as you replace the $600 guitar you left at The Speakeasy, I'll be sure to replace your $200 bass. OK, shithead?"

With that he ended the call.

"I can't believe we got ripped off!!!" I bellowed. "And where the fuck are the cops?!?"

"Relax!!!" Perry yelled back. "It's not that big of a deal."

I'm not sure he realized the extent of *my* losses, but that was definitely the wrong thing to say and the wrong time to say it.

"What do you mean, *not that big of a deal?*" I demanded.

"My guitar is safe," he said with tremendous relief. "I think the only thing they took of mine was a laundry bag."

"Yeah—to carry all of *my* shit out in!!! You should try *using* a laundry bag, you dirty asshole!"

"Then they probably would've noticed the guitar," he said with a smartass grin.

About an hour later the cops showed up, and I cannot find the words to accurately describe their level of indifference. The news of my losses was met with a complete lack of interest, and I would've been satisfied had they demonstrated just a fraction of the passion they would later have for locking me up.

As a matter of procedure, they took a statement and quietly made a list of the stolen items. Then they left without a word.

For a variety of reasons, Perry suspected Crackhead Jim of the burglary, and the more we thought about it—the more it seemed likely. Besides band members and girlfriends, he was probably the only person we'd ever had over, and he was *definitely* the only crackhead. He was also aware of our belongings and the fact that the ground-floor apartment could be accessed through the patio. Although the revelation didn't occur to us until a day or so after the incident, we became certain that Jim had to have been the culprit and once again saw how you can never trust a fucking junky. But on a more positive note, he did teach us how to make crack—so I suppose it wasn't a total loss.

23

On Valentines Day, Venus and I decided to renew our relationship while later that evening, Perry and I decided not to renew the lease and to be out of the apartment by month's end. The decision was spurred on by a variety of factors, including the recent burglary as well as my resurrected relationship.

Though I ended things with Venus immediately after the Halloween debacle, near the end of December she launched a determined campaign to rekindle my interest—culminating on New Year's Eve when she actually *asked* me to fuck her in the ass. I'm not sure whether the request came from a sincere desire, or was just a clever tactic designed to reel me in. Whatever it was, it worked like a charm because for me—this wasn't just a pleasant diversion and an opportunity to have anal sex. More precisely, it was the final frontier and a chance *to boldly go where no man had gone before.* However, unbeknownst to me, by this point Venus' ass might as well have been the *starship, Enterprise*—and my voyage just another footnote in its long history of galactic exploration.

Venus wanted to think that the Valentines Day we'd spent

together served as a catalyst to help realize, affirm, and demonstrate the permanence of our relationship; however, it was clearly the drunken sex that ended the evening. I'd no sooner climbed off—she asked me to move in. Although I thought she might still be a deceptive slut, over the last few months she'd been unusually supportive of my musical aspirations and I could tell that she *really* wanted me to live with her—so I gave in.

As far as *Perry's* immediate options were concerned, he was faced with the prospect of either living with his mommy—or a sexually reassigned prostitute named Clarissa whom he'd met on Tenth Avenue. Regardless of his dilemma, within a week after Valentines Day we'd be packed and ready to vacate the premises, with the beds and furniture already relocated or in storage.

During our final week in the barren apartment, Perry and I decided to rough it out and continue writing and polishing songs, rather than risk interrupting the steady progress made since the Christmas respite. We realized that soon enough, we'd both be subjected to new living arrangements that weren't conducive to the late-night jam sessions which produced the bulk of our music. As a result, on the very last evening in our apartment, we invited Matt over to rehearse the newest material and simply make the best out of the bare and less than comfortable surroundings.

Matt was becoming, without question, the most out of control of the three of us. He lived the biggest lies and did the most drugs, and Perry and I were beginning to grow impatient with his unreliability and inconsistent performance. Certainly, we were both well on our way to full-blown heroin addiction ourselves, but we refused to allow the drugs to negatively affect the music and at least on the surface it didn't. Matt, however, had been screwing up for a long time—arriving late to rehearsals or not showing up at all. Of course, when he did make an appearance he was almost always fucked up and not very helpful.

Don't get me wrong. Matt was still an incredibly gifted guitarist, and in terms of raw playing ability he was in a class by himself. But it was impossible to harness that greatness with any degree of consistency because although Matt was brilliant, his brilliance had strict limitations. The first time hearing a song, he'd immediately join in and amaze everyone with perfectly executed riffs that soared. Unfortunately, we soon realized that for each song—Matt had only one magnificent load to blow. After that he'd be shooting blanks and unable to repeat the performance in quite the same way again.

Initially, we thought we might solve the problem by recording the spontaneous bit of genius in order for him to have something tangible to duplicate. But even after listening to the playback he would seem at a loss. He couldn't really remember the notes or summon the same energy he had previously. Later, while recording the CD, we would use no less than five guitarists to duplicate Matt's recorded brilliance, as none were able to achieve his level of mastery with a wholly original effort.

As usual, Matt was late for that final, 74th Street jam session. He was supposed to be at my apartment by 8 p.m., but it wasn't until 11:30 when I heard him ringing the doorbell. And though it took only about twelve seconds to answer the door, that was apparently long enough for him to get stuck in a nod as I was confronted by Matt with his eyes closed, head tilted upward, and mouth hanging open.

For several minutes I waited, holding the door as he stood there lost in the depths of his nod. In fact, had it not been so late already I would've left him standing there just to see how long he might linger. Unfortunately, after about five minutes my curiosity gave way to an overflowing resentment which I'd now been trying to suppress for hours.

"Who is it—**FUCKHEAD??!!!**" I screamed in his face.

That scared the shit out of him. His eye-slits suddenly burst open and he stumbled backwards grabbing his chest as if he was having a heart attack. Once recovered, he cautiously walked around my fury and into the apartment where he took a seat on the floor of the empty living room. Without a word, Matt then returned to the land of nod while Perry and I remained thoroughly sober and extremely resentful over the way he wasted our time and compromised our effort. Once again he was late, wasted beyond words, and fucking everything up. Perry had to work the following day and by this point I was hardly in the proper mindset, so we gave up on the notion of getting anything accomplished.

As Perry retired to the bedroom, I followed to put away the guitars. When I returned to the living room I found Matt still sitting Indian-style on the floor, and nodding off with a lit cigarette in his hand. He was completely wasted and worthless. I silently glared at him for some time and though he remained sitting cross-legged, at some point I noticed his upper body begin to gradually bend forward until the tip of his nose was actually touching the carpet. It was as if he was seeking a meditative path toward divine enlightenment. In reality, of course, he was just completely mangled and could no longer sit upright.

Not until the cigarette's burning cherry had crept between Matt's fingers did he come back to life—but only long enough to drop the smoldering butt onto the carpeted floor. I attempted to rouse him while stressing the importance of not incinerating us all. He would sit up, agree for a moment, but then light another cigarette as he slowly reassumed the position and again threatened to burn down the building. It was a very long and drawn out process that reminded me of watching a flower die—in slow motion...*over and over again.*

This continued on for about an hour or so until I'd finally had enough. As his nose and cigarette met the floor one last time, I disposed of the burning butt and left him to his meditations. I realized his contorted position was hardly conducive to a restful night's sleep, but at this point it was either him or me. I wasn't his fucking babysitter and it became clear that if I were to rouse him and try to reason—he would only once again humor me, light up another smoke, and then continue with the seemingly endless cycle. So, I chose to leave him there as I eventually passed out not far from where he sat folded-in-half and nodding.

At around 9:30 a.m. I awoke to a madman pounding on the front door. It was The Good Detective. Apparently, Matt's school had called Mr. Anson's home in an effort to determine whether or not his son would be teaching class that day, as he was presently unaccounted for. This set daddy's wheels in motion.

Ernie Anson was a mountain of a man and at six feet tall, weighing in at 300 pounds, he was not to be taken lightly. When he arrived, Perry did try to greet The Good Detective at the door. However, he'd no sooner turned the knob when Mr. Anson blasted over the threshold like a crazed rhino with a force that literally knocked Perry back into the bedroom.

"Matt!!!" roared The Good Detective. "You are so fucking dead!"

Becoming more in tune to what was going on, I looked over at Matt. He was still folded-in-half but now completely alert, and with a look in his eyes that reminded me of a fawn stuck in a mud hole. In order to get a better view of the charging terror, Matt was able to lift his head and rest his chin on the floor in a space previously reserved for his nose. At the moment, unfortunately, this minor repositioning was about the best he could manage as the rest of his body seemed to have petrified overnight. I, however, immediately sprung to my feet unsure if I would be included in the beating that The Good Detective had apparently mapped out for his son.

Thanks to the length of the foyer, Matt had a second or two to get it together before being confronted by the wrath of his father. With a superhuman effort accompanied by a subhuman groan, he managed to straighten his legs and somehow stand. Unfortunately, after rising to his feet he was still unable to unfold himself and was forced to hang on to his ankles and hope for the best.

"MATT!!! I'm gonna kick your fucking ass!" roared Ernie Anson as he raced through the foyer. Little did The Good Detective know what a marvelous position his son was in to help him complete just such a task.

"My back, my back, my back, my back, my back!" Matt cried as he desperately tried to become one of the vertical. It was about the saddest thing I've ever seen.

As his father entered the living room he discovered Matt, pathetically looking up from his ankles and attempting to find a position from which he could better defend himself.

"What the fuck's wrong with you, Matt?!?" The Good Detective bellowed. "Don't you know you're gonna lose your fucking job if you keep missing work?!?!"

"My back, my back, my back, my back, my back!"

Not wanting to be rude, I chimed in.

"What's up, Mr. Anson?"

"Fuck you, asshole."

The Good Detective then totally refocused on Matt.

"You know, Matt—I'm not putting up with this shit anymore! You better get your act together or you're out! What the fuck are you doing with your life anyway?!?"

"I'm trying to run a band!" Matt shouted while looking up from beneath the summit of his ass.

"Yeah, into the ground," Perry astutely pointed out.

Thankfully, and without resorting to physical violence, The Good Detective turned around and stormed out of the apartment for the first and last time. Perry went back to sleep, I made some coffee, and Matt was transported to Lenox Hill Hospital where he was treated for muscle and ligament damage to his back and both legs.

24

We vacated the 74th Street apartment on February 28th, 1992. During the weeks leading up to our departure I never sensed any hesitation or foreboding from Perry. That's because he'd saved it all for the day of the actual move.

I've seen Perry endure some awful things in the past, things that would have most men crying like a baby. However, I'd never actually seen him shed a tear until he was ultimately forced to decide between living with a transgendered hooker—or his mother in Brooklyn. Perry had apparently underestimated the difficulty he would have finding an affordable place to live without a ready-made roommate, and was now faced with a no-win situation. As the lesser of two evils he chose to live with his mother, but he was furious about it and directed all of his venom at Venus, whom he held chiefly to blame. Though he was fine with the idea of relocating he thought it unwise for us to separate and disrupt the recent songwriting spurt, especially since the decision was mostly inspired by my resumption of a relationship with someone he considered a deceptive bitch.

"Nice job, Venus," he snapped at her while she was helping me gather my things. "You know, the band's gonna suffer because of this."

"What are you talking about, Perry?" she asked with some disgust.

"I have to live with my mother because you have to live with Craig. I hope you're fucking satisfied."

"I most certainly am. He's a good pussy licker."

"**All** premature ejaculators are good pussy lickers," Perry replied as he stormed out of the apartment and headed directly to Brooklyn.

Unfortunately, it soon became clear that *my* new living arrangement was not without its own drawbacks and within three days of moving in, Venus had me reluctantly discussing the topic of marriage. Forgive me, but I found it difficult to consider a lifelong commitment to someone I'd recently caught dry-fucking a football player. By moving in, however, such conversations were apparently fair game.

Venus was a mixed bag. She liked the convention of marriage, and did have the potential to become a reliable and trustworthy mate. Of course, she also had the potential to become a terrific slut.

As our first weeks passed as roommates, I could see her begin to try to mold my life in accordance with the future goals she determined we should strive to achieve together. She intended to go to medical school and began suggesting that, given "the relative worthlessness of an English degree," I had few options other than applying to a graduate program as well.

I went along with her delusions to an absurd extent, even applying and getting accepted to Hunter College's graduate program; however, I wouldn't be marrying her or anyone else. All of my focus and commitment was directed toward Sections exclusively. She knew this and though she felt the band was talented, she indirectly dismissed my efforts and aspirations by stressing the importance of a graduate degree. This annoyed me to no end and I realized that when it came down to it, Venus really didn't believe in me. Furthermore, with the exception of alcohol, she lived a drug-free life and was less than thrilled with my fondness for heroin—even though she unknowingly had a bag of dope to thank for a desensitized penis and her very first orgasm.

I decided to go through the motions. Though I had no intention of getting married I would keep this fact, along with my continued drug use, to myself for fear of rocking the boat. Of course, the boat would eventually rock like a motherfucker and sink like a stone.

On a Saturday morning near the middle of March, Venus and I set out to adopt a puppy. Though her landlord didn't allow pets, we reasoned that the studio was now a bit too confining anyway, and if we happened upon a likeable pup we would look for a larger apartment in a building that did.

We walked over to the Humane Society which was only a few blocks away. Upon arriving, we made our way to a room filled with homeless puppies and immediately spotted her. She was an incredibly beautiful, ten-week-old, Chocolate Lab and Doberman mix with a brown coat, hazel eyes, floppy ears, and enormous paws. There was no question that she would grow to become a strikingly beautiful and gigantic beast.

While growing up, I'd always desired the companionship of a dog. Unfortunately, my mother was adamantly opposed to the idea, and instead provided me with a tank full of tropical fish that seemed primarily concerned with eating their young. Though I appreciated how life in the fish tank mirrored my own, the aquatic pet experience left me feeling a bit empty. However, as I stood there in the kennel I could feel that void finally being filled, a void which I hadn't even realized still existed.

A shelter volunteer carried the pup out through a hallway and into the reception area where we waited, along with a writer from *New York Magazine.* He was there to do a story on the Humane Society while his photographer was on a quest for the perfect moment to capture on film. Just as if on cue and as the camera flashed, our puppy lifted her head and draped an abnormally large tongue across the volunteer's hand. We named her Becky.

I couldn't believe how much I loved that stupid dog and I felt like a little kid again. When I would walk her up and down the street, passersby would literally stop dead in their tracks—captivated by how beautiful she was.

About a week after adopting her, Becky and I took a long walk that ended up on the grounds surrounding Gracie Mansion and at some point after we arrived, she appeared to be on a mission of sorts. She sniffed around for several minutes, stalked a few pigeons, and then took an enormous dump on what was the equivalent of the Mayor's front lawn. It was an incredibly satisfying moment for both of us.

We left the steaming tribute and eventually headed toward Venus' apartment. I don't exactly recall how it happened but as we approached York Avenue, Becky's leash somehow worked itself free from my hand. Just as it did, she trotted up a few feet ahead and I could see impending disaster. I knew that if I were to go after her in any obvious way she'd break into a sprint, and we were already so close to York she'd be in the middle of traffic before I had a chance to catch up. This was going to be a **bad** scene. Becky was already increasing her speed and looking back at me tauntingly, daring me to give chase. I had no choice. I started after her, and as she got within 90 feet of the curb she kicked it into high gear with absolutely no intention of stopping.

With a rush of adrenaline, I launched into a sprint that I didn't think I was capable of. I was able to close the gap quickly, but not before Becky was at the edge of York Avenue with cars whizzing by. Fully outstretched, I dove into the street and *knew* I was going to die. At some point between diving and landing, I literally saw my life flash before my eyes. It was as if a long series of photographs, taken throughout the course of my life, was suddenly shown to me in an instant.

I landed halfway in the middle of the right lane, and as my hand came crashing down upon Becky's back she showered me with a boatload of fishy-smelling piss. Then, just as I pulled her to my chest, I felt the rubber tire of a Toyota grip my long, curly, hair as it screeched by—no more than a couple of inches from my head.

I really loved that stupid dog.

25

By the end of March, not even a full month after moving in with Venus, it had become apparent that the health of our relationship was in sharp decline. There were a number of reasons for this, but the prevailing factor had to be that I just didn't like her. Not only did I question her ability to remain faithful, but she was also bossy, controlling, and manipulative—and a living arrangement born partly out of convenience was now steeped in aggravation and turmoil. On a more positive note, my relationship with the dog was going magnificently well. Each morning after Venus headed out for work, as if on cue, Becky jumped in bed to fill the void.

Tensions with Venus reached a boiling point one evening at the home of my childhood friend—Chris Troise—and his girlfriend, Elizabeth. For some reason, throughout the course of the entire evening Venus had been rude, argumentative, and had openly embarrassed me on several occasions. The final straw came as she verbally assaulted me with such venom that even Chris took a step back, and though I can't recall her words precisely, I do remember Chris' response verbatim.

"She's really giving you the fuckin' business," he said in a hushed voice. "You wanna ditch this scene and get a drink?"

"We're gonna ditch this scene and get a drink," I told Venus.

"Do you want us to come?" she asked, unsure if an invitation was being extended.

"No."

After clearing that up, I put on my jacket and headed straight for the door with Chris in hot pursuit. We proceeded to a nearby bar, and

84

as the liquor flowed I began to think that life with Perry and his mom might not be so bad after all.

After several drunken hours in the bar with Chris, I staggered back to the apartment and crawled into bed, thankful that Venus was asleep. Only she wasn't. Like a fanged and hairy beast camouflaged in the thick underbrush of a jungle, she was simply waiting for the perfect opportunity to strike. Just as I positioned myself to pass out, she pounced.

Once again, I can't recall the details of the attack, but this time it was because I wasn't listening. I had already decided that she was a bitch, and that I would be vacating the apartment and the relationship as soon as possible. Of course, in order to minimize any further discomfort to myself, I would withhold that information until the last minute. This may have been a bit deceptive and cowardly but I had no choice. The second she became aware of our demise I'd be in the street and I knew it. It was simply a matter of survival.

I continued to ignore Venus' tirade until I saw sunlight creeping through the window and realized I'd been pretending to listen for over two hours. Up until that moment I was able to ignore her quite effectively, thanks to the intense intoxication. However, the alcohol soon turned on me as the drunkenness transformed itself into a horrendous hangover. My head was pounding and I wanted to puke, which was now exacerbated by the nauseating presence of Venus and her barrage of nasty remarks. Finally, I'd had enough.

"If you don't shut your fucking mouth I'm leaving," I calmly informed her. And then I fell asleep.

That afternoon I awoke in sad shape but was thankful that Venus had apparently decided to spend her Saturday elsewhere.

*Wait a minute... If Venus is out, then Becky would be in bed. But Becky's **not** in bed. That could mean only one thing: VENUS IS STILL IN THE APARTMENT! But it's so quiet, where could she be? She's usually such a noisy bitch. Maybe she's in the bathroom—*

As I turned over to see if the bathroom light was on, I almost rolled into Venus' face as she sat silently on the floor beside the bed, peering at me with bugged-out eyes. Unbelievably, she was there all along—waiting for me to awaken.

"We're getting rid of the dog," she said in an eerie voice that made my skin crawl. Then, for a moment or two she continued to sit silently as though she was waiting for me to dare rebuke her. Of course, I did—but not before asking why she was taking her anger out on the dog.

She explained that by threatening to leave, I demonstrated an obvious lack of commitment. Therefore, it would be unwise for her to relocate to a larger apartment that allowed pets, when there was a very good chance I might abandon her as well as the significantly higher rent.

Obviously, she was once again attempting to manipulate the situation—not to mention my own words in order to exert control over me. I very clearly remembered saying that if she didn't shut her mouth—I would be *leaving* in a temporal sense. I never said I would be *leaving her*, which would suggest a more permanent departure and one that she was now claiming I implied. I decided not to comfort her by illuminating the obvious distinction because she was already aware of it, and it was all just a game anyway. *Fuck her.* Let her pretend to think what she wants.

"So bring the dog back to the kennel today," she told me.

"I'll bring you back first."

Nothing more needed to be said after that.

She gave me until the end of the week to find a place, but I was completely unsuccessful as any apartment allowing pets was clearly out of my price range. Even worse, I was told that the Humane Society offered no guarantee of re-adoption. As a result, Becky and I temporarily moved to my mother's condo in Bayside to buy more time and figure things out.

Perhaps, for the first time in my life, my mother actually rose to the occasion. First of all, it was utterly amazing that she would even allow a shitting, pissing, little puppy in her house to begin with. Beyond that, it was ultimately due to *her* diligence that a shelter guaranteeing adoption was found.

After a few more failed attempts to secure an affordable and pet-friendly apartment, my mother drove us to a Long Island adoption center where I was forced to relinquish my dog.

I cried like a little kid.

26

I spent approximately two weeks at my mother's condo after reluctantly giving away Becky. While living with her on the outskirts of Queens, the commute to Manhattan was a painful ordeal. At the crack of dawn, I would rise to catch an express bus that battled rush-hour traffic from Bell Boulevard in Bayside, to First Avenue in Manhattan. To further complicate matters, Sections had finally begun recording a professional demo tape at a downtown studio where my presence was required almost every evening after work. Then, late at night after the session concluded, I would return to Bayside for a few hours of sleep before beginning the routine anew. It was a grueling schedule, but the demo was an absolute necessity if we were ever going to play any hi-profile gigs.

As luck would have it, Perry stumbled upon a convenient but temporary living arrangement in Manhattan that would at least see me through the late-night recording sessions. He'd recently heard from Rachel Sanders, a friend and former co-worker who was interested in subletting a room in her apartment while her roommate, Melody Richards, was on tour with a theater group. Both girls were extremely talented singers and actresses and both were friends of Perry; however, Melody was especially significant in his life as she would be the second of the aforementioned love interests to fail to reciprocate his feelings.

My new, temporary dwelling was located on 83rd Street between First and Second Avenue. Since the subletting agreement had been entirely arranged through Perry, the first time I met Rachel was when I appeared at her door with a duffel bag in my hand.

Rachel was the working man's blond-bombshell. She was somewhat shorter than you might imagine—but she had the boobs, hair, and makeup to otherwise complete the picture. She was also a bit of a space cadet.

Melody would be on tour for eight weeks during which I could have either the bedroom or the living room for only $300 per month. Honestly, I couldn't have cared less where I slept and was only thankful to be back in the city; however, Rachel was insistent that I have my choice. She guided me toward the back of the apartment to peruse the bedroom, where I encountered a black cat sprawled-out on the bed. Her name was Bridget and as I came closer, she rolled over on her back exposing her stomach. Unfortunately, I'm not much of a cat person and besides, I've always been terribly allergic to them.

"Oh, come on," Rachel said with a smile. "She wants you to pet her belly. She only does that for people she *really* likes."

Not wanting to seem like an asshole in front of my new roommate, I gave in and petted the stupid cat. The moment I began to think that, perhaps, some cats weren't so bad—four sets of razor-sharp claws and a pair of fangs were suddenly plunged into my arm. Even though Rachel seemed shocked by Bridget's behavior, I decided to let the cat have the bedroom.

On the very first evening of my new living arrangement, Perry stopped by to discuss the demo and the final track to be recorded. We had already recorded "Valentines" and "Loud Mouth," and after some debate we settled on "In a Room"—which would finally give Danny a chance to play the sax and shut his mouth.

"Hey, where's Rachel?" Perry asked as it suddenly occurred to him that she wasn't in the apartment.

"She had to run some errands. She should be back in a few minutes," I told him as my eyes had already begun to itch from the cat.

Perry then stood up and produced a plastic bag containing his stash as well as a long, blue, hypodermic needle.

"Nice. When'd you start shootin' up, junky?" I asked.

"Today," he answered.

That wasn't entirely true. Perry had stuck himself once before while visiting his father in California.

I followed him to the kitchen where he found a spoon, into which he emptied a bag of dope and a syringe full of water. Perry then placed a lit match beneath the spoon until the dope dissolved as the water began to boil. The moment it did the match was removed and then, with a piece of cotton to help filter out as many of the "impurities" as possible, he drew the liquefied narcotic into the syringe.

I wasn't exactly sure how I felt about the needle. I must admit, though, I was somewhat mesmerized by the process as I'd never before seen a street drug administered intravenously. I was also incredibly impressed with Perry's expertise as within seconds he located a vein. He slipped the syringe into his arm and then, after maneuvering the needle around for a moment, pulled slightly upwards on the plunger to ensure the intended victim had been penetrated. Then suddenly, **EUREKA!!!** A stream of red rushed into the chamber as a plume of blood slowly rose to mingle with the dirty-looking liquid held within. I began carefully monitoring his behavior to note the effects of the drug once delivered intravenously.

After emptying the chamber's contents into his arm Perry removed the needle, gently closed his eyes, and seemed to just barely clench his jaw. Within four or five seconds he reopened his eyes and I could see he was completely wasted.

"How does it feel?" I asked.

"It feels like heroin," he said. "Yours is on the counter."

I went to retrieve the dope and was disheartened to find only a single bag awaiting me. Of course, I could get high by snorting only one, but to get truly fucked up would require a second bag and I mentioned that fact to Perry.

"The dude only had two left. That's why I got the needles," he responded. Apparently, delivering heroin into the bloodstream intravenously is the most efficient and cost-effective way to manage what could become a very expensive habit. "Booting one bag is like snorting three," he explained.

This was a defining moment in my own drug history as I realized I now had two options before me: I could either head over to Hell's Kitchen for another bag to snort, or for the first time in my life—*plunge a needle into my arm*. Though previously opposed to this brand of drug delivery, watching Perry tap of vein helped demystify the process and remove the aura of depravity I had associated with it. I was now suddenly able to look past the seedier side and accept IV drug use for what it was: *A matter of economics.* So, once again, I would confront yet another line not to cross and take a tremendous leap forward.

I approached the waiting syringe with a mixture of awe and loathing and then realized that these syringes differed dramatically from those belonging to Crackhead Jim. Jim's were orange, fairly short, and designed for diabetics—while these were blue, longer in length, and required assembly as the actual needle had to be attached to the chamber.

Even though I had just witnessed the procedure, I drew a blank when it came time to execute. Fortunately, Perry had always assumed a big brother role with regard to such matters, and once again confidently took the helm. After he combined the ingredients in a spoon, I held a lit match beneath it. As soon as it boiled, I extinguished the flame and tossed the smoldering match into the kitchen's wastebasket.

Perry loaded the syringe, grabbed me by the wrist, and then began to search for the perfect vein. He carefully examined my arms, and though I could see several possibilities and pointed them out, Perry dismissed each as "rolling veins" which are difficult to penetrate.

"Your veins are hard to get at," he told me. "Maybe we should skin-pop it."

"What's a skin-pop?"

"It's when you don't mainline it. You shoot it in your ass, or anywhere other than a vein."

"Fuck that shit. I'm going for glory."

After a few moments of searching, he spotted his target: a barely perceptible, greenish-blue bump located on the top of my left forearm, about two inches from my elbow. As far as I was concerned it barely qualified as a vein at all, but Perry was certain it was the best candidate. Even so, the pressure from a belt wrapped around my arm was required to coax the vein out, and I was again impressed with Perry when he nailed it on the very first attempt. I would later learn that his proficiency with a needle was the fortunate result of a short stint in the army as a medic.

As he emptied the contents of the syringe into my arm, my fascination with his needle-wielding prowess was interrupted by the immediate effects of the heroin. I felt a river of warmth flowing through the penetrated vein, eventually culminating into a rush that can only be described as a body-orgasm. As the climax began to subside, it dispersed throughout—showering me with a million little bursts of euphoria. At one point I could feel my heart tighten, and as the drug traveled through its chambers I could actually *taste* it.

Within a few minutes I realized that the intoxicating effects induced by administering dope intravenously, are ultimately the same as those achieved by snorting it. Cost-effectiveness aside, the only difference between the two delivery methods is in the *immediate* effect. Unlike snorting heroin which results in a gradual, creeping kind of intoxication, booting it provides a rapid rush that many dope fiends become specifically addicted to. This sensation quickly subsides, however, and the hours spent in a nodding euphoria is essentially the same experience—though perhaps for a shorter duration. Although I did find the orgasmic intensity of the IV rush to be pleasurable, and Perry actually preferred it, if given the choice I would've still preferred to put heroin up my nose.

After the rush, I came back down to earth and thought it would be a good idea to clean up the mess, fearing that my new roommate might take exception to the dirty syringes, blood-speckled tissues, and burnt spoons strewn about the kitchen. Although Rachel knew that Perry and I liked to "dabble," this would clearly be too large a slice of life for her to handle.

Once restoring the kitchen to a less traumatizing state, Perry and I relocated to the living room to nod. Then at some point Rachel returned from the store, and immediately greeted Perry with a big hug.

"Hi Perry!" she said. "I love my new roommate!"

"That's nice, Rachel," he responded.

"Hey, how's the demo going?" she asked as she passed the kitchen on her way to the bedroom.

"It's going OK," Perry told her. "If Danny would shut up and Matt could remember how to play his guitar, things would be perfect."

"Hey guys?" Rachel then called out from the back of the apartment; however, failing to hear her Perry and I continued on with the conversation.

"Danny will *never* shut up and Matt can't even remember where he *left* his guitar," I told him.

"Hey, you guys…" Rachel tried again to get our attention.

"Danny's days are numbered," Perry stated.

"Hey guys, excuse me—" Rachel again politely attempted to elicit a response.

Unfortunately, Perry and I were not only engrossed in matters pertaining to Sections, but completely fucked out of our skulls. Thankfully, she got right to the point:

"Hey guys…excuse me, but umm…the kitchen's on fire."

Rachel said it so calmly and without any sense of urgency that it took a moment to register. In fact, I remained in a daze until I saw Perry leap into action as smoke began wafting into the living room, at which point I too jumped to my feet and darted into the kitchen behind him.

The kitchen was filled with smoke, and at first we had no idea of the source or cause. It must have taken Perry a full minute to pinpoint the burning wastebasket, fueled by the smoldering match that **I** failed to completely extinguish, as the culprit.

We mounted an assault on the fire. Perry kicked the smoking wastebasket out from under the sink, I dumped a can of Mountain Dew over it, and Rachel stood by to monitor events. It was a *team effort.* Unfortunately, two fucked up junkies and a messenger from Mars were apparently not the best equipped to deal with the crisis. The Mountain Dew proved itself an ineffective fire retardant, and as the flames grew to within three feet of the ceiling the prospect of an inferno became very real. Then suddenly, throwing all caution to the wind, Perry hastily picked up the melting wastebasket, ran into the bathroom, and threw it in the tub.

27

Rachel was a great singer and had a sultry, bluesy voice that was intoxicating. Before I knew it we were fooling around and within a week, without ever saying a word, we became a very casual item. However, my affair with Rachel took a backseat to my relationship with heroin, which blossomed into something truly meaningful as I became a regular user for the first time.

Although I wasn't getting high on a daily basis just yet, Perry had discovered a new spot in Harlem and I found myself there between three and five times a week to inhale two or three bags of dope. It was located on 110th Street and Lexington Avenue and for a junky—it was the *Mother Land.* In fact, there were not only a number of dope dealers roaming the block, but also a few crack dealers stationed in projects and on street corners. Unfortunately, the increased access to my drug of choice brought new problems to deal with and after two weeks, on days in between using, I began to experience minor withdrawal symptoms that would erupt in the form of headaches, though at the time I didn't recognize them as such.

There were two external factors contributing to the escalated drug use, besides of course, the discovery of 110th Street. One was the minimal amount of rent I was paying while living at Rachel's, and the other was a staff change at Barry's that resulted in more hours on the clock—and more money to buy drugs with.

The primary change at work involved Gina. Along with an associate, she was about to be transferred to the Lexington Avenue store and seemed depressed about it.

"Don't worry, Gina. I promise, I'll write everyday," I told her in an effort to lighten the mood as our final day as co-workers was coming to an end.

"It's not that," she told me. "Paul has been giving me a hard time lately and I think we're gonna call it quits."

Paul was Gina's eccentric, sculptor boyfriend.

"Well, that'll give *Perry* a reason to live," I said, as he often stopped by under the pretense of visiting me, when he was really just interested in boning her.

I gave Gina a hug and left the store as my shift ended. I then headed downtown as earlier that morning Rachel had asked me to pick up a box of headshots recently taken of her at a photography studio in the West Village. She mentioned she was a bit concerned about the final product, recalling that the photographer wore a patch over his left eye. As things turned out, however, the pictures were great. Rachel looked beautiful and her stage history, in resume format, was included on the back of the photos at no additional charge.

As I left the studio I realized that Dabney's was only a few blocks away and that judging from the time, Perry's shift should have been winding down. I decided to see if he was interested in getting high before returning to his mother's apartment in Brooklyn. He was.

We walked toward Union Square to catch the #6 train uptown. Just after crossing Seventh Avenue, progress was halted by a commotion in front of a bodega. Apparently, the little grocery store was in the process of being robbed, as a vertically-challenged Mexican thug was stationed just outside preventing customers from entering and interrupting the progress of his amigos.

The mini-Mexican had apparently felt my path and proximity to the store was somehow a threat to the operation going on within it, and as Perry and I attempted to pass—the little prick actually tried to push me into the street. It was like being roughed-up by a fifth grader.

I am in no way a hero. New York City can be a rough and unpredictable place, and if you choose to live or work there you do so at your own risk. However, I don't take lightly to people putting their hands on me in an aggressive manner, especially when they happen to be…little.

I told him to keep his fucking hands off me and with that, pushed him so forcefully that he fell on his ass. Unbelievably, he then rose to his feet and rushed me. I tossed Rachel's headshots aside, and then courageously showered the little thug with punch after punch as a crowd of onlookers gathered to suggest I pick on somebody my own size.

Believe it or not, the misinformed crowd was becoming hostile and though Perry attempted to explain the situation, a few of them actually threatened to call the police if I didn't stop punching the little bastard. I stopped throwing fists and decided to push him to the ground once more so I could flee the scene before getting arrested for obstructing a robbery in progress. As I gave him one final shove, I noticed that Rachel's box of headshots had exploded onto the sidewalk and was now being trampled upon.

"Shit, Perry—quick! The headshots! Get the fucking headshots!" I shouted, at which point Perry began kicking the Mexican in his head.

28

At the beginning of May in 1992, Rachel left Oscar's for another job at Ed Dibevic's which was located on Broadway in The Village. In New York it was relatively a short-lived, Chicago-based, 1950's-style restaurant that enjoyed some success during the nineties. During this period, such theme-based eateries were all the rage. Among many others, there was Planet Hollywood, Jekyll and Hyde, Ellen's Stardust Diner, The Hard Rock Café, The Fashion Café and The Harley Davidson Café.

In an effort to help emphasize the restaurant's theme, Ed Dibevic's expected its employees to project a certain attitude. A very *bad* attitude. This became immediately apparent to patrons, as they would enter the establishment and be confronted by a sign that read, "EAT FAST, TIP BIG, GET OUT."

As Ed Dibevic's prepared for its grand opening, it conducted auditions as opposed to job interviews because little importance was placed on issues pertaining to table service or past experience. In fact, candidates were instructed to "interview" for positions while assuming the role of an unusual character they felt would best demonstrate the theatrical skills needed to support the restaurant's spirited theme. Perhaps due to my half-serious recommendation,

Rachel auditioned as herself and was hired on the spot.

The idea of being generously rewarded for telling people to fuck off was too much for Perry to resist, and after Rachel secured a spot so effortlessly—he decided to audition as well. Noting the sound advice I provided Rachel, I suggested that he audition with a needle sticking out of his arm. Instead, Perry played the role of a very clumsy nerd, and his performance was so convincing that management thought him an insurance liability and immediately sent him packing. Fortunately, Perry's lack of success was for the better, as Rachel soon realized the job wasn't all that it was cracked-up to be and as a result, her commitment to Ed Dibevic lasted only two weeks.

In mid-May, shortly after Rachel found another job, her roommate—Melody—returned from her theatrical trip abroad and we all got along exceptionally well. So well, in fact, that even though Melody was back in town a month earlier than expected, I was invited to continue on as a member of the household for as long as I wanted. Meanwhile, on the musical front, Casey the Cop had gotten drunk and nearly killed himself along with a friend while racing his Monte Carlo down Park Avenue. So, while the police were busy ignoring the incident and Casey remained in traction, we recruited Colin Emerson—my co-worker from Barry's—to play bass on the demo as well as at any upcoming performances while we continued to search for a more permanent replacement. More suitable to our sound, Colin came from an alternative rock background—as opposed to the funk influences that molded Frank's playing or the heavy metal style that Casey seemed to favor. Unfortunately, Colin's one shortcoming was that he happened to be a complete douche.

His own project was a female-fronted band called Waver. They were very speedy, and their arrangements permitted Colin to adopt some bad bass playing habits. Somehow though, we were able to draw a few decent performances out of him and finish the recording in fair shape.

Although it certainly wasn't perfect, most people thought the demo was shockingly good and having it on hand dramatically increased the quantity, as well as the quality of gigs available to us. The first of these occurred on June 15th when we were invited to play The Blarney Stone. Although there were many dives throughout New York with the same name, this particular installment was located downtown and had developed a reputation for featuring some of the city's more talented bands. It would be our first gig in over six months

95

and though we weren't the most well known band in town, the performance drew a surprising amount of interest and would clearly be the most heavily attended to date. For the first time, we would be performing to a large audience that was there specifically to see us, as opposed to the lingering remnants of another band's following—or a pack of drunks that had just stumbled in from the street.

On the night of the gig, the band showed up about two hours early. Although I had deep reservations about Danny, and of course, Pat, I knew they were both deeply committed to Sections and believed in the quality of the songs. Colin, however, was different. I realized his interest in Sections was based purely on the fact that we appealed to a broad range of tastes, and that the added exposure would eventually benefit Waver. That's why, when I was told that Colin had been trying to convince Danny and Pat to abandon Sections for another project—I wasn't surprised. Of course, that didn't mean I wasn't going to kick the living shit out of him as soon as I got the chance—it just means I wasn't surprised.

Within an hour after the band showed up, Rachel, Melody, and everyone from Barry's had arrived at the Blarney Stone. Cynthia, however, wasn't in attendance and for the first time Matt and Melody were introduced. From the very onset it was obvious to everyone that Melody was attracted to Matt, Matt was attracted to Melody, and Perry wanted to stab himself in the heart. Having been cast aside for a gargantuan penis was one thing, but being passed up for the perpetually unconscious was quite another.

As we waited to take the stage, Melody grew drunker and drunker. Although she was fully aware of the fact that Matt was now living with and engaged to Cynthia, she began wrapping herself around him while he did nothing to discourage the contact. I watched in disgust, Perry watched in horror, and the star-crossed souls simply gazed into each other's eyes as if time stood still—and as if Matt actually needed something else to be doing behind Cynthia's back.

Within a few minutes the two were locked in a deep embrace. Although Matt obviously wanted her, whatever remnants he had left of a conscience compelled him to make sure she knew the score.

The bar rapidly filled and as the noise level increased, Matt repositioned his mouth beside Melody's ear. Then, in an even tighter embrace, as if they were trapped alone on a jagged cliff and about to leap to their very deaths—Matt passionately screamed over the roar of mountain-top winds:

"You know I'm getting married...right!?!?!" he shouted.

Of course she did.

They then celebrated with an impassioned kiss, just before holding hands and jumping over the edge together. Within a few minutes we took the stage, and as Matt began to stumble through the songs, Melody looked as if she wanted to crawl into his amplifier.

After the last song I bid farewell to the audience, and then attempted to insert the mike-stand up Colin Emerson's ass. Unfortunately, within seconds the bouncer was on stage and my arm was twisted behind my back preventing any *real* penetration.

29

Immediately after the Blarney Stone gig, Matt and Melody began a relationship that was even more bizarre than the one I was presently involved in with Rachel. And even though Matt made it clear that he would follow through with the wedding plans, I believe the feelings he had for Melody were actually deeper than those he had for the woman he was about to marry. Whether or not the secretive affection was genuine, however, or somehow connected to his escalating drug use which had now reached epic proportions, I doubt I will ever know. If it was drug related, it was due to the fact that Melody unconditionally accepted Matt for the fuck-up he was, unlike Cynthia who would have none of it. As a result, he lived a double life and began spending more time with Melody who was, to my knowledge, the only living soul on earth who could appreciate Matt for exactly the person he was. Due to the illicit relationship, Matt soon became a fixture at the apartment as school was closed for the summer, and there simply wasn't a more convenient place for him to fuck himself up.

Like Perry, Matt preferred the syringe, and though he never spiked a vein in front of the girls, after scoring on 110th Street he would spend the first few minutes of every visit locked in the bathroom with a needle sticking out of his arm. He would then retreat to the couch for several hours until emerging from his nod with a farewell erection for

Melody—just before rushing back to the Bronx to welcome Cynthia home from work. It couldn't have been the most fulfilling relationship for either girl, but Melody never said a word and Cynthia never even knew he was missing.

I had also been getting high several times a week and though the girls knew exactly what I was doing, they were unfazed and did nothing to try to curb it. I suppose that in the beginning I'd desensitized them to the seriousness of the habit by remaining employed, paying the bills, brushing my teeth, and washing my ass. But still, **there is no question about the fact that while living with Rachel and Melody, two full years after my very first snort, I'd finally become a full-blown dope fiend.** My habit would soon reach a crescendo after Melody told me that she loved Sections—*and that I didn't have to pay rent or household bills, so I could spend less time working and more time focusing on the music.*

"And Craig," she said. "I don't know how and I don't know when, but I know in my heart that someday you guys are gonna be superstars."

I suppose Melody's gesture came from a sincere desire to support the band, and as a result she became my very favorite enabler of all time. Of course, I still frequently made monetary contributions to the household, but due to her generosity I suddenly had enough money to purchase between three and five bags of dope, *daily.*

I was now fully aware of the fact that I was officially a junky—but didn't care and was somehow able to look the other way. I knew I was physically addicted to heroin but was certain that if I wanted to, I could break the habit in a moment's notice. Of course, I had absolutely no intention of doing so because I liked it too much, and had made a conscious decision to remain a functioning addict. But none of that really mattered anyway because eventually, I'd be a star. Perry said so…and now, *so did Melody.*

30

Shortly after attempting to impale Colin Emerson on stage, before the largest gathering we'd ever played in front of, Barry decided to transfer him over to the Lexington Avenue store. In his place and from the same location they sent Kurt Bono. Kurt was a classically trained guitarist who had attended Julliard to hone his skills, but his musicianship was hardly limited to a single instrument. Conveniently, as he stepped in to fill Colin's shoes as bagel boy, he'd soon also fill the void as a bassist for Sections. I had a great deal of respect for Kurt, and was impressed that he'd been accepted into one of the most prestigious music schools in the country, especially in light of the fact that he was a complete burnout. Although now strictly a pot smoker, I had the impression that he was still paying the price for being an acid head in elementary school.

More than any other day, I hated Sunday as it was Megan's only day off and I was forced to open the store. Kurt's first shift fell on a Sunday, and when I arrived at 5:30 he was prepped for the morning rush with an espresso in one hand and a joint in the other.

"What's up, bro? Wanna take a hit?" he asked without hesitation.

I immediately decided that I quite liked my new co-worker.

"Sure—nice combo," I said as he handed me the joint, referring to the mixture of cannabis and caffeine.

"Poor man's speedball," he pointed out.

Yes, Kurt Bono and I would be getting along quite well, I imagined, and by the end of the day I was practically begging him to be our bassist. I then contacted Matt, Danny, Pat and Perry and arranged for him to formally audition later that evening.

Sunday's early morning shift would usually force me to delay the daily dope-pilgrimage in exchange for some much needed slumber. Consequently, the moment my shift ended I jumped in a cab and headed straight home. I then walked into the apartment, kicked off my shoes, and passed out on the couch for several hours.

It was an intensely deep sleep, during which I'd awoken in the midst of a cold sweat and a nightmare that I initially attributed to a wake-up call from the junky monkey. In the dream, I was alone with Perry who, for some reason, was injecting heroin into my feet. It was incredibly vivid and painful as I recall him not only stabbing me with the needle, but also raking it across the tops and bottoms of my toes.

As I sat up and stepped away from the couch, I felt a raw and intense pain in both feet from which blood was now seeping through several tears in my socks. This was obviously the handiwork of the cat, which, as it savored and methodically licked my blood from its claws was now glaring at me from the corner of the room. Bridget had already attacked me several times over the course of my stay, but this was the first assault that occurred while I was asleep and the one that inflicted the most damage.

As I limped around, the pain was so severe that I would've gone directly to the emergency room for pain killers—had I not been going directly to Harlem for heroin. I flagged a cab and headed to 110th Street, where I immediately scored five bags of dope and descended into the subway.

The 110th Street subway station smelled like shit and was completely filthy. The walls were covered in graffiti, and, with the exception of a few homeless addicts sleeping on the piss-stained platform, the station was deserted and lifeless. I quickly moved to the furthest end of the platform and began opening the bags of dope and snorting them, one after the next. Though I never saw him coming, as I was about to tear into my fifth and final bag I heard someone standing behind me.

As I turned, I was frozen with fear as a cop stood no more than three feet away. Fortunately, he wasn't a roid-rager who would've liked nothing better than to kick my ass and then arrest me for it, but an older cop who'd long since given up life on the Mod Squad to walk the beat. He was well into the twilight of his career, and you could tell that by this point he was merely going through the motions and waiting for his pension to kick in.

"What are you doing here?" he asked in a rough voice.

Great question! What was I, a whiter than white boy doing on a subway platform in the middle of Harlem, with four empty dope wrappers crinkling under my feet and a full bag clenched in my fist? I searched the walls for an answer.

"Uhhhhmmm…" was what I decided to go with.

"Waiting for the train?" the cop patiently tried to help me along.

"Uhhhhh…OK," I said.

The officer seemed perfectly satisfied with the explanation he provided, and then left to continue mulling his retirement.

Perry arranged for Kurt's audition to be held at a new rehearsal studio called Big Sounds on University Place in The Village. It was owned and operated by a gentleman named Anton Gifford, who had immediately hit it off with Perry upon meeting him at Dabney's. Anton was a very nice, kind of goofy, 40 year-old guitarist who seemed unable to let go of the past. The studio was his life and the means by which he could earn a meager living to support his family, yet still remain on the periphery of what he loved most. It was really a sad situation because the studio was just barely squeaking by, and Anton was a terrible guitar player.

When I arrived, everyone including Kurt was already there, and we began running through the set list in order to assess his playing. Once again, he wasn't my ideal bassist, but I liked Kurt personally and we decided to bring him aboard.

Beyond Kurt's audition, the evening was notable for two major announcements that were made just prior to breaking down. One was issued by Perry, who informed us that upon receipt of the demo, CBGB's invited Sections to open for PJ Harvey on a Friday night at the end of July. This was a significant accomplishment, not only because PJ Harvey was well established and CBGB's was a premier venue, but because they offered the gig without ever having heard us play a live note. That was very unusual and quite a risk for any club to take, let alone CBGB's, but apparently the demo was stronger than I'd initially thought. As soon as Perry mentioned the gig, there was a palpable excitement in the room and though I didn't say anything—it felt like things were definitely moving in the right direction.

The second announcement was made by Matt, as he and Cynthia had finally set August 29th as the day they would join hands in wedded bliss. However, when he reached into his briefcase for the invitations, it accidentally toppled over and out flew dozens of passed-due bills along with warnings to suspend a variety of services. It turned out that for several months Matt had been juggling debts in a desperate attempt to maintain a façade of domestic normalcy—as he borrowed from Peter to get high with Paul.

31

Before the big performance at CBGB's, we accepted a tune-up gig at The Spiral on Houston Street. Overall, the show was solid and for his first performance with the band, Kurt did admirably. After leaving the stage, Perry and I were greeted by Katrina MacKay and her roommates, Bret and Stacy, all of whom we'd met at the very first Speakeasy gig. They each hailed from Georgia and Katrina, in particular, would become a fixture at our shows and one of Sections' most ardent supporters.

"How were we?" I asked her. Katrina was a devout lover of live music and extremely blunt, so I was both curious and terrified to hear her assessment.

"You guys were great! But nobody got pummeled on stage," she said sounding a bit disappointed.

"Assault and battery is restricted to shows during *odd*-numbered months," Perry explained. "Even-numbers are for stealing liquor and pillaging sound equipment—*so sit tight.*"

"Hey Craig—a buddy of mine is coming into town on Tuesday, and he's gonna have some of that shit you wanted," Katrina suddenly told me.

As if being a heroin addict wasn't enough, ever since the mescaline adventure with Helmer I harbored an intense desire to experiment further with hallucinogenic drugs. Katrina was a card-carrying Dead Head, and her presence was enough to intensify the yearning so dramatically that each time I saw her she was subjected to an interrogation and a frisk. Before we left the club, Katrina and I made tentative arrangements to drop acid on the following Tuesday night. Although I shared my plans with no one, I had the evening mapped out for months and was determined to trip-out and then visit the *Alice in Wonderland* sculpture in Central Park.

When Tuesday morning arrived, I reported to Barry's and was already eagerly anticipating the end of the workday and the beginning of my trip to Wonderland. Then, at around 3 p.m., Gina called from the Lexington Avenue store. For some reason, she'd been terribly affected by a sob story authored by none other than Colin Emerson.

"Hey Craig, Colin is really upset," she said. "He told me to tell

102

you that he really thinks it would be in your best interest to have him on stage at CB's."

In *my* best interest.

Of course, his motivation to speak up had nothing to do with the caliber of the gig, or the fact that we'd be getting some very valuable exposure. I was floored by his audacity. Even after getting attacked on stage before an audience of friends and co-workers, Colin Emerson was still willing to swallow his self-respect and remain the shameless self-promoter.

If the impending trip hadn't so completely captured my fancy, I would've had more to say to Gina—who I was a little annoyed with for speaking on Colin's behalf in the first place.

"You know, we *were* gonna give him a call," I told her. "But then I thought we might try using a good bass player."

Thankfully, 4 p.m. finally rolled around, and as I reported to the apartment for the big trip, the skies opened and a thunderous summer storm began to soak the city. When I finally made it home, Katrina and Rachel were already waiting for me. Although Rachel previously mentioned that she would accompany us on our little adventure, she also said she'd be abstaining from any drug use. I thought this to be a wise decision as certain personalities react poorly to acid, and I had little doubt that Rachel was one of them. Furthermore, this particular batch of Dead Head acid had a reputation for being extremely potent, and I felt that Rachel was far too impressionable to handle it. Besides, I wasn't willing to be anyone's babysitter. I was finally about to attend a never-ending tea party, and would no more allow myself to be deterred by a bumbling blond, than I would be by the rumbling storm outside. So imagine my surprise when Rachel turned to look at me with her mouth opened, and a square of blotter-paper stuck to her tongue.

"You're gonna be sorry," I told her, when I knew it was I who'd be sorriest of all.

I swallowed my own hit and then we waited for the rain to subside. Unfortunately it was to no avail, and by the time we'd finally given up on the possibility of a moonlit evening, two hours had passed and we were tripping our faces off.

At about 9:30 Rachel, Katrina, and I began our trek toward 80th Street and Central Park East. Although I could never quite remember where the sculpture was exactly, I was certain it was on the eastern side of the park between 80th and 90th Streets and assumed we'd bump into it eventually.

As we were about to depart the building and head into the rain, Rachel stopped dead in her tracks—blocking our path to the sidewalk.

"Wait a minute," she said. "I'm not so sure this is such a great idea."

This was exactly what I was worried about.

"Christ! What's wrong, Rachel?" I asked.

"Well, you know, it's just kind of late to be fucked up and running around Central Park. It could be dangerous!"

I'd been getting drunk in the park since I was sixteen years old, and was convinced that at that hour it was as safe as virtually any other part of Manhattan. But make no mistake about it: I was determined to enjoy an evening of wild hallucinations in the middle of Central Park and I was going—safe or not, and with or without them.

We left the building and headed south on Third Avenue, marching silently in single file with me leading the pilgrimage. It had been raining for hours, and as the city marinated in the summer heat it soon produced a warm, toxic, street-gravy that was ankle-deep on certain corners and impossible to avoid. When we finally reached 80th Street, we hung a right and eventually passed my old apartment building just prior to reaching the park. We then crossed Fifth Avenue and as we stood at the edge of the park it began to rain harder. Even with the soggy conditions, it was a monumental occasion and an epic point in my drug consumption history.

While I stood there absorbing the moment and reflecting, for the first time I took a gander at Rachel's outfit. She was wearing a wool hat, sweatshirt and boxer shorts—all of which were outdone by the now completely saturated, fake fur boots that donned her stupid feet.

"What the fuck are those?" I asked.

"They're my special winter galoshes," she said. "Aren't they neat?"

"They'd be neater if it was winter instead of summer, and snowing instead of raining," Katrina pointed out.

"What's the big difference?" Rachel asked, as we stood there in the pouring rain.

"No difference, Rachel," I said. "And by the way: After we spend some time in the park, I wanna sail down the Hudson in a boat made of sponges, OK?"

Then, as I took a deep breath and was about to officially embark on my search for Alice, Rachel opened her mouth once more.

"I *definitely* don't think this is a good idea."

Now I was getting annoyed. If she was going to bail, she should have done so before we left the building. At that point I would have gladly left her behind to ride out the trip in the secure and friendly confines of our apartment. However, if she was to abort the mission now, I'd have no choice but to walk her home and by then I'd probably be too mangled to make it back to the park in one piece.

"Rachel! You will **NOT** ruin this for me," I told her. "Everything will be fine."

She then turned to Katrina.

"Come on—this is crazy! Let's go back," she said, almost pleading with the Georgian.

Katrina paused for a moment to mull the situation over—and then she said it. Though her remark seemed innocent enough at first, it was fully equipped with all the latent implications necessary to ruin my evening.

"I trust Craig," she said. "And if Craig says it's safe…then I believe him."

The fucking bitch.

As Katrina's vote of confidence successfully closed Rachel's mouth it would also dramatically alter my plans, though this was unknown to me at the time. Without further consideration I entered the park and the girls followed.

The intense rain seriously hampered visibility, and as we made our way through an area marked by crisscrossing walkways and maple trees, Katrina's words echoed in my brain:

"If Craig says it's safe, then I believe him... If Craig says it's safe, then I believe him... If Craig says it's safe, then I believe him..."

But what if it isn't such a good idea for two, naïve, country chicks and a skinny junky to be roaming around Central Park in the middle of the night? Now, if something happens to them it'll definitely be my responsibility. Shit! Maybe this isn't so safe after all. I mean, this is New York. What if one or both of them get raped...or even murdered?

As we continued on I tried to calm down and tell myself that the sudden fear was acid-inspired. I looked back at the girls who seemed relaxed as they continued to silently trudge forward.

After about ten minutes of searching for Alice, I stopped for a moment to look around. As we stood in a field of gigantic trees that were no more than ten feet from each other, I tried to get my bearings. As I did, I noticed what appeared to be a Mexican, approximately 50 feet away and darting from tree to tree. For a moment my heart jumped out of my chest. I could see he was wearing a white dress shirt with black pants and shoes, and his attire gave me the impression that he was a busboy or waiter.

I looked back at the girls to see if they noticed anything. They didn't.

*This **must** be the acid.*

I tried to refocus on the task at hand. Then, about 20 seconds later I saw the mysterious Mexican once more and he now seemed to be staring at us. Unfortunately, he was much too fleet-of-foot for me to be able to focus on directly. In fact, I could barely see him from the corner of my eye as he again began to bolt from tree to tree.

*Who the fuck **is** that!*

Now I was *really* getting nervous, and though I still thought it was probably the acid I wasn't entirely sure. All I knew was that if something terrible happened to the girls I would never be able to live with myself. I noticed though, that the suspicious Mexican wasn't a terribly imposing figure. But what if he had a gun, or even a knife?

Wait a minute... this has to be the acid.

It did seem peculiar that although I never managed to look at him directly, through the rain and darkness I was still able to discern his attire and possible ethnicity. I was almost certain that he was a hallucination, but decided not to take any chances.

"Let's go home," I dejectedly said to the girls.

"Why?" Katrina asked.

"It's getting too muddy."

As things turned out, it's likely that the acid gave me the type of experience I was hoping for—but only within a context that would prevent me from enjoying it, which was that of a perceived threat to the girls. It took what, at that moment, was my greatest possible fear and smacked me in the face with it. Instead of conjuring up a vision that was too fantastic to be real—like a fire-breathing dragon or a pirate ship—the hallucinogen merely presented me with a potentially dangerous Mexican, an encounter certainly not unheard of in *this* city.

32

On the night of the big gig at CBGB's, Perry and I once again exercised incredibly poor junky-judgment by sharing a few grams of coke before the show. However, due to my last run-in with the drug, I was fully prepared with a pre-opened bag of dope to immediately rescue me from the dreaded crash.

We were scheduled to open for PJ Harvey at approximately 11p.m. As Perry and I entered the club at precisely 10:50, completely lit-up from the coke, the entire band was there and a little miffed by our fashionably late arrival.

I tried to time things perfectly and reserve the final line of coke for just prior to taking the stage, hoping it would maintain the buzz I was already feeling and serve to *enhance* my performance. So, at just before 11:00, I inconspicuously slid a rolled-up dollar bill into a plastic bag and inhaled deeply. A few moments later, Peggy—the club's booking agent—pulled Perry aside and told him there'd been a change. Things were running late and as a result, PJ Harvey would now be taking the stage and we'd be going on afterwards.

We waited for PJ Harvey to finish and as they did, I realized that the last minute switch had foiled my attempt to correctly time the coke crash. I had initially planned on peaking mid-performance and then crashing as we exited the stage; however, as things turned out I was primed for the PJ Harvey set and completely uninspired for my own.

After PJ Harvey left the stage and we stepped upon it I began to feel the crash. Though I managed to somehow get through the set without killing myself, it would have mattered little as 90% of the audience had already departed with PJ Harvey. As a result, we were left with only 30 or so of our core following which was disheartening, as almost twice that number had showed up to witness my assault on Colin Emerson.

As soon as we finished the set I sprinted to the bathroom, and if the bag of dope hadn't already been opened I probably would've snorted it through the paper. After regaining my composure I returned to the side of the stage and was immediately confronted by Kurt. Apparently, while I was in the bathroom, Danny had given him a tongue-lashing about a minor change he missed during the final song. I don't recall precisely what he said to him, but whatever it was—Kurt was absolutely livid.

"That hairless little fucker needs to learn some manners," Kurt said as he gestured toward the stage in Danny's direction, and though his voice was calm his hand was trembling.

"Don't worry about it," I said, trying to muffle a chuckle. "Danny doesn't matter."

"No, Craig—it's seriously fucked up!"

"I know."

"I mean, come on! Maybe *you* can talk to me that way and maybe even Perry—but that little prick?! No way, bro—fuck him!!" Kurt said.

"Hey man, *no one* has a right to talk to you that way and besides, you know—Danny has no standing here. He's really just a...well, you know, he's a—"

"He's a fucking *ornament*!" Kurt interjected as he hit the nail right on its bald little head. "That's what he is. A fucking ornament."

For a moment I stood there in silence, overcome with emotion.

"YES!!!" I screamed in joyous confirmation while on the brink of tears. "THAT'S **EXACTLY** WHAT HE IS! HE'S AN ORNAMENT! **A FUCKING ORNAMENT!!!** Oh...thank God, man, **THANK GOD!!!**"

After what seemed like years of drifting helplessly in a sea of imperfect pejoratives it felt like I'd finally come home. Ever since our first nasty exchange, I'd been scouring my vocabulary in an effort to help define Danny's role in the band. Indeed, he *was* an ornament. An ornament that we continually tried to reposition more to its liking, but one that would never be completely satisfied with the branch from which it hung.

By now, Danny may well have been confused about what he could reasonably expect from his relationship with Sections, especially given the live dynamic that permitted him to step to the fore during performances. I allowed him that luxury because it was convenient to do so, and though it pandered to his most cherished desires—the whole thing was a bit of a ruse. Inadvertently, we were taunting him with a status he could never truly achieve, and though on stage he was given the freedom to do what he wanted, there was a very clear limit to the extent in which he could influence things. Of course, Danny seemed to have a breaking point with regard to imposed limitations, and perhaps the altercation with Kurt was some indication of that.

33

The day after the CBGB's performance I received a call from Kurt, who said that we needed to "have a talk." Of course, by this point in my life I already knew that any discussion alluded to in that particular way could mean only one thing: My ass was getting dumped.

We agreed to meet at a coffee shop near Lincoln Center that afternoon, and when I arrived I found Kurt sitting alone at a table in the corner of the restaurant. The moment I sat down across from him he let me have it.

"I think I'm gonna leave the band," he said to me.

"Oh come on, Kurt—please don't quit on me," I pleaded.

"Sorry, but I suddenly realized I don't like bald saxophone players. Oh, and that reminds me: I don't much care for singers with curly red hair either, so you and Perry can have these," he said with a smile as he handed me two tickets to see Simply Red at Summer Stage in Central Park that evening. "A friend of mine had a bit of an emergency to deal with and he didn't want them to go to waste."

"Kurt, Danny is **so** not worth quitting over," I told him while ignoring the tickets. "He's probably not even gonna be with us much longer! Why don't you just stick around for another month or so and see what happens?"

"Fuck that," he said. "I don't even wanna look at him anymore and besides, I have so much work coming up this semester that I really shouldn't be getting involved with anything other than school."

After confirming that there were no hard feelings, we wished each other luck before he left and then I called Perry from a payphone in the restaurant.

"Kurt quit the band," I told him.

"Why?!?"

"Danny pissed him off last night."

"That fucking sucks."

"No shit," I agreed.

"Was he a dick about it?"

"No," I told him. "He's just furious with Danny. Oh, and he gave us tickets to see Simply Red tonight at the park.

"Awesome!"

"So I guess you wanna go?"

"Definitely!" Perry replied. "I've still got some of Katrina's acid!"

"OK, but then afterwards we have to pay Alice a visit in Wonderland."

"You're still hung up on that?"

"More so than ever," I said. "I'll meet you by the park at around 7:30."

About an hour before show time Perry and I met on the corner of 72nd Street and Central Park West, right by Rumsey Field which is the Summer Stage venue. We then entered the park while simultaneously swallowing our hits of acid, and officially began the journey toward Wonderland. Of course, there was still the small matter of Simply Red to attend to beforehand, but by the time that wrapped up the acid should have me flying down the rabbit hole at warp speed. And now, THANK GOD, there would be no one to stand in my way. Perry was a big boy and as such, in the event that any gun-toting Mexican should stroll by—*he'd be on his own.*

We silently roamed around the park in a northeasterly direction, killing time and saying nothing until I began to feel the acid introducing itself to the heroin I snorted earlier in the day.

"Hey," I said breaking the silence of a multi-drug euphoria. "Let's go see Simply Red."

We made our way back to Rumsey Field and before we knew it, show time was upon us and we were both feeling the brunt of the acid.

As the lights slowly came up, we could see the band and a silhouette of what appeared to be a bald man with a big head standing motionless in front of the stage. Then suddenly, a spotlight shone brightly. An eight-member band was then completely illuminated and I could see that the bald man was none other than Mick Hucknall himself, wearing a tightly-wrapped, brown, knit hat. Then out of nowhere the band erupted into *Money's Too Tight* and he tore off the hat, unleashing his famous mane of curly crimson as the crowd went wild. Fan or not I have to admit, it was one of the most electrifying starts to a concert that I've ever witnessed.

The first few songs were performed without incident. Then suddenly, during a musical interlude of sorts, I briefly heard what sounded like a tape skipping. In 1987 I attended a Dead or Alive concert, and from the onset it was clear that the band was lip-syncing. However, in this particular instance, though I detected a glitch in the music I was only mildly suspicious because Mick was obviously singing, and I was obviously fucked up. But then Perry weighed in.

"This is fucking bullshit!" he yelled in my ear over the blaring amplifiers. "We're listening to a recording!"

The possibility that we'd experienced the same acid-fueled hallucination was unlikely, and though it seemed something was afoot, I assumed only a small portion of the music *may* have been pre-recorded. However, even with this concession I still wasn't willing to rule out acid as the culprit.

A minute or two had passed and the spotlights were turned on the crowd. For just a moment it seemed as though the audience was largely and oddly made up of guidos from New Jersey and the surrounding boroughs. Then, as soon as the lights again settled on the band, Perry grabbed my shirtsleeve and directed me to an area where the noise was less intense.

"Dude, this show is fixed," he said plainly.

"Huh?"

"They're not really playing. Didn't you hear the tape skip? And just look at all the fuckin' mobsters!"

Perry, not native to the city, had less experience with the variety of New Yorkers that I'd encountered for most of my life, and though there seemed to be a surprising number of Italians in attendance—they hardly seemed Mafioso.

"What the fuck are you talking about?" I asked as he now actually had me looking around.

"Open your eyes, stupid," he told me. "They're not really playing. This is a *mob* concert and Simply Red is a *mob* band."

"That's ridiculous."

"Oh, really? Then why are there so many gangsters here? Do you think that's just a coincidence?"

"What coincidence?! Besides, those aren't gangsters—those are bridge and tunnel guineas. Calm down," I told him but he was insistent.

"Listen to me," he said. "They aren't really playing because the show's fixed, so let's just get the fuck out of here."

"Fixed for what exactly?" I asked. "You can't *fix* a concert. That doesn't even make any sense."

"You don't know what you're talking about. The mob can fix anything! They fixed the fucking World Series, for God's sake."

"That's baseball."

"Baseball, football, boxing," he said. "It doesn't matter. The mob can fix anything they want."

"BUT PERRY!!! WHO THE FUCK IS BETTING ON SIMPLY RED?!?!"

I couldn't reason with him as the acid was obviously having its way with his brain. He was absolutely convinced that Simply Red was up to no good and became increasingly rattled by it. I, however, was determined to ignore him as well as the imaginary gangsters he felt threatened by. That is, until the imaginary gangsters started firing imaginary bullets with deadly precision.

"Get down!!!" he screamed as he tried to pull me to the floor.

"Perry, relax!!" I screamed back as he crouched on the floor with one hand covering his head and the other pulling on my shirt.

"Duck!!! They're shooting at us!"

"Dude, nobody's shooting at anybody," I told him. "Get up off the floor. You're embarrassing me."

"Just get down here before you get shot!" he pleaded.

"Perry! If they're shooting at us, how come nobody else seems to notice?"

"Because it's loud, and they're only shooting at us."

"Why would anybody want to shoot us, Perry?"

"Because they know I'm on to them."

"On to what!?! I swear, Perry—this is the acid."

A moment later, a Jersey guido bent down and put his hand on Perry's shoulder.

"Yo, buddy," said the guido. "You need some help or somethin'?"

With fear in his eyes, Perry sprang to his feet and bolted from the crime scene, dragging me down a hill and out of the park along with him.

Great hair, really, but it was a poor substitute for Wonderland.

34

By the end of August, Matt and Cynthia were married and Perry and I were forced to bear witness to the ridiculous spectacle. Besides the clandestine affair with Melody, the absurdity of it all was heightened by the fact that Cynthia knew nothing about the man she was marrying, or the double life he led in a powder keg of lies. Incidentally, two days before the wedding Melody suddenly decided to return home to visit her family in Michigan, and Rachel went along for the ride.

Regarding the pets that influenced my life, in early September Becky and the Humane Society were finally featured in *New York Magazine,* while Bridget was privately acknowledged for a streak of 21 consecutive days during which she successfully managed to spill my blood. I had picked up a copy of the magazine just prior to returning home from work and getting loaded, and as it was resting on the coffee table I sat there for a moment and reflected on Becky. I thought about how gigantic she'd be by now with those enormous paws, and how wonderful it would be to see her stroll into the apartment, lick my face, and eat the fucking cat.

As I sat there with my musings, I noticed Bridget staring at me as if she was finally beginning to realize just how much I hated her. She then cautiously approached the couch. At some point after I nodded off, she quietly climbed up beside me and rested her head against my right hand. When the little bitch began to purr, I knew it was already too late in the game to prevent bloodshed. Of course, I'd been through this shit before. I knew that if I were to tear my hand away from her head, she'd try to tear that hand away from my wrist. My only option was to remain alert and wait until she was distracted enough by something to put some distance between us. Then, for just a moment I accidentally slipped into a nod. During that brief instant Bridget must have sensed the loss of focus so heavily relied upon by the handlers of other vicious beasts, and launched a bloody assault that resulted in a very deep wound to one of my fingers.

"FUCKING BITCH!!!" I cried with real tears.

God, I hated that cat.

I went to the bathroom to try to get the seeping wound to clot but without much success. I then returned to the living room with a piece of toilet paper wrapped around my finger.

The sight of my flowing blood was simply too much of a banquet for Bridget to resist, and as I again somehow nodded off with the wounded hand lying lifeless beside me she pounced on it once more. The pain from this second attack was so sudden and severe that my heart almost stopped, which would've been difficult to detect because at that point it was only clocking in at about a beat-and-a-half per minute.

As she sunk her teeth into the fresh wound, I instinctively reacted without thinking. Unfortunately, the gut response came in the form of a fist meeting kitty's face.

At first, I was unaware of any damage inflicted as the cat ran away and I was still too consumed by my throbbing finger to care. Somehow though, I managed to nod off yet again without thinking about the attack, or the potential backlash that could result from my retaliation.

Seven hours later at around 1 a.m., my nod was interrupted by a strange, slurping sound coming from the kitchen. From where I was lying, I could see Bridget at her water bowl making the odd noise. Without giving it much concern, I quickly slipped back into my nod, and at some point became aware of an even *more* bizarre, gulping sound. Once again it was Bridget, only this time she was eating—or at least attempting to. Though I am certainly not a cat expert, my layman's diagnosis suggested that I'd damaged Bridget's mouth in some way. Of course, I couldn't be sure because each time I approached her to get a better look at the injury she would run away howling. Finally, at some point she fell asleep on the bed and I thought I had her cornered. Unfortunately, just as I got close enough to execute a more thorough examination, she squirted a gigantic turd and hit the road. Evidently, Bridget was now not only fucked up in the mouth, but even more fucked up in the head than she was previously.

But at least she was finally leaving me alone.

I decided that if the cat was, in fact, damaged there was little I could do about it, so I went back to my nod while Bridget came to terms with life in the physically challenged lane.

On the following day the girls returned to New York and the shit really hit the fan, as Melody almost immediately detected the injury.

"What'd you do to my cat, Craig?!?!"

"Nothing."

"You're a fucking liar."

"What are you talking about?" I asked, trying desperately to sound confused *and* victimized at the same time.

"I wanna know what you did to my cat!!!"

"What could I have possibly done to your cat?"

"I don't know—but you did something! Her face is swollen and she hisses at you whenever you walk by!"

"Oh, *really*? I haven't noticed."

"THE HELL YOU HAVEN'T!!!" she screamed at me.

I finally decided that honesty was the best policy, and then Melody decided that I find another place to live. Quite frankly, though, I thought she was overreacting. For five months Bridget had been tearing me to shreds and I finally *had* to put an end to it. Granted, my instinctive reaction was a bit harsh but the cat had it coming and I really didn't see what the big deal was.

"You're a fucking junky—*that's what the big deal is*," Melody said as Rachel uncomfortably looked on in silence.

"Melody, maybe you're projecting your anger at Matt onto me," I theorized. "He's a self-centered asshole, but I told you that right after you met him. I know he may have misled you during the summer, and it's weird because I think he really does care about you, but it isn't my fault and you shouldn't blame me for what *he's* done to you."

"I'm not blaming you for what *he's* done to me," she countered. "I'm blaming you for what *you've* done to my cat. Craig, you've got a problem and I really hope that for the sake of your music career—not to mention your *life*—you check yourself into rehab. But before you do, get the fuck out of my apartment!"

"Melody, I can stop using anytime I want," I told her. "The drugs don't affect anything and there isn't a problem. I go to work everyday and at the same time front the best band in the city. I may like dope—but everyone else is busy being alcoholics, so what's the fucking difference? Trust me, you're overreacting. I'm absolutely fine and I really don't understand why you're so pissed off."

"Craig!!! You punched my cat in the face!!!" she pointed out.

"It was an accident."

"How the fuck do you accidentally punch a cat in the face?!"

"It was a gut reaction and I didn't mean to do it, but you know what? I'm glad it happened. Really, from day-one your cat's been ripping me apart and you think it's funny!"

"I don't think it's funny," she said. "I think it's cute. Now get the fuck out!"

35

After Melody ejected me from the household, Katrina caught wind of the news from Rachel. The very next day she called me at Barry's to ask if I'd be interested in renting a small room in her Park Slope apartment. It would cost only $350 per month which included utilities, but I wasn't thrilled with the notion of departing Manhattan to become a bridge-and-tunnel Brooklynite. Even so, I accepted the offer and my relationship with Rachel ended without a word, much the way it began.

As things turned out, Brooklyn wasn't so bad after all. Though I was forced to suffer the inconvenience of actually having to pay rent, the added expense was somewhat mitigated by the lower cost of living that exists outside of Manhattan. Ultimately, I would be staying with Katrina and her roommates for less than a year, but I immediately knew we'd be getting along quite well. I always had the impression that Katrina understood me better than most. She related to the band and the music, and even shared a similar opinion regarding drug use. She was an avid pot smoker and had also developed an appreciation for dope, though she would rarely allow herself to indulge. Beyond that, she worked as a receptionist at a doctor's office in Manhattan, where she had access to a steady flow of Xanax as well as a variety of other pharmaceuticals. Yes, Katrina was quite an asset and had moved to New York, not to pursue an acting career, but to experience life in a big city where she would never have to cross paths with another snake... at least of the *reptilian* variety. As a child in Georgia she was once bitten by one, and had ever since harbored an intense fear of all things serpentine.

"I hate that fucking cat," she said to me in her southern drawl as Bret and Stacy, her Georgian roommates, insisted on examining the battle wound to my finger.

The topic of conversation was one that I definitely wanted to avoid. The incident was still fresh in my mind and I was a little sensitive about it all. Unfortunately, for this group sensitivity wasn't high on their list of priorities.

"But you know, Craig, you really shouldn't punch a cat in the face," Stacy said as the others looked on in agreement. Apparently, the Confederacy felt it an inappropriate form of punishment to exact upon a cat.

"Yeah," Bret said. "You can kick a cat, run it over with your tractor, hell—you can even *skin-it-alive* if you want, but you shouldn't try to kill a cat with a punch in the face. That's just weird, man."

"First of all—who the fuck ever said I was trying to kill the cat?" I asked. "And secondly, I shudder to think of the misfortune befallen me to be anywhere even *near* a tractor."

Katrina must have sensed some agitation in my voice.

"Don't worry about it, dude—it's no biggie," she said. "It's just kind of an odd thing to do to a cat—that's all. I mean a dog, well—you know, that's different. Most of the time a dog's just *asking* to get punched in the face. But it's sort of undignified for a cat, don't you think?"

I wanted to throw a snake on her.

"Undignified? Let me get this straight," I said. "It's perfectly acceptable to crush a cat to shit with some fucked up piece of hillbilly farm equipment, but a punch in the face is somehow disrespectful. Is that right?"

"Hell yes!" Bret responded. "It's a much more honorable death."

They *had* to be fucking with me.

"What the fuck kind of redneck-warrior bullshit is *this*?!?" I asked without actually wanting to know, and then fled to relative safety behind a locked bedroom door.

As my living arrangements grew more bizarre with each passing month, Perry's improved dramatically. While staying with his mother he started dating Gina, and though he didn't officially move in—he spent practically all of his waking, sleeping and nodding hours at her apartment on First Avenue in Greenwich Village. However, truth be told, from early on in the relationship Perry realized there were problems. Although beautiful and smart, it became readily apparent that deep within Gina there existed a truly obsessive and domineering bitch just screaming to get out. Ultimately, we would identify and isolate the genetic aberration responsible for her behavior, naming it the "Gina Gene" or for short—*The Gene.*

One afternoon during the middle of September, Gina called me at work to inquire if I'd be interested in seeing Eric Bogosian later that evening.

"Who the fuck is *Eric Bogosian*?" I asked.

"He's an actor," she informed me. "He does this monologue that's supposed to be pretty good."

"What's it called?"

"*Sex, Drugs and Rock and Roll*...coincidentally enough."

"Sounds like a waste of money," said I, the heroin addict.

"Perry already picked up a ticket for you so you might as well come," she added without much enthusiasm.

"All right, fine."

After heading up to 110th Street to score, I took the #6 downtown and caught the F train to Brooklyn. Although I'd fully acclimated myself to the new living arrangement, paying rent forced me to curtail my escalating habit and since I'd cut it down from four bags-a-day to two, snorting my stash on the subway would amount to nothing other than a big waste of dope. So, in order to compensate for the reduction in dosage, I was left with few options other than resorting to the needle, and would now have to wait until I returned home where I could more cost-effectively shoot-up.

The temptation to break out my stash and spike a vein right there on the F train was incredible; however, I didn't yet have the nerve for such a public display of depravity. I made it home safely at around 4:30, at which point I booted and then nodded off. The dope was unusually strong, and although the Bogosian show wasn't until 9 p.m., Sections would be meeting at Big Sounds by 7:00. About an hour before the meeting I showered, got dressed, and headed back into Manhattan.

The band would be reconvening for the first time in almost two months and a few things needed to be discussed. First and foremost on the agenda was Kurt's departure from Sections.

When I arrived at the studio everyone was there except for Kurt, who unlike Matt was made conspicuous by his absence. We immediately dealt with the issue at hand which was, once again, the lack of a bass player. However, on this particular occasion the sudden vacancy, as well as our interrupted momentum, was all Danny's doing. I liked Kurt and quite frankly, was a little annoyed with Danny and the circumstances under which our most competent bassist to date felt forced to leave the band.

I was still extremely high from the dope, which, in combination with the anger I was feeling on behalf of Kurt, resulted in an elixir of nastiness brewed specifically for Danny. It was one that had been fermenting ever since our first unpleasant exchange regarding Matt, and the enormous talent concealed within his pinky.

"Kurt couldn't tolerate being spoken to in such a manner, by someone he considered nothing other than an ornamental member of the band," I explained to Danny while savoring every last word.

"What the fuck is that supposed to mean?!?" he asked, as if I was speaking a foreign language.

"What the fuck do you think it means?!? He said you were an ornament—*a decoration*—and in no position to give him shit about anything.

"He actually called me an *ornament*?!?!"

"And a hairless little fucker.*"*

To be honest, I felt some culpability for allowing things to transpire the way they did. Although I didn't want to control everything with an iron fist, as the singer and primary songwriter there was a certain leadership that I should have assumed from the very beginning, and quite frankly—Perry and Matt expected me to. It was a democratically agreed upon, fascist arrangement concocted by the three of us. Of course, we each had our roles to play—but make no mistake about it: driving musicians out of the band was *my* responsibility. Unfortunately, my reluctance to play front man on stage apparently gave Danny the impression that some sort of power vacuum existed—and one which he was only too willing to fill. Ironically enough, however, as everyone had now improved musically and we had some standing in the local music scene, Danny's value to the band was greatly diminished along with my ability to tolerate his nonsense.

We wrapped up the meeting with a general advisory for everyone to keep their eyes and ears open for a bass player, at which point we would again schedule auditions and attempt to get back on track.

At around 8 p.m. Perry and I left Big Sounds and headed uptown to meet Gina at the theater. Before boarding the train, however, he brandished a bag of dope and offered me a snort. I was still entirely loaded from the previous dose and hardly needed anymore, but was somehow able to accommodate his generosity.

By the time we found Gina in front of the theater I needed Perry's help to safely make it inside, and the moment he dumped me into my chair the lights dimmed and I realized I was too mangled to enjoy the show. My eyes had become a couple of paper cuts through which I could barely distinguish the outline of a man who I assumed was Eric Bogosian. For about two hours I drifted in and out, occasionally trying to focus on the performance as I heard strings of meaningless words followed by moments of laughter.

Eventually, while resting on the periphery of consciousness, I detected an explosion of applause that seemed to come from very far away. Moments later, Perry shook my shoulder.

"Time to go, dickhead," he said as he attempted to gather my lifeless form.

"It's over?" I lamented. "I can't believe I missed the whole thing."

"It was great. You really missed out, stupid," was Gina's sympathetic response.

"Fuck you," I tried to say, but I don't think it quite came out.

"Bogosian's awesome," Gina said. "I knew he was a good actor, but I didn't realize how intelligent and funny he is."

"I'm surprised I haven't seen him in anything else," Perry remarked.

"Really?" asked Gina. "I think he's in something else that's out right now."

"What's it called?" Perry asked.

"I forgot, but it's supposed to be really good."

"I'm so glad we went. That's the best film I've seen in months," Perry decided.

Wait a minute … That was a fucking movie?

36

Within a few months, Perry had convinced himself that Gina's primary goal was to pin him down, and somehow get him married and herself pregnant. That perception resulted in an uncomfortable moment when Perry was caught desperately rummaging through the garbage in an attempt to recover a hastily discarded condom and thus, prevent Gina from "kidnapping his sperm." As a result, the relationship immediately went south and Perry soon became a boy-toy for a sexy guitar-tech named Karen, who in exchange for services rendered compensated him with a beautiful Les Paul. But Perry must have missed the fine print for in addition to the guitar, he was also rewarded with a raging case of gonorrhea that he was kind enough to pass along to Gina. In fact, Gina was the first to become aware of their mutual infection after a thick, yellow, discharge dotted with bloody specs began appearing in her panties—which Perry brazenly dismissed as "just a bad period." After a gynecologist offered up the correct diagnosis, Perry—never missing a beat—actually threw Gina's fidelity into question and then immediately found himself once again bonding with his mother in Brooklyn.

By November, Perry recruited Justin Filmer to play bass for Sections. Justin had grown up in Australia and South Africa, and it was difficult to determine where one accent began and the other ended. What wasn't difficult to determine was the fact that he was clearly the most talented bass player we'd seen thus far, and his style and disposition were perfect additions to the lineup. Beyond that, he was pretty to look at which was always a plus. I was finally at peace. Justin's musical instincts perfectly complimented our songs and I knew that the search for a bassist had finally come to an end. Now, if only Pat would get with the program we'd be in decent shape.

Perry scheduled a gig at The Bank on Houston Street. It would be Justin's first performance with Sections and the first time we'd taken the stage in almost four months.

On the day of the gig, just before my shift ended at Barry's, Megan stopped me at the door.

"Here," she said. "I have a present for you."

In my hand she then placed a tiny blue pill.

"What's this?" I asked.

"It's a valium. Try it."

"What's it gonna do to me?"

"Don't worry about it. You'll like it. But these are pretty strong, so you might wanna start off with half.

Half?

"Thanks," I said as I popped the whole thing in my mouth.

After leaving the store I realized I had six hours to kill before the show, so I decided to return home to Brooklyn. I walked over to the 77th Street subway station, boarded the #6, and as I sat down I began to feel the effects of the valium. I eventually transferred to the F at Bleecker Street, and as the train pulled out I felt a potent little buzz come over me. Then, seemingly within the blink of an eye, I found myself in Coney Island as the train came to a rapid, thudding, halt and pulled me out of my stupor. I'm not sure exactly when, but at some point the valium had hit me like a ton of bricks. Well over an hour had disappeared from my life as I suddenly found myself in the southern-most part of Brooklyn, fifteen stops past my own.

"FUCK!!!" I said out loud.

As tourists returning from the aquarium boarded the train, I couldn't believe that the stupid little pill caused me to miss my stop. It was already after 5p.m., and I knew that I now wouldn't be home until at least six. Then, all of a sudden there was another thud, only it wasn't at all sudden as I realized I was back in Manhattan.

"FUCK!"

I couldn't believe that I actually passed out and missed my stop *again.*

The train rapidly filled with men and women in business suits returning home to the borough of Brooklyn, and I can only assume they did—as I returned to the state of unconsciousness. When I realized that the same thing happened yet again, it was exactly 8:00 and I was back in Coney Island.

"FUCK! FUCK! FUCK! FUCK! FUCK! FUCK! FUCK! FUCK!!!" I screamed, marking the hour like a vulgar cuckoo as I'd now been traveling back and forth on the F train for four hours.

I eventually made it home at 9:00 to shower, and then immediately returned to Manhattan for the gig. By now, the valium had worn off sufficiently enough for me to maintain consciousness and without a moment to spare, I arrived at The Bank just as Sections was about to take the stage.

37

I don't know exactly what I was thinking, but in December I decided to accept Hunter College's invitation to attend graduate school. The semester started in January of 1993 and for me it would end that very month, though I did learn a few interesting things during my brief stay. Most notably, I learned that graduate school was no place for a junky.

Meanwhile, Anton asked Perry if he would be interested in

managing Big Sounds during the evening hours in exchange for free rehearsal time. Though the bartering arrangement was a valuable asset to the band, a cot in the back room was an even greater allure to Perry as he could no longer tolerate living with Felicia. Though his belongings and mailing address remained in Brooklyn, he now spent the majority of his time at the studio.

Perry's arrangement at Big Sounds was an extraordinary benefit to Sections, as some or all of us were there virtually every night working on material. One evening in late January Perry, Matt, and I convened at the studio to discuss a letter of interest we'd received from Boomerang Productions, a small management company that handled a growing list of rising bands signed to independent labels. The general consensus was that they were relatively smalltime for a band of *our* caliber and as a result, the letter was immediately set aside. In reality, however, the cavalier disinterest in the management company was due less to cockiness, and was mainly the result of a rumor that our demo was being passed around Atlantic Records. Though Boomerang's interest in the band would go ignored—it was still cause for celebration. Accordingly, Matt and Perry left to score while I stayed behind to mind the shop.

A couple of hours had passed and I began to grow restless as they'd gone to score on 18th Street near the Beth Israel Medical Center, which was only eight blocks from the studio. By around midnight my junky impatience had finally gotten the better of me, and I decided to venture over to the spot to investigate the matter.

When I arrived nothing seemed out of the ordinary. There were a few junkies roaming around, and the dope dealer was manning his usual post outside the doorway of a rundown building. As soon as he saw me he motioned me over.

"Hey, papi. Your friends got busted," he said.

"What!?! Are the fucking cops out?" I asked as I looked around.

"They were watching from the roof," he explained as he pointed to a building across the street. "They're gone now."

"Good, then give me three."

There were no works in the area, so I decided to take a day away from the needle as three bags was enough to snort and still catch a buzz.

As I headed back to the studio, I realized the arrest would probably be Matt's great undoing. It was quite likely that The Good Detective would eventually get wind of his son's brush with the law, and at that point Matt's double life would finally come crashing down around him. Of course, Matt could probably prevent the news from reaching Mr. Anson; however, that would require him to suck it up like a brave little junky and resist mentioning his father's name in exchange for preferential police treatment.

"DETECTIVE ERNIE ANSON! DETECTIVE ERNIE ANSON! DETECTIVE ERNIE ANSON!" Matt cried over and over again as he and Perry were placed in general population, which, besides the likes of child molesters, petty thieves, prostitutes, pimps, drunk drivers, drug dealers and drug buyers—also included a nice sampling of violent felons. They were then relocated to a cell with 20 others, and as Matt's desperate chant continued—Perry considered bitch-slapping him to avoid the pussy-by-association beating that now seemed imminent.

"Matt!" Perry said with real fear in his eyes, "For the sake of my own survival, I don't fucking know you right now! OK?!?" He then nervously attempted to conceal his long, girly, black hair beneath the collar of his shirt.

Within seconds a corrections officer appeared at the cell as Matt continued to cry out.

"Who the fuck is Detective Ernie Anson?" was the same old response from a brand new officer.

"He's my father," said Matt in between sobs. "Detective Ernie Anson...He works at the 45th Precinct in—"

"SHUT THE FUCK UP YOU JUNKY CUNT!!" interrupted the officer.

Unbeknownst to Matt, New York City corrections officers were an entirely different breed of cop. Whereas street cops would almost always feel a bit of sympathy for The Good Detective and the indignities heaped upon him by his junky-son, corrections officers—known as C.O.'s for short—really didn't give a shit. They spent the whole of their days in what was tantamount to a chamber of horrors, and had become far too detached to be affected by Matt or his father's status in the police department. However, Matt's relationship to The Good Detective had now been revealed to a cell full of thugs, and the C.O.'s only concern was that if he left him there—he'd only be back in a minute to mop him up off the floor. With no other choice, he unlocked the gate to move Matt to a safer location.

"Come on you fucking pansy. Do you wanna bring your girlfriend with you?" the C.O. asked, as Perry was doing his best to blend in with a group of Puerto Rican gangsters.

They were both transferred to a private cell and remained in the system for almost 25 hours, after which each was sentenced to three days of community service and released. It was quite the traumatic experience for Matt who was convinced that his father was eventually going to find out about the arrest. To lift his spirits, on the following day Perry purchased him a harmonica with an inscription that read, *"For My Cellie."*

38

Oddly enough, Perry's mother somehow got wind of the arrest before Matt's father. As a result, while Matt would maintain his secret life a little longer, on February 6th Perry returned home to find his things neatly packed and sitting on the curb. Not one to share his indignities with anyone, he picked up his belongings and checked into the Whitehouse Hotel on Bowery, where he would stay when he wasn't working at the studio.

Although no foreign dignitaries ever checked in, the Whitehouse still maintained an impressive guest list of ex-cons, drug addicts, and vagrants—along with a few of the city's more colorful schizophrenics just to spice things up. For a nominal fee of ten dollars per day, guests were provided access to a locker-room shower, and what the establishment referred to as a "room." However, the 8 x 5 foot space didn't exactly qualify as a room, and much more resembled the stall of a barnyard stable where one could actually stand up, look over the wall, and sneak a peak at the horse living next door. Of course, this could be risky as the unsuspecting horse might be smoking crack, masturbating, or changing his dressings and not exactly in the mood for company. It was truly a very sad and depressing place to be.

On February 25th Matt's double life finally came to an end as his father was made aware of the arrest. Then, without saying a word to Matt, The Good Detective went directly to Cynthia to report his findings which included a detailed summary of the monies owed to a variety of creditors. Unfortunately, though, he didn't stop there. To top it off, going above and beyond the call of duty, Mr. Anson then sold most of Matt's belongings to help compensate Cynthia for the cost of marrying his son.

The fallout was severe, but quite frankly—it was amazing that Matt was able to maintain the charade for as long as he had. In fact, this time he was lucky because although his marriage was in tatters, he was still somehow able to maintain his teaching job. The day after the drama unfolded he appeared at the studio as Perry and I were running through new material.

"My life is completely over," Matt lamented as he stepped into the room.

"Are you and Cynthia getting divorced?" asked Perry.

"We're getting an annulment."

"An annulment! There you go," Perry said as he tried to sound comforting. "Just like it never even happened."

"Too bad you can't get the warts annulled," I pointed out.

"You're real funny," Matt said. "Oh man, what the fuck am I gonna do? I don't wanna live with my father after all this shit! I don't even have a guitar anymore."

"But at least you've got that nifty-looking harmonica," I reminded him. "Look at it over there, so bright and shiny. It's almost as if it's *mocking* you."

"You're moving back in with your dad?" Perry asked him.

"Where the fuck else am I gonna go?"

"I don't know, but that should definitely teach him not to stick his fat ass where it doesn't belong."

On February 26th, 1993, I went to work and Ramzi Yousef attempted to blow up the World Trade Center. While the event was unfolding, a news report could be heard on the store's television. As I made change for customers I listened to reporters question a Port Authority official, who was quick to brag about the buildings' structural superiority in light of the failed attempt to bring them down.

After momentarily stepping out of the store, I peered down Second Avenue and could see a gigantic plume of smoke surrounding the towers. I didn't realize it at the time, but the image was a prophetic one with regard to not only the buildings' destiny—but also Matt's double-life, and though for the moment they managed to stand upright amidst smoldering flames, it was only a matter of time before *all four* came crashing down.

As I returned to the store, the Port Authority official concluded his remarks:

"If this had happened at the UN, you'd be looking at a big hole in the ground," he said with a swagger that would ultimately prove itself to be not so justified.

39

By the beginning of March, Perry's new arrangement at Big Sounds encouraged us to dedicate more hours to rehearsing, and after Barry caught me smoking a joint in the basement of his store I found myself with plenty of time to fulfill the commitment.

After getting canned at Barry's I made a decision to change my life. *"I'm gonna quit using,"* I said. Unfortunately, I was already fucked up when I made the statement so it ended up being inadmissible. In fact, within 36 hours of making the empty promise I was beginning to regret it, as I'd detected a sudden irritability in my bowels which is an early precursor to dope sickness. To make matters worse I was jobless, had no money to alleviate the oncoming withdrawal symptoms, and was now hardly in the mood to rehearse or discuss the rejection letter we'd recently received from Atlantic. Of course, I knew that Perry would get us high afterwards, but the notion of enduring the next couple of hours was tortuous.

The matter of being rejected by a major label went unaddressed and that was fortunate, as the rehearsal left me with enough to be agitated by. During the past month I'd become even more disenchanted with Pat's playing and now, while Justin desperately tried to hold it together with a bass line that was beautiful unto itself, he busily clamored through each measure with his usual brand of jazz-infused bullshit. Of course, there was no need for Justin to address the issue:

"WHAT THE FUCK ARE YOU DOING?!" I screamed into the mike as Matt was about to launch into a solo.

Just then, Danny decided to handle the situation. Unfortunately, he began reprimanding Justin.

"Yeah man. You gotta do a better job of staying with Pat or you're gonna have to go," he said, incredibly.

"SHUT THE FUCK UP, DANNY! JUST SHUT THE FUCK UP!" I roared as I whipped around to cut him off.

I was on the verge of unloading a torrent of pent-up, withdrawal-driven aggravation that was now bolstered by Danny's inability to know his place. After all, what exactly did he think was going on here? Not to belabor the point, but the band was mine—**MINE, MINE, MINE, MINE, MINE.** If he was ever going to come to terms with this critical detail, now was the time.

"Don't say another fucking word Danny, not another fucking word! Just stand there and keep your mouth shut," I warned him. I then unleashed my fury upon the drummer.

"Pat—what the fuck is going on with all the busy bullshit?!"

"What are you talking about?!" he shot back with some disgust.

"More snares and bass—less high-hat. Got it?"

"I'm trying to capture the vibe, man," he said.

"What *vibe, man*? Just play the fucking song! If you think that stifles your creativity then maybe you should pick up another instrument."

"We don't wanna sound like all the other bands out there," he said in defense of his playing. "I want Sections to be known for something different."

"And what's that, Pat? **SUCKING?** Because that's what we'll be known for. Sucking big, fat, motherfucking dick and nothing else! Is that what you want, Pat!?! *IS THAT WHAT YOU FUCKING WANT?!?!*"

"Craig, shut the fuck up," was uttered by someone with a death wish. Of course, it could be none other than Danny.

"What did you say you little prick-motherfucker?" I inquired.

"OK," Perry interrupted. "The little clock on the wall tells me rehearsal time is *over*."

I was beyond enraged but before I was able to grab Danny by the throat, Perry ushered me down the staircase and out into the street.

"Just relax, man," he said. "This isn't worth beating anyone up over."

"Well I don't have time to lose another bass player, especially one that I wanna keep around," I told him. "I just lost my job, I'm broke, and I'm a fucking dopesick junky! I can't afford to let that little fucker hold things up anymore with his big mouth!"

Just as I finished my sentence, I noticed Danny and Pat standing behind me.

"He guys, listen, it's nothing personal," Danny said. "But I think the drugs and shit are getting out of control, and we'll never get anything accomplished when you guys are so fucked up all the time. So, we thought about it for a while, and feel it would be best if me and Pat left the band."

"See that!" Perry said to me with a big grin. "Problem solved."

With that settled, we headed in the direction of a new spot on Sixth Street and Avenue D, as the only other options were Harlem or Hell's Kitchen. Unfortunately, the 18th Street location was now out of the question as the memory of Perry's recent bust lingered ever present.

"Guys!" Danny called out as we walked away. "Don't leave like that...come on!"

We weren't leaving like anything. We were leaving to get fucked up and not a moment too soon. I felt a fart developing somewhere around my intestines, but in my dopesick condition I couldn't at all guarantee that the matter being detected was only gaseous in nature.

As the new spot was located on the outermost edges of the East Village and about a block away from the river, we had at least eight avenue blocks to traverse. Making matters worse, withdrawal symptoms were coming on strong and given the unreliability of my bowels, we wisely stopped at a Barnes and Noble to use the facility. I no sooner plopped myself down on the bowl, I felt a hot gush of burning, fecal-colored liquid immediately shoot out of my ass. That was hardly the end of the deluge, however, as a steady flow of clear liquid followed until the bowl was almost filled to capacity.

We eventually reached Avenue D, and by the time we crossed Sixth Street the dealers were obvious. We quickly copped two bags of dope and two sets of works, and then headed back in a westerly direction toward something that resembled civilization.

The next closest junky-friendly bathroom to which we could gain access was located in a pizza restaurant on St. Mark's Place. Though it was only four blocks away, my stomach began making an extremely loud, industrial-sounding gurgle as another vulgar discharge seemed imminent. I definitely had to get that dope inside of me as soon as possible or things were going to get messy.

"Perry, I gotta get off," I told him.

"Just relax," he said as he tried to calm me down.

"No, you don't understand. If I don't get off soon I'm gonna take a shit right on the fucking sidewalk!"

"We'll be there in three minutes."

"I don't fucking have three minutes!" I said. "I've got about 30 seconds."

With that, Perry whipped out his stash and we immediately ducked down the basement steps of an old brownstone.

My veins had deteriorated extensively over the past few months, and since we were operating right out in the open I decided to defer to Perry's expertise and allow him to perform the procedure. He loaded the needle and due to my ravaged arms, several nerve-racking minutes passed before he was able to locate a battle-worthy vein. Eventually, a useable pathway was at last identified and penetrated as sidewalk pedestrians passed by in broad daylight without noticing. However, just after inserting the needle but before he could pull the trigger, we were interrupted by the sound of a door opening directly behind me. I couldn't believe my shitty luck. After ten courageous minutes working under extremely risky conditions we'd finally found a vein, and now the entire effort was about to be compromised along with my underwear.

With little in terms of choice we temporarily suspended operations, scrambling back up the staircase to escape detection. Then, to further complicate matters, just as we stepped onto the sidewalk a police car was seen patrolling its way down the street and in our direction. There was simply nowhere to turn.

Now the challenge was to make haste and not attract any unwanted attention, so we continued on as I moved quickly and inconspicuously. That is, as quickly and inconspicuously as one can be expected to move with a syringe dangling out of one's arm.

40

I was in a bad place. No job, no money, no idea of what to do next. I was having serious concerns about Sections, our perceived talent, and if any of this was at all worth it. I was discouraged by the way the band's progress had completely ceased, though I did find solace in the fact that we finally had a great bass player to work with.

Unfortunately, beyond that one bright spot I really didn't know what to do to get things back on track. I felt that, for really the first time, we were floundering and I was beginning to question my decisions. Perry, however, never seemed to think that our eventual success was ever in doubt.

"I wish I could take what I knew to be true in my heart, and put it in yours...But I can't—so fuck off and just believe me," he once told me when my confidence began to wane.

Ultimately, I decided that I was in too deep to quit and would see things through. I reasoned that the only thing worse than wasting anymore time on a musical journey to nowhere was the thought of ever having to say, *"What if I'd stuck it out?"* Of course, it eventually made no difference as I would later adopt the slightly revised, *"What if I'd stuck it out—without a needle sticking out of my arm?"*

By the middle of March I was still jobless, but as my rent was paid and Perry kept me flushed with drugs while also supporting my less expensive *eating* habit, I had a hard time finding motivation to re-enter the workforce. My lack of drive was due less to drugs, and more to a painful acknowledgement of what would be my only, viable, employment option.

Perry suggested that I come to grips with the fact that, at least for the short term, I'd be working in a restaurant.

"Stop being such a pussy," he told me during a phone call. "Face up to it and get it over with."

"Strong words coming from someone who's still running from the law," I responded, referring to his failure to perform the community service he was sentenced to after getting busted with Matt back in January. "You know, eventually, they *will* come and get you," I told him—and we both knew what that could mean. New York addicts may have enjoyed relatively relaxed penalties with regard to drug possession, but when bad little junkies disobeyed and didn't follow through with their punitive commitments the result was often 30 days at Riker's Island.

"Don't worry. They won't catch me," he bragged. "Besides, I'm gonna take care of it in a few weeks anyway. I just don't have the time right now. Meet me at the Whitehouse tonight after I get out of work. We'll talk about everything then."

In reality, though we weren't gigging, the band was slowly

evolving into what it needed to become in order to perform the songs the way they were intended. The moment I wrote a song, I heard the finished product in my head. It was this mental prototype that I attempted, but was never able to fully realize with any of the previous configurations of musicians. Adding Justin to the lineup and subtracting Pat and Danny were the first solid steps taken to achieve this end. Of course, we were now without a drummer.

Before heading over to the Whitehouse, I was supposed to meet Justin at Tower Records with a copy of the demo. He had mentioned a friend from church named Chris Duncan whose drumming style might be compatible with our songs. Before wasting any time with formal rehearsals, however, we thought it might be a good idea to have Chris listen to the tape and decide if he was even interested. After arriving at Tower I found Justin and gave him the demo. I then walked four or five blocks to the Whitehouse to meet Perry.

The Whitehouse Hotel was located on Bowery, just south of Cooper Union and north of CBGB's. It was a very old, grimy, four-story building, and the only thing it had in common with its D.C. namesake were the security measures one was confronted with when attempting to enter the shithole.

As I stepped over the building's filthy threshold I was immediately struck by degradation in every corner, as homeless men wandered around intermittently muttering to themselves as well as the lifeless drunks scattered around the lobby. Within a few seconds I was then confronted by a shabbily dressed, unshaven, middle-aged man whose status as either a guest or employee was at first, somewhat in question.

"What do you want?" he asked me.

"I'm looking for someone."

"Who the fuck are you looking for?" he demanded.

"Who the fuck are you?" I demanded back, a little put off by his tone.

"I'm the fucking hotel manager!"

"Way to go," I said. "I'm supposed to meet Perry Ward here."

"Who the fuck is he?"

Now how in the world was I supposed to answer that?

"He's a homeless fucking drug addict that just *happens* to live here," I told him.

Obviously, that wasn't going to be a specific enough description, but I didn't know what else to say and was beginning to get impatient.

Without another word, I took a step forward to continue the search when the shabby one raised his hand to stop my progress.

"Only hotel guests are allowed to be on the lobby floor," he said, forgetting about the piss stains and beer cans that were apparently also permitted. "What's that name again?"

"Perry Ward."

He thought about it for a moment and then a light suddenly flickered.

"Hey Ward...Get down here!" he shouted toward a dark staircase that rose up beside him.

While waiting for Perry to get it together, I snuck into the bathroom to take a leak. It was completely filthy, and as I stepped into the very first stall I noticed a sign that read, *"Attention Passengers: Please remain seated until the shit comes to a complete stop."* I peed, exited the bathroom, and then approached the manager to check on the status of my friend.

"Did you heed the sign?" he asked me with a smartass grin.

"I would have, but I didn't wanna get my turds dirty."

"Oh, really?"

"Uh-huh."

"Ward!!!" he roared again. "Get down here!!! There's someone *special* here to see you...Hey Ward!!! Are you up there or what?!?!"

Indeed, he was up there. Way up there. On the roof, in fact, completely wasted and desperately trying to concoct an escape route that would help him elude the special someone who was waiting in the lobby—and certain to be wearing a badge and brandishing a baton.

*"Someone special...*They must think I'm a fucking asshole," he said out loud as he tried to calm his palpitating heart and collect his thoughts.

The Whitehouse was one of several adjoining buildings that ran the length of Bowery, from Great Jones to Bond Street. To avoid "capture," Perry would have to flee the property and somehow make his getaway down the fire escape or stairwell of one of the connected buildings. Unfortunately, the adjacent rooftops were all of varying heights and lengths and in the darkness of night—a perilous, urban, valley stood between him and freedom.

Perry mounted a barefoot assault, scaling peaks and paying little heed to the dark chasms that lay in wait as he blindly jumped from one cement summit to the next. Fortunately, a junky's bitter disregard for his own well being—combined with the thought of going to jail—can

produce Spider-Man like feats of strength and agility. Only, he wasn't
Spider-Man…he was Junky-Man.

Junky-Man, Junky-Man
Does whatever a junky can.
Evades police at any price.
Escaped arrest once or twice.
LOOK UP!
Here comes the Junky-Man.
Is he strong?
Listen bud,
He's got opiates in his blood.
Can he rise from the dead?
Take a look overhead.
Hey, there
There goes the Junky-Man.
In the chill of night
When The Man came to call
From the roof he jumped
But the dope broke his fall!
Junky-Man, Junky-Man,
Friendly neighborhood Junky-Man.
Cops and courts he's ignored
Nodding off is his reward.
Hey, there
There goes the Junky-Man.

41

My arms were beginning to look bad. Since I was booting only
once a day I never developed track marks, but I did sport a fair share
of bumps and bruises from injecting heroin into places where there
really wasn't anywhere for it to go. But even though my needlework
was questionable, I was a stone-cold junky and knew it. Hence,
relocating to the belly of the beast was probably not the wisest of

decisions.

After his death-defying escape from "the police," Perry voluntarily fulfilled his community service obligations and decided to move out of the Whitehouse Hotel. Within a week he found a large studio apartment located in Hell's Kitchen on Tenth Avenue between 45th and 46th Streets. His new living arrangement, however, would require me to reprise my role as his roommate now that I'd found a job and was once again a contributing member of society. Of course, I was still a drug addict contributing to the *decay* of that society; but at least now I was legally employed, so as far as I was concerned—*me and society were even.*

I ended up getting hired as a waiter at Serendipity 3 on 60th Street. Although homosexual men largely populate the rank and file of the city's food service industry, Serendipity was unusual as not only the staff—but the management, ownership, and décor of the restaurant was so *flamboyantly* gay. Decked out in pinkish tones with tiffany lamps hanging from almost every ceiling, it was clear the establishment and its employees were more concerned with how things looked as opposed to how they actually tasted, which also helped explain the number of hours dedicated to the procurement and consumption of sperm.

Besides myself, there were only three other confirmed, straight waiters. When I say "confirmed," I mean their heterosexuality was vouched for by a gay wait staff that was always on the lookout for someone who might even be just *a little bit gay*—but unwilling to admit it. At some point, I came to the conclusion that heterosexuals were employed at Serendipity simply because the restaurant could never manage to recruit a completely gay staff. This is supported by the fact that during my tenure, the only employees ever dismissed were straight men. It quickly became apparent that if you didn't fancy the taste of penis—you'd better tow the line.

The confirmed straights were Renee Lewis—an actress from Los Angeles, Bill Sorvillo—an artist from Florida and a kid from New Jersey named Ian Brewster who, to my knowledge, had no ulterior career motives. Serendipity was led by Debbie Christie, and as the restaurant's apex predator and general manager she terrified me from the very beginning. Of course, Serendipity's owner was and still is Mr. Stephen Bruce, and though it would be years before the movie was released, due to his efforts the restaurant enjoyed a great deal of exposure even back then.

Though Serendipity was much more style than substance it mattered little, as tourists and natives alike were somehow drawn in by the glitz and glamour of it all. I must admit, though, it was always a very beautiful atmosphere to dine under, and the rich and famous were even more sucked into the allure than the average person. Celebrities regularly frequented the restaurant not only for its aesthetically pleasing quality, but also because a dark atmosphere and an unaffected waiter allowed them to maintain the anonymity they seemed to cherish so dearly. In fact, during my stint at Serendipity I personally waited on Jackie Onassis and her grandchildren, as well as Neil Simon, Martin Short, Alyssa Milano, Jim O'Brien, Andre Previn, Tim Robbins and Susan Sarandon among a host of others.

Hollywood and Broadway elite were a constant presence at Serendipity, a fact shamelessly promoted and often printed in the New York dailies. As a matter of fact, though I cannot personally attest to it, it was once allegedly reported that Madonna had popped in for one of Mr. Bruce's famous foot-long hot dogs. Of course, the singer's staunchly vegetarian status might have made the story a bit difficult to swallow.

42

In mid-April, Perry and I moved into the $800 per month studio apartment in Hell's Kitchen and for the first time, I could see how my habit was beginning to affect my standard of living. But even with the concession of living in a rundown part of town where rent was cheap by Manhattan standards, my overall cost of living was dramatically increased. Of course, my overall cost of living included a healthy dope habit to contend with and if I wasn't careful, I knew it would be only a matter of time before I was checking into the Whitehouse myself.

The apartment was on the fifth floor of a five-story walk-up, and featured a kitchen/dining room that led into a bedroom/living room. What made *this* shithole unique was that the bathroom plumbing couldn't support anything beyond a tiny toilet and as a result, the apartment's only sink was situated in the kitchen alongside a rickety, modular, shower stall. Well, at least it was a *quaint* shithole.

As far as the band was concerned, although we hadn't gigged for over five months, progress was being made in giant, albeit, very sporadic steps. Justin's friend, Chris Duncan, ended up liking the demo as did his brother, Leslie, and both signed on as drummer and alternate guitarist, respectively. They were both very competent, very black, and very much members of the same church where Justin not only worshipped, but where his father actually led the flock as minister.

We quickly realized that our new band mates were not only deeply religious but also living completely drug free lives—while Perry, Matt, and I...*weren't*. Obviously, we thought it wise to keep the lifestyle disparities under wraps as much as possible. Unfortunately, this would be easier said than done while living in Hell's Kitchen and hardly oblivious to the abundance of crack and heroin being peddled right outside our building. In fact, within a few weeks of moving in, Perry and I were doing more drugs than ever before.

Since I lived almost directly across town from Serendipity, each morning I would make the eleven block journey on foot as attempting the cross-town subway connection never seemed worth the effort. Of course, the return trip home would almost always involve a cab, as I could hardly wait to get completely annihilated the moment my shift ended. Like clockwork, each and every afternoon Perry and I would meet at the apartment by 5:15. Then, for most of the evening we would gorge ourselves on a crack cocaine buffet, followed by a decadent trip to the dope dessert bar.

On the subject of employment, my overall experience at Serendipity was much worse *and* much better than I could ever have imagined. On the upside, I developed some very close and long-lasting relationships with a few members of the wait staff. On a less enchanting note, I found Mr. Bruce to be offensive and Debbie an incredible bully as they both made it exceedingly clear that I wasn't one of their favorites.

Among the wait staff Evan Bennett, Bill Sorvillo and Jeff Kirby soon became like brothers to me. Bill and Jeff were both completely straight; however, Jeff—a very talented actor—was never able to firmly establish his heterosexuality, as Serendipity's ruling body on straightness refused to recognize the claim. Though he would never publicly admit it, he found it unsettling as some of the gay waiters made conspicuous remarks about what they believed to be his latent longing for a pair of testes on the chin.

One afternoon as our shift was ending he privately shared his concerns with me. Although I personally knew that, without question, Jeff was totally straight—for some reason I could see why there were lingering doubts.

"Why's that?" he asked me.

"I'm not exactly sure," I said. "It's just that sometimes…I don't know, man, it just seems like every now and then you get a little too artsy-fartsy or something."

"That's ridiculous," he responded. "*Everyone* here is artsy and I happen to be a heterosexual pig! I go through a different chick every week and for nothing other than to satisfy my own lustful urges."

This was true, and in the wake was a trail of warm bodies to prove it.

"Listen," I said. "The next time you do something especially gay I'll be sure to point it out. OK?"

"I'd appreciate that. Now—I'm off to dance class!" he said as he pirouetted out the front door of the restaurant.

43

According to Dictionary.com, the definition of the word "serendipity" is: *"An aptitude for making fortunate discoveries accidentally"* or *"an instance of making such a discovery."*

While working at Serendipity, I personally made such a discovery. I discovered that being a heterosexual man drifting in a sea of homosexuality was not without its advantages. Of course, hitting on straights is seriously frowned upon by the gay community, but that didn't prevent my co-workers from showering me with the same degree of attention that a straight man might bestow upon a woman he wanted, but knew he could never have.

I often found myself being spoiled by doting homos and must admit—*I milked it for all it was worth.* I also began to question some of the wisdom behind the feminist movement. Whether my sidework involved maintaining the ice cream cooler, preparing condiments, or setting tables—on most days I would arrive at the restaurant to find most of it already completed. *Fuck holding the door open!* If you wanna burp the worm while I step into my uniform—THEN GET TO IT, MAN!!! *Just drain the coleslaw for me...OK?*

One afternoon in June as we awaited the lunch rush, Ricky Diaz—a chubby but loveable queer—was polishing my shoes (which were still on my feet) when Andy Hupperts—Serendipity's host and resident closet-case—had entered the kitchen. Andy was, of course, the subject of great derision as he refused to come to terms with his occasional but overtly gay tendencies, which only added fuel to the speculative fire. And although the committee could be harsh and not always correct when assessing sexual orientations, as far as Andy was concerned they were spot-on. For the most part, Andy was able to subdue any openly homosexual displays; however, he harbored a passion for designer clothing that couldn't be suppressed. Whenever a conversation about fashion erupted Andy was on it, and if the discussion involved one of his *favorite* designers he'd immediately launch into a gushing review of their latest offerings.

Initially, besides the fact that his façade of straightness prevented him from doing my sidework, I bore no ill will toward Andy. But unfortunately, by this point he'd become a real pain in my ass and quite frankly, a bit of a threat. Although I had yet to tell anyone in the restaurant about my drug habit, Andy would regularly drop little hints that suggested he knew something he shouldn't. I assumed that in the past he'd been a junky himself, or had an intimate experience with one which provided some insights. Then again, it also could have been the tiny bruises dotting my left arm which usually went unnoticed by most. Regardless of the cause, Andy soon became a constant source of commentary that I found invasive and unsettling.

"Craig, you have a table," he said as I noticed that my Doc Martens were shining like diamonds.

"Thanks."

"You don't look so hot," he said. "Is anything wrong?"

"No, not really. I'm just feeling a little under the weather today," I said like I did every other time he asked me the same, fucking, question.

"You look a little underweight," he went on. "Sure there's nothing wrong?"

"No, Andy!" I said with obvious annoyance. "There's nothing

wrong."

"Relax," he said. "It's just that for a young guy you seem really unhealthy."

"That's alright, Andy. For a straight guy you seem really obsessed with Versace."

He was on the brink of tears.

"You have a table," he said again and then ran away.

I exited the kitchen and found a middle-aged woman sitting in my station with two spoiled brats. The kids ordered burgers and after about 20 minutes of serious consideration, mom settled on the barbecued chicken casserole. When the food was ready, Aaron—the daytime cook—put the order in the window and I immediately brought it out to the table. Not more than a minute passed before I was back at the table dealing with a dissatisfied customer.

"What the hell is this?!?" she asked, referring to a cigarette butt that had apparently been fished-out of her casserole.

This wouldn't qualify as a serendipitous discovery.

"Oh…" I said. "That shouldn't be in there."

She then stood up, gathered her brats, and stormed out of the restaurant.

44

New York City summers suck, especially in Manhattan. The intense heat and humidity become trapped within its concrete confines, providing natives and tourists with a vague idea of what it must be like to live in an oven that hasn't been cleaned for a century. To make matters worse our apartment had no air conditioning, which would have been troublesome each night had I not been so completely wasted and oblivious to my surroundings. Of course, the heat had inspired Perry to rekindle his relationship with Gina and the centrally air-conditioned apartment she lived in. So now more often than not I found myself alone, sitting cross-legged on the living room floor like a wayward Indian who had emptied the peace from his pipe to fill it with crack.

One unpleasant side effect of my escalated crack-smoking was an inability to resist picking at my face, as the increased toxins entering my body resulted in the occasional blemish. On one particularly sweaty evening spent smoking rocks and shooting dope, I noticed what felt like a pimple erupting on—of all places—the very tip of my nose.

I knew full well that picking on a zit would do nothing to camouflage it, and would only cause it to be redder and more pronounced. But the junky in me was convinced that by applying just the right amount of pressure, I'd be able to expel the puss (which had yet to even form) without causing a great deal of damage. Unfortunately, I was so high that I completely lost track of time and space and before I knew it, I was the proud owner of a swollen, bloody, protrusion which at one time was my nose.

Thankfully, that false sense of well being soon kicked in. I left the bathroom and proceeded to nod off and then fall asleep on the futon. When the alarm sounded, I immediately became aware of the soreness and without even looking in the mirror I began to concoct a lie to justify my new face:

Ummm...I was uhhh...cleaning the stove and uhhh...it's one of those new glass-top ovens and uh, I kind of just lost my balance and sort of slammed my face into it.

As soon as I arrived at Serendipity that morning my deformity was immediately addressed by Andy, and after offering up my lame excuse I scurried into the kitchen as Mr. Bruce was fast approaching.

"What is that awful thing on his nose?!?" Mr. Bruce asked, with a degree of disgust that he simply couldn't disguise.

"He burnt it on the stove," said Andy.

"Oh. Was he trying to stick his head in the oven again?"

45

As the summer wore on it seemed my life and aspirations were caught in a downward spiral, and even though Perry said he had a plan, I increasingly turned to drugs in order to distract myself from the realities around me.

"Everything's going great," I tried to tell myself as the crack pipe sizzled and I strained to hold in the fumes. "Couldn't be better." Then, at the last possible moment I would exhale the vaporized rock only to cap off the evening with a dope-loaded syringe.

But things definitely *could have* been better. I hadn't seen Justin, Chris, or Leslie since April and though we hardly cared, no one had heard a word from Matt in almost six months as he remained completely unreachable since his arrest. Perry tried to call his Bronx residence on several occasions, but Matt never seemed to be home and would never return the call.

As it turned out, his parents had hatched a plan designed to sequester Matt from the world in a desperate attempt to save him from a life of hopeless drug addiction. He was forced to remain imprisoned in their home, except on Monday through Friday between 7 a.m. and 4 p.m., when he was permitted to drive himself to work and somehow maintain his teaching job. Of course, had he been teaching a group of students expecting anything even remotely close to an education he wouldn't have been so lucky. Appropriately enough, however, he led a class consisting exclusively of drug abusers and delinquents bound for nowhere. As such, they were perfectly willing to allow him to nod off in class, fucked from the dope that he'd purchased on his way in to work. Most of his students would be dropping out by the end of the semester anyway, so there'd be no one running home to tell mommy or daddy that the teacher wasn't teaching. As far as his class was concerned, Matt was a refreshing diversion from more annoying teachers who actually gave a shit.

Essentially, Matt's quarantine was tantamount to being grounded. As far as The Good Detective and the Missus were concerned—he woke up, went to school, returned home, and then reported directly to his room. No playing outside after school, no friends, no phone calls, and no heroin.

I think The Ansons really believed their semi-isolation therapy was working, especially when Matt chose to remain "productive" by finding a summer job, rather than laying back and collecting Department of Education checks. In reality, though, Matt *needed* a second job to help pay for what had now become a gargantuan heroin habit, and the reason he'd finally resurfaced in the first place.

In mid-July he called Perry at Dabney's, who had actually been promoted to a waiter/manager capacity. This wasn't as amazing as it

142

might sound because regardless of its size, Perry always had the remarkable ability to completely camouflage his habit.

"Hey!" he greeted Matt and the overdo phone call. "We thought you'd died. We actually picked up a substitute guitarist just in case you OD'd."

"No man, I'm fine," Matt said, without even asking about the status of the band. "Hey dude, do you think you can get me a job at your restaurant for the summer?"

"I don't know. We've already got a dope fiend on board."

Perry did manage to secure Matt a temporary job in the kitchen, as one of the regular prep cooks had just left for vacation. As a matter of fact, it was a great job. For fifteen bucks an hour Matt hid in the basement—high as a kite—chopping celery stalks and carrot sticks.

With both incomes Matt was earning enough to maintain his enormous drug habit and still have money left over, especially since he was living with his parents. Pardon the pun, but Matt was definitely living the high life and apparently letting it go to his head. On a daily basis he would brag about how much more money he was making than Perry—while he worked fewer hours and did even more drugs.

"Hey, Perry: How many hours do you think I worked last week?" he asked, even though he knew exactly how many.

"I don't know, Matt," said Perry who just happened to be cutting payroll checks at a desk behind the prep area.

"I'll tell you how many," Matt slurred with eyes barely open as he continued chopping celery. "Thirty four point five hours, exactly!"

"That's great, Matt."

"You know what that means, Perry?"

"What does that mean, Matt?"

No answer.

"What does that mean, Matt?" Perry tried again but to no avail, as the new prep cook was suddenly stuck in a nod.

"MATT!!!" he bellowed, finally losing patience.

"WHAT!!!" Matt shouted back as the cleaver fell out of his hand.

"You just asked me a fucking question!"

"What question?"

"You just asked me what it meant that you worked 34.5 hours last week," Perry reminded him.

"I worked 34.5 hours last week?"

"Well that's what you just fucking told me!!!"

"Oh yeah!" Matt said as he returned to a more thorough state of awareness and resumed chopping. "I worked 34.5 hours last week, which comes to…"

He thought about it for a few moments.

"That comes to $517! Do you know what that means?" he asked once more.

"No Matt, I don't fucking know what that means. Can you hang in there long enough to tell me?"

"Sure. That means that with my teaching check I've made almost $1100 for the week," he pointed out, as visions of loaded syringes danced in his head.

"That's great, Matt."

"And it also means that for same week, you've made about half of what I've made. You hear that, buddy? **HALF!!!**" Matt said, as he aggressively slammed the cleaver down on the celery stalk to accentuate his point. However, upon a closer analysis it became clear that although Matt would be enjoying a 90% gain in gross earnings, it would come at a 10% loss in net fingers as the cleaver came crashing down on his hand along with the unsuspecting stalk of celery.

Of course, this wasn't the first time nor would it be the last that Matt found himself in need of emergency medical attention, as once again he chose to do the wrong drug at the wrong time. As a result, he was immediately transported to St. Vincent's Hospital to undergo surgery and have the severed part of his left index finger re-attached.

Fortunately, *his pinky* remained unscathed.

46

Though the summer finally neared an end, my spell as not only a junky—but also a crackhead—was just beginning. Of course, I never actually considered myself *addicted* to crack. After all, I was already a heroin addict and as far as I was concerned, a significant dope dependency clearly marked the end of the drug-addiction line.

By now, my chemically altered brain considered even the regular use of any drug other than heroin to be insignificant. It sounds crazy—but my daily, summertime, crack-dabble seemed nothing more than a symptom of living in an area that was inundated with crack *dealers*. I'm fairly certain that had they not been stationed in such close proximity to my building, the thought of smoking crack everyday would've never occurred to me. However, they were and it did.

One particular afternoon, just before returning home from Serendipity, I purchased two rocks outside a schoolyard on the corner of 47th Street. Shortly thereafter, as I attempted to cross Tenth Avenue in order to score my daily dose of dope, a car pulled up and blocked my path to the other side of the street. Meanwhile, the dope dealer, who only a moment ago was patiently awaiting my arrival, suddenly sprinted in the opposite direction as if he'd seen a cop or something.

"Get your fucking hands against the car, asshole!!!" came a greeting from one of New York's Finest, as he exploded out of the unmarked vehicle in front of me.

Without thinking I complied with the command, and it wasn't until he patted me down and found the crack in my pocket that I realized what was going on.

"Fuck!" I quietly muttered to myself as I didn't want the little children looking on to be traumatized. However, expletive aside, I realized I was a bit lucky for had the cops waited just a few moments longer they could've busted me twice.

"Turn around and smile for the camera you fuckin' crackhead," said a cop and of course it *really* pissed me off.

"Where?" I asked.

"On the roof of the building across the street," another cop said to me and pointed. "Do you see the guy with the camera waving to you?"

Indeed I did and would've waved back—but my hands were cuffed. Besides, I was a little miffed that the cocksucker was collecting evidence against me from the roof of the very building I lived in. I must say, even now I was a little cavalier about it all, but that was only because it was my first arrest and I had yet to learn of the plague of miseries awaiting me.

I was loaded into a white cargo van and then chained to a collection of crackheads, heroin addicts, and a few drug dealers that included my own. There, bound together on the floor of the van, we were to be transported to the local precinct responsible for hosting the event.

I realized that rush-hour traffic, distasteful under normal conditions, was utterly revolting when chained to a group of dirty drug addicts on the floor of a hot and stinking police van. While sitting in the vehicle with temperatures approaching a hundred degrees, conversations soon began to revolve around the fate of its passengers. Essentially, predictions involved one of two scenarios: You would either be "going home," or cast off to Riker's Island for an indeterminate period. Fortunately, based on the fact that this was my first arrest, I would be part of the former group.

Eventually, we reached our destination. The chain gang was then led off the van, fingerprinted, and moved to a cell where we sat and awaited our destiny.

"When the fuck are we gonna get out of here?" I said to my dealer.

"Get out of here? You're not going nowhere for a while, papi," he said.

"You said I was going home!!!"

"You're in the system now," he informed me. "You go home when it's through with you."

"When the fuck is that gonna be?!?!"

"Twelve hours...maybe 24, maybe *more*. It depends on how business is."

The "business" he was referring to was operated by the Department of Corrections and from the looks of things, business was fucking booming.

Eventually, we were re-chained to each other and led back to the van for a journey downtown to Central Booking. My crack dealer and I were now chained together and I began to sense him playing the role of my own, personal, jail-house escort—as if the service was included with the price of the drugs.

As we exited the van and entered the monstrously large facility, it was all really beginning to sink in.

"The *system*?!" I said with disgust, as I looked around and was faced with the scourge of society decaying right before my very eyes.

"*Corrections* system," my chaperon elaborated.

"Fucking *digestive* system, maybe."

We were unchained and then herded into an area to undergo additional processing procedures. First, I had to drop my pants and underwear and then squat and cough before a corrections officer, whose job was to ensure that I had no objectionable materials stowed away in my ass. After passing inspection, my belt and shoelaces were removed and my belongings were confiscated.

Finally, we each waited in line to undergo health assessments

146

performed by a member of the facility's medical staff. When it was my turn I stumbled over to her desk with my hands cuffed, my shoes falling off my feet, and my pants sliding below my waist. Out of respect for the lady, a disgusted C.O. was forced to return my pants to their regular position as the detailed evaluation began.

"Name?" she asked.

"Craig Goodman."

"Date of birth?"

"May 27th, 1968."

"Married or single?"

"Single."

"Any children or dependents?"

"No."

"Any food allergies?"

"No."

"Taking any prescribed drugs?"

"Prescribed? No."

"Any pain or discomfort?"

"Not yet."

"Diabetes, epilepsy, or heart condition?"

"No."

"Any known physical illness?"

"No."

"Any known mental illness?"

"Yes."

"Thank you. You're done."

I stood up and with my hands still cuffed before me, tried to hold up my pants. I was then escorted to another area where I was to consult with my court appointed, public defender. As he discussed the charge, I was given the impression that my sentence would involve community service. He also mentioned that as long as I didn't get arrested again within a year, the conviction would remain sealed.

After the consultation, I was led to an enormous jail cell that held at least a hundred prisoners. For the first time since the ordeal began, my handcuffs were removed and I was ushered in. I made my way toward a desolate corner of the cell and passed a young Latino who wasn't as lucky, as he was not only cuffed—but hanging from an extension of thick pipe that ran from floor to ceiling. With cuffed hands held above his head and draped over the outcropping of pipe, he struggled to remain on the tips of his toes and only partially suspended in order to reduce the pressure on his wrists. Even in such a painful and vulnerable position, he glared and taunted the C.O.'s as they passed.

"You fucking pig motherfuckers!" he screamed, as a C.O. then reached up to tighten the cuffs. "Yeah? Good!!! Fuck you!"

All of the benches were taken, so I was resigned to remain standing as the cold cement floor was soiled with substances and matter I don't know how to describe. Unfortunately, after about three hours of standing I realized I wasn't going anywhere for a while and finally gave in.

"Fuck it," I said, and staked out a small spot on the vile floor.

It was three in the morning and I was tired and filthy. By this point, I'd already been in custody for close to nine hours and if I didn't need a bag of dope so desperately—I would've sworn off the habit again. I decided to try to relax and hopefully sleep through some of the nightmare because after all, *I was going home*...someday. I allowed fatigue to overcome me until I finally heard the magic words.

"Goodman! Craig Goodman!"

At last! The moment my name was called, I sprung to life and could almost taste the heroin.

"Thank God! Oh thank GOD!!!" I rejoiced out loud.

However, my jubilance was premature, for as the sun began to rise they were now preparing to transport a group of us to "The Tombs," which was a complex of cells located directly beneath the very courtrooms in which we would be tried and sentenced.

Before departing, we were provided scrambled egg sandwiches for breakfast. Afterwards, we were once again chained together and crammed into another van to continue the odyssey at The Tombs, which was only a minute away. Unfortunately, it took two hours to get there as the van sat motionless for almost the entire duration while the rising sun intensified. These two hours were the most unpleasant of all in what would be a 27-hour ordeal—from arrest to release. It was so bad, in fact, that another junky—apparently further along the road to withdrawals than I—began spewing up chunks of scrambled egg. This was just too much. Keeping twenty of us bound and baking together in a dirty, stinking, van was one thing—but being chained to a vomiting junky had to qualify as cruel and unusual punishment. I banged on the wall which separated the cops in front from the cargo in back.

"Hey!!!" I screamed as I continued to slam my fist against the partition. "This fucker's puking all over the van!"

148

Suddenly, a panel on the wall slid open and revealed the fat, food-filled face of a cop.

"What'd you say!?!?!" he barked, annoyed that I'd distracted him from a breakfast cake.

"Somebody fucking puked back here!!!" I shouted again.

"Alright!! Just don't play around with it!" he bellowed, and it's a good thing he had because Lord knows—there's nothing I like better than a good game of vomit.

Finally, the van started to move. Although at first I was horrified by the puke, it was obvious that had the junky not heaved, we would've remained stationary for who knows how much longer. With 20/20 hindsight I now recommend that if you ever find yourself holed up in a police van, vomit—or better yet, *shit your pants.* Your fellow prisoners may be a little put off at first, but trust me—they'll thank you later.

Within less than a minute we arrived at The Tombs, and were led to a cell equipped with a sink and a metal toilet bowl sitting right out in the open. Then, at about noon we were served lunch, and not a moment too soon as I was starving and willing to eat just about anything—as long as it didn't involve mustard or bologna. Of course, I would soon learn that mustard and bologna sandwiches happen to be the official lunch item of the NYC Department of Corrections. I traded mine to a cellmate in exchange for a cigarette.

In jail, candy and cigarettes are treated like gold and were each worth two dollars on the jailhouse black market, as sugar temporarily staves off withdrawals and almost everyone's a smoker…or at least decides to become one. I staked out a corner of the cell, and crouched down with my back against the wall as I lit the butt and took a deep drag.

As I sat there with the cigarette between my fingers, I detected another kind of smoke lingering in the air and was immediately able to identify it. The fact that somebody was able to smuggle a rock into the facility was impressive enough, but how those motherfuckers could smoke crack in jail without wanting to kill themselves afterwards was simply beyond me.

Another five hours in the cell would pass before my name was called, during which time I began going through the beginning stages of withdrawals. I spent four dollars on two, fun-sized Butterfingers and tried to hold it together.

Eventually, I was escorted up to the courtroom and led to a row of empty wooden chairs where I waited until further notice. Within about ten minutes my name was called and I was told to stand beside my public defender. I pleaded guilty and it all seemed extremely routine, though a bit embarrassing.

I was provided the option of performing my community service in Central Park or the subway system. I knew that both would involve something vile, but I assumed the park would be the lesser of two evils.

As I left the courthouse, I realized that the trip to jail was intended to teach me something about drugs, which it did. It taught me that nothing could make me want them more than a trip to jail.

47

I was very lucky that the arrest occurred just prior to my day off from Serendipity, otherwise I most certainly would have been fired. Upon returning to work on the following day I was determined to keep the news classified, and thought it wise to avoid early morning conversations that might result in a dangerous slip of the tongue and self-incrimination. So, without saying a word to anyone, I immediately reported to the kitchen to consult my daily sidework assignments and to thank whoever was responsible for completing them.

"Did you have an interesting day off?" Aaron suddenly asked in a tone that implied he knew exactly where I'd spent it. *But how could he?* I found the probing nature of his question a bit troubling as I certainly wanted my alternative lifestyle to remain under wraps. Of course, as far as Manhattan Criminal Court and the Department of Corrections were concerned, the cat was already out of the bag.

"Yeah," I said to him, and was then able to escape the conversation as Andy told me I had a phone call. It was Perry.

"Katrina OD'd last night," he told me.

Apparently, Katrina's cat might have made it out as well.

"Oh shit!" I said. "Is she OK?"

"If dead's OK she's doing great."

"Oh my God!!! How could—"

"Just kidding," he interrupted after only a moment of gut-wrenching agony. "She's at a hospital in Brooklyn."

As soon as my shift ended, I met Perry at Dabney's and we headed to the hospital. Along the way, he filled me in on the details which I was eager to hear as dope-fueled experiences with Katrina were very rare, limited to snorting a single bag, and only in the event of a Sections gig. Aside from those occasions, I never saw her high—even while I was living in her apartment. Furthermore, since it's difficult to overdose by *snorting* dope, I assumed that at some point Katrina must have graduated to the needle which was hard to believe.

Perry informed me that about a month after I moved out of her Brooklyn apartment, a friend of hers from Georgia named Doug Gentry moved in. Doug happened to have been a vein-tapping junky and apparently, Katrina was under his influence when she picked up the syringe. Even so, I couldn't help but feel partially responsible for the overdose because *I* was the one who introduced her to heroin in the first place.

Perry and I arrived at the hospital by 5 p.m. We were then sent to the third floor and roamed around until we came to a room with the name "MacKay" posted on the door.

Although I knew she was OK, as Perry turned the doorknob I was half-expecting to see her on a ventilator with tubes and hoses protruding, but that was hardly the case. As soon as we walked in, there was Katrina—propped-up against a pillow and wearing the sweet smile of a southern belle.

"Hey guys," she said, a little embarrassed but extremely happy to see us. "Perfect timing! I'm being discharged any minute."

"What the fuck, dude?" Perry said.

"I'm sorry," she said. "I hope I didn't freak anyone out."

"Perry told me you were dead."

"I swear I'm not."

"*You* can't OD, Katrina," I said. "I'd feel responsible. Perry can OD anytime he wants because he's a fucked up junky and I had nothing to do with *his* problem—but you don't have that luxury. Got it?"

"I don't have a problem," she said. "I just lost track of what I was doing."

At that moment—two, fat, uniformed cops stormed into the room and toward the bed like there was a pig in the blanket instead of

Katrina. Then, one of them made the unfortunate mistake of attempting to say something.

"Miss MacKay? I'm Officer Marty Da—"

"Get out," Katrina interrupted, at first calmly.

I'm not exactly sure what the police expected to accomplish but whatever it was, they weren't going to get very far because the only thing Katrina hated more than snakes—*were cops*.

"Miss MacKay, I know you're not in the mood to discuss this right now, but—"

"You don't know fucking shit!" she screamed at the cop, and I suddenly realized I loved her.

"That's fine," the officer said as he finally gave up and turned to leave. "But I certainly hope you've learned something from all of this."

"I certainly have," she said. "I learned to put a little less in the needle next time, which from the looks of things should be in about 20 minutes—so if I run into any problems I'll be sure to give you guys a call. But until then, **FUCK OFF!!!**"

I actually felt an erection coming on.

For a moment the cops just stood there, flabbergasted and silent.

"Let's go!" Katrina shouted as she actually snapped her fingers at them. "Out!! What the fuck are you waiting for!?!? Are you dumb *and* deaf? GET THE FUCK OUT!"

And so they did.

"Katrina!" I said, "I really can't believe you!"

"What?"

"You still have some dope left and you didn't tell us?"

48

I am not, nor have I ever been a big fan of the handshake. A lot of guys believe that a noticeably firm handshake tells a lot about a man. It tells *me* he's an asshole. In fact, it seems in some testosterone-driven instances the gesture can actually transform itself into a brief but primitive display of chest-pounding dominance, as each hand momentarily attempts to overpower the other.

In mid-October Serendipity hired a new waiter, and when we met I shook his hand. His name was Randy Stewart and he was a big, strapping, Californian who looked as if he'd just stepped off the football field. At first I thought he was straight, but then his handshake told me otherwise. It said:

"I'm totally gay. Not only am I totally gay, but if I wanted—through brute physical force and sheer will alone—I could bend you over and make you my honey. But I won't do that because I'm a really nice guy."

Actually, Randy *was* a nice guy. But he was different. He was, for lack of a better term, *straight gay*. Though certainly not in denial, this variety of homosexual *appears* straight when in reality he's as queer as the others. Though I would later encounter straight gays in Florida, for whom keeping a low profile was a matter of survival, in New York they live openly but in a shadow cast by their more flamboyant peers.

"You wanna get high after work?" Randy asked me as our first shift together was nearing an end.

A loaded question for some, but I knew I could fly *this* plane blindfolded.

"Of course," I said without knowing exactly which substance he was suggesting we abuse.

Bearing in mind that Randy was queer, I assumed getting high would involve cocaine as it seemed, along with ecstasy, to be the drug of choice amongst my gay friends. Armed with that bit of knowledge I wasn't going to be stupid, and insisted on first heading uptown to "pick something up" before meeting him at his apartment.

I jumped in a cab, headed up to 110th Street, purchased the dope, and then immediately flagged another cab to Randy's building which was across the street from Serendipity. The round-trip journey took only 20 minutes which, given rush hour traffic, was remarkable time though apparently not fast enough. When I entered the apartment the stereo was blasting, cocaine was cooking, and Randy and his friend Jack were about to torch the first batch of homemade crack. Clearly, I was beginning to think that my fear of exposure at Serendipity was an overreaction, as it was now obvious that I wasn't the *only* fuck-up employed there.

As the two of them sat on a couch hitting the pipe, I tossed my jacket onto a chair.

"Help yourself," Jack said to me. "There's another pipe on the table."

I walked over to the table and just as he said, there was a glass pipe loaded with a rock that seemed to be calling my name. I hit it hard as a Concrete Blonde CD played in the background.

"This shit is fucking good," I said and then checked my back pocket for the waiting bag of dope. It was there. Now I could relax and enjoy the free cocaine without worry.

A plugged-in synthesizer happened to be sitting on the table which was too good to be true. When lit up, most people have their little obsession and mine was jamming to recorded music. It didn't matter what the music was, or what musical equipment I had access to. If cocaine was involved, I'd almost always find myself mindlessly playing whatever instrument was available until the drug wore off. Beyond that, I also happened to have been a devoted Concrete Blonde fan.

I struck the keyboard and for a while was lost in a reverie as the cocaine seemed to intensify the gothic undertones of the music.

Wait a minute... Free drugs, a plugged-in synthesizer, and Concrete Blonde!!! Are they trying to seduce me? No, of course not! Evan told me that hitting on straights is frowned upon by homosexuals. Even so, I would watch for the slightest indication of impending intimacy and swore that if they so much as even turned down the lights—I was fucking out of there.

"Hey man, can I have another rock?" I asked.

Randy looked up from the blowjob he was administering just long enough to give me the go ahead—and then got right back down to business.

Once I knew what they were up to, it seemed like it really didn't matter anymore. Now at least it was out in the open and after all, you can't blame a guy for trying.

Homosexual gratification continued as I smoked crack and played the synthesizer. Unfortunately, however, all good things must come to an end as the supply of cocaine and erections was eventually depleted. Of course, although I abstained from the latter—I may have overindulged in the crack.

"Craig, you smoked almost all the coke!" Randy said as he went to hit the pipe.

"Well...you guys were smokin' the poles," I responded with a nervous chuckle. "Listen, I'm sorry. I got a little carried away. Let me run uptown and I'll replenish the supply."

I knew that within a matter of moments I'd be feeling the coke crash, so I quickly ducked into Randy's bathroom to tap a vein before heading up to Harlem to score.

Although I had never purchased crack anywhere other than Hell's Kitchen, I knew there were several coke dealers lingering in and around the projects of 110th Street. Upon arriving I exited the cab, entered the nearest building, and was immediately confronted by a crackhead dealer who was intermittently smoking and selling his stash. I bought four rocks and then turned to leave. Just as I did, I noticed a very young, white, uniformed cop approach the building and I immediately wet my pants.

Hoping he didn't catch sight of the transaction—or the piss—I walked toward the doorway as if absolutely nothing of interest was going on, and causally dropped the rocks into an empty paper bag sitting on a nearby windowsill. I was extremely subtle and except for the spontaneous bit of peeing, was impressed with my ability to remain calm and collected in light of certain doom. Of course, I was sure I was going to jail anyway.

Just before we brushed by each other I was trembling and hesitant to meet his gaze; however, after summoning the courage I was acknowledged with a friendly head nod as if I were another cop. He didn't say a word to me and fortunately, this brush with the law ended without incident. I decided to cut my losses and call it a night.

Clearly, for the first and only time in my junky experience, my whiteness—along with a bit of flawed racial profiling—saved me from almost certain arrest. This extremely rookie cop had gone into the building with a preconceived notion of what to potentially arrest and apparently, a white boy wasn't on the menu. Now, this is not to suggest that the cop was necessarily a racist. More likely, at this early stage in his career he simply wasn't programmed to associate a Caucasian with the illicit activities known to occur in this particular part of town. Ironically, a more seasoned cop would have stopped me at the door, and taken my whiteness as a sure-fire indication that I didn't belong in the area and was up to no good.

49

I was overwhelmed by the smell of rot and decay and at first, was puzzled by it. As the rising sun began to illuminate the park, I scanned the surface of the lake. My eyes suddenly settled upon a bloated body floating just on its surface, and then of course—I recognized the smell. *It was the smell of death.*

He was perhaps 20 years old, and at that age the loss was especially tragic. I took a step closer to the lake, and upon further examination made the horrifying discovery that he wasn't alone. There were others...*many, many others.*

I hadn't seen or heard from Perry in at least a week and was getting a little agitated. It appeared as though he'd grown a bit complacent living in the sweet surroundings of Gina's apartment, while I was living the lonely life of a drug addict in a shithole. Sections had done nothing in months, and though I didn't mind being a junky, I didn't want to be a *shiftless* junky.

On October 30th I reported to Central Park at 7 a.m. to commence with community service and repay my debt to society. When I arrived at the ranger's office I was met by a police officer and told to sign-in which I did, along with six or seven other incorrigibles.

"Oh boy," said the officer. "We have something *really* special planned for you guys today!"

At around eighteen acres, The Boathouse Lake in Central Park is surprisingly large, and there are areas so secluded that if you didn't know any better, you might think you were in the middle of the woods and not the middle of Manhattan. As a matter of fact, in some of the park's most isolated patches there's no visible skyline, and the sounds of city life are somehow muffled by the noise of nothingness.

Though many are surprised by it, the lake is brimming with bluegills, carp, koi, perch, catfish, and who knows what else. But the rulers of the lake are, undoubtedly, the carp. Central Park carp have no natural enemies, and as a result some are almost 30 years old, over three feet long, and weigh as much as 50 pounds. They are *true* abominations. In fact, I once saw one swim up and swallow a rat like it was a grain of rice. As traumatized as I was by the experience, I realized that these deranged fish were a novelty of sorts, and what better place for a rat-eating breed of carp to call home than in the middle of Manhattan.

There was no doubt, the carp were on top of the lake's food chain and had been for years. That was, until the fall of 1993, when an algae that had been forming all summer finally decided to extinguish scores of them the night before I was scheduled to perform my community service.

At first glance it appeared as though the oldest and largest fish were among the most prevalent victims, as hundreds of giant carcasses floated on the water's surface or had already drifted ashore. Since retrieving and disposing the bodies of decomposing monsters would make most people turn to drugs, the task was left to a squad of already established addicts. For almost six hours we hauled dead fish from the edge of the shore to dumpsters positioned around the lake's perimeter. It was such a horrifying experience that the park rangers actually took pity on us, and historically broke with precedent by allowing us to leave early.

50

Once again, I hadn't seen or heard from Perry for several consecutive days. I decided to leave him alone because he was supposedly sick, but I was also sick—sick of his fucking bullshit. Nothing was getting done, and as it was my responsibility to ensure the songs were written—it was Perry's to ensure they were heard by the right people in the right places. Unfortunately, it seemed he wasn't living up to his end of the bargain.

In reality though, Perry *did* have a plan for Sections. While working at Dabney's he had recently made the acquaintance of Catherine Walter, who was originally from Westchester County and nothing if not ambitious. More importantly, however, Catherine was well-positioned with influential music-industry contacts that could facilitate our eventual success, if it behooved them. After hearing the demo Catherine eventually convinced Perry, who would then easily convince me, to sign a contract which would enable Sections to record a CD with Son's Comic—a new, independent label she was involved with.

On a Sunday afternoon in mid-November I finally got a phone call from Perry, who wanted Matt and me to meet him at Dabney's in order to discuss the details of the recording agreement.

"Fine," I said. "I'll be there right after work. By the way, I was wondering if you were ever planning on coming back to the apartment. Or have you finally decided to give Gina some of your vile seed?"

"I'd chop up my dick first," he said which probably wasn't too far from the truth. "Actually, I've been getting *really* sick at night and I don't know why. Right now I'm more comfortable over there, but I'm seeing a doctor this week and I'll find out what's going on."

"You're probably just dopesick," I offered.

"No, I'm not. I drank a bottle of methadone three days ago just to make sure, and I'm still getting sick. It's gotta be something else."

At about 5 p.m., I met Perry at Dabney's and he did look sick. He was pale and even skinnier than usual.

"You *do* look like shit," I told him. "Where's Matt?"

"He said he'd be here an hour ago."

Shortly thereafter Matt appeared and believe it or not, he actually looked worse than Perry. But Matt, unlike Perry, *was* dopesick. Perry outlined the details of the recording arrangement and it finally seemed as though things were moving in the right direction. We would begin recording on December 10th.

"I'm calling Justin today to arrange rehearsals so we can figure out what we wanna record," Perry said.

"I know what we wanna record," I told him.

During the discussion I asked a variety of questions regarding the details of the contract, the timeline, and what level of control we'd be afforded. Matt, on the other hand, said not a word and only sat there staring off into space like a little kid waiting to be excused from the dinner table. When he sensed the conversation was winding down, he finally made an inquiry.

"Hey, can either of you guys lend me 40 bucks?"

Apparently, Matt was having a hard time supporting his habit on a teacher's salary alone.

"I've only got 20 but I can spare ten," I said. Though I needed a bag to avoid my own withdrawals, I was willing to sacrifice the $20 nod.

"That's not gonna be enough," Matt said.

"I have ten I can give you," Perry said. "There, that's 20 bucks."

"It's *still* not enough."

"Matt!!!" Perry exploded. "What the fuck is wrong with you?!? If you don't have enough money to completely obliterate yourself, then you're just gonna have to settle for getting straight! Is that OK, you gluttonous dickhead?!?"

"I need 40 to get straight!!" he fired back.

Holy crap! His disclosure amounted to a cost of $280 per week—just to avoid withdrawals. That was some pretty serious shit. Apparently, the reckless abandon with which Matt indulged in heroin during the summer, had resulted in an even *bigger* habit that was now impossible to maintain without the help of a second income. And a 40 dollar-a-day addiction meant that he now needed at least $50 to actually get high.

"Then we can't help you."

"Well, if you don't lend me the money I'll sell my car," Matt threatened.

"Then sell your fucking car," Perry said as if he couldn't have cared less.

"Matt," I said. "If you sell your car, then how the fuck are you gonna get to work?"

"I'll worry about that later. Perry—I'll give it to you for a $1,000."

"Matt! Are you crazy?" I interrupted as I tried to talk some sense into him. "It's worth at least three times that!"

"I don't care. Come on, Perry—give me a thousand bucks and take the keys."

"Matt," Perry said, "there's no way I can come up with a thousand dollars and since I don't really want or need a car, I wouldn't give you that much anyway."

"Then how much would you give me?"

"I only have 300."

"Three-hundred-fucking-dollars!?!" Matt screamed. "Come on, man. Give me at least 800."

"Three hundred's all I have."

"How about 700?" Matt countered.

"Nope."

"Then 600."

"Can't do it."

"What about five?"

"No way, man," Perry said refusing to yield. "Matt, I really don't want your fucking car."

"Four hundred is as low as I can possibly go," Matt said.

"Matt!" Perry screamed. "What the fuck is wrong with you? I just told you I only have $300 to my name and I really don't want a car to begin with!"

"FINE!!!" he roared back. "Three hundred dollars then! **ASSHOLE!!!**"

"Matt, you're an idiot," I said. "You could drive into Queens right now and get five times that amount from a dealer—and you'd *still* be getting ripped off."

"Mind your own business."

Perry opened his wallet and counted out the *agreed* upon sum.

"Wait a minute, Matt," he said. "I forgot I bought a cheeseburger for breakfast. I only have 298."

"Perry, I have to have at least 300."

At $300, Matt apparently drove a hard bargain.

"Matt," I decided to try again. "Why don't you forget about it, or at least get a thousand bucks from a dealer? This just doesn't make any sense."

"Asshole!!! If I wanted your fucking financial advice I'd ask it for it!"

Wow. He was getting really nasty. The withdrawals must have begun to set in.

"Fuck him, Perry," I said. "I'll lend you two bucks. Buy the fucking car."

We gave him the money and he signed over the title.

"You're a fool, Matt," I told him.

Of course, the moment Matt had the money in his hand, he needed to score. Unfortunately, in order to do so he would now also need a ride from Perry. Withdrawals were well on their way and his bowels were in no condition to complete the journey by foot.

We jumped into Perry's new Ford Taurus and, selfless as ever, he was kind enough to give Matt a ride to Avenue A and Houston. There, he and I waited as Matt bought drugs.

"I hope he gets busted," I said, which would mean he'd lose his car, money, dope *and* freedom in one, felled, swoop. Unfortunately, I had no such luck as Matt returned to the car with not one, not two—but three *bundles* of dope. With ten bags to a bundle, he now found himself in possession of 30 bags of heroin and yes, he blew the entire wad in one, magnificent, load. Honestly though, I don't think I ever saw Matt happier, and this is precisely why I've always considered his addiction to have been the most dangerous. He had absolutely no sense of self-control and gave no forethought to anything, which is why he would often find himself the subject of ridicule, derision, and his own humiliation. Now, he would also find himself penniless and without transportation.

Matt fixed five bags of dope in the backseat of the car and booted. Within seconds his eyes rolled back in his head, and I could tell that if you were going to blow your bottom dollar on a batch of dope—this was probably the one to do it with.

"You guys wanna get high?" he asked.

Matt may have typically been a selfish junky, but with 25 bags of dope to spare I suppose he felt he could afford to be generous. Then again, with the enormity of his habit, that amounted to no more than a week's supply.

I grabbed a needle and tapped my own vein. The heroin was strong. In fact, it was clearly the most potent strain I'd had to date, so when Matt started opening another bag I had no choice but to smack him in his face.

"Leave me alone, asshole—I know what I'm doing!" he said, which would have been more believable had we not been sitting in what was now **PERRY'S** car.

"Matt, you're gonna overdose and when you do, I swear to God I'll leave you lying in a puddle of your own piss," I warned him.

"Go fuck yourself. I can handle twice as much dope as you two pussies combined," he said as if that was something to brag about, which, I suppose in some twisted way it was because that was a shitload of dope.

Regardless, Matt ignored my threat and proceeded to go back for seconds. As he plunged the needle into his arm for the second time in two minutes, I could see his eyes roll back once more.

And then he was unconscious.

"Watch," I said to Perry. "I'll bet you 20 bucks his heart stops."

"Ten," he countered, as apparently Matt's heartbeat wasn't quite worth twenty. Perry then jumped in the backseat and felt for a pulse as he monitored a clock on the dashboard.

Ten seconds passed.

"Anything?" I asked, not entirely sure of what to hope for.

"I can't tell yet. I'm not even sure he's breathing."

Twenty seconds passed.

"How about now?"

"I don't hear anything," Perry said as he put an ear to Matt's chest.

"Maybe we should take him to the hospital," I told him. "But first—*pay the fuck up!*"

"Wow. I really don't think I hear anything," Perry said again, ignoring my demand as 30 seconds had now elapsed.

"OH FUCK!!!" I screamed in horror as I finally realized what was happening. "You spent all your fucking money on the car—and you already owe me two bucks!"

"Holy shit, Craig! His heart really isn't beating!"

"Don't worry about it. You can just pay me twelve when you get it."

Suddenly, with his head against Matt's chest, Perry's eyes lit up at the 40-second mark.

"I've got a heartbeat!" he said triumphantly.

"Liar!!!"

"No really," Perry protested. "I *definitely* have a heartbeat…Come listen."

I jumped into the backseat and it was clear that not only was Matt's heart beating, but he was breathing as well.

"Fuck!" I said as I handed Perry his winnings, but not before rummaging through Matt's pockets to recoup any losses resulting from his pesky heartbeat. After a lengthy search I eventually found one of his bundles and extracted a bag to enjoy later in retribution.

"We should probably walk him around some," Perry suggested.

We dragged Matt's worthless and seemingly lifeless body out of the car for a stroll along Houston Street. After about five minutes he returned to consciousness, though just long enough to angrily push us away and then pass out in a mountain of garbage on the corner of First Avenue.

"Come on, douche bag," I said as I tried to return Matt to his feet.

"Get off," he slurred.

"Matt! You're lying in a pile of garbage."

"I don't care. Leave me alone."

Perry bent over to help and once again an attempt was made to bring Matt to his feet.

"Get your fucking hands off me!" he slurred, and then passed out once more.

"Man, I could really go for a pastrami on rye," I said, changing the subject as I noticed Katz's Delicatessen almost directly across the street from where Matt was relaxing in the refuse.

"Yeah, me too," Perry agreed.

"Then you watch stupid while I get the sandwiches."

I went to the deli and bought two sandwiches and two cans of Pepsi. When I returned, Matt was still lying in garbage as Perry sat and waited on the steps of a nearby building.

I took a seat next to him and we ate. For about fifteen minutes we tried to enjoy the pastrami, while intermittently chasing pigeons and curious school children away from Matt's body.

"Is he dead?" a little boy asked, as he poked and prodded Matt with a stick.

"Yeah, he's dead. Now get the fuck away from him you little shit," Perry said.

"How'd he die?" the little shit asked as he pinched Matt's nostrils to see if he was faking.

"He died from AIDS," Perry said. "So you better get outta here before you catch it."

"You can't catch AIDS that easily," the fourth grader informed him.

"Yes you can."

"No you can't."

"Yes you *can*."

"No you can't."

"He died from *Junky* AIDS—not regular AIDS," Perry clarified.

"There's no such thing."

"Oh *really*? You think I'm lying?!? Go home and tell your mother you caught AIDS from a dead junky and see what she says."

"She'll say you're a liar," the boy responded and we were beginning to think this kid wasn't so cute.

"GET THE FUCK OUT OF HERE!!!" Perry roared as he finally lost all patience and threw what was left of his sandwich at the kid. Although the little pain in the ass finally left, the pigeons returned with a vengeance to claim pieces of pastrami that were now scattered around Matt.

We were beginning to attract attention and that was a bad thing, as I had a bag of dope in my pocket along with a set of works—which was everything a cop could ever hope for in a junky. Of course, Matt still had over *20* bags of dope in his own possession—which might be enough for a distribution charge. Unfortunately, he concealed most of the heroin so well that it would take more than a few moments to locate and remove and now, with the neighborhood becoming aware of his condition, it just wasn't worth the risk. I knew that with the increasing amount of attention a cop would be rolling by any minute, and if one or both of us were caught rifling through Matt's pockets—we'd *all* be going to jail.

As three or four pigeons boarded Matt's chest to gain better access to a few hunks of pastrami, we realized that we had no choice other than to step away from the spectacle and leave Matt to his fate. It was simply a matter of survival.

51

*"Although the bicuspid aortic valve is the most common heart valve defect at birth, it is found in only 1.36% of the population. Although many people live a normal life without even being aware of this condition, bicuspid aortic valves are still more prone to disease than the normal three cusped valves. Over the years, conditions such as restricted blood flow to the aorta (aortic stenosis), backflow of blood from the aorta into the heart (aortic regurgitation) and valve infection (**endocarditis**) are often detected with associated symptoms during adulthood as progressive damage is done to the bicuspid aortic valve.*

***Endocarditis** is an inflammation and deterioration of the inside lining of the heart chambers and heart valves (endocardium). Bacterial infection is its most common source as bacteria may deposit on the malformed bicuspid aortic valve, causing the condition. Recent dental surgery, prior valve surgery, and weakened valves are risk factors for developing endocarditis. A history of congenital heart disease, rheumatic fever, or **intravenous drug use raises the index of suspicion**."* *

* Ahajournals.org

###

As Perry and I left Matt lying there in the interest of self preservation, the cops drove by and apparently, unable to distinguish his body from the pile of garbage—they kept right on driving. It was either that, or the fact that a dead or dying junky wasn't nearly as much fun to bust. Regardless, an ambulance was there within minutes and Matt was once again whisked away to St. Vincent's Hospital.

I'm sure that treating heroin overdoses was fairly commonplace in this West Village medical facility. Not surprisingly, however, administering to those that ended up on a pile of garbage was probably less routine, especially when that pile of garbage turns out not to be a pile of garbage but rather, a pile of garbage *bags* brimming with towels that had been soaked in bleach. As a result of Matt's insistence to use them as a recliner, he suffered second degree burns to his hands, legs, and ass as the bleach soaked right through his Levis while he was too fucked up to notice or tell anyone.

He spent several days lying on his belly in the hospital, and though the dope was so well-concealed that Matt was able to hang on to it along with his freedom, The Good Detective had finally had enough and decided to kick his burnt ass out of the house. That night Matt ended up on my doorstep with a sob story and a rationalization. He said that everything had turned out for the best, as he could now be in Manhattan full-time and devote more of himself to the CD.

Hooray!

Unfortunately, being in Manhattan full-time apparently also meant becoming my roommate, and I wasn't thrilled with the idea. Nonetheless, although his value to the band was rapidly diminishing, I just didn't have the heart to send him away—especially now that he was officially homeless. To dramatize things further, that same evening Perry had become so ill that he left Gina's and checked himself into Lenox Hill Hospital. At about 4 p.m. on the following day he called me at Serendipity.

"What's up dude? I'm glad I caught you before you left," he said.

"What'd the doctor say?"

"I have endocarditis. It's no big deal."

"What the fuck is that?"

"It's a bacterial infection on my heart," he explained.

"Are you gonna be OK?"

"Yeah. But I need to have heart surgery," he said as though it was nothing out of the ordinary.

"WHAT?!?"

"They have to replace a valve."

"Holy fucking shit!!!" I went on, still floored by the news.

"It's from all the dope, but don't worry about it. Right now I need a favor."

"What do you want?"

"I want you to get me some dope."

"Are you fucking serious?!?"

"Yes."

"Don't you think that now's a good time to quit," I asked, "at least for a fucking day or two?!"

"I haven't had any dope in almost a week. I'm not sick, I'm just bored. Please. Bring me a bag. Just one. It'll help pass the time."

"You just told me that you have to have heart surgery because you're a dope fiend, and now you're telling me to bring you dope. Seriously, Perry—you're stupider than Matt."

"Listen, it's not *actually* because of the dope," he said. "It's because of the *impurities* in the dope and the dirty needles I've been reusing—so don't worry about it. Besides, they've already got an IV pumping me full of antibiotics and antifungal medications to kill the infection. Trust me, I'm impenetrable. I couldn't even catch a cold if I tried."

"Fine," I said with some disgust. "Give me an hour."

I left Serendipity and caught the #6 train to 110th Street, copped two bags of dope, and then headed back downtown to 77th.

I entered the hospital and was eventually directed to Perry's room, where I found him sitting up in bed and attached to an IV. Without a word I immediately handed over the heroin and a syringe. He then loaded the needle and after disconnecting the IV for a moment, injected its contents directly into a catheter that was, for the time being, a permanent and very convenient fixture in his arm.

"You should see if they'll let you take that home with you," I suggested.

"I actually thought about that."

"So when's the surgery?" I asked.

"In three weeks."

"Three fucking weeks! Isn't that right around the time we're supposed to begin recording?"

"You don't need me right now. Just get everyone together and start things off. You know how everything's supposed to sound."

That reminded me:

"By the way, Matt finally got kicked out of his house last night and showed up at the apartment with nowhere else to go."

"Perfect!"

"*Perfect?* Perfect for you, maybe! You don't have to live with him," I pointed out.

"Yeah, I know. But we're finally recording and now we'll definitely be able to get a hold of him. Besides, I won't be working for a while, and he can help pay rent until I'm back on my feet."

"Do we really even need him anymore?" I asked. "He still can't remember the riffs, and we're probably gonna have to replace him anyway."

"Yeah, but since I'm in here we can use him to lay rhythm tracks and keep things moving along."

"Man, I *really* don't want to deal with Matt. Why don't you just schedule the surgery for earlier so you can be ready?"

"It wouldn't matter because I'll have to spend a month in here recovering and besides, they first have to kill the vegetation growing on my heart," he said, which made me want to puke.

"Then what?" I asked.

"Then they go in and replace the valve, which is bicuspid and the reason I got sick in the first place...besides the heroin."

Apparently, most people are born with a tricuspid valve, as a bicuspid malformation is an extremely rare defect. However, many of the afflicted never even become aware of the condition unless they happen to be an IV drug user, in which case there is a good probability of endocarditis developing on or around the faulty valve. Though I was sensitive to Perry's plight, not to mention worried about him, I couldn't help but resent the fact that I'd now have to manage the recording effort.

"Listen," Perry said to me. "I know this isn't supposed to be your job, but you're gonna have to step up and rise to the occasion or else we might lose the opportunity."

52

Matt became a fixture in my apartment and by December, was spending most of his days glued to the couch. Supposedly, the reason behind his continued presence was an early and extended faculty recess, as the Bronx high school that employed him was being renovated. As a result, while Matt sat around watching Ricki Lake, his students were temporarily farmed-out to other schools in order to ensure that construction efforts were completed before the winter semester commenced in January. Making matters worse, he also mentioned that he wouldn't be receiving any paychecks until then. Predictably, when rent was due he asked for a loan. Although he promised to reimburse me in January when he was paid retroactively, the whole thing sounded a bit fishy. Regardless, the bottom line was that it would be *my* responsibility to cover *his* half of the rent. Unfortunately, I knew it would be impossible for me to pay the entire rent single-handedly while already supporting both of our drug habits.

As desperation set in, I strolled into Hunter College's financial aid office to claim loans for the second semester before it ended, and before they realized I hadn't even attended the first. I collected $1500, half of which was spent on rent and household bills. The rest would eventually go to drugs; however, I temporarily suspended my crack habit because with Matt around, the remaining cash would've gone up in smoke immediately.

Meanwhile, each day after work I would report to Lenox Hill to deliver Perry a pack of cigarettes and a bag of dope. Certainly, I knew I was breaking hospital regulations. "No Smoking" reminders were plastered everywhere, and though there was nothing posted about shooting dope—I assumed that was against the rules as well.

Of course, we weren't fooling anyone. Doctors, nurses and hospital administrators knew that Perry was still using, and every other day he was administered a blood test that would remind them of the fact. But how was he getting it? Perry received regular visits from not only me—but Gina, Katrina, Justin, Anton, Leslie, Chris and many others, all of whom could have been the culprit or culprits. Although they didn't think he would dare sneak out of the hospital to score for himself, just to be on the safe side the nurses confiscated his street clothes to eliminate him from the list of possible suspects.

On the afternoon of December 8th I made my daily delivery to the hospital, but Perry was nowhere to be found. I would soon learn that just days before surgery, he once again found himself bored and thought he might pass the time by seeing a movie. So, in his gown and with a catheter sticking out of his arm, he snuck out of the hospital and walked nine blocks in 30 degree temperatures to a theater on 86th Street. And yes, once he paid for the ticket he was permitted entry—catheter, gown, slippers, and all.

I waited in his room for about a half-hour, and just as I was finally about to give up—in walked Perry along with two security officers who caught him traipsing through the lobby on his way back from the theater. When I saw him, I could tell he had somehow scored for himself and was already wasted.

"Where were you?" I immediately asked.

"Dazed and confused," he slurred.

"Obviously."

"No, the movie."

"Oh… How was it?"

"I'm not sure."

From that point on hospital officials were convinced that Perry had somehow been escaping on a regular basis to buy drugs. As a result, they were constantly on high alert and on the verge of chaining him to his bed.

The next day I left work and again headed up to 110th Street to score; however, upon my arrival I immediately realized that something had changed. At first, I wasn't quite sure what it was, but within a moment or two I realized that the dealers were nowhere to be found, and that nobody was selling anything to anyone—*not even a set of works*. Typically, 110th Street was pure paradise for a dope fiend. At any given moment there were usually several dope dealers roaming about, as "Hot City," "Hot Party," and "Black Flag" could be heard as they strolled by and openly peddled their respective brands.

Although the same, old, addicts still lingered—they looked nervous, moved cautiously, and no one said a word to me as I headed east on 110th. Then, as I made a left onto Third Avenue and rounded the corner of 111th Street, I was horrified to see three white junkies with their hands against the wall of a building.

Holy shit! This was the first time I ever remembered seeing a bust go down in this part of Harlem, known as *Spanish* Harlem due to the area's high concentration of Latinos. I instinctively turned around and headed back toward 110th Street when I was approached by an old, vaguely familiar-looking junky.

"It's hot out here and 5-O's lookin' at you **hard,** son!" he said to me as he passed.

In junky-speak that meant people were getting arrested while the police were closely monitoring my behavior.

"What the fuck are they watching *me* for?" I turned and asked as innocently as possible.

"Maybe cuz you a white boy tryin' to buy drugs in Harlem," he said and kept right on walking.

By this point I'd been a white boy trying to buy drugs in Harlem for about as long as I could remember. Why should things suddenly be different? Here's why:

The previous month, our beloved Mayor Dinkins was dethroned by Rudy Giuliani who had already made good on his campaign promise to eliminate the "open-air drug bazaars" that plagued the city. Now, I realized two things: one—it took a black mayor to make a white junky feel safe from white cops in Spanish Harlem and two—*you never know what you've got until it's gone.*

I turned around to see a cop in the driver's seat of a patrol car staring intensely at me. It had become clear that the climate in Spanish Harlem had changed. *Now*, if you were white and in the area you'd better have a good reason for being there—*and a sudden craving for cuchifritos just wasn't gonna cut it anymore.*

I hopped in a cab and decided to give the Hell's Kitchen spot by my apartment a try. When I got there I was mortified. My slippery-looking Colombian with bad skin had his hands against the wall and was about to be loaded into a police van.

"Holy fucking shit!" I said to the cabbie. "Change of plans. Bring me down to Avenue D and Sixth Street."

Amazingly, when we got downtown the scene was much the same, as the new mayor's drug crusade had apparently penetrated all of my regular haunts. Although I didn't notice anyone getting busted at this particular location—cops were everywhere. The only other spot left to try was 18th Street, and those dealers didn't come out until later.

That was it. I was out of resources. I went back uptown to Lenox Hill, and by that point I'd already spent over $50 in cab rides just to come up empty.

"Where the fuck have *you* been?!" Perry demanded, obviously referring to my much later than anticipated arrival.

"Trying to score."

"Did you get anything?" he asked, expecting me to answer in the affirmative.

"Negative."

"FUCK!!! Where'd you look?"

"Everywhere."

"Did you try on 106th Street?"

"A hundred and sixth?" I asked, as I was totally unaware of the spot's existence.

"They sell nickel bags out of an apartment on the corner of First Avenue, and they're actually pretty good if you boot two."

"I've never been there and I'm not gonna knock on some dope dealer's door."

"Don't be such a pussy. He'll buzz you in."

"Fuck you!" I said. "Wait until the dealers on 18th Street come out."

"By Beth Israel?"

"Yeah."

"That's not until at least 9:00 and visiting hours are over by then," he told me.

"Well then I guess you're shit outta luck."

"Fine! I'll go to 106th Street myself, you big pussy."

"Just wait a second," I said, trying to dissuade him from yet another stupid escape. "I'll go downtown and wait for the dealers to come out. After I hook it up, I'll cab it back to the hospital and talk my way in."

"They'll never let you back upstairs. Come on, let's go," he said and of course there was no arguing with him.

Perry and I were forced to leave the hospital through a fire exit, as merely the sight of him in the lobby was enough to sound the alarms. Then, the moment he tasted freedom, he flagged a cab and within minutes we arrived at his secret, 106th Street location.

"Wait in there a minute," he said to me while pointing at a White Castle located just across the street.

I went inside, ordered four cheeseburgers, sat down and waited for Perry. Within minutes I noticed him enter the restaurant and dart into the bathroom, and I quickly abandoned the tiny burgers and followed him in. After getting off, I returned to the table with Perry in tow to finish eating, though the dope made consuming any more than two of the cheeseburgers an impossibility.

"You want one of these?" I asked as I offered him a cheeseburger.

"Get that shit out of my face!" Perry said with a bit more passion than I expected.

"Why?"

"I'm not allowed to eat cheese right now...it's against medical advice," he said while high on dope, dressed in a hospital gown, and wearing a catheter at a White Castle in Spanish Harlem.

53

Recording sessions were to begin on December 10th at Fast Trax Studios on 28th Street and Eighth Avenue, two days before Perry was scheduled to undergo heart surgery. That afternoon, I had arranged for Justin and Chris to meet me there along with Matt at 7 p.m.

I was worried about the session. I really had no idea where to begin, especially while Perry was in the hospital and there was such an emphasis placed on being cost efficient. This urgency was stressed by Catherine, who was a little annoyed by our refusal to record digitally and instead opt for an analog recording which was considerably more expensive. In the mid-nineties, many musicians weren't yet convinced of the merits of the new technology, and a rumor persisted that the warmth and resonance of certain instruments couldn't be reproduced digitally. Of course, this was pure rubbish as the "warmth and resonance" we were all so mesmerized by would eventually be identified as hiss and background noise. Had we gone along with the digital option we would have saved thousands, and the CD would have sounded even cleaner and better produced.

On December 10th I decided to delay the dope purchase until after the session concluded, as Matt was scheduled to record guitar tracks and I thought it wise to keep him as sober as possible. Unfortunately, upon returning home from Serendipity I discovered him too dopesick to function, and this was far too important of an occasion for me to just sit back and enjoy the sight of him suffering. With that in mind, I headed back downstairs to score each of us a bag. Thankfully, ever since his last visit to the emergency room Matt had no choice other than to wean his habit down to a single bag a day.

"We're gonna be in there for at least five hours," he said as I handed him his dope. "Maybe you should get another bag or two."

"Maybe you should get some money," I suggested.

"Oh, don't worry about it, man—it'll work out. I have some weed and a six-pack of Old English that we can bring along."

"Oh good, because I was really worried that you weren't gonna be fucked up enough," I said, as once again Matt demonstrated the fact that he was always cocked and loaded to get out of control. Although one bag of dope would be sufficient to keep him straight, it certainly wouldn't be enough for him to obliterate himself. As a result, he felt he had no choice other than to supplement his buzz with marijuana and alcohol. And incidentally, though Matt really didn't care for Old English 800—I absolutely despised it so it was always his six-pack of choice as he could rely on being able to hoard it all. The fact that he purchased the malt liquor with my money seemed to matter little.

We headed downtown to the studio, and when we arrived Chris was already arranging the drum mikes with Nick Vera, the engineer who would be recording the CD. I liked Nick. He was from New Jersey and had volunteered for the project because he was impressed with the old demo.

"I think their might be a problem with the sax, though," he said.

"Don't worry about it," I told him. "The problem's been eliminated."

For two hours, while Chris and Nick worked diligently to arrange the microphones, Matt strutted around the studio—smoking blunts and drinking malt liquor.

"Hey Dr. Dre!" I snapped. "Why don't you tune your guitar or something?"

"I already did!"

Sometimes I really hated him.

"By the way, can I have one of these?" I then asked, pointing to the six-pack of Old English 800.

"Really?!"

"Yeah, fucking really!"

He begrudgingly handed over one of the cans, and as I went to the bathroom to pour it down the drain I was yet again mesmerized by his selfishness.

Justin arrived at about 9:30 and shortly thereafter we started. "The

Wish" was the obvious song to begin with, not because it was possibly our strongest—but because Matt was the only one who could play the rhythm guitar track. The fact that he was presently living in my apartment offered little confidence with regard to his reliability, and since he was at the studio and in working condition I thought it best to complete the one portion of the CD for which his talents were indispensible. Unfortunately, while running through the song, the complexity of the chord progression prevented Chris from coming up with anything cohesive, and for almost two hours they bumbled along, never capturing the energy that the music was written with.

"Hey guys, you know what?" I said to Chris and Justin. "Why don't you call it a night? Matt and I'll try to get this straight so you have something decent to work with later."

Although it hardly justified the expense of the evening's session, with the help of a click track to compensate for the lack of percussive time-keeping, Matt was able to record a perfect rhythm-guitar track. But unfortunately, with all the time wasted it took us five hours to do what should have easily been accomplished in one. Obviously, even with that one success the session was considered a waste of time and money.

The day after the session, which was the day before Perry was to get cut open, I made my usual visit to the hospital. However, I decided to spare him the news about our lackluster recording effort and instead save it for a post-operative surprise. Before surgery could commence, however, Perry had a big decision to make.

When I arrived at Lenox Hill, Perry and his heart surgeon were discussing the pros and cons of replacing his damaged valve with that of a donor's, or with a synthetic valve made of metal. The metal version was generally more durable and less likely to require surgical maintenance in the future; however, it did require a specific blood consistency, so much so that not only would Perry be forced to take blood thinners for the rest of his life, he would also be prohibited from ever again sticking himself with a needle. This was no idle warning. Even though the valve was synthetic, Perry would still be entirely susceptible to a reoccurrence of the infection due to the development of infection-friendly scar tissue and other factors resulting from the upcoming surgery. Consequently, if endocarditis was to reappear, and even a tiny piece of bacterial vegetation was to break off into his bloodstream, the synthetic valve would likely suffer a catastrophic failure resulting in almost immediate death. As far as the donor valve was concerned, it was better equipped to endure such rigors without immediately shutting down; however, any transplanted valve made of tissue had an expiration date of approximately ten years, at which point it would again have to be replaced—regardless of whether it was attached to the heart of a junky or not. Of course, a valve made of tissue was—in and of itself—also susceptible to a reoccurrence of the infection. For a committed junky it was simply a no-win situation.

"So, Perry—what's it gonna be?" asked Dr. Wendel who for days had been desperately trying to persuade him to swear off heroin, and take the synthetic option which would likely spare him from having to undergo future procedures. Of course, the notion of wasting a perfectly healthy donor valve on a junky who'd probably just fuck it up anyway, must have raised some ethical questions for the doctor as well. "You are going to quit using…aren't you?"

"Of course (not)," Perry said. "But just out of curiosity: Let's say I was to choose the donor valve and then for some reason had a relapse. What would happen?"

"There'd be an increased likelihood of a recurring infection, which could result in vegetation entering your bloodstream followed by a major stroke, possibly a heart attack, and then another valve replacement. **Trust me**. Your best option is to quit using and choose the synthetic valve. If you stay clean and take the blood thinners it'll probably last forever."

"OK, OK, I know. But if I chose the donor valve and then had a relapse, would I die?"

"Well like I just said, Perry, you could have a stroke, and yes, as a potential candidate for a heart attack and a second heart surgery you would ultimately be putting yourself in—."

"Yes, I know—but could I immediately drop dead like I might with the synthetic valve?" Perry interrupted, finally cutting to the chase.

"In the event of a relapse the donor valve would allow vegetation to pass through without shutting down, so in that situation *immediate* death is unlikely but—"

"I'll take the donor valve."

As far as the doctor was concerned, for someone with Perry's obvious inclinations it was ultimately a choice between life or death, but as far as Perry was concerned, it was merely a choice between life—*or life without heroin.*

"Alright Mr. Ward," Dr. Wendel said as he heaved a great sigh and then left the room, fully disenchanted by Perry's selection criteria.

"Maybe you should reconsider your options," I suggested carefully, as Perry was not one to be told what to do.

"Let me worry about it," he said.

"Well then you better quit poking holes in yourself."

"Alright, I will."

No he wouldn't. Perry was going to do what Perry was going to do. If you tried to suggest otherwise, he would tell you exactly what he thought you wanted to hear—and if that didn't work he'd tell you to fuck yourself.

"Where's my heroin?" he asked.

Just as I was handing over the dope, Gina walked in.

"Oh Christ!!!" she said as she saw the transfer. "Is that a bag of heroin?!?"

"No," Perry said.

"Are you out of your fucking mind?"

"Yes."

"And what the fuck are *you* doing here?" she said to me.

"I'm always here."

"No doubt," she said. "You're the reason *he's* here."

In recent months Gina, as well as Felicia, had convinced herself that I was the cause of Perry's drug problem. Yes, it was all painfully ironic, and if I gave a shit about what either of them thought I might have been offended. Admittedly, I was bringing Perry drugs while he was is the hospital suffering from a condition brought on by the very substance I was delivering; however, I knew that if I didn't he'd simply escape and get it himself. And let's not forget, I was also a junky and the antibiotic IV rationale still sounded like a pretty good one.

"Go away," Perry said to her on my behalf.

"Go away?" Gina said in a shocked voice. "Do you actually think I'm the only one who feels this way? Your mother doesn't want Craig around you either."

"I'm 28 years old and my mother's a cunt."

"That's not fair, Perry," I said. "Gina's a cunt too."

"Fuck you," she mentioned to me and then continued on with Perry. "Look. I know you two are friends, Perry, but he's always talking you into getting high."

That was like saying the Jews were always talking Hitler into getting them dead.

"I've already told you about a billion fucking times, *I* turned *him* on to dope and you wanna know something? My habit is *twice* as big as his," Perry said.

"At least," I threw in my two cents.

"I don't care," Gina said. "He's not my problem—*you are*. I don't want you around him anymore aside from the studio. OK?"

"OK."

54

"Uh-uh. No fucking way! I simply refuse. Go ahead and see what happens, you shithead motherfucker! You'll be amazed. I swear to God, the moment you stick me in there I'll shrivel up into nothing before you ever get a chance to close the deal. Fuck you, dude. I don't care; I'm not going into that fucked-up place. You know what goes on in there and you're *still* gonna go through with it, aren't you? OK smart guy, **try it!** You college boys are all the same. You think you're all so smart with your fucking *procedures*."

Three days after surgery, Perry was removed from intensive care and returned to his room to begin the recovery process. That day after I got out of work, Matt and I headed to the hospital bearing the usual gifts, but Perry was so wasted from the morphine drip that there was no need to hand over the heroin.

"Then can I have it?" Matt asked me.

"Of course you can't."

Although the surgery was a success, Perry looked like death. He was attached to a variety of devices and drips, had no color in his face, and appeared extremely frail. We hung around for about an hour filling him in on the less than stellar, first-day recording details when Dr. Wendel entered the room. It was the first time he'd seen Perry since sewing him shut.

"How are you feeling today, my boy?" Dr. Wendel asked his

patient.

"Pretty good, I guess."

"The surgery went incredibly well, but we couldn't use the donor's valve," the doctor explained.

"What happened?!" Perry asked, fearing a metal valve and the end of life as he knew it.

"I'm not exactly sure. The valve seemed perfectly alright after the harvesting procedure, but during surgery it shriveled up into nothing before I ever got a chance to close the deal. Unfortunately, the other donor options were too small to plug the gap, so I had to use something else."

"So you put a metal valve in me?!" Perry cried out as the tears began to roll.

"No, I put a pig's valve in you," Dr. Wendel said with a smile. "They're used all the time and it was the only other option, especially since you didn't want any part of the synthetic replacement."

Perry looked on in confused silence—but I had so many things I wanted to say.

"You should have nothing to worry about," the doctor went on. "Your body accepted the pig's valve without any complications, and for some reason it turned out to be a much better match than the donor's."

I covered my mouth with both hands and held on tight.

"As a matter of fact," the surgeon continued, "I've never seen that happen before with a healthy human valve, the way it just deteriorated mid-surgery. I was really amazed. But that pig valve was something else, I tell ya! It took to your heart like a, like a—"

"Like a newborn takes to its momma's titty?" I suggested.

"No, not exactly," said the doctor, a bit dismissively.

"Like a long-lost baby chick at last returning to the brood?" I tried again.

"Perry," said the doctor who was now completely ignoring me. "For about a billion reasons it's really important that you quit using. And whatever you do, you're never, **ever** going to stick yourself with a needle again. Right?!?!"

"Right!"

Wrong!

55

Perry was supposed to remain in the hospital for 28 days recovering from heart surgery and endocarditis, brought on by the use of dirty needles and unsanitary street drugs.

"Where's my dope?" he asked me on day ten.

At some point after surgery and in accordance with pain management procedures, his morphine was gradually being reduced in order to prevent, ironically, an addiction to opiates. Unfortunately, the greater irony was that Perry, who had managed to maintain a large habit and complete numbness during the pain-free weeks prior to surgery, immediately began to suffer from withdrawal symptoms afterwards as he was slowly being weaned off his medication.

"This can't be a good thing," I said as I handed him the heroin.

"It doesn't matter," he responded, referring to the massive dose of antibiotics he was now being given to prevent post-operative infections. "Besides, I'm still recovering from surgery and I'm not healthy enough to go through withdrawals."

So, every day after work I would continue to score for both of us and then deliver Perry's portion to the hospital. Afterwards, I would meet Matt at the studio where relatively little would be accomplished. In fact, during Perry's recuperation only three rhythm guitars were recorded to click tracks, though we did manage to completely record the music for a song called "Araby."

Although Chris was a vast improvement from Pat, the CD had to be perfect and it quickly became apparent that we would eventually need the services of a second drummer, at least for some tracks. And although I was willing to pick up some of the organizational slack resulting from Perry's absence, I would have no part of recruiting musicians. Consequently, I decided to suspend recordings until Perry was fully recovered, which probably wouldn't be until the end of January.

In the meantime, Matt was driving me out of my mind. He did nothing but sit on the couch, watch television, and sweat as withdrawals erupted while he waited for me to return home from work.

"Matt," I said to him as I handed over his daily feeding. "Rent is coming up. When are you getting paid?"

"Oh, any day now."

For some reason I didn't believe him. He already owed me for December's rent—not to mention December's drugs and alcohol—and January was just around the corner.

On Christmas Eve I received a call at Serendipity from none other than The Good Detective himself.

"You know, Craig, I'm really pissed at Matt," he told me. "But I still don't like what you're doing to him."

"I'm giving him a place to live," I said, straining to be as polite as possible.

"That's only because you're using him."

At that point my politeness flew right the fuck out the window.

"You know, you're right. If he wasn't attached to my couch, I don't know what the fuck I'd do. And by the way, your son owes me at least $350 for rent and bills," I said, neglecting to mention approximately $400 for heroin, weed, and Old English 800.

I was offended to say the least, and as I thought about the rising debt, the upcoming rent, and the fact that I seemed to be everybody's favorite scapegoat I became increasingly angry.

"And," I added, "if the lazy fucker doesn't come up with some money pretty soon, I'm gonna kick him off my couch and into the street."

"Go ahead," said The Good Detective.

Go ahead? Apparently I needed to crank it up a notch.

"First though, I'll be sure to inform the Board of Education that they have a junky teaching in the Bronx."

Apparently, a homeless son was one thing but a jobless son was quite another, because when I returned to the apartment Matt was gone and in his place was an envelope containing exactly $350.

Although I didn't know it at the time, I would never see Matthew Anson again.

56

On December 26th I arrived at Serendipity for work, and upon perusal of the upcoming week's schedule I noticed I'd been given only a single shift. Apparently, a former employee and one of Debbie's favorite waiters was back in town and needed a job. I believe the pared-down schedule was part of a plan hatched by Debbie to encourage my *voluntary* departure, which would not only provide the necessary vacancy—but also eliminate the obligation of having to dole-out unemployment benefits. *It worked like a charm.*

Rent was due in about a week and I was suddenly unemployed. Although I still had Matt's $350 and about $500 in student loans stashed away, given the job situation I felt the funds were better left for drugs and to a lesser extent food, rather than being pissed away on January's rent. Besides, Perry, who was broke and still in the hospital recovering from surgery, had made it clear that he'd soon be heading directly to Gina's apartment to ride the gravy train for as long as he could keep her running, which left me with no option other than to vacate the apartment as I would never be able to afford it alone.

Fortunately, losing my apartment *and* job during the height of the holiday season stimulated a genuine concern for my well being. As a result, virtually every waiter at Serendipity offered me a place to stay until I was able to resettle myself. Ultimately, I accepted Jeff's invitation as we had become fairly good friends and shared some interesting things in common. Though Jeff was an actor, he was also from Queens which was unusual as the starving artist sect consisted of people mostly hailing from places other than New York. I had also become quite affected by not only the passion he displayed for his craft, but the mastery with which he executed it and to this day I credit him with being my greatest artistic inspiration. Jeff was one of the only actors I've ever known to be completely unconcerned with the prospect of fame or fortune. He was in it purely for the love of the theater, and for that I held him in extremely high regard. But most importantly, I found his invitation to be specifically appealing because by now, Jeff was one of the few individuals who knew I was a dope fiend.

Jeff's apartment was a few blocks away from Central Park, and not far from Bloomingdales. Besides the prime location, he was lucky enough to have inherited the rent-controlled lease from his deceased father who held it for close to 30 years. As a result, the cost of his split-room studio near Manhattan's Gold Coast was a mere $140 per month, while at the same time similar apartments in the area fetched close to 1500. Due to the ridiculously inexpensive rent, Jeff and his unnamed, free-ranging pet toad lived very comfortable lives together.

The day before I actually moved in, I met Jeff at Tony Roma's near Times Square for happy hour and to make a quick stop at his apartment afterwards. At the time, he was also providing temporary refuge to another friend with issues, and I suppose he felt an introduction was in order before I came storming in on the following day.

"We should go soon," he said as he drained the last of his drink. "Elliot's waiting. By the way, you know you can stay with me for as long as you need to. I just hope you don't mind me banging on the piano in the middle of the night." Besides being a talented actor, Jeff could also play the piano like Mozart.

We left the restaurant and after making a quick detour, decided to walk to his apartment on the east side. Then, upon crossing Broadway at 42nd Street we encountered a particularly aggressive group of Black Israelites, and as a preacher cloaked in purple explained their militant belief system, another politely informed passing white pedestrians that they were bound for hell.

"You see, in the first place it's you white devils that have been leading society, which is why there's rampant homosexuality, drugs, and child pornography in this country," said the preacher in purple. "All nations have seen you devils abuse your power. After all your transgressions—the slavery, the lynching, the church bombings, the financial exploitation, the racial profiling and far too much more to completely recount here—do you think you white people are gonna get away with it? Do you honestly think so?! We suffered as a people under your power; **therefore**, when Christ comes back to put this world in the order that God intended, what do you propose the blacks, Hispanics and Native Americans do with their newly acquired white slaves? Would you then like us to forgive you for everything you've done and continue to do to this day?"

"But why be a hate group?" asked some poor, white-devil-passerby.

"Don't call us a hate group!" bellowed the preacher in purple. "No, no, no. We do not hate. We are a *spiritual* group."

182

"Oh."

"And by the way," the preacher continued, "we are not a group that makes excuses for evil black people. Wicked blacks share a fate similar to that of the entire white race. They too are devils, and this message will be preached throughout the world as we slowly build our nation. You see, nation building is what we're primarily concerned with, and accomplishing that requires us to embrace common laws that entirely exclude you white devils. This doesn't have to be achieved through the use of violence, but since you whites refuse to give up everything you stole, your empire will be taken away from you by force. What else would you propose that the minorities, who are actually the majority, do to remedy the problem of racially-based oppression in this country? It has been going on since the very beginning when your white forefathers conquered a land that didn't belong to them, and set boundaries for those that it did belong to. Yes, all of you white devils should die a most brutal death!" suggested the spiritual leader. "In fact, you should buy a gun from the CIA—who sells them to blacks in the ghetto—and go home, kiss your family goodbye, shoot them, and then kill yourself. If you white people want to do anything that would benefit humanity as a whole, then do as I've instructed so we have less of you to deal with. If any white person will do as I request, I thank you in advance for your forethought and willingness to rid the world of Satan, but of course—*you will still go to hell!!*

Jeff then caught the preacher's eye for just a moment, but it was apparently long enough to warrant a response.

"What are **YOU** looking at, white devil?!" asked the preacher.

"I'm looking at a man," Jeff said. "What do you think I'm looking at?"

"Your future taskmaster!"

We tore ourselves away from the preacher as Jeff was eager for me to meet Elliot, who had been a friend of his since childhood. Elliot was supposedly suffering from a life altering, identity crisis of sorts, and had ended up on Jeff's doorstep after losing his job and getting evicted from his apartment.

"Actually, I think he's just stuck in the closet and a little afraid to come out," was Jeff's analysis.

57

Some people have an uncanny ability to spot a heroin addict from a mile away. Even dope fiends who go the extra mile by camouflaging themselves in what they perceive to be a cloak of normalcy, are usually unable to escape *this* level of scrutiny. As with Andy from Serendipity, Elliot had a dangerously discerning eye, and from the moment he saw me he knew I was a junky—*and didn't like it.* Fortunately, however, Jeff was unaffected by my lifestyle. As a matter of fact, Jeff, who is six years my senior, usually remained uninfluenced by the behavior of others and I believe he is a rare example of a *truly* non-addictive personality. He'd dabbled with heroin and morphine before, mainly in Asia, but had never developed a habit and perhaps that was the cause of his indifference toward my own situation. As far as Jeff was concerned, I was a big boy and could make my own decisions. Elliot, however, felt differently and found it difficult to be around me—*especially when I was high.*

"You know, he's *really* freaked out by you," Jeff said with regard to the effect my presence was having on Elliot.

"Sorry."

"Oh no, man, don't worry about it. Actually, he's been here way too long and I'm kinda hoping you drive him out anyway."

Good. My life had purpose. And besides—fuck Elliot because I quite liked it there, thank you very much. Jeff's apartment was on the top floor of a four-story building that was otherwise occupied by business tenants. The split-room studio was larger than most, and the windows offered direct access onto the roof of the adjacent, three-story building. Essentially, the neighboring rooftop functioned as Jeff's patio, as well as a small marijuana farm he'd been seasonally cultivating for years.

On January 1st, 1994 came rolling in as Perry rolled out of the hospital against medical advice. He then relocated himself to Gina's with strict orders from Dr. Wendel to remain bedridden until at least January 15th. So, on January 2nd, when he left an urgent message for me to call him at her apartment I had a feeling he was probably up to no good.

"How're you feeling?" I asked as soon as he answered the phone.

"Shitty. Come over and bring some dope."

"Later," I told him.

"No. NOW."

"Listen—my money's running out and I've gotta find a job. If you've got so much time on your hands, why don't you use it to make some calls and start looking for another drummer?"

"I can't," he said.

"Why not?"

"Because I'm all fucked up."

"So why do you need more dope?"

"I'm not fucked up on dope; I'm fucked up on *acid*."

A hit of acid would certainly increase the rate of his recently stitched heart, and that seemed like poor decision-making.

"Where the fuck did you get acid, Perry?"

"Katrina gave it to me a few hours ago."

"Katrina gave you acid after you just had heart surgery?"

"I promised her I wouldn't do it until next month."

"That's amazingly stupid, Perry."

"It's some fucked-up shit, too. I think my head's gonna spin off my shoulders. Please, man. I really need some dope, bad."

I wasn't sure whether his request for heroin was the result of withdrawal symptoms, or simply a need to mitigate the anxiety brought on by the acid. Regardless, I wasn't willing to let him have his way that easily, especially when he was being so reckless while he was supposed to be recovering.

"You just had open-heart surgery three weeks ago and now, a day after checking yourself out of the hospital *against* medical advice, you drop a hit of acid. Did you think that was a good idea, Perry?"

Perry—normally very quick-witted with his one word, bullshit responses—was having a difficult time with this one. I hadn't immediately realized it, but by framing the question in a past-tense context and utilizing the word "Did" as opposed to the word "Do," I had unwittingly complicated things for him. Forcing him to look back and assess the intelligence of his decision at the very moment he executed it, made it impossible for him to appease me with his usual brand of bullshit. If he was to answer "No," *I did not think it was a good idea to drop acid after having open-heart surgery* and then dropped it anyway—he was an idiot. On the other hand, if he was to answer "Yes," *I thought it was a good idea to drop acid after having open-heart surgery*—he was, well, an even *bigger* idiot. I clearly had him cornered and he knew it.

The silence on the other end of the phone went on for a few moments as he struggled to find an answer. Typically, Perry wouldn't have cared whether I was satisfied with his response or not. But since he was interested in not only shutting me up, but having me do his dirty work as well—there was a bit more riding on this particular load of crap than usual.

"Well, Perry. Did you?" I asked again.

"Did I what?" he replied, desperately hoping that I might lose track of the conversation.

"Did you think it was a good idea to drop acid after having open-heart surgery?!"

I could hear him squirming.

"Did I think it was a good idea to drop acid after having open-heart surgery?" he rolled the question around for a while. "Did I **think** it was a good idea to drop acid after having open-heart surgery? Did I think it **was** a good idea to drop acid after having open-heart surgery?"

Apparently, by accentuating different parts of the question Perry thought he might discover a new way to answer it, and thus, a way out of the predicament.

"No, I definitely don't think it's a good idea" he said.

"Of course it's not a good idea you moron, but that's not what I asked."

"Yes it is."

"No it isn't."

"Yes it is."

Obviously, he ignored my question and rather than explain what was going on in his head when he made the stupid decision, he instead provided a 20/20-hindsight assessment as a way out. Unfortunately, I just didn't have the fortitude to press the issue knowing that in the end, it would have been pointless anyway.

"Alright," I said. "I'll get you the dope, but only if you promise not to boot it."

Technically, I suppose this wasn't a direct question and so, of course, Perry said nothing and hoped he'd be able to slide right by without making any kind of a commitment.

"Well, do you?!" I demanded.

"Yeah, fine."

No he didn't.

Though it was difficult to give in, I again knew that if I didn't he would just go out and get it himself. Besides, my own monkey was awakening and since I was about to score anyway, I reasoned that—given his fragile health—it would be foolish for him to risk arrest and exposure to the less than sanitary conditions of jail.

Incidentally, the notion of permanently abandoning heroin was never really a consideration for either of us—even after Perry's surgery, which was in no way the wake-up call that it should've been. As far as Perry was concerned, his fate was the unfortunate result of a bicuspid valve and incredibly bad luck. Of course, he would now have to be more vigilant when it came to cleanliness—but that was where the lifestyle adjustments ended because the dope was here to stay. In fact, *it was written into the business plan.* We wanted nothing other than to be junky musicians, occasionally pumping out a CD or two to support ourselves. We really didn't care about fame or fortune—and we certainly didn't care about what anyone thought. Our only concern was having enough money for a decent place to live and a lifetime supply of dope, but not necessarily in that order.

I left Jeff's and took the #6 downtown to Alphabet City. Given the new mayor's mission to rid the city of drugs, scoring continued to be a complicated affair. Rather than positioning themselves on the usual street corners and waiting for addicts to arrive, dealers were now constantly in motion and transactions were made on the go. Fortunately, on this particular occasion my junky timing was perfect and I scored immediately. I copped two bags and then walked over to Gina's apartment on First Avenue, where I would be permitted entry only because she wasn't home. I met Perry in front of the building and almost immediately noticed the strain of dopesickness on his face as we rode the elevator up to her ninth-floor apartment.

"Wow. I feel sneaky," I said as we crossed the threshold.

"Yeah—Gina would fucking kill me if she knew you were here."

"Should I suck your dick and *really* piss her off?"

"That would be entirely unnecessary. She's already really pissed off."

I laid the dope down on the table and Perry wasted no time fixing the syringe. After a few seconds passed, he tapped a vein.

"That is just *so* much better," he said, and let out a huge sigh of relief as the drug-induced anxieties dissipated.

Perry then opened his wallet and pulled out the sheet of LSD that Katrina had given him.

"Take a hit," he said.

Needle

I carefully tore a little square away from the perforations and placed it under my tongue. Then, I loaded a syringe and booted.

For about a half-hour we discussed Sections and the need for a second drummer. Then suddenly, Perry changed the subject.

"You wanna get some ice cream?"

"No."

"OK, let's go."

We left the apartment and headed to Baskin Robbins, only a few storefronts away from Gina's building. When we arrived the line of customers was not only surprisingly long, but very slow-moving and as we inched our way toward the counter I could feel the acid creeping into my brain. Though only ten minutes had passed, it seemed like hours.

"Hey Perry," I said. "I don't even want any ice cream. Let's go."

"No. I wanna waffle cone."

"Well, you better have some fucking money because I spent all of mine on drugs," I told him along with a group of children waiting in line for ice cream.

"Shit...Alright," Perry said. "I'll run upstairs to get some cash."

"Please don't leave me here alone. I'm beginning to trip."

"Don't be such a pussy. I'll be right back."

He then left me standing in line at Baskin Robbins surrounded by screaming kids, a pink and brown motif, and 31 shades of ice cream that were now fusing into one. I knew that a very bad trip was on the way and I started getting upset.

Fucking asshole! Leaves me standing here by myself, and I don't even want any ice cream. Who the fuck eats ice cream on acid anyway? And on dope too! In January!! I'll bet right now I'm the only idiot in the world that's fucked up, tripping balls, and waiting in line for ice cream at a Baskin Robbins in the middle of the winter. There are Baskin Robbins' all over the world—aren't there?

I wasn't sure.

"Hey lady—are there Baskin Robbins' all over the world?" I asked a woman behind me.

"All over the *universe*, I think," she said.

Haaa! She must be high. But that would be cool, wouldn't it? "31 Flavors on 31 Planets." I should've been an advertising executive. I would've been if it wasn't for Judy. No, I wouldn't have. Ahh, but fuck her anyway. She's probably telling Gail that she was a fool for ever getting involved with me. And Venus...That bitch! Poor Becky. Poor,

188

*poor, Becky. I miss that stupid dog. Shit, I almost died for her. I'm gonna get that dog back someday. No, I'm not. Becky's probably happy now. No, she isn't. She deserves to be happy, though—she was such a good little puppy. I really miss her—but fuck it. I don't have time for a dog anymore because I'm gonna be a rock star. Perry said so. Hey! Where the fuck **is** Perry? Shit! He's been gone for a while. Maybe he had a heart attack and died. I should try to find him. But I'm so fucked up! I can barely see straight. I can barely see at all. Huh, what?*

"Next customer, please."

Somehow, seemingly in the blink of an eye, I had been transported to the very front of the line. Confronted by a pimply-faced kid wearing a brown visor and a pink and brown striped shirt, I suddenly realized I had no idea where I was or what the fuck I was supposed to be doing.

"How can I help you, sir?" the polite young man asked me.

"HEY!!! You need to fucking relax, OK???!!!" I demanded, before bolting out of the store and wondering if I was in trouble.

I suddenly found myself roaming up and down First Avenue, completely confused with one eye closed and the other half-opened.

"Hey, are you OK? Are you OK?" I heard from indiscriminate voices that seemed to be coming from nowhere. Then, I felt a firm grasp on my shoulder.

That's it. I'm going to jail.

"Hey!!! I want my fucking waffle cone!"

58

By the end of January, although Perry had returned to work—I was still jobless, rapidly running out of money, and convinced that Rudy Giuliani was the devil incarnate. In fact, the lengths we would go to score were becoming more ridiculous with every passing week, as the out of shape, uniformed cops that pretended to patrol the drug infested areas of Manhattan were mostly replaced by undercover, steroid-injecting psychopaths that had joined the police because they were too unstable for the marines. We were definitely in need of a weapon to assist us in the war against the war on drugs. Little did we know, that weapon would come on *wheels*.

On January 29th we were scheduled to resume recording efforts after almost six weeks of inactivity. Unfortunately, my enthusiasm for the upcoming session was dampened by the fact that Chris was still missing the point musically, and I had a feeling that little to nothing would be accomplished.

Under normal conditions, drums and bass are the very first tracks to be recorded; however, due to Chris' difficulties, only one of the songs had been performed with a rhythm section. Beyond that, Matt managed to record three rhythm guitars to click tracks, but there was some question as to whether or not the respective drum and bass lines could be added later—in this unconventional, reversed-recording order.

"When we get inside let's try 'Sitting in the Sky,'" Perry suggested. He seemed to think that this particular song was tailor made for Chris' drumming style; however, I still had my doubts.

"Listen, I really like Chris and he's a great drummer," I said. "But eventually we're gonna have to find somebody else to help out on a few of the songs. Trust me. His range is a little limited."

We were due at Fast Trax by 8 p.m., but with dopesickness on the horizon Perry first needed to score or else he didn't think he would survive the session.

We made the usual stops throughout the East Village, but there was no one selling anything and if they were, they were getting busted. As a matter of fact, just after spotting a dealer operating on Avenue C, three roid-raging cops came out of nowhere and threw him against a wall. Things were becoming *surreal*. One day we would have no trouble scoring and on the next it would seem as though the same area had never been anything other than a completely drug-free zone.

"You wanna try uptown?" I suggested.

"We don't have time for that. I'm gonna look for Winston."

Although I hadn't met him prior to this point, I'd heard Perry mention Winston's name on several occasions ever since they first met at the Whitehouse Hotel. Winston was a middle-aged gypsy cab driver who, for the past 20 years, had supported his sizeable habit by stealing fares from yellow taxis in Manhattan. What made Winston a valuable asset was that for the price of a bag, he would transport junkies to the closest and safest place to score before returning them to whatever rock they crawled out from under. It was a pretty good deal, especially if your objective was to buy drugs and not get busted in the process because Winston was nothing if not cautious. Although getting arrested is always traumatic, for Winston it would be truly disastrous because not only did he lack the proper insurance and permits to operate a taxi—*he didn't even have a fucking driver's license.* As a result, in the event of a police encounter Winston would end up in jail and his 20-year-old, emissions-failing cab would end up permanently impounded. That would effectively end life as he knew it because for all intents and purposes, Winston *lived* in his cab. With the exception of two nights a week when he checked-in to the Whitehouse for a shower—Winston ate, drank, slept, scored, fixed, and booted in his cab, all while maintaining a semi-respectable front transporting passengers around Manhattan.

Perry and I headed west on Houston until we came to a navy blue sedan sitting on the corner of Essex Street, where a hippyish-looking man wearing sunglasses and a beret was nodding off at the steering wheel.

"Winston!" Perry greeted the cabbie, rousing him from his stupor.

"What's up, my brother?" replied Winston as he emerged from his nod.

"Hey Winston, this is Craig."

"What's up, my other brother?" the wasted cabbie said as he held out his hand.

"Man, I'm glad we found you," Perry said. "The police are everywhere. We were about a minute away from getting busted ourselves."

"Sometimes it can be difficult to know where it is hot, and where it is not."

"Well then why don't you show us," Perry suggested as we climbed into the back seat of the cab.

Although I considered myself well informed with regard to heroin spots in lower Manhattan, I was very much mistaken. Winston must have scrutinized over a dozen locations that were previously unknown to me as he searched high and low for a safe place to score.

"How about here?" Perry suggested as we passed a familiar spot near Delancey Street that seemed to be police-free.

"No way," Winston replied. "Something's going down...I know it. I can almost *smell* the little piggies."

At first we were unaware of the cause for his concern but sure enough, as we turned the corner we spotted two men that were too white, too big, and too wholesome-looking to be anything other than a couple of narcs. Winston had been a junky for so long that he'd developed a sixth sense for detecting police activity by somehow gauging the energy in the street.

Eventually we ended up at the corner of Rivington and Clinton Streets, a couple of blocks south of Houston. Winston then illegally parked the cab and immediately ran into what *appeared* to be a women's clothing boutique on Clinton. Costume jewelry and handbags sat on display in the store's window, and above the merchandise hung a black sign with the name, "Angelina's" written in shiny gold lettering. We were waiting in the car for less than a minute when Winston returned with a hairclip in one hand and a bundle of dope in the other.

"Where do you guys wanna go?" Winston asked as he then put the car in drive and handed over our share of the treasure.

"Could you bring us up to 28th and Eighth?" Perry asked.

"No problem," he said, and then made a quick left onto Rivington while fixing his dope and dismissing stop signs as suggestions.

Always the consummate host, Winston soon noticed we weren't indulging and offered us each a fresh set of works.

"No thanks," I said. "We're gonna wait until we get to the studio."

"Groovy, brother."

As we approached Allen Street the cabbie made a sharp right and the car fishtailed, clipping the back bumper of a *real* cab and subjecting it to a 360 degree spinout in the middle of the intersection.

"Shit—that was fuckin' close," Winston said, and at once stumbled upon a whole new dimension of adjective. He then crossed Houston and sped up First Avenue rolling through red lights as he tapped a vein.

My heart was pounding out of my chest. I was amazed how someone could exercise such extreme caution while buying heroin—and then go on to commit a multitude of traffic violations with a needle sticking out of his arm.

As he made a 50 mile-per-hour left turn onto 23rd Street I could actually smell burnt rubber.

"At best, we die. At worst we go to jail," said Perry.

Somehow we arrived at the studio in one piece and as Winston popped the trunk, Perry retrieved his guitar.

192

"Thanks for the dope, brother," Winston said to me as I exited the car.

"No problem, brother. Thanks for the brush with death."

We went upstairs to Fast Trax and before saying anything to anyone, Perry and I locked ourselves in the bathroom to get off. By the time we made our presences known we were already an hour late, but otherwise—fucked up and ready for business.

Although only one song was attempted, the session ended up being our most productive thus far. Perry recorded the rhythm guitar track for "Sitting in the Sky," I recorded the vocal, and Chris put down a solid groove which allowed Justin to do the same. Furthermore, Leslie came up with a riveting lead which made Matt's unreliability somewhat less of an issue. At last, one of our songs was almost completely recorded. Of course, it was just a small step, but at least a step in the right direction.

59

In early February we learned from Katrina that Matt had finally lost his teaching job. Interestingly enough, however, he lost the job not long after moving in with me and had just managed to keep it a secret. Apparently, his poor attendance record and proclivity for ending up in the emergency room had finally taken its toll on somebody's patience.

By the middle of the month, Perry was once again ousted by Gina who had become disgusted with his inability to comply with the medical advice intended to save his life. Within a week, however, he found a new living arrangement and then called to share the news.

"Hey, I found us a place to live."

"Where?" I asked.

"On 51st Street between Eighth and Ninth."

That couldn't be good.

"How much?"

"A hundred bucks a week," he told me.

"That sounds like a very hotelish-sounding price to me, Perry, and

I can't be living in a hotel. My life is fucked-up enough. It's not good for my self-esteem."

"Then tell your self-esteem to come up with some fucking money."

"Listen—I'm not living in a crackhead hotel and sharing a bathroom with 200 homeless drug addicts."

"It's not like the Whitehouse," he tried to reassure me. "They have private bathrooms."

Within a few days I would agree to join Perry at the Midtown Hotel, but not before successfully ejecting Elliot from Jeff's apartment by simply leaving a bloody syringe next to his toothbrush. *Mission accomplished;* however, I was still reluctant to abandon my rent-free arrangement with Jeff, for what I knew was going to be a less than savory situation with Perry. Unfortunately, Perry needed a roommate and the CD had to be completed, so if moving into the hotel would bring our ultimate goal to fruition more quickly, then I would do whatever was required…as long as the room came equipped with one thing.

"Perry, you *are* sure about the bathroom—right?" I asked once more before officially giving in.

"Yeah, don't worry about it," he said.

But I *was* worried. I was worried about everything. I was also getting depressed as work on the CD was advancing at a snail's pace and I couldn't see the light at the end of the tunnel. We'd already been recording for two months and there was so much left to do, not the least of which was recruiting a second drummer as we'd discovered a few more chinks in Chris' musical armor. But perhaps worst of all, I noticed a pattern developing as each new living arrangement was less desirable than the previous, and the one looming ahead sounded about a step above the Whitehouse. It ended up being exactly that, but in some ways it was actually *worse.*

The Whitehouse Hotel, though its guests were mostly homeless men and drug addicts, in some ways seemed like a halfway-house of sorts where behaviors and visitors were at least *partially* monitored. The Midtown, however, had a completely different energy about it. In fact, this shithole was *the wild fucking west.* Although many of its guests were drug dealers and users, most were hookers and pimps with clients in tow and nobody ever said a word about it.

For a hundred dollars a week, Perry and I were provided a small room equipped with a sink on the second floor, and a "private" bathroom conveniently located next door. However, the privacy of this particular bathroom was a luxury enjoyed by not only Perry and I, but about 20 crack-whores who also resided on the floor. It was cleaned once in the morning at around 6:00, but that did little to alleviate the biohazard that would eventually develop as a troop of hookers used the facility to freshen up in between assignments. Needless to say, by the end of the workday the floor, sink, toilet bowl and shower would be covered in a cumulative stew of biological debris that had at some point been expelled from a variety of different orifices and canals.

60

Living in the Midtown Hotel certainly did nothing to improve my mental outlook as I seemed to be creeping ever closer to rock-bottom. "Everything's gonna be great and it's just a matter of time," I would constantly tell myself, but at the pace things were going my words were practically meaningless.

Exactly how far my life had deteriorated became clear one morning during our first week at the hotel, when Perry awoke at 5:00 to use the facility. Although I didn't notice him leave the room, I was certainly awakened by his return.

"Don't go in there, man, don't ever go the fuck in there again!" he said to me as he stampeded back into the room with a nightmarish look in his eyes.

"Don't go in where?" I asked.

"The bathroom! It's the most awful thing I've ever seen in my life."

That was definitely saying something.

I looked at the clock and realized it was just before the HAZMAT team typically arrived to decontaminate the second floor facility. Even so, my curiosity had gotten the better of me and I decided to investigate the matter myself.

"Where the fuck are you going?" Perry asked me.

"I wanna see."

"Dude, you're crazy. Don't go in there. You're not up to it. It might make you cry."

"I'll take my chances. Besides, I've gotta take a leak."

"You'd be better off peeing out the window."

"It can't be that bad," I said.

I left the room, and as I cautiously opened the bathroom door and turned on the light I was shocked by how Perry could mitigate the horror of it all. A whitish-yellow gelatinous goo clung to the sink and dangled from the faucet, while a mixture of feces and blood smeared the toilet bowl and floor. When I noticed a moist, bright-red, foamy-looking lump nestled in the corner of the shower stall I finally had to puke.

I ran back to the room and apparently, the expression on my face said it all.

"Told you so," Perry said.

"That was horrible, man...just horrible!!!" I said as I tearfully peed out the window. "And what the fuck was that red thing in the corner?!?"

"I don't know. I think it was a slice of pizza...or maybe a fetus."

From that day forward, Perry and I pledged to never again enter the bathroom between 5 p.m. and 6 a.m., as that was when the hookers seemed most active and before the facility was sterilized. To help combat the problem, we resorted to relieving ourselves in empty beverage bottles and would soon amass a variety of different containers filled to the rim with our bright-yellow, junky urine. Notwithstanding the occasional spillage, the system actually worked out quite nicely. Unfortunately, however, the room would soon become inundated with bottles, and we'd eventually be confronted with the unenviable task of having to empty them into the sink in order to start anew. Of course, in no time at all, the piss menagerie would once again accumulate to a point that would make even a *serious* collector proud.

On a *slightly* less revolting note, I managed to secure another restaurant gig. On February 20th I was hired at Ellen's Stardust Diner which was located in midtown on Sixth Avenue, but has since relocated to Broadway. Although I was pleased with its proximity to my new residence, there was no question that it was a step down from Serendipity in terms of staff and earning potential. Ellen's was another theme-based restaurant that attempted to replicate a 1950's-style diner with a wait staff outfitted in baseball caps, bowling shirts, and shorts. On the self-degradation scale it was about a nine-and-a-half.

The restaurant was owned and operated by Ellen Hart, formally Ruth Ericsson, who was apparently a "Miss Subway" pageant winner from 50 years ago. This little bit of local lore was documented by old, black and white photographs of her and other pageant winners that were plastered around the dining areas. The restaurant, its décor, and menu was a shrine to an era that hadn't been in the collective consciousness since *Happy Days* went off the air, and a tribute to a long forgotten beauty pageant that few seemed to know anything about.

61

"Hey, I think I found us another drummer," Perry told me.

"Well it's about time you got something constructive accomplished," I said as I withdrew the needle from my arm.

It was already well into March, we hadn't set foot in the studio in almost seven weeks, and Perry was beginning to feel the heat from Catherine.

"Who'd you get?" I managed to ask before the dope had its way with me.

"Marc…from Sound Advice."

Marc Jordan was not only a great drummer, but he was also calling the shots for what I felt was one of the best bands in the city. His status in Sound Advice was the result of him being the most gifted musician in the band, and even with a relatively weak bassist they were still impressive enough to be well regarded. Certainly, his involvement with Sections was very good news for the moment, and it provided me with a respite from the depression I'd been experiencing.

"How'd you get him to agree to it," I asked Perry.

"It wasn't difficult. He knows we're great. Besides, I think he's really into the idea of working with Justin."

"Yes. We *are* great," I said as I drifted away.

A few minutes, or perhaps, a few hours had passed before another word was spoken.

"Hey! The light's on in my toe, but I'm stuck in the elevator."

What? Did I just say that? I wasn't sure.

"My watch hurts. Hey Perry!!! Are you gonna wake up or am I gonna have to stand on the roof again? Perry...Answer me you fucking asshole!"

"Would you shut the fuck up?!?" Perry shouted. "You're talking shit again."

"I most certainly am not."

"Yes, you are."

"No, I'm not," I insisted. "Hey Perry!"

"WHAT?!?"

"Isn't spinach brave?"

Oh shit, that was definitely me.

Actually, I had a long history of talking shit whenever seriously fucked up, which—unfortunately for Perry—was every night.

"If you don't shut the fuck up, I'm never getting high with you again," he said.

Empty threat.

Then there was a knock at the door.

"Who is it?!" Perry yelled from his bed, further agitated by yet another slumber interruption.

"Yo, man—there's a fire! You better get outta there!" shouted a stranger from the hallway.

"Don't worry about it and just go away!" Perry shouted back.

"Seriously man," the stranger went on. "You guys better hurry up and get out."

Perry, who was seriously fucked-up himself, stumbled out of bed and opened the door to assess the threat, not to mention the source from which it was revealed. A skinny, black, crackhead appeared in the doorway and continued to urge us into flight mode.

"Let's go guys. The smoke is getting thick," the crackhead said.

Perry stepped out into the hallway and took a look at the commotion going on around us. In a sober state of recollection, I'm not sure if it was the fact that Perry had little faith in crackheads, or he was just too fucked-up to notice smoke billowing into the room.

"Fuck it. We're staying," he said with a surprising amount of conviction.

"Are you crazy?" responded the crackhead in disbelief.

"Fuck it all," Perry told him. "Now please go away."

"You guys are gonna die."

"Don't worry about it and just get the fuck outta here!" Perry shouted as he slammed the door shut and the frightened crackhead fled the building.

62

As much as I didn't care for certain aspects of his personality, Marc seemed to be the missing link. Remarkably, during his first session he was able to add drums to several guitar tracks that Matt had recorded previously, and though forced to adapt to such an unorthodox recording methodology—he was flawless and his rhythms were electrifying. In fact, the only interruption in progress occurred when Justin was unable to develop a proper bass line around Marc's performance on "The Wish."

"What the fuck are you doing?" I said, interrupting Justin who was only about 30 seconds into his initial effort.

"What's wrong?" Justin asked with a smile, probably because this was the first and only time I'd ever questioned his playing. But then again, this was the first time I'd ever heard him play anything that wasn't perfect. In a tactful manner I attempted to explain the error of his ways. Unfortunately, my ability to question or communicate musical direction was compromised by an extremely limited command of the proper terminologies.

"You're coming in on the wrong beat or measure or time signature or something," I stated plainly.

"Sorry. I must have lost my mind," Justin admitted.

"It's probably my fault," Marc interjected as though he felt his limited exposure to the song might have somehow contributed to the miscue.

"No, it's not," I said.

"But what you said doesn't make any sense," he replied.

"He means the *progression*," Perry clarified, who by now had an advanced degree in my musical doublespeak. "He wants you to play basically the same thing you're playing, but try coming in on the first progression instead of the third."

With that one correction Justin nailed it in a single take, and I thought it was the most beautiful bass line I'd ever heard. That session had proven to be the most productive to date, and with the music to four songs now virtually completed, Perry and I decided to celebrate in the usual way. We bid Justin and Marc farewell and flagged a cab to Clinton Street.

"What time is it?" Perry asked me as we exited the cab.

"Just after six."

"I have to be at my mother's in Brooklyn by 7:30," he said.

"What the fuck for?"

"She's making pot roast."

"So?"

"She's been at it all day."

"And?"

"I fucking want some, alright?!?"

Ever since Winston introduced us to Angelina's we had become frequent shoppers at the dainty, little, lady's boutique—owned and operated by Colombian dope peddlers. It was, without question, the most extravagant and successful drug front I've ever seen, and had come into existence as dealers found it increasingly difficult to safely do business in the street—especially around Greenwich Village.

The secret behind the boutique's success was its attention to detail. The store was filled with racks of women's clothing and accessories, which, although a complete ruse were actually for sale to customers unaware of the core product. There were even women inside, arranging merchandise and posing as sales associates. It was a remarkably well thought-out operation; everything in the store had a price tag and junkies were required to purchase a legitimate item in order to help maintain the facade. For that very reason a basket of twenty-five cent hairclips sat on a desk in front of the cash register—which was located just above a hidden garbage pail filled with dope. After transactions were completed the boutique even provided its junky clientele with a receipt...*for the hairclip,* that is. Unfortunately, on this particular afternoon they were fresh out of hairclips, so Perry selected a cheap pair of fishnets that were **very** slutty.

We left the store, purchased syringes from a homeless junky, and then headed toward Houston in search of an appropriate place to get off.

"There's a Chinese restaurant," Perry said as he spotted Ming's Dynasty on the corner of Houston and First Avenue. "Besides, I could go for an egg roll, anyway."

"Me too," I said. "Especially since I don't have your fucked-up mother's pot roast to look forward to." Obviously, I knew I wouldn't be invited to the home-cooked extravaganza because if there was one person who hated me more than Gina—it was Perry's mother, Felicia.

We entered the restaurant and made our way to a back table strategically located near the bathrooms. As Perry headed to the facility, I placed an order for an appetizer portion of egg rolls and two cokes. Shortly thereafter he returned.

"How is it?" I asked.

"Two semi-private, well-equipped stalls with fully functioning toilets," he told me.

"I mean the dope."

"Dope's fine."

About fifteen minutes after I booted and returned from the bathroom the egg rolls had arrived and were rapidly consumed. We then lingered for a half-hour, paid the tab, left Ming's and were almost immediately descended upon by police.

The moment Perry caught sight of the cops he knew we were busted. He dropped his fishnets on the floor and then instinctively threw himself against the nearest wall, which happened to be a fence. Unfortunately, I wasn't quite as quick on the take.

"Get against the wall, dickhead!" said the first little piggy to arrive.

"You mean the fence?" I clarified.

Apparently, that was exactly what he meant, evidenced by the fence-like indentations that were then immediately imprinted on my forehead.

"Where's your fucking dope?" the cop demanded, as he continued to press my face against the fence with one hand while patting me down with the other.

"What dope?" I asked, and then he pressed a little harder.

"We saw you scumbags buy the fucking works!" he screamed into my ear.

Ducking into Ming's Dynasty after we secured the works, but before the cops had a chance to grab us, not only delayed—but had apparently compromised their poorly thought-out operation.

Once my face was peeled from the fence, Perry and I continued to be subjected to a very aggressive interrogation and a more thorough search right there on Houston Street. It was a tad humiliating but overall, it was definitely the most satisfying moment I've ever spent with the NYC Police Department. Once again, they demonstrated a shortsighted and bloodthirsty passion for busting addicts without considering the nature of the addiction—or that a junky might prioritize a bag of dope over an egg roll. Although they correctly assumed that we'd already purchased the heroin, they foolishly believed we'd still be in possession of it after leaving the establishment. Apparently, they may have overestimated a craving for Asian cuisine, which was really just a passing fancy brought on by the never-ending quest for a bathroom door that we could shut and tap a vein behind.

"Why the fuck did you assholes go into the restaurant?" asked the other cop.

Yes, *we* were the assholes, but they still couldn't figure out why we went into the restaurant.

"It's the egg rolls, man. It's all about the egg rolls," I told him.

"I'm not fucking around with you!" he said, as if the pattern of diamonds stamped on my face left any question about his level of seriousness. Actually though, by this point the cops were beyond serious; they were absolutely livid. It was bad enough that they'd already wasted an hour on a couple of dopeless junkies without an arrest warrant between them, but it was also becoming clear that the evidence they sought was now coursing through our veins.

Unfortunately, a third search of Perry did yield a used syringe, and the residual dope left in its chamber was enough to get him busted for possession. Thankfully, I had already discarded my own set of works in the bathroom at Ming's.

I stood on the sidewalk and watched the police confiscate Perry's fishnets, and then handcuff and load him onto a van filled with several other unfortunate souls. As a cop aggressively pushed him by the only open window facing me, he resisted for a moment—straining to rattle off one, last, desperate message:

"Craig! Call my mom. Tell her I'm not gonna be there for dinner tonight," he shouted as the cop steadied himself, grabbed Perry by the neck, and then threw him into the back of the van.

Quite frankly, as delectable as dinner sounded, I doubt it was worth mentioning his mother in front of a van full of thugs, especially since his fishnets had just been confiscated. Of course, I would do as he asked even though it was likely to put me in a very uncomfortable position. Perry's mother not only hated me, but still held me responsible for her son's health problems. Nonetheless, as soon as I found a payphone I summoned the courage and made the call. Fortunately, she wasn't home so I left a message on her answering machine.

"Hey Felicia? Yeah, uhhh, this is Craig... How's it going? Ummm, Perry got busted with a dirty syringe, so he won't be making it over there for dinner tonight. But don't worry—everything's OK. He managed to scarf down an egg roll just before they got him. OK—talk to you later. Bye."

63

By the end of May, Perry completed his community service just two days before he managed to get busted again, and once again the only evidence found on him was a syringe. Like before, the police had witnessed the purchase of a needle, but on this particular occasion they executed the bust before he ever had a chance to score. As a result, the only available evidence was a brand new, *sealed* syringe.

Since there was no dope, no residue in the needle, and no possible way to charge Perry with possession it was a very unglamorous arrest. So much so, in fact, that I was surprised they would even bother with the effort as paraphernalia-related arrests were becoming a thing of the past. Most junkies now belonged to the Needle Exchange Program, which was intended to control the spread of AIDS throughout the city. The organization provided heroin addicts with free access to sterile syringes, and ID that verified program membership and served as a get-out-of-jail-free card should they be caught with nothing other than unused paraphernalia.

The program's existence obviously compromised police motivation with regard to such arrests, as Needle Exchange addicts caught with nothing beyond a sealed syringe were typically let go. It was like catch-and-release fishing for junkies. Unfortunately, Perry wasn't a member of the program—*so he was gonna be a keeper.*

"I can't believe they actually busted you for that," I told him the night he returned from jail. He had just spent a whopping 60 hours in the system, which was a personal best for Perry and now the new milestone to shoot for.

"I can't believe it either," he said. "Sixty hours in the system for paraphernalia."

The worst of the repercussions was that Perry was in police custody, withdrawing—while he was supposed to be at Dabney's, working. Somehow, word had gotten out about the arrest and an hour after Perry returned from jail, Gabriel—Perry's boss and the owner of Dabney's—called to have a heart-to-heart with his favorite employee.

Initially, Gabriel was only concerned for Perry's health and at one point actually seemed on the verge of overlooking the entire incident. However, before that happened Perry would have to answer some tough questions.

"Perry, why did you have a syringe?" Gabriel asked with a seemingly endless amount of patience. "You didn't have any drugs in your possession, but you had a syringe. It's OK…You can tell me the truth. Really, I'll understand."

Though the question was absurd, I think Gabriel was desperately trying to provide Perry with a way out of the predicament, or at least a flimsy excuse that might prevent him from having to end their relationship. Unfortunately, after 60 hours with the Department of Corrections, Perry was in no mood to humor anyone and the two bags of dope he'd just booted did little to improve his disposition.

"I don't know," was the eagerly anticipated but very disappointing response.

"What do you mean *you don't know*?" Gabriel asked. "How could you *not know*? Were you planning to do drugs or not?"

"Maybe I was and maybe I wasn't," Perry told him and then hung up the phone.

"What the fuck are you doing?" I asked.

"Fuck him."

"Now you're *definitely* gonna get fired."

"He won't fire me."

A moment later Gabriel called to tell Perry he was fired.

I couldn't understand how Perry was so cavalier about a job that he really didn't mind, while each day I was forced to endure the diner. Of course, I was never completely thrilled with Serendipity either, but at least there I found some solace in my co-workers. This certainly wasn't the case at Ellen's, however, where I was surrounded by bitter, old, queens and arrogant starving artists. Management, too, had its shortcomings and prominent among them was an asshole named Vincent. He was extremely old-school, completely out of place, and bitterly disliked by the restaurant's homosexual employees whom he'd snidely refer to as "The Fruit Loops."

Although the staff had its imperfections they paled in comparison to those of the customers, who were constantly lured in by relatively cheap menu prices for a restaurant operating in that part of town. Unfortunately, from a waiter's perspective, the business model was less than lucrative as these patrons were hardly the big spenders that were constantly rolling into Serendipity.

In the middle of a June evening, just before the thrust of the dinner rush stampeded into Ellen's for Elvis Melts, Be Bop a Lula Burgers and Leave it to Beefer Wraps, I discovered four elderly women sitting in my station and eagerly awaiting my arrival. However, as I approached the table and they realized I was to be their waiter, I could see excitement and anticipation transform itself into restlessness and concern.

"Hey ladies," I said as I greeted the table with the usual degree of make-believe enthusiasm. "My name's Craig. Can I get you something to drink while you take a look at the menu?"

"We'll hayav four swait tays," said one of the ladies in a deep southern accent.

"Sorry ladies, we don't have sweet tea," I said, trying to break the news as delicately as possible. "We do have unsweetened tea that I can bring over with some sugar and sweetener if you'd like."

"That won't do!" shouted the same woman as she continued to speak for the group with a twang that made Long Island accents sound sophisticated. "Oh, jes go on en git us four Sprites theyen!"

I left to "go on en git'em" their Sprites, and when I returned to the table they seemed more than ready to order dinner. Before they did, however, one of them attempted to broach an unusual subject given the nature of our relationship.

"Doncha thank yer hayer's kina lowung?" I was asked by a truly ancient woman that had yet to utter a single word—and from the way things were sounding she still hadn't managed to pull it off.

"*What???*"

"I sayed, doncha thank yer hayer's kina lowung?" she said again while pointing to her head.

I was about to consult my English to Hillbilly Asshole / Hillbilly Asshole to English Dictionary, but then one of the younger women with a more discernable tongue chose to serve as the group's interpreter.

"My mom thinks yer hayer is kina long for you to be workin' in a restaurant," the woman said with a smile, as she seemed to be enjoying my humiliation. "It's jes a little unappetizin' at the moment—thas'all."

Oh, was that all you fucking bitch?

I wanted to give her a look at the bloody trail of injection wounds dotting my left arm and ruin her appetite for **life**.

"Sorry about the *unappetizin' hayer* ladies, but what are you eating?" I asked, trying to mask my rage.

They ordered three Dean Martins and a Frank Sinatra.

Unfortunately, upon placing the order, I learned that the kitchen was out of mozzarella cheese and therefore unable to capture the delicate mingling of flavors synonymous with The Frank Sinatra (a cheeseburger with marinara sauce). With no other option, I returned to the table as the bearer of bad news.

"Weyel, you shoulda tollus dat ta begin wit," said the fossil.

"I'm sorry. I was just made aware of it myself."

"Relax mom," interjected the interpreter. "After all, he is some poor ole' woman's son."

"Weyel....den I guess I'll jes hayav the Dean Martin (spaghetti with meatballs and marinara sauce) too," the old lady said with a good deal of disappointment.

I re-placed the order and as their meals appeared in the window, the restaurant was slammed by the dinner rush and my station was filled within minutes.

As I hastily ran around and greeted my new tables, the lady rednecks wolfed down their Dean Martins like they'd never seen a bowl of pasta named after a guinea singer before. The moment I noticed that all four had finished, I returned to the table to absorb the next round of abuse.

"Where ya been?" the relic asked.

"Gettin' a *hayer* cut."

"Weyel. We want dessert!"

"OK. What do you want?"

"We wanna shayer a Chubby Checker Sundae (Oreo Cookies, vanilla ice cream, whipped cream, chocolate sauce and a cherry)."

I placed the order with Pedro, the dessert guy, and the moment it was put in the window I rushed it over to the table.

As luck would have it, just as I was about to set the dessert before the women I noticed a baby roach doing the backstroke in a sea of chocolate sauce. Although I'd already had my fair share of revolting restaurant experiences, one of this magnitude was exceptionally rare and I decided that it couldn't have happened to a bigger bunch of bitches.

"Oops!" I said as I became aware of the tiny invader, and without ever actually placing the dessert on the table I whisked it away and returned it to Pedro for another. Then, after I delivered a freshly made, roach-free, Chubby Checker Sundae to the ladies they ravenously consumed it, paid the $60 check with four credit cards, stiffed the waiter, and left the restaurant.

I was able to forget about the unpleasant experience until the following morning, when I went to the computer to clock in and Vincent put his hand against my chest.

"Don't worry about it, asshole," he said to me. "You don't work here anymore. Ellen fired you yesterday."

"What the fuck for?!?"

"Because you served a cheesecake with a roach in it…**AND YOU DIDN'T RING IT UP!!!**"

"Ring up what? The fucking roach?!?!"

"No, the fucking cheesecake!"

"First of all," I said, "it wasn't a cheesecake. It was a Chubby Fucking Checker Sundae and amazingly, *I did ring it up!*"

"Oh," said Vincent, looking at the actual check. "Lemme look into this."

After he corroborated the story with Pedro and established the fact that there was never a cheesecake involved, I followed him to the register where Larry Mills—the general manager—was in the midst of a discussion with his assistant manager, Jessica.

"I think there's a mistake here," Vincent said to the GM.

As they backtracked through the chain of events leading to my dismissal, it became clear that Ellen was far more concerned with the potential threat of internal theft than any posed by the Health Department.

"I don't think I served a piece of fucking cheesecake all night," I said with indignation.

"Oh, don't worry about it, Craig," Jessica tried to comfort me.

"It's obviously a mistake."

"I don't understand any of this," Larry remarked.

"Oh—you know Ellen," Jessica said to the G.M. "She probably just got confused."

Larry told me to take the morning off and he would iron everything out with Ellen by the end of the work day.

"Just give me a call tomorrow morning before you come in."

Assuming all was well, I went back to the Midtown and got wasted. Then, on the following morning I called Larry to make sure everything was kosher before heading in to work.

"Sorry, Craig—Ellen said she doesn't want you back."

"Didn't you tell her I rang up the fucking dessert?!"

"Yeah, but she didn't wanna hear about it."

"That's fucked up."

"I know, man. I'm sorry."

I couldn't believe it, and if I didn't hate the job so much I might have protested a little further. None of it made sense. Ellen was either stubborn beyond words, or had been moved by something the hillbillies said about my service, my hair, or who-knows-what-the-fuck. In any event, she refused to look into the matter simply because she couldn't be bothered. I was just a number to her, and she knew I could be replaced 20 times in ten minutes.

64

Psychiatric News / April 16ᵗʰ· 1999

"When New York City Mayor Rudolph Giuliani announced last July that he was planning to phase out all city methadone programs, the reaction of the addiction treatment community was in some cases unprintable.

But through a combination of highly public criticism and quiet diplomacy, New York's outspoken mayor was persuaded that he was wrong, and announced that he had changed his mind. The addiction treatment community and methadone addicts who had come to rely on the drug to function normally breathed a collective sigh of relief.

*The story, unfortunately, does not have an entirely happy ending, as U.S. Sen. John McCain rushed into the breach this February with federal legislation that would, if approved, drastically curtail access to methadone treatment. The provision that would **terminate treatment immediately if an addict had dirty urine, that is, urine that showed evidence of illegal drug use,** is of particular concern to methadone advocates.*

'Methadone is a tool—it's not a cure—but anyone who knows anything about methadone treatment knows you are going to have relapses,' explained Dr. Donald Vereen Jr., Deputy Director of the Office of National Drug Control Policy. 'The critical issue is how you deal with those relapses.'

*While some politicians would like to tighten the circumstances in which methadone or other addictive drugs could be dispensed to opiate addicts, **the mainstream addiction treatment community appears to be moving in the opposite direction.***

'The idea of less restrictive dispensing of methadone or similar drugs is consistent with the notion that addiction should be treated like any other clinical problem,' Vereen continued. 'Why is it if you're an opiate addict and you're a [treating] doctor, you have to go to the one place that gives methadone every day and is only open from 10 a.m. to 2 p.m.?'

***'Some addicts may have to be on methadone indefinitely,'** Vereen said. 'Medicine doesn't yet know enough about who is best suited to achieve abstinence and who is most likely to need methadone indefinitely. **The current system doesn't encourage physicians to make that distinction,'** Vereen observed."*

So, may the streets run orange with the meth of the non-believers.*

*Author's remark

###

After getting the boot from Ellen's, it would be weeks before I'd manage to land another miserable restaurant gig. Though Perry had just gotten hired at Oasis, a Mediterranean cafe on the Upper East Side, he was in the midst of an unpaid training period and we were forced to fund our drug habits with the carefully rationed-out proceeds of a pawned guitar. This was perhaps the best indication of the condition we were in. Our instruments had long been considered sacred, not only as indispensable tools of the trade, but as future artifacts from a period of suffering and sacrifice—just prior to a grand and inevitable destiny. But a few stomach cramps and a little bit of diarrhea was all it took before an East Village pawnbroker became the proud owner of Perry's beloved, twelve-string Rickenbacker.

As the cash continued to dwindle, we could no longer afford to get high and had to settle for not getting sick. Soon, I realized that my tolerance for heroin had clearly increased, as a single bag booted every 24 hours was now just barely enough for me to avoid serious withdrawals. Due to these extended bouts of borderline sobriety, I was beginning to experience an altered state of self-awareness. For really the first time I could no longer ignore my surroundings or even momentarily look away, as I was forced to come to terms with my sordid condition. Whereas in the past, salvation could be found at the sharpened end of a loaded syringe, now I was beginning to think that being a junky wasn't so cool anymore. The starving artist thing was finally getting old, and the never ending words of praise as well as the countless predictions of success were beginning to wear thin. We hadn't recorded a note in well over a month, and as the recent spate of job dismissals and arrests disrupted our lives, it was one step forward and two steps back with no end to the slide in sight. I was already 26-years-old and it seemed the anticipation of becoming a *junky-rocker* had at last given way to the reality of being a *junky-waiter*, and I wasn't very happy with the transformation. *"I didn't go to school for this shit!"* became the shriek of the week, as I sat in squalor surrounded by hundreds of dope wrappers, dozens of dirty needles, and 44 bottles of piss.

I was down to my last 20 bucks. That amounted to a two-day supply of heroin, after which I'd be staring directly into the face of a dopesickness that I'd luckily managed to elude for years. Beyond that we were a week behind on rent, and I knew the only way to really improve the situation was for both of us to be working and making money. However, before that could happen I would not only have to find a job, but ultimately survive a dopesick training period during which it would be impossible for me to leave the bathroom—let alone impress anyone with my passion for serving assholes and being treated like shit. Of course, had it been Saturday—also known around meth clinics as "take-home day"—I would have been able to purchase a bottle of methadone on the street and avoid withdrawals. Unfortunately, it was Monday and besides, a single dose of meth would only eliminate the physical aspects of withdrawal, and I'd still have to deal with a deep depression and the psychological cravings until I could afford to reengage my habit. Maybe a more drastic measure finally needed to be taken. Regardless, I saw only two options available to me: score some dope, remain straight for a couple of days, and hope that Perry generated some cash by Wednesday or—spend the money registering for one of the city's methadone programs, something we swore never to do only moments after we swore never to pawn our instruments.

Though I had taken methadone before, it was purchased illegally on the street as a last minute and temporary substitution for heroin. Until now, I had never seriously considered joining a long-term maintenance program, which is how the drug is typically and legally administered. This was something very different and a good indication of my mental state as I knew that meth maintenance programs had a well-earned reputation for turning desperate junkies into permanently-tranquilized zombies. Each day as they report to their local clinics for monitored treatments, the vaguely sedated but clearly condemned carry on as they imitate the living. It's a dimension of existence reserved for the truly forlorn, as they wander through Methadonia without any real hope or aspirations for the future—and it's about as close to a lobotomy as you can get.

The attraction of methadone to a recovering addict is that it not only blocks the physical withdrawal symptoms, but also the depression and psychological cravings—which is at least partially because it replaces heroin with its own intoxicating effect. However, once the meth wares off and physical symptoms have subsided, the more enduring psychological symptoms return unless followed-up by another dose. Unfortunately, methadone is even more addictive than heroin and as a result, another dependency with almost identical withdrawal symptoms can develop more rapidly and be harder to overcome. The bottom line is that junkies hoping to escape the horrors of heroin by resigning themselves to a methadone maintenance program are simply substituting one addiction for another.

Of course, in theory, the program is supposed to conclude with a detoxification period of an indeterminate length, during which daily doses are gradually reduced until the patient is completely weaned off the drug. Unfortunately, that seldom seems to happen and many relapse at some point during the process. This is evidenced by the methadone flea markets that pop up around clinics every Saturday which, as previously mentioned, is referred to as "take-home day." On take-home Saturday, addicts are dosed and then provided with a sealed, prescription bottle of meth to be self-administered on Sunday when the clinics are closed. However, for many, Saturday tends not to be *take-home day* but rather, *sell-your-meth-to-a-dopesick-junky-and-use-the-money-to-buy heroin day.*

Even those who managed to avoid relapse rarely permitted their dosages to be reduced, and counselors quietly looked the other way—just as they did for program violators with traces of heroin or other forbidden substances in their randomly administered piss tests. I'm not exactly sure what the clinics' policies and penalties were with respect to such infractions, but it seems they were often overlooked—possibly to prevent junkies from permanently returning to the street's version of the same drug they were distributing. Consequently, most patients who successfully avoided relapse remained indefinitely addicted to the same levels of meth that were first prescribed, while some bad apples simultaneously maintained two habits.

At best, meth maintenance served only to further marginalize junkies by keeping them permanently sedated and off the streets, while robbing them of any chance they might have at recovery or a normal existence. Once again, complete indifference or at least a failure to understand addiction at its most basic level was demonstrated by yet another city-funded agency, as the band-aid solution was to simply replace one tainted brain chemistry with another.

Of course, it wasn't as if I didn't know any of this. Throughout the course of my junky odyssey I'd gotten to know many addicts who had been on methadone maintenance and there was no shortage of horror stories. But just as the thrill of getting high enabled me to turn away from the reality of heroin addiction, the fear of being dopesick now enabled me to turn away from the reality of methadone maintenance. Obviously, I knew I could report for just the first few days of treatment to eliminate withdrawals and buy some time without risking an addiction to methadone, but in my fear-induced state of reasoning I considered that a maintenance program might have been precisely what I needed. Quite frankly, I could never imagine myself completely abandoning opiates and thought that by giving-in to the stupid substitute I might at least stay out of jail.

Regardless of how thoroughly I would commit myself to the program, I decided that for the moment I simply had no choice. It had been only 22 hours since my last fix and I was already beginning to feel a syrupy sweat collecting on the back of my neck—a sure sign that more serious withdrawals were on the way.

I quietly left the room being careful not to wake Perry, who would have talked me out of the idea as he was entirely opposed to methadone. His objections probably stemmed from the fact that he, unlike I, was largely hooked on the orgasmic rush and the actual process associated with mainlining heroin, which is also known as being "addicted to the needle." It's an element of the addiction that meth does little to mitigate, and another reason why the program has such limited success.

At about 7 a.m., as I left the hotel and headed to the nearest bodega for my daily bacon, egg, and cheese bagel, I passed a crackhead hooker who was hobbling toward me and in very bad shape. She was visibly filthy, her hair was matted together, and the edges of her mouth were lined with bulging red sores. Her "dress" was torn from her shoulder, and as she limped closer compensating for a broken heal that desperately hung on to what was left of her right shoe, I could see she also had a black eye.

"Hey, have you seen Jacky, have you seen Jacky yet?!?" she croaked with desperation in her raspy voice to a man who was just a few paces in front of me.

"Lookin' great, babe, lookin' great," he replied, at first ignoring her question. "No, I haven't seen him."

I continued on, trying to wipe that bit of human degradation away from my brain as I now tried to come to terms with my own.

After eating breakfast, I jumped on a downtown train and headed for the clinic on Delancey Street. As I began the journey toward Methadonia, a tiny part of me was fiercely protesting against any long term commitment to the program; however, my reservations were more than counterbalanced by the harbinger of dopesick sweat now soaking through my shirt.

Within ten minutes the train reached the Delancey Street subway station, which was three blocks away from the clinic and quite ironically—only two blocks from Angelina's. The clinic's proximity to the boutique made me again momentarily question whether or not methadone maintenance was the right decision, but once more I was able to look past my doubts and continue in the direction of the clinic.

When I entered the building I made my way to the appropriate suite of offices and after signing in, sat in a waiting area which remained empty except for the occasional junky wandering from room to room. As I filled out the questionnaire a loud, ripping, gurgle echoed from my stomach and I knew the game was on. I informed the clinic's receptionist that if need be she could find me in the bathroom making my case for admission into the program. I then headed directly to the lavatory and thought that for once, perhaps, I might have been exactly where I needed to be.

I took care of business and returned to the waiting area. Within a few minutes the intestinal grumbling resumed, and as I rose to return to the bathroom I was re-directed to an office that was only a few feet from where I was sitting.

"The counselor will see you now," the receptionist said.

I ignored my boisterous bowels and entered the office where a middle-aged woman sat behind a desk awaiting my arrival. From the very beginning, I could tell she'd long had her fill of junkies. Without introducing herself, she immediately commenced with a quick review of the program's details that were first and foremost on my mind.

"The fee is six dollars per week and that covers the cost of seven, daily treatments," she said before I even had a chance to sit down.

"Fine. I'll take 21 then—*just in case.*"

"It doesn't quite work that way," she told me. "First of all, we don't dispense methadone from this office and secondly, there's a five-day waiting period to process your Medicaid information."

"Oh, don't worry about that," I told her. "I don't have Medicaid. I'll just pay for it in cash."

"Then it's $40 per week and there's *still* a five-day waiting period."

"Listen, I don't have $40 and I don't have one day to wait let alone five," I said as another round of intestinal gurgling helped emphasize my point.

"I'm sorry, but if you don't have Medicaid we require a $40 deposit for the first week of treatment," she explained again. "But either way, we first have to schedule a blood screening and a physical examination."

"What the fuck for?!?"

"To test for chemical dependency!" she fired back, apparently offended by my choice of words. "Who *the fuck* knows—you might not even be an addict."

"Oh really? Well I've got a belly full of brown piss that begs to differ with ya...*ma'am*."

"Look—I'm sorry, but those are the rules."

I was stunned. Why in the world would a junky spend $40 on methadone that he couldn't even have for a week, when he could walk to Angelina's and score a bag of dope and a pair of fishnets for $10.99 plus tax?

"You gotta be kidding me," I said as I was beginning to realize that there'd be no methadone for *this* rock star.

"I don't kid, Mr. Goodman."

"But this doesn't make any sense."

"It makes perfect sense," the counselor told me. "You might just be looking to get high."

"Oh come on!" I shouted in disbelief. "If I was looking to get high, I'd be outside copping a bag from your fucking neighbors! I'm trying to get clean!"

"Yeah, sure, I know...rules are rules."

I left the office and the building in a blind fury, unable to see more than just a few feet in front of me. I continued down the street propelled by nothing but rage and then, in a brief moment of clarity, I realized I didn't know where I was going or what I was going to do. So I screamed.

""FUUUUUUUUUUUUUCK!!!!!!!!!!!!!!!! FUUUUUUUCK!!! THIS IS SUCH A BUNCH OF FUCKING **BULLSHIT!!!!!**" I bellowed as I fell to my knees and began pounding my fist on the pavement.

As I knelt on the corner of Delancey Street, panting from the outburst and the amount of energy it expended, I realized I'd finally become one of those that I used to walk in the opposite direction of.

"Fuck it all," I said as I headed to Angelina's.

65

After failing to convince the Delancey Street drug dealers that I was a dope fiend, I went to Angelina's and scored two bags of heroin which left me penniless and with no choice but to make the 60-block journey back home on foot. It took me over an hour as I threw-up my breakfast bagel several times along the way—much to the disgust of passing pedestrians and about a million tourists.

By the time I made it back to our room, it was nearly lunchtime and Perry was already at Oasis in the middle of another training shift. I quickly threw my stash on the table and opened the top dresser drawer to retrieve a syringe.

"Fuck!"

The only remaining, remotely useable syringe was quite old, dirty, and had a needle that was bent. With no money to speak of, no time to spare, and my bowels ready to discharge once more I was forced to make the best out of a bad situation. I immediately prepared the dope in a spoon and without bothering to cook it up, attempted to draw the drug into a needle that had long outlived its usefulness. Somehow, I managed to finesse the reluctant syringe into service one last time as I then bent back the needle and prayed to the IV drug gods above that it didn't snap off in my fingertips—much less my vein when I pulled the trigger. Though I was able to return the needle to a somewhat straightened position, I realized it was far too dull to penetrate a vein and instead skin-popped the loaded syringe in my shoulder. It was like getting stabbed with the prong of a rusty fork.

The dope was much better than usual, even for Angelina's always-potent blend. Within just a few minutes—even without being able to tap a vein—I could feel the tide of intestinal fluids recede upwards while simultaneously, a wave of comfort and relief washed over me. Amazingly, I'd used only one of the bags and was not only straight, but high enough to actually catch a nod.

As I drifted in and out, I realized that registering for the meth program would have been tantamount to a death sentence. Of course, I was high at the time of this chemically-concocted conclusion, but it was still more qualified than earlier decisions egged-on by the panic-stricken fear of dopesickness. I realized that if I genuinely wanted to quit using heroin, the meth program was definitely the wrong way to go about it. I mean, things weren't that bad... *were they?* Besides, I reasoned, if I was going to be addicted to a drug, it may as well be one of my own choosing. Fuck the city, fuck the police, and perhaps most of all—fuck the methadone clinic.

With the fear of dopesickness eliminated, I was able to recognize the fact that I wasn't at all sure about ending my relationship with heroin. Like writing music, shooting dope had become a fundamental component to my daily life, and the two routines were so closely intertwined that I wasn't even sure one could exist without the other. As a matter of fact, whereas before we would use drugs to make music and secure our future as contented, working musicians—we were now trying to use music to make money and secure our future as contented, functioning drug addicts. Heroin had become such a vital part of our lives that the thought of doing without it was almost inconceivable.

Of course, somewhere deep inside—perhaps without actually acknowledging it—I knew my longstanding philosophies about drug use were flawed. Just like Nancy Reagan and the Just Say No To Drugs Choir, I too was guilty of over generalizing. However, *my* drug policy was centered on reckless experimentation—and I was now clearly suffering the consequences. Unfortunately, so many years were spent forging this path to self-destruction that I didn't want to admit I was wrong, as Perry and I now began to take perverse pleasure in unapologetically defining ourselves as junky musicians. Out of what can be described as nothing other than spiteful stubbornness, I relished the thought of remaining exactly as I was and somehow making it work to our benefit. Somewhere along the line, adolescent passion and a rebellious sense of adventure had crossed wires with a very grown-up fear of wasting time and being proven wrong.

For the past few weeks, I'd been meaning to write the acknowledgments for the CD's insert, and in the heat of the moment I began by first giving credit to my own arrogance and combativeness:

"Additional thanks go to the Delancey Street Clinic for convincing me to bypass methadone and remain faithfully addicted to heroin, New York City's Legal Aid Society for keeping us out of jail and in the studio—most of the time, Dr. Wendel for keeping Perry's drug-ravaged heart beating long enough to see the completion of the disc and last, but not least, the former members of Sections for calling it quits so we could get a real band."

I went on unrepentant, and after selecting each word based on its ability to offend the intended target, I decided that the inclusion of some additional imagery might better emphasize the point.

One afternoon several months earlier, Jason Fontana—who was responsible for designing the CD cover—had stopped by the apartment with a camera to, as he put it, *capture our purest essence.* For about an hour he quietly snapped a myriad of pictures and within a few weeks we received a proof. It was a hand-sketched depiction of a few packs of Marlboros, an ashtray filled with butts, and a bottle of booze overlooking the terrain of slop that continuously blanketed our dirty, little, Hell's Kitchen dwelling. As unflattering as that may sound, it was actually quite a good rendering and very symbolic of the mess that cluttered our lives. Unfortunately, however, though the cover was pleasingly unconventional, I suddenly decided it was missing something. I picked up the phone and called Jason to share my vision.

"Hey Jason—this is Craig from Sections," I said after he answered.

"What do *you* want?"

I'm not sure Jason was ever a big fan of the band.

"I want you to add something to the CD cover," I told him now, about six months after I'd already signed-off on it.

"Ah, man—come on!"

"No—really, Jason. I think something needs to be added to truly *capture our purest essence,*" I said, repeating his own words back to him with hopes they might stir up a little inspiration.

"Listen," he said. "I've already spent an hour capturing your essence and I still haven't been able to disinfect my camera."

"Trust me," I told him. "There's something you can include that'll really show the world who we are and what we're about."

"And what's that?"

"A syringe!"

"Wow…You really are fucked up, aren't you?" he asked without really asking.

"No, man—seriously," I pleaded. "A syringe with just a drop of residual blood left *tastefully* dangling from the needle. What do you think?"

"I think not," he said and then hung up.

I was not to be deterred. Although I might not have my way on the CD cover, I still had one more card to play: a kid named Adam who was responsible for the artwork, liner notes and font selections in the booklet. He was only sixteen years old, and I thought I stood a good chance of exploiting his innocence. I decided to give him a call.

"Hello?"

"Hey Adam, this is Craig."

"What's up, Craig? How's everything?"

I cut right to the chase.

"I want you to draw a picture of a bloody syringe."

"For the booklet?"

"Yeah."

"Ummmm…OK," he said. "I already have a few good sketches but I could definitely use some more. You know, I'd love for you to drop by and take a look at them."

"Cool, I'll stop by next week."

As I disengaged with Adam, Perry returned from his training shift and threw $80 on the night stand.

"Where'd you get that?" I asked.

Apparently, the waitress charged with training Perry had a sudden audition that surprisingly took precedence over the fine Mediterranean fare she was doling out. Consequently, the restaurant had no choice other than to prematurely put Perry on the floor.

With $80 now burning a hole on the nightstand, any lingering notions I may have had about cleaning up my act were entirely squelched as I booted the other bag.

66

Although it wasn't easy I did eventually find a daytime waiting job at La Trattoria, a little Italian restaurant in the West Village, while Perry continued on miserably at Oasis. Each day he seemed on the verge of quitting but was always held in check by a habit that was now approaching four bags-a-day. My own remained at about two, and that was fortunate because any more would have been difficult to afford while working at La Trattoria.

Finally, in early July we managed to get back in the studio. The rhythm sections for three more songs were recorded and I was able to complete vocals for two of them. Things finally seemed to be getting back on track, albeit precariously, until the end of the month when Perry was fired from Oasis.

Apparently, an unhappy customer made a scene over a sub par dining experience and as a result, the restaurant's manager made Perry the sacrificial lamb by publicly firing him. To add insult to injury, he then presented the unhappy gentleman with a gift certificate to compensate him for his troubles.

"I got fired because the fucker didn't like his couscous," Perry explained.

"So what are you gonna do?" I asked.

"Borrow this for a while," he said as he handed me an American Express gold card.

"Who's Michael Bonomo?" I asked, as I read the card member's name.

"The dickhead that got me fired."

Apparently, before Mr. Bonomo left Oasis, he forgot to retrieve his card. I could only imagine the brand of poetic justice now awaiting the gentleman and his credit limit.

Each day for the next few weeks Perry would meet me at 4 p.m. in the West Village with a big bag of cameras, radios and other electronic devices purchased with the "borrowed" line of credit. We would then make our way up to Harlem for a spontaneous liquidation sale and unload the entire stash of merchandise. It became such a regular routine, that at around 4:30 people began assembling right outside the 110th Street subway station to welcome our arrival. Within a matter of minutes, the inventory was cleared and we'd immediately score. It was all very convenient. In fact, one of the more regular shoppers was a dope dealer who gave us a few bags for any item he wanted and as a result, we were often able to kill two birds with one camera.

Throughout August the reckless use of Mr. Bonomo's credit card went unabated; however, purchases were hardly limited to electronics. We charged everything from snakeskin boots to expensive dinners in some of the city's more exclusive restaurant's, each time tipping the waiter or waitress a great deal more than Mr. Bonomo would have thought necessary.

Although I considered myself a law abiding junky, I was able to rationalize the fraudulent use of a stolen credit card. To my way of thinking, stealing from a greedy and powerful financial institution was much like rebelling against a corrupt and oppressive government

220

and equally permissible. Of course, the fact that our actions might have a negative impact on the interest rates of innocent card holders was never considered, nor was the plight of Mr. Bonomo, who—as far as we were concerned—was only getting what he deserved.

Eventually, our cluttered hotel room began to take on an almost surreal appearance. With dirty syringes strewn about and bottles of piss on display everywhere, ten pairs of new boots lined the closet and a stack of stereo equipment stood in the corner. Unfortunately, however, at the end of August the gravy train would finally stop running. It happened when Perry attempted to buy—of all things—a pack of cigarettes at a pharmacy near the Midtown and the cashier was provided with a security alert.

"This card's been stolen!" she announced to Perry and any other customers within earshot.

Perry then immediately bolted out of the store, and the summer shopping spree had officially come to an end.

As if that wasn't bad enough, I happened to have quit my job on the very same day when Leon—the cook at La Trattoria—and I had gotten into a nasty argument about sidework responsibilities. To teach me a lesson he began sabotaging my food orders and as a result, a very dissatisfied group of customers left me with shit for tips and I threatened to choke Leon to death. Apparently, the prospect of losing his cook was too much for the restaurant's manager to bear and he sided with Leon, so in the heat of the moment I told them both to fuck-off and walked out. Of course, had I known about the confiscated line of credit I might not have. No, actually, I probably would have anyway.

Since we were both now unemployed again, it was incredibly fortunate to still have a variety of expensive merchandise ready for sale. For the moment, I didn't think I could summon the courage to find another restaurant job—dopesick or not.

67

At the beginning of September, Perry was hired at a restaurant in Greenwich Village. That, along with the line of merchandise still stashed away in our hotel room allowed me to remain temporarily unemployed in order to focus on a busy week of recording.

Things were now running dangerously behind schedule. I suggested to Perry that in the interest of productivity, I should permanently forgo another restaurant job and concentrate exclusively on the music—while he work to support us from day to day. The upcoming sessions were of particular importance as Catherine had yet to hear a completed song, and the reassurance she needed was long overdo. Although I cared little about what people said, rumors regarding our extracurricular activities were now circulating and Catherine had actually threatened to pull the plug if we didn't show her something to justify the time and money being spent. You couldn't really blame her; after all, we'd been in and out of the studio for over eight months and still weren't halfway finished. Although there was no particular time-frame to complete the project, I doubt whether Catherine or anyone else expected it to drag on for as long as it had.

Unfortunately, even in light of the costly delays, Perry wasn't as open to my suggestion so I agreed to hit the pavement and find a job...eventually. Right now, at least for the week of recording, I really believed it was more important to make progress in the studio and after some cajoling Perry agreed.

I was scheduled to begin a string of ten-hour recording sessions and was very serious about getting the bulk of the vocals completed during the weeklong stint. So, when the day arrived, I woke up early and headed to Angelina's to do some shopping before getting down to business. Ten hours was a long time to be singing, and I assumed I might need an extra bag of motivation to see me through the session. However, since it was well before my usual feeding, I decided to hold off on booting until I was safely in the studio.

When I arrived at Fast Trax Nick was already at work listening to "Sitting in the Sky," and I realized I quite liked the idea of working alone with the sound engineer. I gestured a hello and proceeded to the bathroom where the song was being piped-in through a set of speakers.

As I ripped into the bag of dope, I was horrified by what I heard. Although my performance was technically passable, there was a slurring sluggishness in my voice. It didn't take a genius to realize that the heroin had somehow affected my vocal chords while recording, not to mention my ability to detect the audible abomination on the playback afterwards. This was the first time I'd ever listened to the performance in a sober state, and I was now both disgusted with myself and a little annoyed with everyone else for not having the balls to mention that it absolutely sucked. But could I really blame anyone for wanting to avoid an altercation with an egomaniac junky? No, I suppose I couldn't, but what was Perry's excuse? His stake in this four-year odyssey was as great as mine, and he had never before hesitated to share his thoughts with me on *any* matter.

Feeling desperation set in, I decided to put the dope aside. Of course, I was then forced to briefly leave Nick at the studio while I hailed a cab to Washington Square for a dime bag of weed. Fuck it—I wasn't trying to be anyone's hero. Although I would be able to postpone the dope-doing until afterwards, I surely needed something to help me through the extended session.

Within 45 minutes I made it back to the studio, got completely stoned, and then stepped into the booth.

"Let's try 'The Wish,'" I suggested to Nick. In order to keep my chemically-enhanced enthusiasm peaked, I wanted to start off with something new rather than become aggravated by a track that I should have performed correctly the first time. Unfortunately, although the weed left my voice in tact, it compromised the integrity of my brain. With each take the tape rolled, the music played, and my mind began to wander as I continually missed the fifth measure which is when I was supposed to start singing.

On the fourth take, like those that preceded it, I once again lost track of where I was in the song. With the tape still rolling I looked to Nick for help.

"Do I start to sing?" I whispered into the mike, as if by whispering my voice would somehow go unrecorded.

Nick just nodded and looked at me like a man who has simply given up.

Eventually, I did manage to begin singing during the correct measure—and Nick liked the whispered inquiry so much that he actually mixed it in. I finished the song and then recorded background

223

vocals and harmonies which took considerably longer. I then decided to re-record all the vocals to "Sitting in the Sky" which sucked up the remaining time.

When we finally wrapped everything up and Nick dubbed a copy of the effort for Perry, it was almost 11:30 and I was beginning to feel sick. I darted into the bathroom to tap a vein and then returned directly to the Midtown.

68

"That's it, man. I tried to be down with it. I tried to go along with *everything*. But look here: I got this disgusting shit growin' all over me! I'm tellin' ya, I gotta get the fuck outta *this* shithole!!!"

"Hey, watch it!" shouted Perry's anus from below, apparently offended by the pig valve's choice of words. "You should see the crap that *I* have to deal with."

"Sorry man," the valve apologized. "But I can't take it no more. I'm through with this!"

"Relax!" said another of Perry's more indigenous organs.

"No, muthafucka—**YOU** relax!!! I didn't ask for this shit! This is *your* deal, not mine."

"Well, we're all in this together now," said the lungs in unison.

"Fuck **that** shit!!!" rebutted the pig valve. "I was taken against my will!"

"You know, you've got a really bad attitude on you there, porky," the two chimed-in again.

"Fuck you and fuck you."

"Nice language!" said one of the group's less vital members. "Were you raised in a barn or something?"

A ripple of laughter could be heard reverberating throughout Perry's chest cavity.

"You all wanna make fun of my shit—then go ahead, but lemme tell ya that this right here is the most grotesque muthafucka I *ever* did see. So fuck ya'll...*ya dirty bitches!*"

###

As the summer began to wear away, so did the pig valve's willingness to acclimate itself to the new—but less than savory surroundings. Its displeasure became apparent one evening when Perry suddenly awoke with a fever and night sweats before heading to the emergency room at Lenox Hill Hospital.

After a few preliminary tests determined that his life wasn't in any immediate danger, Perry was released from the hospital—though he would have to return within a week to see Dr. Wendel for a battery of more thorough examinations. Based on his symptoms, however, it was likely that vegetation was developing on or around the pig valve and the need for additional surgery was a distinct possibility. As ominous sounding as that was Perry would continue on, unfazed, with a four-bag-a-day habit delivered over the course of two feedings—once in the early afternoon and then once again in the evening.

On the morning after Perry's trip to the emergency room we'd received a call from Adam.

"Hey, are you ever gonna come over and take a look at the artwork?" he asked me as it had been well over a month since I last agreed to stop by within a week.

"Yeah, man. No problem," I said. "When do you want us to come over?"

"Is Perry there too?"

"Yeah,"

"Well then why don't you both come over right now?"

Adam gave us his Madison Avenue address and after making the necessary stop at Angelina's, we took the #6 back uptown to 77th Street. Within a few minutes we arrived at his building, checked-in with the doorman, and entered the lobby which was lavishly adorned with mirrors and brass. Adam lived on the 14th floor, and as we stepped into the elevator I noticed that it too was furnished with the same splendid motif.

"Wow. Adam must be rich," Perry said.

"Adam doesn't have shit!" I shot back with bizarre resentment. "He lives with his fucking parents. He's still in high school, for God's sake."

It was just after 1 p.m. and I was completely fucked from the dope. Furthermore, through a perverse extension of my own inebriation, I somehow lost sight of what was going on and began to associate Adam with the general debauchery. When we reached his apartment he was waiting at the doorway and my big brother instinct suddenly kicked in.

"Adam!" I shouted. "Why the fuck aren't you in school?!"

"It's Sunday," he said.

We followed Adam down a long foyer and into a small office, carved out from beneath a grand staircase that led up to the second floor of the apartment.

"Wow! Adam *is* fucking rich," I accidentally blurted out loud.

"I don't have anything…but my dad does OK," Adam said.

"See that, Perry—I told you so. Adam doesn't have shit!"

After Adam made his way to a desk, he began rifling through a drawer of papers and extracted a series of sketches for us to review. They were all vaguely offensive in some way, but I picked out a few of my favorites to help him narrow the field.

"Oh yeah," Adam said suddenly and then turned to retrieve a notebook that sat on a shelf behind his head. "These are the sketches of syringes I was working on. My dad had some lying around, so I actually had a few good examples to work from."

"Your father's a junky?" I asked.

"No. He's a surgeon," he said as I flipped through several pages with illustrations of hypodermic needles.

"This one's great," I said referring to the image of a shiny, metallic, cartoonish-looking syringe that appeared to protrude from the page as a gigantic drop of blood dangled from its needle. "But I think you should make the blood look like a teardrop."

Just then my critique was interrupted when, from the opposite end of the foyer, we heard the front door unlock and open.

"Speak of the devil," said Adam. "That's my dad right now."

As I continued reviewing the syringes, Adam's father greeted us from the doorway of the office.

"Hey guys," he said. "How's everything?"

Although I didn't recognize him at first, Perry did and he immediately turned white.

"Dr. Wendel!" Perry exclaimed. "Holy shit! What a surprise."

"Yeah, what a coinkidink," I pointed out as I was suddenly caught up to speed. And despite the fact that I'd apparently been encouraging the teenage son of Perry's heart surgeon to draw pictures of bloody needles, I continued to flip through the notebook, undaunted—on a

226

quest for the perfect syringe.

"Yes, it *is* a surprise…and a coinkidink," said the cardio-thoracic surgeon. "Nice to see you again, Perry… this time in my own home."

"Very nice to be here, sir," Perry said as he inconspicuously seized the Book of Syringes.

"Hey man, I was still looking at that!" I shouted.

"We'll look at it later," he said. "We have to go now."

"So I'll see you next week then….*at the hospital*… right, Perry?" Dr. Wendel cautiously asked as he left the room.

"Right."

Adam led us out of the office and when we reached the front door, Perry turned and grabbed him by the shoulders.

"Adam," Perry said in a desperate whisper. "I want you to gather up any other drawings of syringes and throw them away. No, actually, just burn them. OK?"

"Sure."

Before I could protest, Perry ushered me out of the apartment and down the hallway toward the elevators.

"Why the fuck did you tell him to do that?" I demanded.

"Because I don't want his father fucking around with my heart after he learns you've been telling his son to draw pictures of bloody syringes…*asshole*."

69

By September 19th things were looking bleak. Perry's battery of tests showed signs of new vegetation developing on his pig valve and as a result, though it would not require surgery, he would now have to spend several weeks in the hospital attached to the usual combination of intravenous drips.

Although we managed to momentarily pacify Catherine with two finished songs, I was still jobless and our total assets had dwindled down to just two CD players and three cameras. To make matters worse rent was due, and Perry would be relinquishing his own job in lieu of the upcoming five-week stint at Lenox Hill that was to commence in only two days. I knew once again that even if I was to find a job immediately, it would be at least a week until I generated any cash and before that happened I'd likely be dopesick, homeless, or both. Certainly, at least while Perry was in the hospital, it seemed a reprieve from the financial pressure was definitely in order and as a result, we thought it best to check-out of the Midtown Hotel.

I decided to use my sister's recent return home from college to justify a family visit to Stamford, where my mother had relocated a year earlier, and knew I could bolster the length of the stay by mentioning the fact that my "lease" was up and that I was now in between "apartments." Before temporarily going our separate ways, however, Perry and I decided to liquidate the remaining electronic assets, which amounted to about $130 each. Given the circumstances, I knew exactly where a good portion of my bounty would be spent. I left the Midtown for the second-to-last time in my life and headed directly to Delancey Street. Before stranding myself in Connecticut, I knew I needed a good dose of methadone to be free from the threat of withdrawals, or at least those of the physical variety which was all that I was really concerned with.

Fortunately, it was Saturday, so I assumed that procuring a sealed bottle of take-home meth wouldn't pose that much of a problem. *But it did.* After about a half-hour of pacing up and down Delancey and attempting to locate a credible program violator, all I came across was a dirt bag with an unsealed bottle.

"Where's the seal?" I asked the "recovering" junky.

"It fell off."

Sure it did. On Saturdays, besides peddling their sealed doses, many patients weren't above selling their *daily* doses by somehow smuggling them out of the clinics in their mouths, and then spitting the contraband back into empty meth bottles. Unfortunately, there were also quite a few junkies who weren't above drinking it.

"No, thanks," I said and decided to take a pass.

"You should go up to 125th," said another of the Delancey Street Undead.

"Why, what's up there?" I asked.

"About like ten clinics."

That was good enough for me. I took the subway uptown to 125th Street and Lexington Avenue which was as far into Harlem as I'd ever ventured. The moment I ascended the staircase I was inundated with sales pitches for a variety of different dosages and flavors of methadone, though orange was clearly the most prevalent.

"Sealed 60," was immediately offered, but this porridge was too small.

"Sealed 90," was another opportunity.

"What flavor?" I asked.

"Orange."

"Nah. I wanna try cherry."

"I got cherry!" said another passing program violator.

"How many milligrams?"

"Seventy."

Seventy would have been sufficient to do the trick, but I wanted to see what else was available. I headed west on 125th Street toward Park Avenue which was only a block away, and realized I'd accidentally stumbled upon the Promised Land. Not only was there an enormous supply of methadone available, but dope dealers were out in such force that for a moment I thought Dinkins was back in office. It was like a flashback to the drug conventions held on 110th Street back in 1992, and though police could be seen patrolling the area they seemed to do so without any real sense of purpose.

I circled the block and was bombarded by offers from both meth *and* dope dealers. I soon realized that, unlike the rest of Harlem where my whiteness was usually interpreted as police activity or at the very least, *police-chum,* here it signaled nothing other than a potential shopper with money to burn. It was as though I'd inadvertently stumbled upon a sanctuary for junkies and drug dealers alike, where on this little island of cement we could find shelter from a sea of bloodthirsty predators able to do nothing but lurk harmlessly along the street-lined shore.

It wasn't long before I discovered the reason for my perceived safety. Upon entering Manhattan, Metro North and Amtrak trains en route to Grand Central Station at 42nd Street travel along an elevation until reaching 105th Street, at which point they descend beneath the city and continue on to 42nd. However, commuters are provided with the option of disembarking at Grand Central, or the preceding stop which just happens to be at 125th Street and Park Avenue in Harlem. Although most passengers from both rail systems detrain at Grand Central, a good number are bound for destinations too far north of 42nd Street for the stop to be convenient, and instead opt for the Harlem station followed by the nearby Lexington Avenue subway line to complete the journey. As a result—at least between the hours of 8 a.m. and 6 p.m.—police were reluctant to scour away the unsavory from this tiny transit hub as they feared accidentally ensnaring respectable commuters in the trap.

"A hundred milligrams—sealed," I heard as I turned a corner.

What? A hundred milligrams? I'd never before come across such a high dosage.

"What flavor?"

"Cherry."

My search was over. I paid him $30, removed the seal, and gulped it down right there on 125th Street before returning the prescription bottle to its owner. According to program policy, on the Monday following take-home Saturday, patients were required to return their empty bottles in exchange for the next treatment—which, of course, was intended to prevent them from selling their to-go dosages in the first place.

After the transaction was completed, I took two steps and descended into the subway station. Due to the incidental discovery of a new dope spot, I realized I now had an uptown location offering a similar level of security and convenience to that of the downtown boutique.

Fifteen minutes after swallowing the methadone I began to feel the effects as I boarded a train. Given the size of my habit, 100 milligrams was roughly quadruple the dose that I would have been prescribed had I been on the program. Needless to say, I was completely wasted; however, even at such an extraordinarily large dosage the inebriation was controllable, and in this way the drug differs significantly from heroin. Although I could have easily nodded off, it was just as easy to remain fairly alert and aware of my surroundings—*regardless of how I may have appeared.*

Now that I was "clean," I returned to the Midtown for one final evening.

70

Upon awakening at 8 a.m. to the splendor of the Midtown for one last time, I felt entirely refreshed. It was, without a doubt, the most restful night I'd had in years, as methadone is more conducive to sleep than heroin.

I packed a bag, left the hotel, and rather than walk eight blocks and catch the train to Connecticut from Grand Central, I opted to depart from the 125th Street Station which was 80 blocks away. Of course, there was absolutely no need for me to be going to Harlem. A hundred milligrams was quite a bit of methadone for me to have consumed, and the high was so powerful that I was feeling almost the same degree of intensity I'd experienced the previous day. Furthermore, since the half-life of methadone is about 48 hours, I could look forward to the buzz maintaining itself until at least the following afternoon. But even though I knew I would remain inebriated for some time and completely free from the threat of physical withdrawals, there was no question about it: I chose to use the Harlem station because I intended to buy heroin before boarding the train.

It must have been that altered brain chemistry thing again. I rationalized that after three days of methadone-fueled abstinence, I would break the physical addiction to heroin and could therefore justify an afternoon nodding off somewhere in the city of Stamford, without becoming physically re-addicted to the drug.

Obviously, even at this point I never intended to permanently eliminate heroin from my life. Just as Perry's ultimate goal was a prolonged retirement involving a dope-laden IV, a room full of books, and an assistant—mine was much the same, *minus the books and the assistant*. Hence, in reality, the methadone was merely a safety precaution designed to temporarily curtail my habit as money was scarce and I was terrified at the prospect of being broke and dopesick in Stamford.

After scoring the dope, I climbed the stairs to the station's platform and waited for the train to Connecticut. Fortunately, an express quickly appeared and I arrived in Stamford within 45 minutes.

As the train entered downtown Stamford a few tall buildings rose up in the distance. They were very new, very shiny, and wholly uninspiring—and from the most prominent, a greenish emanation returned a gesture from the sun which blazed across windows tinted a similar hue. When I stepped off the train and took in the sad little skyline, I couldn't help but be reminded of the Emerald City from *The Wizard of Oz.*

I absolutely despised Stamford. It was yuppie nirvana; a place where Wall Street wizards and corporate conquerors eagerly ascended to after years of raping and pillaging their respective ways to the top. When they finally did arrive, they would openly champion their new and improved quality of life at the expense of the very city that provided it. What was once a shining testament to the magnificence of their own accomplishments was now a place to be loathed, condescended to, and criticized for its moral decay and tendency to broadcast the seamier side of life, which is—of course—best kept behind rural ranch-house doors.

As far as my mother was concerned, I would manage to mostly avoid her even though I was sleeping in the living room of a small, two-bedroom version of the same, spiritless, condo-style apartment she was always drawn to. Ironically, my sister, who's return home from school was the first reason cited to help justify my visit, had just left again to embark upon an extended cruise to the Caribbean.

A couple of days after arriving in Stamford, and three full days after swallowing the meth, I booted the dope purchased on 125th Street. As predicted, even though only four days had passed since I'd last tapped a vein, the meth-sponsored respite prevented the rekindling of any physical re-addiction to heroin. However, two days after this last indiscretion, the psychological withdrawals that were lying in wait had finally made their presence known, and were much worse than anticipated. I began to experience a severe state of depression that would continue unabated until my brain finally decided to again produce the endorphins that the dope had long since banished. Unfortunately, from what I understood by way of the experts roaming Methadonia, due to the number of years I'd spent as a hardcore dope fiend it could take anywhere from six months to as much as a year before these naturally occurring hormones felt safe enough to return. Of course, I was unwilling to think logically or recognize the importance of riding out the discomfort, resisting temptation, and trying to stay clean. Instead, I was able to strip away any tangential concerns and cast aside the potential consequences. It didn't matter that I was 26 years-old and living with my mommy. It didn't matter that the CD was languishing, half-finished now for almost a year. It didn't even matter that I was squandering an opportunity that any other musician would have killed for. None of it mattered because I knew that if I could just get loaded—everything would be fine. I could then escape not only depression, but the blandness that sobriety had come to represent. I even concocted a justification for the addiction, providing it functionality as a buffer zone between me and the pain of being, I daresay—*a starving artist.* And though the drug may have contributed to the starving, I felt it was also an essential component to the artist. Hence, I would do everything in my power to mitigate any suffering in the short term and worry about the long term later, as I somehow convinced myself of the wisdom in remaining fucked up.

I still had about $50 left over from the last electronics sale that Perry and I had staged in Harlem before closing our doors to the public forever. Unfortunately, a round-trip ticket to Manhattan from Stamford was about $17, which would leave just enough money for two bags of dope, a set of works, and a couple of packs of cigarettes. What I would do after the money ran out was again, something to consider later. With that in mind, and after only four days in Stamford, I set out for Manhattan to score and to check in on Perry.

My mother's apartment was only a five minute walk to the Stamford train station, where I proceeded to catch the 12:53 p.m. express to the city. At about 1:30 it arrived at 125th Street, where I disembarked and copped two bags of dope and a syringe without breaking stride to the subway station.

In order to get off as quickly and as safely as possible, I took the #6 downtown to 86th Street and walked four blocks north to my favorite Polish diner. There were other restaurants closer to the score, but I was drawn to the quaintness of this particular establishment as it offered a tastefully decorated, single-occupancy bathroom affording one the luxury of shooting-up in complete privacy—*if one so desired.* Once inside I ordered a cup of coffee and then immediately snuck off to the bathroom with the spoon. After getting high I left the bathroom, paid the tab, and walked thirteen blocks to Lenox Hill Hospital to see if Perry was still alive. He was.

"Where the fuck have you been?" he asked the moment I stepped into his semi-private room.

"Stamford."

"Well, it would've been nice of you to call," he lectured me. "You have to get back in the studio next week and finish up some vocals before Catherine flips the fuck out."

"I thought she liked 'The Wish?'"

"She does, but she doesn't think it should've taken eight months to record."

"Whatever," I said. "You can't rush genius."

Perry got out of bed and ventured over to the closet with his IV in tow. He then reached inside a jacket pocket for his wallet and pulled out two, crisp, hundred dollar bills.

"Go to Angelina's and get us each a bundle," he said as he handed me the cash, which I took without mentioning the fact that I'd already scored some dope...*for myself.*

"Where'd you get the money?" I inquired.

"I told Catherine we needed strings."

"Two hundred dollars for fucking guitar strings?" I asked as they typically sold for about seven dollars a set.

"The best strings money can buy," he said. Then he handed me a little orange pill.

"What's this?" I asked.

"Forty milligrams of meth."

Perry's doctors were now actually providing him methadone with the foolish hope that it might discourage him from having dope delivered to the hospital or even worse, sneaking out to get it himself. Of course, Perry didn't care for methadone.

I left the hospital and took the subway downtown to Angelina's to get the dope. Although 125th Street was closer in proximity to Lenox Hill, I felt more comfortable purchasing 20 bags of heroin in the secure and friendly confines of a ladies boutique. Later, when I returned to the hospital to give Perry his half of the stash, he informed me that he'd scheduled a session on the following Tuesday evening, during which I was expected to record two more vocal tracks.

71

"Get down here," Perry said to me in a tone that I always hated. "Fuck you!"

"Come on, dude. I need you to run to Angelina's for me."

"Forget it."

"Please! Hurry up and catch the train and I'll pay you back when you get here," he said as he was beginning to sound desperate.

"Get it yourself," I told him.

"I can't."

"Why the fuck not?"

"Because they're watching me like a hawk."

"So what," I said as the threat of being declared medically noncompliant never deterred him before.

"You don't understand," he said. "They actually have a security guard posted in the hallway right outside my room. It's way too risky. Come on, man—please! I'm beginning to get really sick."

"Then just swallow your fucking methadone for once."

"They're cutting back on the dosage and it barely even takes the edge off," he said.

"Perry, you're gonna have to let it make do."

"I can't. I traded it to this guy across the hall for a big bag of weed," the liar finally admitted.

"You're *definitely* more fucked-up than I am."

"I know. Please come down here."

"Listen, I don't even have enough money to get there," I told him. "You're gonna have to rough it out until I can find a way to sell something."

After angrily hanging up the phone, Perry shut the door of his room and proceeded to get dressed. A few moments passed before he cracked it back open and peered down the corridor at a patrolling hospital guard. It was 11:30 a.m., and as lunchtime was fast approaching Perry knew the guard would be temporarily leaving his post to grab a sandwich.

By 12:30 the guard did leave, and without a moment's hesitation Perry darted out of the room, down the staircase, and out of the hospital through a service exit going completely unnoticed. He then flagged a cab heading downtown and arrived at Angelina's within minutes.

The boutique had been out of hairclips and nail polish for quite a while, so after selecting a silky, purplish-looking scarf, Perry brought it to the front of the store.

"Give me two," he said in a hushed voice to a dope dealer manning the register.

"Be careful, papi," the dealer cautioned him. "It's hot out there."

Not overly concerned with the warning, Perry grabbed the dope and scarf and headed in the direction of Houston Street.

Although once again the dope purchase went unseen, Perry was in the wrong place at the wrong time as the police were about a half-a-block away busting dealers that were fearlessly operating in the street. Unfortunately, since Perry had already been a guest at the local precinct on two occasions, his face and tendencies were well known to narcs patrolling the area. As a result, when they caught sight of him they had a feeling he was there for one thing and one thing only and of course, they were right.

As Perry turned onto Houston he suddenly felt a firm grip on the back of his neck.

"Hey dickhead!" said a voice with an all too familiar ring. "Nice of you to drop by. Get your hands against the wall."

"Ah Christ," Perry said as he looked back in disgust to see one of the cops that had attempted to bust both of us near Ming's Dynasty in April.

"Where's your fuckin' boyfriend?" asked the officer as he pushed Perry firmly against the wall of a building.

"He died."

"Well then I guess you should be thankful we got to *you* in time."

This was going to be a bad scene. Unless he was able to talk his way out of the predicament, Perry was about to be arrested for the third time in six months and the fourth time in less than a year. With those numbers it was quite likely that after seeing the judge, he'd be spending 30 days at Riker's Island for being such a stubborn junky.

"Come on, man—give me a break. I'm supposed to be in the hospital right now," he pleaded while brandishing his catheter. "I've got a really fucked-up heart."

"Don't worry about it—we'll send you back with a note."

Perry thought his medical condition would save him, but the cop either didn't believe the seriousness of the situation or didn't care. Regardless, as far as Perry was concerned, there was absolutely no way he could afford to get arrested…and I suppose desperate times call for desperate measures.

"Hey listen," Perry said as he was being searched. "What if I tell you who my dealer is?"

Note, I said *desperate*—not moronic and self-defeating.

"I don't think we need your help," the disinterested cop told him, obviously dismissing the offer as insincere or not of any real value. "In about two minutes he's gonna be sitting right next to you in the van, anyway."

"Not *my* dealer. He's too smart for you stupid fuckers."

That definitely raised the cop's level of interest, and about a millisecond before he inquired further with a punch to Perry's midsection, the rat started squealing.

"WAIT-WAIT-WAIT, I swear!!! Look at the dope in my wallet. There's no stamp on it."

One common feature to every bag of dope in the city is that each had a stamp identifying the operation that provided it, and most of the bags in this part of town were marked with the image of a skull and crossbones and the word, "POISON" appropriately emblazoned beneath. Bags of dope originating from Angelina's, however, were completely and uniquely *unmarked*.

As the cop found and inspected the bags, a light bulb, though not fully lit had at least begun to flicker. Unfortunately, his partner, apparently much less impressed with the discovery had proceeded to usher Perry into the van.

"Oh come on, man!" Perry squealed as he was led away. "Fine, go ahead! Lock me up and you know what'll happen? I'm gonna come right back down here tomorrow for two more bags and a fuckin' blouse!"

"Wait a second!" said the first cop who was still pondering the unmarked bags. "What did you just say?"

"I said I'll be back tomorrow for more," Perry repeated.

"No, dickhead—I mean the blouse. You said something about a blouse."

Now Perry *knew* he had him, which sparked-up a bit of belligerent bravery.

"Yeah, a blouse! Preferably purple to match the scarf you just knocked the fuck out of my hand," Perry said. Actually, the scarf was more of a deep lavender but either way, that bulb was now burning with the white-hot intensity of a thousand suns.

The now intrigued cop removed the cuffs and then pulled Perry to the side as he officially became a police informant—giving away the greatest, safest, dope-dealing operation the city had ever known, just to save his own miserable ass.

"Listen," the cop said. "If you're telling me the truth and we make a bust, I'll send you a page on your little beeper there, and you can come pick up part of the seizure for yourself. And then we can continue to do business together. But if you're lying to me, you're gonna be the sorriest motherfucker there ever was because when I find you—and *believe me,* I **will** find you—I'm gonna slap these fucking cuffs right back on those skinny, little, junky-wrists. Only this time we won't be loading you into a van. You'll be getting on a boat. Catch my drift, motherfucker?"

I'm not sure whether I was more shocked that Perry had become a police informant, or that the cop couldn't come up with something a little more original than throwing his puny body in the river. Regardless, when I finally heard about the boneheaded betrayal I was more than a little miffed.

72

By the middle of October and over the course of three weeks and four recording sessions, I had managed to complete two more vocal tracks while Perry remained fucked up, in the hospital, and strapped to an IV.

The routine was always the same. Each week I would head into Manhattan to score at 125th Street, bring Perry his share of the dope, and then proceed to the studio where—if scheduled to sing—I would act responsibly and refrain from using until the session concluded. And by carefully managing a drug regimen consisting of almost daily but alternating doses of heroin and methadone, I was able to remain high on *something* while convincing myself that I was physically addicted to *nothing.* Whether or not this was actually the case I haven't a clue because I never ran out of drugs, as Perry kept me stocked with meth and I would usually find a way to raise the funds necessary to replenish my stash. On one occasion, I sold my father's sapphire ring. Over the course of several others I would relinquish the expansive collection of books that I'd accumulated during college.

Unexpectedly, upon hearing the recorded fruits of my labor for the very first time, my mother was actually impressed enough to ignore the fact that I remained unemployed while continuing to live under her roof. And, incidentally, though she was somewhat upset by the bartering of my books for "spending money," she was hardly affected by the fact that my father's ring was now sitting in a pawn shop in Harlem.

On October 15th, I returned to the city to record vocals for two songs that Perry had escaped from the hospital to work on the previous night. Of course, I would first have to provide him with a care package of dope, so after exiting the train I walked over to a dealer on the corner of 125th Street and Lexington Avenue.

"Give me a bundle," I told him.

"I've only got four bags left," he said. "Take these now and I'll go re-up."

We made the exchange and I then pretended to wait for a bus. I stood there pretending for almost fifteen minutes, and as I allowed a procession of busses to pass by I began to feel as though I was attracting attention. In Manhattan, you rarely wait more than a few minutes for anything, especially a bus, and because it was a weekend with few commuters milling about—I felt especially conspicuous. I decided to make do with what I had, at least for now, and descended to the subway knowing that I could always make a stop at Angelina's later.

When I arrived at Lenox Hill, Perry was in his usual, reclined, and medicated position.

"I was only able to get you two bags," I told him as I tossed the dope onto his bed.

"That's not enough."

I noticed he was beginning to sound a lot like Matt.

"I'll stop at Angelina's on the way to Fast Trax and bring you some more later," I said.

"I don't think that's such a good idea."

"Why not?"

"Because I have a feeling the cops are watching them, or they may have been raided already."

"How do you know?"

"I ratted them out."

"YOU WHAT!?!"

"I had no choice," he said, and then explained the circumstances surrounding the awful betrayal.

"I can't believe you did that," I told him as it felt like my heart had been ripped in half.

"I couldn't help it," he said. "If I got arrested I would've ended up at Riker's."

"Big deal? You should've taken one for the team you stupid fucker! I would've."

"Sure you would've," he responded. "Get the fuck off my back."

"Yeah, I'll get off your back until I get busted…you fucking rat!"

"Stop being such a pussy," he said. "You still have 125th Street and I'm sure you'll learn to live with it. Besides, the cop promised me some of the stash after they bust the place."

"So what! It wasn't worth giving up a safe place to score for some free dope and a quick fix."

"Just listen to yourself," Perry said. "You're not thinking like a junky."

"I'm thinking like a junky that doesn't wanna get busted you fucking moron! What the fuck were *you* thinking?! You're a selfish, stupid, rat-motherfucker, Perry, and once again you've managed to—"

At that point we were interrupted by a knock at the door as the hospital nutritionist had stepped in to inquire about Perry's lunch selection.

"Good afternoon Mr. Ward," she said. "Today you have a choice of either baked chicken or tuna casserole."

"Sorry ma'am," I interjected. "Mr. Ward is now restricted to a diet of lettuce and cheese."

With that, I stormed out of the room in a blind fury. After returning to 125th Street for the rest of the dope, I took the #6 downtown to the studio and completed the tracks that were expected of me. I then got myself completely loaded in the bathroom as I thought about Perry and the new development.

What a spineless, rat-fuck.

I was beyond upset and just couldn't get over it; however, I realized I would have to shelve my anger and attempt to make peace if we were ever going to successfully see things through. So, before heading back uptown to give the coward his dope, I decided to stop at a pet store for something to raise his spirits while he was still in the hospital, though, given his disgusting behavior he hardly deserved it.

"Here's your dope you fucking rodent," I said to him after making it back to his room.

"I can't believe you're so pissed off."

"*I* can't believe you're so stupid."

"Here you go you big pussy," he said with a smartass grin as he handed me a lavender scarf. "Keep it… as a memento of Angelina's. You'll feel better."

"That's so weird."

"Why?"

"Because I have a present for you too," I said as I tossed him a plastic exercise ball, complete with oversized air vents and rounded foot-treads to ensure comfort. "Actually, it's designed for hamsters, but I'm sure you'll *learn to live with it*…you rat-face fuck."

73

I stepped outside the building for a cigarette and realized I had about an hour to kill before the next train would be departing from Stamford. I had dedicated the better part of the morning to drug-fundraising by selling several text books to the University of Connecticut, and though Perry and I had an ample supply of dope—I decided to stay on task and head into the city to score, anyway.

"What's up?" a voice suddenly said from behind.

I turned to notice a fourteen or fifteen year-old boy lighting up a smoke. At first glance, he seemed much like the other overindulged, snot-nosed kids seen wandering around the malls of Stamford, wrapped in Ralph Lauren and armed with their own lines of credit.

"How's it going?" I asked.

"I don't know, man," he said. "It's pretty beat around here."

"Don't you go to school?"

"I got kicked out for a semester," he said. "I'm just here visiting my mother for a few months."

Following the divorce of his parents, Brandon Lutz was sent away to a prestigious, New England boarding school that offered a privileged education for anyone who could afford it, regardless of academic qualifications or intellectual capacity.

"What'd you get kicked out for?"

"A security guard found a vile of liquid in my locker."

For those out of the drug loop, the "liquid" Brandon was referring to was *liquid acid*, which I had heard of but never actually seen before.

"Did they call the cops?" I asked.

"No."

"What'd they do?"

"Nothing…besides kick me out of school," he said. "But they said I can come back in January."

That was quite a display of commitment to the young man's education, not to mention the $20,000 a year tuition attached to it.

"That was nice of them," I said.

"And they didn't even take the acid away from me," he added.

"What?"

"They never took the shit away. I still have it."

"You're fucking with me."

"I swear. They just called my father and told me not to come back until 1995."

"No fucking shit!"

I was impressed by the lengths the school would go to protect its profit margin because that was a lot of acid. Even for a minor, getting caught with such a sizable load should have been much more trouble that it was worth.

"You wanna do some?" he asked. "I haven't even tried any of it yet."

By now I normally wouldn't have bothered with acid, especially after the nightmarish pink and brown episode I'd recently suffered through at Baskin Robbins. But this was *liquid* acid. I had never tried liquid before and again, as my dope supply was far from depleted I knew I could forgo the trip to the city and satisfy my curiosity.

I followed Brandon upstairs to his mother's apartment and was offered a seat at the dinner table.

"Wait here a sec," he told me.

After a minute or two he returned with a pack of Rolos, and a Visine eye-dropper filled with the drug. He then extracted two Rolos from the pack and placed a large drop of acid on the surface of each. I noticed how nicely the drops settled within the rim of the candy—resembling a tiny, chocolate, pool of acid.

We each carefully picked up a piece of candy and consumed it. Then we sat there staring at each other for about fifteen minutes.

"This shit is weak," I said.

I knew that typically, paper hits of acid require about an hour of digestion before the drug actually enters the bloodstream and the effects are noticed. But this was *liquid* acid, and due to a past experience with magic-mushroom tea I knew that once hallucinogens are liquefied, absorption rates dramatically increase. Armed with that bit of knowledge I had a feeling that something was terribly amiss.

"I think this shit is bogus," I announced.

"Let's try some more," Brandon offered as a solution to the problem.

We each swallowed another pool of acid, waited a few more minutes, and no one felt anything.

"I don't get it," Brandon said.

"Looks like you got expelled for nothing," I said, even though I could tell that to Brandon the loss of an academic semester paled in comparison to another sacrifice he made.

"I spent $300 on this fucking bullshit!"

"That seems like a lot of money for *water*."

"It's not supposed to be *water*," Brandon agitatedly pointed out. "Each of those drops is supposed to be like five hits."

"Five fucking hits? Then I'm glad it's water. I wouldn't have been able to hold it together."

"And we both did two, so that would've been about ten hits each," he added.

About a minute after he arrived at that calculation, I began to feel the anxiety that always accompanies a hallucinogenic as it enters the bloodstream.

"You know what? I think I'm beginning to feel it," I said.

"I think I am too," Brandon agreed. "This is gonna be some fuckin' shit!"

Now knowing that the stuff was legitimate, and that I'd ingested roughly the equivalent of ten hits of acid, I couldn't quite share in his enthusiasm. *Two* hits—let alone ten—would have been too much acid for me to handle, so I sat there preparing myself for major problems. Realizing what was in store, and that I'd be better off losing complete control in the more familiar surroundings of my mother's apartment, I got up to leave.

"Hey man," Brandon said as I was walking out of the apartment, "I'll come down and check on you in a few, alright?"

Without saying a word, I left Brandon's apartment and headed down the staircase to my mother's. However, after several minutes of attempting to open her front door, I became convinced that while I was upstairs someone had changed the locks. Although the key seemed to slide into the lock perfectly, when I attempted to turn it toward the unlocked position it refused to budge.

"Motherfucker!!!" I screamed as I tried to unlock the door with all my might.

Then, to make matters worse, the key got stuck in the keyhole.

"I can't fucking believe this shit," I said almost on the brink of tears.

While trying to pull the key out of the lock, I slipped on the welcome mat as it somehow slid out from under me. Then, as I grabbed the doorknob to steady myself, I accidentally turned it and opened the door—which was apparently unlocked to begin with. Unfortunately, I still couldn't get the damned key out of the lock.

As I finally got inside, I slammed the door shut and tried to regain some composure. Then, after a minute or two of uncontrollable panting, I went to the kitchen for a glass of water and realized I was even more uncomfortable in my mother's apartment than I had been in Brandon's.

The trip was coming on hard and fast and there was no doubt about it: Given my surroundings and the amount of acid I'd so rapidly consumed, this was going to be a very bad experience. My eyes had already become a kaleidoscope that distorted and fused the details of my mother's apartment into a single, indistinguishable mass of nauseating swirl.

As I walked around the apartment, intermittently taking sips of water and muttering to myself, I noticed that my trembling hands had apparently helped some of the water out of the glass and onto the floor, forming a trail of wetness behind me. That was all it took for me to grab a roll of paper towels and become twelve years-old again.

Oh shit—look at what I did! Mama's gonna fuckin' kill me when she gets home. There's water all over the place and someone's gonna step in it and track up mud, and then she's gonna beat the living shit out of me. She's probably gonna kick me out of the house and then what the fuck am I gonna do? Fucking loser-junky on acid. She must be so proud of me. I deserve to get kicked out. BUT FUCK HER!!! I don't owe that bitch anything...but she could still kick me out. Did I wipe up the kitchen floor yet? I can't remember. Fuck! Let me see. Yes, I did. Oh, but what about the fucking key in the door? It's jammed in there like a motherfucker. I'm gonna have to find a tool or something to get it out. Shit! Did I spill water in the bathroom? I better check. Nope, there's no water on the floor. There sure is a shitload of water in the hallway, though. Wait a minute: If there's water on the floor in the hallway, then there's probably water on the floor in the bathroom and I just didn't notice it. OK—let me get this water in the hallway first, and then I'll take another look in the bathroom and...SHIT!!! Who the fuck is that!?!?

Just as I sat there on the hallway floor having a nervous breakdown and wiping up imaginary drops of water, Brandon walked in.

"Dude, my mother just came home early from work!" he said with excitement. "That never happens. Can you fucking believe it?"

He seemed to be amazed by the coincidence of his mother's impromptu appearance just 30 minutes after he swallowed ten hits of acid. I, however, couldn't appreciate the moment and knew that had I suffered a similar fate, I'd find nothing remarkable about it other than the fact that I soiled myself.

After sharing the news of his mother's arrival—Brandon took one good look at me, paused, and then actually fell to the floor laughing hysterically.

"OH MY GOD, HE'S CLEANING THE FLOOR! HE'S CLEANING THE FUCKING FLOOR!!!" he screamed in between fits of uncontrollable laughter.

Suddenly, this kid was really annoying me. I decided right then and there that I didn't like Brandon, and had my eyes been able to focus on him at all—I would have hit him.

"Hey," he said to me as he finally collected himself. "Here's your key, dude. It was still in the lock."

He handed the key to me and for a moment, I thought that Brandon might not be so bad after all. Getting that key unstuck had to have taken some effort.

"What'd you use to get it out with?" I asked.

"My hand. Hey—wait here a minute and I'll be right back," he said and then left my mother's apartment.

I immediately jumped up, locked the door, and tried once again to compose myself.

I sat down on the couch and turned on the television which marked the beginning of the end. CNN was on, and though my eyes were focusing better, my ears were starting to give me problems as I was hearing the news broadcast in reverse. At first, I really didn't think the problem was with me, and for a second assumed the newscasters were enjoying a momentary, lighthearted reprieve from the day's events. Then, after about an hour I realized that English, something I had once known intimately, was now completely foreign to me.

It'll pass. This has got to pass.

But it didn't pass, and for an undetermined period I sat there listening to gibberish. I eventually tore myself away from the television to use the bathroom and then, while looking at my reflection in the mirror I decided to have a heart-to-heart.

*People have been telling you you're fucked up for years...Well now, you're **REALLY FUCKED UP!!!***

Standing in front of the mirror was obviously doing me no good. I returned to the living room and considered the pros and cons of an assisted living facility located in Connecticut as opposed to Manhattan.

"This can't be happening," I tried to tell myself. *"It's just a bad trip...that's all."*

I decided to call Katrina. She'd been a Dead Head for years and had dropped more acid than anyone I'd ever known. She'd be able to calm me down and talk some sense into me before I really *did* have a nervous breakdown. Unfortunately, when I called, it was one of her roommates that answered the phone.

"Katrina went back to Georgia," Stacy told me in a tone suggesting I bore some responsibility for her departure. At that point, however, I was hardly concerned for *Katrina's* well-being.

"FUCK!!!!"

It's interesting to note that the auditory problem I was calling about had apparently subsided, as I not only understood that Katrina had gone back to Georgia, but was also able to detect Stacy's subtle yet accusatory tone. Somehow, though, at that point the revelation hadn't occurred to me.

"What's the matter?" she asked in her southern drawl.

"Stacy, I just dropped a shitload of acid and I think I may have really fucked myself up. It'll pass, right? I mean, I know I'm having a bad trip and all, but this will definitely go away...won't it? I mean, shit—I'm OK, aren't I?"

Even though she was apparently a little peeved with me, Stacy was a Dead Head as well and I was sure she'd be able to offer a few, much needed words of comfort:

"Well...who'd you get it from?"

That wasn't quite what I had in mind. I hung up the phone before her question began to echo in my head, along with the fucked up answer to it.

I then decided to call Perry in the hospital. He'd know what to do…or at least what to say.

"Hello?"

"Perry. Thank God you're there. I just dropped about ten hits of acid and I'm gonna die."

"You'll be fine."

"No, seriously man, I need some help."

"Where are you?"

"At my mother's apartment."

"First of all, just calm down and get out of your mother's apartment," he said. "That *can't* be a good place for you to be. Go into the woods and try to enjoy it. Just sit down under a tree, watch the show, and relax. You'll be fine, trust me. You won't hurt anyone, and nobody will hurt you. Everything will be OK, I promise."

He was right. I was probably just exacerbating my own problems and being in my mother's apartment certainly didn't help matters. A little bit of getting back to nature along with some peace and serenity might've been just what I needed. The woods definitely *sounded* like a good idea. Unfortunately, the moment I stepped out of the building I was nearly hit by several speeding cars leaving trails of light wherever they went, and as far as "the woods" were concerned—there was barely a blade of grass to be found *let alone a fucking tree.* Although Stamford has its share of countrified areas, they are in no way a significant part of the downtown landscape which is precisely where my mother's apartment was situated.

At some point I regained a bit more composure and though I realized I would probably survive the experience, I also realized that the only cure to my affliction was time. I would simply have to wait for the trip to run its course and try not to get killed in the process. For about five hours I paced the sidewalks surrounding my mother's building, occasionally ducking behind a bush when things became a little too hectic to handle.

Eventually, the sun began to set and as it did I began to more fully regain control of my senses. However, as that bright, sickly-sweet glow emanated from the buildings and began to engulf the Emerald City, my anxiety again emerged. I decided to head back to the apartment before the Wicked Witch of the West returned home with a flock of flying monkeys.

74

On October 20th Perry left a message on my mother's answering machine, saying that he was about to be discharged from the hospital and that he'd be calling me back on the following day. I hadn't heard from him, however, and was beginning to get concerned. I was suddenly down to my last few bags of dope, very little cash, and only about 60 milligrams of methadone. Then, at about 8 p.m. on October 23rd, the phone rang and it was Perry.

"Hey, what's happening?" he said with slurring jubilation.

"What's happening with you?"

"I finally escaped from Gina's."

He sounded fucked up. Typically, even when Perry was completely annihilated I could rarely, if ever, detect it—so if he was slurring his words he had to be close to comatose.

"What the fuck were you doing at Gina's?" I asked.

"Withdrawing."

"Did you?"

"Yeah."

"Then why do you sound so fucked up?"

"Because I'm completely wasted. Meet me at the Polish diner."

I caught the 8:53 express train into the city and met him at the diner just before 10 p.m. Apparently, the moment his regimen of antifungal medications had run its course, Perry was ejected from the hospital by administrators who saw him as nothing other than a continued flight risk and a dangerous liability. Completely broke and with nowhere else to go, he managed to weasel his way back into Gina's good graces and her new apartment in Sunnyside. I'm sure he assumed that, as usual, she would lend him some money until he got himself re-settled. Unfortunately, Gina had decided that she would no longer be an enabler, and seized the opportunity to exact her brand of tough love upon his broken junky spirit.

During his stint in the hospital, Perry had been doing between three and six bags of dope per day, which he managed to pay for by selling his methadone on the street or by crying about recording costs to Catherine. As a result, for three days he went through a horrid detoxification and no matter how much he begged, Gina refused to give him a penny or even a chance to step outside the apartment. She even confiscated his beeper, which, in the most painful example of poetic justice doled-out so far, prevented Perry from getting that all-important page from the cop, as well as several bundles of dope that were promised in exchange for his treacherous testimony.

popped out of the darkness from around a corner and then vanished as quickly as it appeared. Perry immediately moved in the direction of the vanishing head which belonged to a dope dealer who'd set up shop in one of the building's decrepit rooms.

"You sneakin' out of the hospital again?" the dealer asked.

"No," Perry responded. "Give me a bundle."

"You is one fucked up white boy…sneakin' out of the hospital and shit…*crazy muthafucka!*"

As I came into view and the dealer caught sight of me for the first time, his demeanor changed from amusement to paranoia.

"Who the fuck is that?!" he asked.

"Don't worry about him," Perry responded.

"You a cop?" the dealer asked me.

"He's the furthest thing from a cop," Perry explained before I had a chance to giggle. "Here's the money. Give me the fucking dope."

At that point I knew we *had* to be crazy. Neither of us was even dopesick and yet we still found ourselves buying heroin in the bowels of a condemned Harlem building after dark.

"Come on," I said. "Let's get out of here before we get killed."

We headed out into the darkness and toward the subway when Perry suddenly descended to the lower level of another deserted brownstone. Initially, I thought it was a bad idea, but when I saw the expression on his face it wasn't long before I was joining him at the bottom of the staircase to tap a vein.

The next thing I recall was my seemingly lifeless body being dragged back up the stairs and onto the sidewalk. Later, Perry would tell me that for a moment he was certain I'd died. But of course, I wasn't at all dead but had merely returned to the womb right there on 111th Street.

"Come on, dude," Perry tried to rouse me. "You better get up before this gets ugly."

Unfortunately, by this point it was already ugly as I was much more an observer than an actual participant in the events surrounding me. Certainly, I was aware of what was happening—but unable to move, speak, or react in any way. Although my consciousness still lingered it had in some way become detached, and though at no point did I leave my body to hover over it all, I would definitely describe it as an *out-of-body* experience.

Eventually, I found myself being flung like a rag doll over the shoulder of a gigantic black man who then proceeded to throw me into the backseat of a cab. I remember feeling helpless and thinking he could have easily killed both of us and might have, had Perry not commissioned him to scoop me up off the floor.

Somehow, as we neared the train station at 125th Street, I sobered-up just enough to be able to step out of the cab and have Perry lead me in the right direction. As we approached the staircase leading up to the platform, we were confronted by a rush of police activity. Fortunately, on this particular occasion, junkies weren't the intended prey and crackheads scattered like roaches as the hunted and the hunters sprinted by.

Perry waited with me at the station for about an hour. At around 11:50 the train arrived and I was back at my mother's apartment by 1 a.m. As I unlocked the door and gently turned the knob, it seemed as though I had again been transported back to 1980. I nervously felt my way around the dark apartment, careful not to bump into anything or even turn on a light and chance waking her.

With my right hand feeling for the wall, I tiptoed toward the couch and decided to call it a night right then and there. I was still very obviously fucked up and refused to compromise the safety of silence with a noisy trip to the bathroom. Apparently, even a bladder full of urine and a mouthful of grimy teeth failed to provide the incentive necessary to risk awakening the beast.

With tiny steps and in complete darkness, I very slowly made my way through the living room until at last, my left foot grazed the base of the couch. Mission complete. I heaved a huge sigh of relief and then turned to sit down. However, I must have misjudged the target or overshot my landing, because what I assumed would be the edge of the couch—was actually the edge of a glass end-table that noisily shattered under the weight of my bony ass. Then, for an immediate encore, as I landed on the chard-strewn floor my head hit the wall and the impact brought down a set of shelves. It was a remarkably loud and drawn-out demolition.

"WHAT WAS THAT!?!?!" my mother screamed from her bedroom as the last, glass, trinket finally exploded onto the floor.

"It was the wind—go back to sleep."

Unfortunately, she didn't take my advice. After providing an on-the-spot assessment of the damage, my mother suggested that I find someone else to visit. Interestingly enough, my stay was terminated before I ever had a chance to see my sister.

The very next day, I packed up my belongings and headed for the train station under the assumption that I could stay with Jeff until things got sorted out. It was probably for the best anyway, now that Perry was out of the hospital and would eventually be looking for a place to live.

I boarded the 7:38 a.m. express train to Manhattan, and took a seat next to a middle-aged woman with a briefcase on her lap and a newspaper in her hands. As the train left the station she turned to me.

"Look at the filth they print in that cesspool of a city," the woman said in complete disgust as she showed me the front page of the New York Press.

She had an old issue of the paper and though I can't remember exactly what the headline read, she was offended by the cover story. It began with a blow-by-blow account of the writer's first experience with heroin, and then provided a glowing endorsement for the drug, as well as the impression that it can be casually used and safely experimented with.

"Isn't that just the most irresponsible piece of journalism you've ever seen?" the woman asked me.

In the article, it was clear that the writer was enjoying the honeymoon stages of what would likely become his own addiction to heroin. He explained how the buzz was the most pleasurable he'd ever experienced as well as the most cost-effective, and that the side effects were negligible. In fact, he likened the nausea to "a toothless baby alligator trying to gnaw its way out" of his stomach. Three years earlier, I could have written virtually the same article.

"Yeah… It is."

75

"Hey man, I really need a favor," I said to Jeff from a payphone in Grand Central Station.

"Forget it."

"I haven't even said what it is yet!"

"OK, what is it?"

"I need to stay with you for a few weeks until I get an apartment."

"Nope."

"Come on—man!" I pleaded. "I really need to get back in the studio and finish this thing. I promise, just a few weeks—and you'll never have to look at me again."

"Fuck you and your shitty band."

"Please?"

"No problem. Come over whenever you want," he said. "But I probably won't be here. Do you still have a key?"

"Yeah."

"Then I'll see you when I see you. And don't smoke all of my fucking weed!"

Thank God for Jeff. If it wasn't for him, I definitely would've ended up at the Whitehouse Hotel, which is precisely where Perry was banished to after he outsmarted Gina, got us high, dropped me off at the train station and then returned to her apartment. So, before October was over, I relocated to Jeff's and prepared myself to look for another miserable waiting job. I still had about 30 bucks and 60 milligrams of meth, so I felt confident that I could find one and make it through training.

During my very first afternoon back in the city, I secured a position at Blockhead's Burritos on Third Avenue, about a mile from Jeff's building. I then headed over to his apartment and found him there, banging out Beethoven on the piano.

"How's it going, junky?" Jeff asked as he stopped playing and I crossed the threshold of his dwelling.

"I found a job," I answered without much enthusiasm.

"That's good. At least one of us should be slaving away in a shitty restaurant."

"What do you mean?"

"I got fired from Serendipity three weeks ago," he said joyfully with a gleam in his eye.

"No shit?"

"I kid you not, sir."

"Then what the fuck are you so happy about?"

"Oh, nothing much…just **THIS!!!**" he said as he gleefully waved a slip of paper in the air—*like a lady trying to flag a cab with a hanky.*

"By the way—**that's** why everybody thinks you're gay," I pointed out while realizing that the slip of paper was actually a check.

"What the fuck are you talking about?!?!"

I couldn't elaborate on his girly gestures any further as I was suddenly overcome by both envy and admiration. After years of contentedly waiting tables and performing in fringe productions, Jeff must have finally landed the role of a lifetime.

Lucky motherfucker!!! I can't believe it. OK, fine, I love Jeff and this is exactly the break he deserves. But fuck! He wasn't even looking for it and it just fell into his lap. No, that's not quite true. He's been at it for a while. Maybe that's how it happens. Maybe you just have to be patient and work hard and then suddenly—after a lot of blood, sweat, and tears—someone walks up to you and hands you a check that changes your life. I wonder how much it's for. I bet it's for at least ten grand. Shit, I think I can see a one and a two. Maybe it's 12,000. Fuck—I wonder if it's for a $120,000!!! From the way he's acting, it might be. God, I can't stand the suspense any longer. I wish he would just tell me already!

"A hundred and twenty bucks!" he announced, as he continued to wave around an unemployment check like he was planning his retirement.

"Big fucking deal," I said. "Perry pumps that much into his arm every other day."

One of the many downfalls to working as a waiter or waitress is the limited compensation provided in the event of termination. Because incomes are gratuity-based and impossible to determine precisely, restaurants typically claim them as being roughly ten percent of an employee's sales, which translates into about half of what is usually generated. Although the conservative estimate is beneficial at tax time, as far as unemployment compensation and social security benefits are concerned, it has *severe* drawbacks.

Although the check's lack of zeroes was a disappointment to me—as far as Jeff was concerned he was on easy street for six months. In fact, he was so thrilled about being on the dole, that after his benefits ran out he intended to apply for an extension. His bounty may have only amounted to $120 per week, but his rent-controlled apartment was a $140 per month, and as a result his bills were covered and he was still left with plenty of money to burn on whatever he chose—which was usually rice, beans, and rolling papers.

"By the way—why'd they fire you?" I finally asked.

"I got into an altercation with Mitch."

Mitch was one of Debbie's favorites and though I never had a problem with him personally, there was always an underlying tension that existed between him and Jeff. One afternoon during a shift change Mitch made a smartass remark that, as usual, threw Jeff's heterosexuality into question. Apparently though, this time Jeff had taken exception to the comment and responded with some sort of a threatening, physical gesture. Then the shit really hit the fan.

"The next day Debbie got wind of it and called both of us into her office," Jeff recounted. "Then she sat there for a half-hour kissing Mitch's ass right in front of me, and telling me that I was envious of his professionalism. Can you fucking believe that? Like I could give two shits about Mitch's professionalism."

"So she fired you because she thought you were jealous of Mitch?"

"Not exactly," he said. "So anyway, that night I went home stewing about it and when I came into work the next day I was *still* totally pissed off."

"So you *are* jealous of Mitch's professionalism!"

"Fuck no, I'm not jealous of that little prick," he said. "Let me tell you something about Mitch: Whenever he doesn't like the way a customer talks to him—he spits in the poor bastard's food. How's that for professional?"

"You should've mentioned that to Debbie," I told him.

As a matter of fact that's precisely what Jeff did, which, when verified by other staff members resulted in Mitch's immediate termination.

"But it gets better," he said.

"It must," I agreed. "How the fuck did *you* get fired?"

"I'm getting to that," he said. "The night they gave Mitch the boot, Renee called my house and left a really nasty message on my answering machine."

Renee, one of Serendipity's few female employees, was totally straight and extremely attractive with long blond hair and a pair of enormous breasts. However, from the tone of the message it became clear that she was now furious with Jeff, which was notable because in addition to the aforementioned attributes, Renee also happened to have been over six feet tall and one of Mitch's most fiercely protective fag-hags:

Jeff, you two-faced-fucking-faggot. When I find you I'm gonna kill you, you little piece of shit queer! I'm gonna wait for you in front of the restaurant and then I'm gonna drag you out back and beat the fucking shit out of you! Then, I'm gonna rip off your dick and shove it right the fuck up your ass because we all know that's what you really want anyway—you little, fucking, faggot-ass, queer!!!"

"Holy shit!" I said, half wanting to laugh out loud and half fearing for Jeff's life.

"Uh huh," he agreed. "And what do you think I did after hearing that?"

"Jerk off?"

"After that."

"I can't imagine."

"I let Debbie listen to it."

"No fucking shit!"

Debbie then decided to not only fire Renee, but to go for the trifecta by giving Jeff *his* walking papers as well.

"She said she was firing me because I ratted-out Mitch only to settle a personal vendetta, rather than because he wasn't performing his job correctly."

"How typical," I said. "I can't believe I missed so much."

"That's not all," he said. "Aaron OD'd and died."

It had been so long since I'd thought about Serendipity that it took a moment to remember who exactly Aaron was.

"Aaron...the cook," Jeff said and successfully jogged my memory. "Two weeks ago there was a strain of dope going around that was killing addicts on Avenue D. One of the newspapers actually did a story about it that featured him."

"You're kidding," I said in amazement. "I didn't even know he was a junky."

"No one did until the cops found his body on a park bench."

"Oh my God," I said and for a moment recalled the cook who always seemed to know a little too much about the secret life I tried to keep hidden from the world.

"Hey junky!!!" Jeff ripped me away from my reflections. "You wanna go get some now?"

"Get what?"

"What do you think?"

"You're not seriously thinking about doing dope, are you Jeff?"

"Yeah, so?"

"You're crazy," I said with genuine concern. "You don't need this shit in your life, trust me."

"Listen, junky. I was doing dope in China while you were still suckin' on your mama's titty."

"Uh, for your information: the only part of my mother that ever

256

ended up in my mouth was her fist—so fuck you."

Within seconds, as if on cue, the door opened and in walked what I immediately knew was a middle-aged dope fiend in distress.

"Hey-hey! Speak-of-the-fucking-junky!" Jeff exclaimed. "How're you doing, dude? Craig, this is Stephen—fresh out of Central Booking. *He's* a fuck-up just like you!"

Not quite.

Stephen Livingston was a hardcore, 24-hour-a-day junky and he didn't care what anyone thought about it. He was dirty and disheveled with long, greasy, hair and a demeanor that not only screamed dope fiend, but crackhead as well. In fact, he could have easily been Crackhead Jim's older, *smarter* brother.

"Hey man, how's it going?" he asked me in a nervous way as he strangely scanned the apartment.

"OK. How's it going with you?"

"Better—now that I've clearly been sprung," he said as if he wasn't entirely sure a moment ago.

"Stephen got busted trying to score on Houston yesterday," Jeff said as he brought me up to speed.

"Twenty-nine hours in the fucking system," Stephen added, which was a decent stint but nothing to write home about.

"Then I suppose you wanna score a few bags and make it a memory," Jeff said as if he needed to egg-on the bundle-a-day junky who'd just spent 29 hours in jail. "Let's go to The Laundromat."

"The what?" I asked.

"The Laundromat," he repeated. "Let's go."

As we jumped on the #6 and headed to the East Village, I was surprised that Jeff would know about a spot that I was unaware of. I was also very excited at the prospect of finding a safe, downtown option to replace the loss of Angelina's with. We disembarked at Astor Place as Jeff and Stephen led the way to what was once a laundromat in a deserted old building on Sixth Street in Alphabet City.

Though I'd never previously seen or heard of the spot before, I must have been in the minority as I noticed a long line of addicts waiting to be served. Given the mayor's obsession with eradicating the city's drug problem, it was quite a spectacle to see such a robust business operating right out in the open, especially in Greenwich Village. And by the way, these guys were dealing dope *and* crack cocaine from the very same stoop.

76

"We need to finish recording," Perry told me on a Saturday afternoon from a payphone at the Whitehouse Hotel.

Although I'd heard the tired, old, refrain on several occasions, he sounded more serious than before.

"Well if you could stay out of the hospital for a minute, then maybe we would."

"Catherine's issuing direct threats," he said. "She wants the disc completely finished within a month."

"It'll never happen," I told him. "Only seven tracks have vocals and *none* of the songs are completely finished."

"Then put it in overdrive!"

"YOU PUT IT IN OVERDRIVE, FUCKFACE!!!" I shouted and then slammed the phone down.

"You're getting nasty," Jeff commented. "Are you feeling a little dopesick today, junky?"

As a matter of fact, I wasn't at all dopesick as my methadone and heroin maintenance program was working beautifully. I'd been staying with Jeff for two weeks, and on Saturday mornings I'd head up to 125th Street for a bottle of meth which would keep me medicated through Sunday. Then, on Monday or Tuesday at the latest, I would return to my 20 dollar-a-day heroin habit. Of course, the whole routine was really just a ruse designed to convince myself that I was in control of something.

"That reminds me," Jeff said. "Stephen should be stopping by. He still owes me money from last week."

During my stay with Jeff, almost everyday Stephen dropped by unannounced for one reason or another and it seldom had anything to do with drugs, as Jeff remained exclusively a Weekend Warrior. Today, however, was Saturday and though it was methadone day for me, I thought Jeff might have other plans as he seemed to be eagerly anticipating Stephen's arrival.

I didn't care for Stephen because he was a shiftless junky. He lived in an abandoned antique shop located on Madison Avenue and owned by his extremely wealthy parents, while he sold weed in Central Park to support a monstrous dope addiction and a diet consisting of Raman Noodles and Butterfingers. And yes, he looked like complete shit.

Although in many ways he reminded me of Crackhead Jim, while Jim was a reckless, damaged, and unrestricted drug receptacle, Stephen was a thoughtful junky who carefully managed and maintained his lifestyle. Of course, he had the benefit of a free place to live, but beyond that he always paid his bills on time without ever burdening anyone or any government agency with requests for assistance. He never panhandled, never freeloaded, never slept in a shelter, never stole and never seemed in need. Mind you, he still wallowed near rock bottom, but he was fine there and perfectly content to live out the rest of his life in an opiated stupor. He had no goals, no aspirations, and no reason to live other than the needle he arranged his days around.

It may seem peculiar, but at the time I didn't consider Stephen and myself to be at all similar in terms of lifestyle, and I really thought he was a terrible influence on Jeff. Although I may have been a junky as well, I was a junky on a mission that still managed to maintain a legitimate job as well as a facade of sobriety, both of which would remain in place until I achieved my goals. Of course, once the CD was completed and my success certain, I would tear away the cloak of normalcy and happily offend the sensibilities of everyone around me. In the meantime, however, I was able to look away from the fact that my daily life really didn't deviate much from Stephen's.

Before nightfall, Stephen made his appearance and it soon became clear that getting fucked up was, in fact, on the agenda.

"Hey—I think my shirt's beginning to smell a little gamey," Jeff said, tacitly suggesting a trip to The Laundromat.

"I have some for you at the lair," Stephen replied. "But if Craig wants any we might have to do a load or two."

"No thanks. I'm good," I told him. "What's 'the lair?'"

"My pad," Stephen said.

"Why do you call it that?"

"Because it looks like a dirty, disgusting, animal lives there," Jeff blurted out.

Stephen's *lair* was only a few blocks away, and by now the old antique shop was virtually an antique itself as it had been permanently closed in the mid-1960's. We arrived at just after 8 p.m. in almost complete darkness, which was only accentuated by the seemingly uninhabited store.

Stephen unlocked the front door and felt for a light switch as he walked in. A single bulb burned brightly in the center of the room, illuminating a volcano-like pile of trash consisting of empty bottles, Styrofoam cups, paper plates and fast food containers. The mountain of mess took up perhaps as much as a third of the room's area, and was surrounded by newspapers, garbage bags, and a variety of other refuse. I was amazed that a single person could produce such an immense heap of shit.

"Wow! It actually looks cleaner in here," Jeff commented, unbelievably.

"Excuse the mess, boys," Stephen said, "But I've fully devoted my lair to the city's recycling effort."

Apparently, along with the rest of Manhattan.

The condition of his "lair" was so deplorable that at first, it distracted me from the unusual choice of wall covering that adorned the store. Lining all four walls was white construction paper, almost completely covered in what appeared to be tiny splatters of watery red paint.

"How many do you want?" Stephen asked Jeff, as he pulled his stash out from under the dirty mattress he slept on.

"Just one."

Jeff quickly inserted a dollar bill into the bag and inhaled, while our host emptied six bags into a spoon and began to cook. Somehow, Stephen managed to fill a single syringe with the massive dose of dope, but he had more difficulty locating a usable vein in an arm ravaged by scars, track marks, contusions and open sores.

After a few minutes and finally resorting to his *hand*, he found a vein and pulled the trigger. Then, with eyes wide open and mouth agape, Stephen removed the syringe and stared in awe at the needle as if it was telling him just how incredibly fucked in the head he was. He then stood up, pointed the syringe at one of the few white spaces remaining on the wall, and forced out what little liquid remained in the chamber. It amounted to no more than a raindrop's worth of bloody residue, but like thousands of others it found its place in the grotesque, slice-of-life display.

After finally stepping outside to throw-up in the comparatively sterile conditions of 63rd Street, I regained control of myself and returned to the shop. As disturbing as it was, the bloody walls of the antique store were not only a fair depiction of how terribly lost Stephen was, but how terribly long he'd managed to remain lost.

77

On November 24th, Perry and I gave thanks and then booted.

But there were other things to be thankful for. Two weeks prior, Perry had found employment at The Boulevard—a pricey rib joint on the Upper West Side—just as I finally realized that Blockhead's was a dead-end gig with little earning potential. The revelation prompted me to quit, and within a day of my departure I was hired at Texas Grill, also a rib joint but located on the Upper East Side and not nearly as lucrative as The Boulevard. Texas Grill had its perks, however, and preeminent among them was a staff consisting of fewer actors and actresses than one might expect in a Manhattan restaurant. Among my new co-workers was Marie O'Donnell, a recent college graduate from Ireland and Jill Simpkins, a violinist from Norfolk, Virginia. The three of us immediately became good friends as we all shared something in common: We were fucked up.

Of course, I was the only dope fiend in the group, but I would soon learn that Marie had anorexia and Jill suffered from a panic disorder which, at times, was so debilitating that she couldn't leave her apartment. Although we didn't share our personal issues with each other at first, it wasn't long before the open forums began.

Jill had thrown a dinner party around the middle of December. Though at this point I seldom attended social engagements that didn't involve heroin with individuals who weren't junkies, that evening I broke with precedent and decided to delay the doping until afterwards. Besides, Jill's apartment was located just a few blocks from The Laundromat which would be convenient enough when the festivities ended.

I arrived at her 10th Street apartment at 11 p.m., and by that point everyone had already left except for Marie and, of course, Jill who were watching a video of Jill's recitals. At one point during a performance, another young woman sang for a few moments and I was moved by an almost ethereal resonance in her voice.

Before the night was over, the three of us horrified each other with intimate details of our respective dysfunctions. Eventually, Jill mentioned that she desperately needed to get away from the city before she had a nervous breakdown.

"Craig, I'm going home to Virginia for a while to get my head together," she said. "Would you do me a favor and house-sit while I'm gone?"

"Sure, no problem."

"Oh, thank you *so* much. I would hate to have to leave my kitty with a complete stranger."

"Oh, I mean absolutely not," I said. "I forgot that I'm really busy."

"Oh, don't worry. I'm not leaving for another week and a half."

"It doesn't matter. I'm busy for the rest of my life," I said as Jill looked confused by the sudden reversal. "Listen: it's nothing personal, but I'm known far and wide for having a killer left hook and a bad track record when it comes to cats."

"Please, Craig, I really need your help! I'm in a bad situation right now and besides, how could you *possibly* refuse me?"

"Because I've worked long and hard at building a reputation and I'm just not willing to throw it all away yet. I don't care how fucked up you are."

"Craig! Chester's just like me," she said, perhaps not taking me as seriously as she should have. "He hides under the bed trembling in fear, and then sneaks out once or twice-a-day to eat and take a shit. You'll never even see him."

Actually, that sounds like my kind of cat!

I reluctantly agreed to be a cat-sitter, and by 1 a.m. had left Jill's apartment to score some dope at The Laundromat. Then, before heading uptown to Jeff's, I stopped at a bodega for some water and used the bottle cap to fix the dope and load the syringe while waiting for a train at Astor Place. As soon as I booted the first bag I immediately realized the dope was much stronger than usual, and the kind that typically produced an overdose or two. Fortunately, by booting only one bag I avoided that fate. Jeff, however, wasn't so lucky.

When I arrived at his apartment I stumbled into chaos. Brad Winslow, Alex Broderick and Jeremy Kettering—all childhood friends of Jeff's from Queens—were there berating him and snarling at Stephen who was oblivious and nodding in a corner of the living room. I'd met all of them previously, and though Brad was aware of Jeff's occasional dope-dabbling, he'd remained unconcerned as his nearest and dearest friend always seemed in control. But now Jeff had suddenly ventured into forbidden territory and Brad's confidence in him was completely shaken. Earlier in the evening and for the first time in his life, Jeff had booted a bag of dope—the very *same* dope that I was lucky enough not to have overindulged in after leaving Jill's. He then immediately stopped breathing which required Stephen to do so on his behalf for approximately ten minutes. Eventually, Jeff was able to resume the task himself, and then in an overly-medicated condition he decided to call Brad and share the gory details. Within 20 minutes Brad and the others were at the apartment raising hell.

"I can't believe you stuck a fucking needle in your arm!!!" Brad roared. "What the fuck is wrong with you?! Are you trying to kill yourself?!"

"Calm the fuck down!!!" Jeff slurred belligerently with his eyes half open.

"Hey man, you need to make some serious changes in your life. Why don't you give Denise a call? She really likes you and she'd be good for you," Brad continued as Alex was visibly put off by the suggestion.

Denise Wexler, originally from Maryland, was a high-ranking administrator at New York University Medical Center and responsible for overseeing a large portion of the hospital's organ donations. About a year earlier, she and Alex had been a fairly serious item and it was now obvious that he wasn't too thrilled with the notion of her becoming involved with Jeff. Fortunately for Alex, Jeff was mainly attracted to *Asian* women.

"Look at what your life is turning into," Brad went on. "You're unemployed and your best friend is Skeletor," he said gesturing toward Stephen's wasted body.

"Why don't you just get the fuck out of here?" Jeff suggested to his old friend.

"You know what? Why don't *we* just get Skeletor the fuck out of here?" Alex countered as he glanced at Brad.

Brad and Alex then approached Stephen with the intention of flinging his worthless body out the fourth-floor window. Truthfully, part of me was hoping they would, because when Jeff foolishly tapped a vein it was under Stephen's deranged auspices. Of course, had *I* been there, Jeff's arm would have been broken in two before he had a chance to stick it with a needle.

Brad and Alex took two menacing steps toward Stephen, but before they were able to lay a hand on him, Jeff cleaned house and ejected everyone from the apartment that wasn't a junky. Then, without another word, he climbed up to the loft and passed out. A few minutes later, I followed to make sure he was still breathing and then passed out beside him. When I awoke at 11 a.m., Jeff sat up and announced that it was *I* who was, in fact, the homosexual—and then went right back to sleep.

I was supposed to be at the studio by 1 p.m., so I left the apartment at noon and ventured over to Central Park for a bag of weed to get me through the day. Jeff had previously introduced me to a Rasta working out of a gazebo on a hill near the southern end of the Park, who sold the greenest, stickiest, buds I'd ever seen in my life. I climbed the hill, made the purchase, and then immediately headed back down.

As I descended and nearly reached the bottom of the hill, I was suddenly pulled aside by an undercover cop. Much to everyone's surprise, a posse of police dressed in leisure-wear was there observing the illicit transactions; however, rather than arresting anyone they were actually handing out tickets—assembly-line style—to startled potheads as they passed.

The officer calmly confiscated my beautiful buds and gave it to one of his cronies in exchange for a bag of twigs and dirt. "Alleged marijuana," he then said with a smile, as he placed the substituted bag in a manila envelope and issued me a ticket.

"Even a pothead wouldn't be stupid enough to buy that shit," I said with a make-believe smile as I turned to continue down the hill. "But a cop might be."

"What'd you say?"

"Nothing."

78

Toward the end of December, Perry had actually reduced his habit to just a few bags-a-day. That, combined with the fact that he was making incredibly good money at The Boulevard, stimulated a desire to again flee the Whitehouse.

"Hey, I found us a place," he called to tell me.

Of course, I was once again more than comfortable at Jeff's, and as I was about to begin a cat-sitting stint at Jill's, I was reluctant to embrace another of Perry's questionable living arrangements.

"Where?" I dared to ask.

"A hotel on the Upper West Side."

The mere mention of the word "hotel" now instantly conjured-up horrific thoughts.

"Fuck off," I told him.

"No really, this one's nice!"

"Sure it is," I humored him. "Where's the bathroom?"

"In the hallway right outside the room," he had the nerve to say.

"You see, Perry, that's where you get yourself in trouble. I'm telling you, once you give up exclusive access to the bathroom you're just asking for problems."

"Well, I'm sick of the Whitehouse and I'm moving in there today," he said. "When you get tired of being a freeloader, let me know."

"Will do."

On Christmas Eve I was supposed to begin cat-sitting duties, as Jill caught a flight to Norfolk earlier that day. After working the lunch shift at Texas Grill, I headed to 125th Street to score and then stopped at Jeff's apartment for some clothes before continuing on to Jill's. When I arrived, Jeff was there with Denise, who he'd been spending a good deal of time with in recent weeks. Following the overdose, Jeff had taken steps to distance himself from heroin, and since I was departing and he had severed all ties with Stephen, perhaps this new relationship was intended to further change the cast of characters surrounding him. Actually, Denise seemed like a good person for him to have around. She was cute, lived a healthy lifestyle, and the only self-destructive obsession she harbored was a desire to fuck Jeff. As much as I would miss him, I knew he hardly needed his life to be influenced by the dark forces that affected my own, regardless of how in control he usually seemed.

"Hey Jeff," I said. "After I finish the cat-sitting gig, I'm gonna be moving into some place on the west side with Perry."

"Good. It's about time you got the fuck out."

"Is it alright if I leave some of my shit here?" I asked as I was about to hit the road. "I'll drop by in a few days to pick up the rest of it."

"Yeah, that's fine. You're not leaving right now are you?"

"I most certainly am."

"Why don't you wait until tomorrow?" he asked. "Hang out for a while with Denise and me. We have some big plans for tonight."

"Yeah—we're gonna drink until we puke, and then we're gonna get all fucked up on some skunky weed," confirmed the healthcare professional.

"I think it's better if I head downtown," I said. "You know, I've got a kitty to tend to."

"You can punch it in the face tomorrow," Jeff pointed out. "Right now you should hang."

"Come on, Craig," Denise piped-up again. "You're really gonna dig this weed."

"Yeah," Jeff chimed in with a smile. "Maybe you can figure out a way to boot it."

The evening went on as advertised, with Denise and Jeff drinking it up and smoking in style. However, since I'd already tapped a vein, I knew it would be fairly pointless to indulge in any of the party favors so I mostly abstained.

By around 3 a.m. I felt fatigue and heroin join forces to produce a deep nod. Sprawled out in the bottom bunk-bed, I was then suddenly jolted out of my reverie by a burst of activity coming from just above, which was unusual because Jeff typically slept in the loft. Then, within a few seconds I recognized the unmistakable sounds of a healthcare professional getting the shit fucked out of her. It wasn't long before I realized that Jeff had deliberately staged the event on the top bunk for my very own benefit. I suppose he hoped it might in some way be frustrating for me to listen to while he brandished his heterosexuality, especially since *I* hadn't in years. But more importantly, his behavior demonstrated that Jeff was never truly in touch with the value system of a junky, because even though a piece of ass sounded pretty good—*a piece of cake sounded even better.*

While they remained in the throws of drunken passion, I roused myself to make the craving for cake a reality. I also decided that since I was up and dressed and heading out to satisfy the sudden urge, I might as well kill two birds with one stone and continue onward to Jill's. I quietly placed a few essentials in a backpack and then made my way to the front door.

"By the way," I said before leaving the darkened apartment. "Nothing's changed. Everybody *still* thinks you're gay." I then headed downtown to Jill's apartment where I immediately returned to my nod and eventually fell asleep on her couch, but not before throwing up two Suzy-Q's and a Twinkie.

For some time now—in one form or another—I'd remained a

houseguest and as a result was prevented from ever feeling truly comfortable and self-destructive. Though I was still *technically* a guest, for the first time in months I could finally enjoy the pleasures of being entirely left alone.

I woke up at about 5:30 p.m. on Christmas Day, and though I was excited about the prospect of complete solitude, the gift-giving ritual I'd experienced for most of my life sparked-up a bit of holiday melancholy. So at about 6:30 when I headed out to score my daily dope, I also picked-up some Christmas crack as a present to myself. I then bought a set of works from a homeless junky dressed as Santa, and a crack pipe from a head shop with a Nativity Scene in the window.

I sprinted back to Jill's apartment and as soon as I got inside, I laid all the drugs out on a kitchen table along with their respective paraphernalia. Unfortunately, just as I was about to dive into the dope the intercom rang and I was forced to tear myself away from the Christmas celebration.

"WHO THE FUCK IS IT?!?" I demanded.

"Merry Christmas, Craig—**YOU FUCKING ASSHOLE!!!**"

It was Marie.

Apparently, homesickness had begun to affect her as she recalled a lifetime of Christmas memories with her family back in Ireland, celebrating the birth of our Blessed Lord and Savior, Jesus Christ.

"Hey—you wanna get drunk?" she asked.

"Come up," I said as I buzzed her in and then rushed back into the kitchen to hide the drugs. Marie knew I was a dope fiend, so I didn't want her to see the crack and lose respect for me.

"Merry Christmas!" she said as she barged in through an unlocked door and almost caught me red-handed, stashing the drugs in a cabinet. She then opened the refrigerator and grabbed each of us a beer, which was about the *last* thing I wanted.

Had she been anyone else in the world, I would have concocted a lie to get rid of her. But Marie was special and she happened to have looked worse than ever. As she walked from the kitchen attempting to mask a limp, it was obvious that even at the age of 23 a diet of tortilla chips and Guinness had finally taken its toll. I was awed by the fact that for the first time ever, a concern for someone else's well being had actually supplanted my own selfish determination to get high. We sat down for a while and talked about what was going on.

"I saw a doctor today," she confided. "He suggested that I go back home and I think it would be wise to heed the advice."

"That sucks, Marie. Coming here fucked you all up and now they're telling you to go back."

"It has nothing to do with being here," she said. "I used to think it did…but it doesn't."

"You know, I'm the last person on earth who should be judging anybody. But you're beginning to look really sick, and I'm beginning to get, you know, kind of worried."

That was about the best I could offer beyond listening, which I continued to do for two hours as she attempted to explain her illness. Eventually, Marie likened her condition to my own drug addiction and though I couldn't see the similarities then, I do now. Apparently, by starving and depriving herself of food, she managed to achieve something similar to the false sense of well-being, security, and control that I found at the end of a needle.

Marie had been in the states for only a year to launch a career in charitable fundraising and given her condition, it wasn't surprising that she met with limited success. But the grave risk to her health was overshadowed by a fear of going back home empty-handed, as some of her compatriots apparently looked down upon those returning from America without the success they set out for.

"Going back to Ireland will be horrific. They'll torture me. I think when I get back I'll just hide in my room until everyone forgets that I ever left," she said with a sad giggle.

"Give me a break," I said. "What's the worst that can happen? When you go home just tell them you went to New York to get your career started, but got sick and had to come back. What the fuck are they gonna say?"

"They'll say it serves me right for trying."

After two hours of mutual commiserating, I began to feel a churning in my belly and that could mean only one thing: anorexia or not, Marie had to go.

"Are you sure you don't wanna go out for a few drinks?" she asked as she could sense our chat was coming to a close.

"No, really. I've got a session tomorrow and I should be getting some sleep," I said as I walked her to the door and sent her on her way.

With that I was free to open my Christmas presents while Marie booked a flight to Ireland.

79

As 1995 commenced, Perry got himself situated at the West Side Inn located on 108th Street between Amsterdam and Columbus Avenues. In the meantime, I became even further immersed in my own debauchery. Throughout the month of January and on into February, each night immediately following my shift at Texas Grill, I'd be at The Laundromat for two bags of dope and as many rocks as the evening's earnings would allow. Then, I would look forward to getting high for hours and putting my body through the ringer. Night after night I found myself sitting in Jill's living room with her ukulele in my hands and a sizzling crack pipe between my lips, as I played along to a recording of whatever was last completed in the studio. Then, just as the pipe crackled for the final time I would plunge a loaded syringe into my arm, well before the horrid cocaine crash ensued.

Although I had passing dalliances with crack cocaine before, mainly at the grimy Hell's Kitchen apartment, I had never before hit the pipe with such ferocity as my intensified drug use had now spun me into a whole new dimension of fucked up. For really the first time, I was no longer rationalizing my addiction as a coping mechanism designed to help me survive the Herculean trials of a starving artist. Now, rather than using drugs as a buffering agent and to help me convince myself that everything was fine, I was using purely for the sake of getting loaded. Although I probably didn't recognize it as such, issues pertaining to Sections and the CD had clearly become secondary. I was also beginning to look worse than ever, as not only my arms but my face showed signs of the abuse. Like most junkies, I had dark circles under my eyes and was skinnier than I should have been. However, the incessant crack smoking was beginning to wreak havoc with my complexion as well. I looked like an AIDS patient suffering from multiple afflictions, but I didn't care. Armed with a tube of flesh-toned Oxy-10 I was prepared for anything.

On Valentines Day, which commemorated a month-and-a-half since we'd resumed our relationship, I found myself whispering sweet nothings into one end of a crack pipe while my rekindled passion burned brightly at the other. Then things abruptly hit a snag. As I sat on Jill's living room floor Indian-style, thrilling imaginary audiences with spine tingling leads on the ukulele, I suddenly went into convulsions; however, at the time I was completely unaware of what was happening. Actually, it seemed as though someone had grabbed me by the nape of the neck as my head was violently thrust downward, my body folded in half, and my nose was repeatedly smashed against the floor between my knees. While the punishment continued and my nose absorbed at least six or seven solid shots, never did I once even consider the role that intensive drug use may have played in relation to the attack, as I was consumed with the question of how the fuck Gina managed to get into the apartment.

Of course, Gina was nowhere to be found but Perry, who was making an unscheduled visit, had inconspicuously entered the apartment through an open door just as the seizures began. Apparently, besides the cocaine crash, heroin also eliminated those pesky feelings of paranoia that often have crackheads bolting doors, boarding windows, and securing perimeters.

"That was the most fucked up thing I've ever seen," Perry said as the convulsions subsided and I sat there rubbing my forehead and wiping a bloody nose. "It was like 'The Exorcist.'"

I took a deep breath, leaned back on my elbows, and completely unfolded my body and legs.

"Holy shit," I sighed as I exhaled the first, post-convulsive breath.

I then rose from the floor and with Perry in tow, made my way to a bathroom mirror to inspect the damage as blood steadily flowed from a nose that was now slightly bent.

"Do you think I look tough?" I asked.

"No," Perry said. "I think you look like a crackhead with a busted-up nose."

80

On the morning of March 1st I finally joined Perry at the West Side Inn as Jill's lease had expired. Rather than renew it, she decided to remain at her parent's home in Virginia and like Marie, confront her problems in more familiar surroundings.

My new residence was located just south of Harlem. Regardless of its location, this particular hotel was actually respectable and though the bathrooms were communal, they were in much better condition than those of the Midtown and the Whitehouse. Here, residents were mainly graduate students from Columbia University, and I quickly realized that academics were much better neighbors than hookers and pimps. I also temporarily ended my romance with cocaine and to the untrained eye, it may have seemed as though we were beginning to get our lives together. Unfortunately, although my complexion had cleared up, this was hardly the case as I continued to look the other way and slide deeper into an opiated abyss.

"You know, after today, we only have three scheduled sessions," Perry informed me as I entered my new dwelling for the very first time.

Although nine tracks were almost finished, we had initially slated ourselves to record twelve, and I knew that another fifteen hours of recording would be nowhere near enough time to complete the project as it was originally intended.

"We're gonna need at least another 50 or 60 hours to completely finish everything," I plainly stated.

"It'll never happen," Perry told me. "Catherine isn't even returning my calls anymore...and that isn't a good thing."

"Fuck Catherine," was my usual response, which made no sense whatsoever as I foolishly permitted my ego to pretend to call the shots. Launching our careers with the CD would obviously entail a greater effort than merely recording it. Unfortunately, for well over a year now we'd missed virtually every deadline we were faced with and as a result, the promotional trip that Catherine had planned for the college radio circuit in April was now impossible.

That day the recording session would begin at noon and conclude sometime around 4 p.m., and even though I wouldn't be getting high until after it ended, I decided to get the daily dope purchase out of the way beforehand. Unfortunately, however, the Laundromat didn't open for business until well after nightfall. Given the circumstances, I could either take advantage of the daylight by heading uptown to score, or scour the downtown area around Houston Street, which, with the dismantling of Angelina's, was now frequented by several dope dealers bravely peddling on foot. Since police activity had recently increased in Harlem, I foolishly chose the downtown option.

I took the subway to the Second Avenue station, and then headed east on Houston until I reached Clinton Street and made a right turn. I continued on in that direction until I noticed two junkies getting busted by narcs on the corner of Delancey. I immediately turned around feeling very fortunate that I hadn't arrived two minutes earlier, and wisely resigned myself to somehow scoring later in the day when things cooled down. Then, as I got back within 50 feet of Houston Street, I recognized a Colombian dope dealer exiting a building.

"Right here, papi," he said to me as I casually walked past.

"Be cool, people are getting busted down there," I turned and said nervously as he followed from a few paces behind.

"Don't worry, papi," he said as we neared the corner. "How many do you want?"

At first, I thought it unwise to proceed with the transaction in such close proximity to a drug bust and almost kept walking. After all, the last thing I needed was to get arrested and miss the recording session. However, since the dealer had even more to lose, I ignored my instincts and assumed he must have known it was safe.

"Three," I told him.

He turned around, walked over to a payphone, and then stashed the dope in the coin return. After waiting a moment I then made my way to the phone, retrieved the dope from the slot, and replaced it with $30. With three bags of dope cupped tightly in my hand, I casually continued toward Houston.

As I stepped off the curb, I noticed a black sedan heading in my direction that seemed to be strangely telegraphing my pace. It intermittently fluctuated in speed, either accelerating too quickly to allow me to cross Houston safely, or drastically reducing its pace so it wouldn't pass me by.

As the car pulled within three feet of me it made an abrupt stop, and as the doors were flung open I knew I was going to jail. Things then proceeded in the usual way, with a direct order followed by a personal attack.

"Put your hands on the car, scumbag!!!" screamed a skinny, black, female police officer who looked not unlike a crackhead herself.

Unfortunately, my right hand was full of heroin, so in order to better comply with the police directive I did what any other junky would do: *I swallowed the dope.*

Although her partner seemed unaffected—as though he'd seen this tactic used before—the skinny, crackhead, lady-cop became incensed. She then shoved me into the front of the car, grabbed me by my hair and began banging my head against the hood.

"Spit it up," she said as she continued to bang away. "Spit it up you junky fuck!!!"

Though I had no idea the gag reflex worked this way, I still managed to keep down the dope.

Of course, swallowing the heroin would do nothing to persuade the police to abandon the arrest and allow me to attend the recording session, but I still took some pleasure in the fact that once again a lack of evidence compromised their level of enjoyment. After a few minutes of interrogation, denials, and some name calling, I was thrown into a van right behind a cop in the passenger seat.

"You know," he said to me, "we saw you swallow the dope, and when it opens up in your stomach you're gonna be a dead fucking junky."

Wonderful. As if things weren't going badly enough already, now there was a chance I might end up dying in prison. I decided to deny the allegation, at least until the autopsy.

"I have absolutely no idea of what you're talking about…officer."

Although I continued to deny the charges, by openly divulging the manner by which I disposed of the evidence, the cop had put me in what would later turn out to be a very uncomfortable position.

By the time I made my way through the initial processing stages, Central Booking, and then on to the tombs to await the judge—I'd been incarcerated for over 30 hours which was already a lengthy visit. Apparently, business was again booming, and due to the length of my incarceration I was beginning to feel the onset of withdrawals. Some of my cellmates, however, sported much larger habits and were suffering severely, as their pain would undoubtedly worsen until they saw the judge and were released or placed on the jailhouse methadone program.

One of the truly afflicted was Jake. Approaching seven feet tall he was a monster of a man—not only in terms of height, but in waste line as well which was unusual for a junky. He was big, black, and sweating profusely, and when word got out that I had three bags of dope lingering in my digestive system he started looking at me like I was a pork chop dredged in dope. Even so, in his extremely weakened state, Jake instilled feelings of sympathy rather than terror.

"Please bro. Go over there and take a shit for me," he pleaded with tears in his eyes while pointing at a metal toilet that was sitting in the center of the cell.

"You're kidding me, right?" I asked.

"No, man…I'm *begging* you."

Call me crazy, but I've always been a sucker for a big, sweaty, black man who could swallow me whole. And though taking a dump on the cold, metallic, bowl in front of a jail cell full of addicts was a bit unsettling, I knew what Jake was going through and decided to give it the old college try. Unfortunately, I had yet to experience the brunt of my own dopesickness and was still extremely constipated. Even so, I sat there for a while trying to summon forth something that might offer Jake the buried treasure he was looking for.

After about 20 minutes of straining I finally relinquished a rather meager-looking turd and some blood. Although I didn't say anything, I very much doubted that this particular dump would provide Jake with anything beyond a hunk of petrified fecal matter. Regardless, I stood up and with my hands on my knees, leaned over the bowl to better assess my effort. As I did, Jake pushed me out of the way and pounced on it. He then pulled the bloody turd out of the water and gently cradled it in his hands like a baby bird that had just fallen out of a tree.

"Goodman! Craig Goodman!" roared a corrections officer who was suddenly standing right outside the cell, unlocking the gate.

As soon as the C.O. made his presence known, Jake bolted to a corner with the excrement and left me standing there—bent over—with my underwear still wrapped around my ankles.

"It's not what it looks like," I told the officer.

I pulled up my pants as the C.O. led me out of the cell and down a series of corridors, which brought me to a bench in a courtroom where I'd wait an hour until my name was called. Unfortunately, my own withdrawals were now beginning to intensify and after about 40 minutes I felt my bowels suddenly become liquid.

"Hey C.O.," I said with desperation in my voice, "I *really* need to use the bathroom."

"Relax," he said. "You'll be out of here before you know it."

Shortly thereafter my name was called. I then made my way to a little podium where a public defender—whom I'd met earlier—patiently awaited my arrival. Within a few minutes the allegations were read, at which point my attorney stated that there were never any drugs found in my possession and that accordingly, the charges should be dropped.

"He swallowed them!!!" exclaimed the assistant district attorney, somewhat peeved by the defense.

Although I appreciated my counsel's effort, this was only dragging things out because everyone knew I was guilty. I knew it, the cops knew it, and opposing counsel knew it and if we didn't wrap things up pretty quickly, the judge was going to find out for himself when the proof came pouring out of my ass in open court.

I managed to hold it together just long enough to be ordered to perform three days of community service in Central Park. I then befouled the courthouse facility before heading over to The Laundromat.

81

In mid-April, despite the fact that we'd managed to arrange for a few additional recording sessions the previous month, Perry had to confront Catherine and address the fact that we were *still* recording. As a result, the disc probably wouldn't be mixed-down, mastered, manufactured, shrink-wrapped, and ready to be distributed until June or July. As far as Catherine was concerned, this was disastrous. Although she still intended to promote the band on the college radio circuit, for that to be truly effective the CD should have been available by early May—*at the latest.*

"What did she say?" I asked, before leaving our room and heading to the studio for the second to last time.

"She really didn't say anything," Perry told me. She sort of just frowned at me and left the restaurant. But that's it as far as recording goes."

"What do you mean?"

"She's not paying for any additional studio costs," he said. "After today we have one more session."

"Then what?"

"Then I guess we pay for it ourselves."

Fortunately, since we scaled back the project and resigned ourselves to just nine songs, we expected recording efforts to conclude that day. However, there still remained the issue of mixdown, at which point the many, individually-recorded tracks would be balanced and merged together to achieve a single, cohesive, and clean-sounding track for each song. This would take at least two or three more sessions, and at a hundred bucks-an-hour that was easier said than done.

In order to finish recording, and, since it was Sunday and the studio was typically empty, Perry convinced Nick to extend our session from five hours to ten. Fortunately, Nick really believed in the project and had already contributed well beyond the scope of a sound engineer, in terms of not only time and effort but in musical collaboration as well.

At noon I'd begin the session alone with Nick and then after working the lunch shift at The Boulevard, Perry would arrive at around 5 p.m. to finish any remaining guitar tracks. Although I had no need or intention to get high until much later, Perry would be dopesick in a matter of hours and due to the hectic schedule, he asked me to score and have the dope ready by the time he arrived at Fast Trax.

Ever since getting busted the previous month, I'd been trying to avoid downtown operations during daytime hours and was again scoring on 125th Street. But unfortunately, Giuliani's war on drugs had suddenly expanded to include the little Harlem oasis I once thought impenetrable due to its constant throng of respectable commuters. Although I hadn't yet personally seen anyone get busted, there'd been a rash of recent arrests—and the dealers who once flocked to me on sight were now missing in action and likely sitting in jail. Of course, an entirely new crop of dealers immediately emerged, but I was completely unknown to them and they were far too paranoid to even consider serving me. As a result, I had to adapt by taking advantage of a few liaisons, all of whom were black or Latino junkies that blended into the landscape much more indigenously than my pastiness would permit. For the price of a bag, any one of them would make the purchase while I waited at a bus stop for them to return. Among them, Arnold was my favorite. He was a black, 60 year-old junky, and though not as fleet of foot as he may've once been, he was extremely trustworthy and always had his ear to the ground. That morning, I had no difficulty finding him lurking around the bus stop. After he purchased a bundle for me, I descended to the subway and headed to Fast Trax. There, I would try to complete any remaining vocal work in order to allow the one, final, session to be exclusively reserved for mixdown.

After arriving and sharing a joint with Nick, we listened to all nine tracks and surprisingly, very little needed to be completed. However, although Nick thought it was fine, I noticed that a three-part harmony I'd developed on "Valentines" was lacking in some way, and the solution to the problem didn't immediately occur to me. But this was a minor concern, and I knew that I could devote the first few minutes of the final session to figuring things out. In the meantime, however, I was inspired to completely alter the lyrical content of the CD's final song, and what was once a tribute to a James Joyce story became a confession of my own addiction. Hence, the title of the song was changed from "Araby," to "Living in the Land of the Lilies."

At just before 5 p.m. Perry arrived at the studio and like a baton, I passed him a loaded syringe to finish the final leg of the session. And, since I had no plans for the evening that required any particular level of sobriety, I tapped my own vein.

"I'll catch you later at home," I then told him as he tuned his guitar and I staggered out of the studio.

As I stumbled in the direction of the subway, I strapped on a set of headphones to isolate the harmony issue with "Valentines," but I was puzzled. I must have rewound that tape five or six times until finally, just as I was crossing Broadway—it hit me…a cab, that is.

As I bounced off the hood, the momentum of the moving vehicle caused me to tumble backwards until I collided with the edge of the taxi's windshield. Had I landed any nearer to the center, I would have gone straight through it—*assways* first. However, as things turned out I landed unceremoniously enough on the street, bringing rush-hour traffic to a standstill.

"Oh shit, man!!! Are you OK?!?!" asked the distraught taxi driver as he jumped out of his cab.

"Yeah, no problem," I said, a little dazed as I rose to my feet. Just then, two women came rushing out into the street.

"Don't get up so fast, honey, you might've hurt yourself," said one of the women.

"I'm fine," I said again, now becoming a little agitated and embarrassed by all the attention.

"There's an ambulance right over there. Why don't you let them take a look at you before you leave?" someone else suggested as traffic began to build but patiently wait for me to recover.

"Don't worry about it!" I said as I finally made my way out of the street and on to the sidewalk. Just as I did, however, I was descended upon by two emergency medical technicians who were apparently watching from the nearby ambulance.

"Hey buddy," said one of them. "Why don't you let us check you out? The ambulance is right over there."

Yes, in fact, the ambulance was "right over there." However, there was also a police car sitting beside it and since I still had a set of works and four bags of dope on my broken body, the last thing I needed was to draw any *additional* attention from any *other* municipal employees.

"Listen," said the other EMT. "You took a really hard hit and you're gonna feel it later. Most people wouldn't have gotten up from that."

This was true; however, most people also wouldn't have been fucked on three bags of dope and besides, *later* was all I was looking for. If I could just manage to make it down the street before a kidney fell out of my ass—*later* would be perfect.

I ignored all offers of assistance and kept walking towards the subway. As I descended the staircase, I felt a sudden pain in my lower back which would remain until I was able to return to the hotel and stretch out in bed. By around 7 p.m. I'd made it back to the West Side Inn, and after a few hours I fell into a deep sleep that went undisturbed even after Perry returned from the studio.

By the very next morning the heroin had completely worn off and I became one with the pain. It was so intense that before heading off to work I booted, which was a first as I always considered shooting dope to be an *after* school activity. But Mondays were typically slow and since I took half my usual dosage, I was certain I'd make it through the shift without incident.

I arrived at Texas Grill at 10 a.m. to commence with opening sidework. Then at noon, just after the first customer of the day was seated in my station, Denise walked into the restaurant. She looked bad. I hadn't seen her in four months and she'd gone from cute, slim, and sexy—to chubby, oily, and blemished and it looked as if she could've fallen victim to Jeff's darker side. Even though most addicts tended to *lose* weight, it wasn't unheard of to occasionally encounter a chunky-junky who, like Jake from jail, had gotten hooked on Milky Ways as well.

"Hey Craig," she said as she came over to the bar where I was awaiting my customer's Heineken. "How've you been?"

She seemed nervous and distracted.

"Fine," I said. "How's it going with you?"

"I'm pretty good," she said while looking at me with a strange expression. "Hey…are you high?"

"No," I said firmly.

"Yes you are."

"No, I'm not."

"I'm not stupid, you know," she said. "Christ! I have a nursing degree. I can tell you're fucked up. I need you to score for me."

"Are you fucking crazy? Forget about it."

"Please, Craig!"

No way. I'm not gonna do it. Shit, people's lives are depending on her! And besides, I already dodged one bullet of responsibility with Katrina, and now that she's safely tucked away in Georgia there's just no way in hell I'm gonna be responsible for this bitch's fate.

"I'm not copping for you, Denise," I told her. "I'm not high, and when I get a hold of Jeff I'm gonna kick him in his ass."

"How can you say you're not high when you're standing there with your eyes closed?!" she said as her voice grew louder. "You're a liar—just like Jeff! A fucking liar!"

"Would you please shut up and get out of here before you get me fired?" I asked. I then tried the, *I quit using and can't risk putting myself in that kind of environment again*, excuse.

"YOU ARE SUCH A MOTHERFUCKING LIAR!!!" she once again announced to the restaurant.

"Denise, I swear to God, I'm not high. Don't you think they would fire me if I came into work all fucked up?"

Without answering the question, she stormed out of the restaurant—and about 20 seconds later I was fired for nodding off at the service bar.

82

Looking back at the final years of my addiction I remember that, in many ways, life was simpler. It was either black or white. I was either scoring or had scored. Everything else was barely on the periphery, if at all. Of course, there were isolated moments when the horror of it all had crept into my consciousness, but by that point my ability to look the other way had become the stuff of legends. If such thoughts occurred during a sober moment, I simply postponed them for reconsideration later because I knew they would fade away with the help of another fix. And if at some point I felt uncertain about carrying on like a stone-cold junky, then all I had to do was tap into a reservoir of ego that was specifically maintained for just such an occasion.

"Hey, I listened to that tape you gave Jeff. You guys are really good...No, I'm fucking serious! I don't usually like demo tapes but I mean it—you guys are really, really good."

Honestly, if I heard something like that once—I heard it a thousand times. Now, however, the CD was practically finished, and I was sure I was about to have my cake and eat it too.

But you're a junky.

"It doesn't matter, we're gonna be famous."

Yeah, but you've been living like a crackhead for years.

"It doesn't matter, we're gonna be famous."

But you fucked up Catherine's promotional plans.

"It doesn't matter, the cream always rises to the top and besides—we're gonna be famous."

One of the best examples of my ability to ignore the gravity of it all occurred in mid-April, when I blew off the community service I was ordered to complete as a result of my arrest on March 1st. To this day, I can't explain what I was thinking. Perry—of course—warned me, and somewhere in the back of my mind I knew that if I didn't report to the park they'd eventually come looking for me. But even as a fugitive from justice, I simply spiked a vein and was magically able to look the other way as I reasoned that the police had bigger fish to fry. Within a week, however, a knock at the door was heard, and I was carted away for an impromptu get-together with an irate judge who was floored by what she interpreted as my blatant disregard for the city's judicial system.

"Alright Mr. Goodman, I don't know who you *think* you are exactly—but drug addicts are not afforded any special privileges in this courtroom. So let me make this perfectly clear to you: You are hereby sentenced to appear in Central Park on the morning of May 5th to begin three days of community service. This is **not** an option. I strongly suggest you make an appearance because if you don't, when I see you again you'll be with us for an extended stay."

On May 5th I reported to the park where I, along with a crew of mostly addicts, was ordered to "help relocate the park's homeless campers." Essentially, this was a euphemism for gathering up their belongings, carting them off to dumpsters, and then re-directing the "campers" to city shelters while they tried to kill you. In order to complete the sentence I had taken three days off from Bella Luna, an Italian restaurant on the Upper West Side, where I was somehow hired immediately following my dismissal from Texas Grill.

After my final hour of executing park evictions, I decided to take advantage of the night off and pay Jeff a visit since I was in the area and hadn't seen him in months. When I arrived at his building he buzzed me upstairs, and as I entered the apartment I could see he was in the midst of entertaining a very young, very beautiful, Asian woman.

"Hey brother," Jeff said as I sat down on the couch. "This is Li."

Li said "Hi" which seemed to be the extent of her English.

"OK, now baby," Jeff said with more affection than I thought him capable off. "I'll see you later."

He then gave her a very tender kiss, walked her out, and then turned to me.

"She is such a cutie, isn't she?" he asked me.

"Yeah. Why don't you leave her alone?"

"Why? She really digs me and I think she wants us to spend some time together."

"Because you ruined Denise's life and all *she* ever wanted to do was fuck you."

"Listen," he said. "Denise is cool and everything and I'm always up for a party and shit, but if I get into a serious relationship there's only one thing I expect from the other person and *she* just doesn't have it."

"Oh, and what's that, Jeff? A dick?"

"A little self control!" he answered. "You leave to cat-sit and I no sooner get rid of one fucking junky—I've got another one on my hands. Only this one can't even score for herself. Every few days she came over here asking me to cop for her, and then she actually started showing up with her friends! Eventually, *they* all realized what they were getting themselves into and stopped bothering me, but not Denise. I actually had to yell at her and tell her never to come back again. Nothing personal, Craig, but I just can't have this crazy shit in my life anymore. And besides, you know, I'm more into Asian chicks."

"Well, the last time I saw her she was a mess."

"Hey, man—look, I know," he said with a sad reflection. "And what's fucked up about it is that the day you left, I actually decided it was good time to quit using. But about a week after that Denise and I got drunk, and she caught me snorting my leftover stash in the bathroom… And she wouldn't take no for an answer."

Incidentally, a *real* junky would never have "leftover stash in the bathroom," especially after quitting, which further supported my theory about Jeff's superhuman immunity to *real* addiction.

"So you gave her a bag of dope?!"

"Not that it's any of your fucking business, junky, but no—*I didn't give her a bag of dope!*" he said sounding somewhat offended. "She snatched it out of my hand…which fucking pissed me off because I only had two left and wanted them both for myself."

"Have you seen her recently?"

"She took-off two weeks ago," he said as he looked away.

"Where to?"

"Back home to Maryland."

"Did she get fired from the hospital?"

"I don't know, man," he said. "God, I hope not. Everybody already wants to kill me as it is."

83

On May 10th, Nick was able to secure a freebee at the studio in order for us to finish mixdown. Remarkably, during the previous session and in one of those extremely rare instances of productivity, we managed to mix seven of nine tracks. However, time ran out before we could fully complete "Valentines" and "Living in the Land of the Lilies," and this next session would clearly be our last opportunity to finish the project. The budget was spent, and Catherine had already scheduled manufacturing processes to begin as the tapes and artwork were due at a company called Ballistic Communications by the following day. Apparently, Catherine was still determined to have things ready for a promotional campaign, at which point she would attempt to convince college radio stations to include the CD on their playlists. The campaign would commence on June 1st, which was just in the nick-of-time for the CD to be heard by no one as the campuses, dorms, and student unions would already be abandoned for the summer.

Since the session would be complimentary, it would have to occur on a Sunday at midnight. It would also have to forge ahead without the help of Nick, who would be there only long enough to unlock the door and let us in as the graveyard session wouldn't conclude until well passed his bedtime. Though *I* was free for the evening, Perry was scheduled to work the dinner shift at The Boulevard. Nonetheless, he agreed to meet me at Fast Trax by no later than 12:30 a.m.

I had initially planned on scoring at The Laundromat; however, I was still smarting from the downtown arrest of two months prior, and the recent stint of community service only helped freshen the memory. As a result, at around 7 p.m. I decided to take advantage of the lingering daylight and venture up to Harlem. When I arrived at 125th Street, however, addicts were in the process of going to jail, and with the unexpected police presence I decided to take my chances further south.

I walked over to 111th Street, and the abandoned brownstone looked the same as it did when Perry first introduced me to the location back in October. Unfortunately, after stepping inside the building it didn't take long to realize that for some reason, the dealer was nowhere to be found. Soon enough, however, a baton-wielding reason came strolling in.

"What the fuck are you doing in here," the cop said to me and then immediately called for backup.

Think fast, Craig, think fast… But don't look like your thinking fast.

"Oh…I'm, uh—looking for maintenance work," I said as I pretended to peruse several official-looking documents plastered to a wall. "But I can't find the landlord's contact information."

"It's right there," the officer said with some suspicion.

"Right where?"

"Right where you're pretending to look."

At that precise moment we were interrupted by a very obvious-looking crackhead who was now on a hunt for dope, and happened to have wandered in through a back entrance. His appearance alone was enough for the cop to pounce, and the moment the wretch was searched, four rocks were quickly uncovered. Even though crack wasn't sold out of that location, the discovery was sufficient enough to send **both** of us to jail.

"You almost had me fooled there for a minute," the cop said to me as backup arrived.

I was charged with *trespassing*; however, in order to better justify an arrest he tacked on *intent to purchase illegal narcotics.* Although he was, of course, correct in his assumption, I was offended by the circumstances under which the added allegation was made, which enabled him to send me to jail on a trumped-up charge without a stitch of evidence to support it. There were no dealers in the vicinity, no drugs or needles in my possession, and I'd never been arrested in Harlem before; so, why should he automatically assume that my reason for being there was to score? Regardless of the lack of evidence, I was going to jail and as a result would once again be absent from the studio.

Within a few minutes a van loaded with junkies, crackheads, and drug dealers arrived to collect us. As I stepped inside the vehicle, I was surprised to find Crackhead Jim chained to the other "passengers" and sitting on one of the benches that lined either side of the van.

"Dude!" he exclaimed the moment he saw me, and before I could even acknowledge his presence he suddenly spilled his guts with some very disturbing news.

"My girlfriend's dead," he told me.

"What do you mean?!?

"What did I just say?!"

"So you're in here for murder?"

"No, I got busted on 125th."

"Oh," I said. "Sorry to hear that—I mean, about your girlfriend. What the fuck happened?"

"She OD'd!" he said as if I should've known.

"When?"

"I don't know," he said looking at his Swatch. "But I found her about an hour before I got busted."

Apparently, Crackhead Jim was so grief stricken by the tragic loss of his girlfriend, that he immediately sought comfort in the arms of two rocks and a bag of dope. And rather than first informing the proper authorities about her passing, he instead headed out to score while her body now grew colder and stiffer as he told the tale. Of course, I'm sure he had some completely fucked up reason for letting her death remain a secret, but I didn't have the courage to ask.

After checking in at the local precinct, we were then re-loaded onto a van headed for Central Booking. I sat there next to Crackhead Jim, silently cursing the fact that I would be unable to attend mixdown, and noticed a dirty, white, addict sitting across from us and nodding—*and I was jealous as hell.*

"I wish **I** had a chance to tap a vein before **I** got busted," I mentioned to Crackhead Jim while gesturing to the dope fiend.

"He isn't nodding," Jim informed me. "He's passing out. His mother died last week and he's been up for five days blowing his inheritance on crack."

Even so, I thought that unconscious was definitely the way to go.

As the crackhead drifted off, his neck began to slowly bend to the right until his head bobbed just above the shoulder of an already miffed Hispanic drug dealer seated next to him. Fortunately, at the last possible moment before any head-to-shoulder contact was made, an internal alarm would sound and the crackhead's neck straightened out—but only to begin the sequence anew. After about three or four minutes, however, his warning system began to fail as his neck finally gave way and permitted his head to land gently on the drug dealer's shoulder. It was actually a very tender moment, especially in a police van, though not everyone seemed to agree.

"Yo—get the fuck offa me muthafucka!" the drug dealer said as he jerked his shoulder upward.

"Oh, shit—I'm sorry," the roused crackhead said, but within 20 seconds his head was back on the same shoulder.

"I'm not playin' around witchoo, man!" the dealer warned him. "Get the fuck off me!"

"Oh shit! I'm really sorry, man, **really** sorry," was again the reply.

Unfortunately, the same thing happened again. This time, however, as contact was made the drug dealer sprung to his feet, and even though our wrists were shackled together he still managed to get off several solid shots to the sleepy crackhead's face.

My jealousy evaporated.

The sleepy crackhead was now fully revived, as blood started oozing out of several gashes in his cheek and forehead. Though he did his best to minimize the injuries and stop the flow of blood, he met with little success.

After we arrived at Central Booking, a cop opened the back door of the van and was confronted by a significant amount of blood and the crackhead's extensive injuries.

"Who did this to you?" the cop asked.

"Nobody."

"I *know* somebody in there hit you."

"Don't worry about it."

The crackhead knew better than to snitch because even though the cops wouldn't hesitate to slap the drug dealer with an assault charge, they also wouldn't hesitate to let him loose in the jail's general population after doing so.

I was in police custody for about 20 hours before I met my attorney. He was fresh out of law school, principled, and under the misconception that providing me with a competent defense would actually make a difference.

"We shouldn't plead guilty to any of this," he said. "They've got nothing."

"Forget about it," I said with disgust. "It's not gonna change anything and they're gonna do what they want anyway. Let me just plead guilty and get this shit over with as quickly as possible."

"Plead guilty to what?" he asked incredulously. "There were no signs prohibiting anyone from entering the building, there were no drugs or paraphernalia in your possession, and there wasn't even a dealer on the premises."

"And your point?"

"My point is that they can't *prove* anything. We'll go in there and plead *not guilty*. They'll schedule a hearing, release you, and then I'll take care of everything else. Just make sure you show up for court."

"Yeah, OK—whatever."

About two hours later I was led to a courtroom and did as instructed, but without any real conviction or interest in the proceedings. I was consumed by only my emerging withdrawal symptoms and the fact that I'd missed final mixdown over nothing other than police suspicion. Regardless, the hearing was scheduled for July 15th.

I was released at around 9 p.m. on Monday evening, and after visiting The Laundromat I returned to the West Side Inn. When I arrived, Perry was missing and I decided to give Nick a call to see how things had transpired at the studio in my absence.

"How'd it go last night?" I asked him the moment he answered.

"What do you mean?"

"What do you mean, *what do I m*ean?"

"Nobody showed up."

"Perry didn't stop by?"

"Nope," he said. "I waited there until one, and then gave you guys a call but nobody answered the phone. I assumed you decided you were happy enough with the last two tracks as they were, so I dropped the tapes off at Ballistic this afternoon."

Without another word, I slammed the phone down and started cursing. Of course, I wasn't angry with Nick because the tapes had to be at Ballistic that day, finished or not. However, this did little to mitigate the fact that the final product was now compromised. Although seven of the tracks were clean, balanced, and virtually flawless, "Valentines" was far from crisp and "Living in the Land of the Lilies" sounded like it was recorded in a can—and it broke my heart. Now I would break Perry's face. Unfortunately, when I awoke on Tuesday morning he was still nowhere to be found.

That junky motherfucker! He gets himself all fucked up, blows-off the session, and now he just happens to be missing in action. OK. FUCKING FINE!!!

I placed a call to Gary Reinstein at Ballistic Communications. Gary was charged with overseeing this stage of the project, and I needed a moment of his time because there were going to be some changes. I decided that if all aspects of the recording were ultimately my responsibility, and everyone else was willing to let things slide—then fuck it; they were all expendable and I wanted there to be some indication of that on the disc.

"What are the changes?" asked Gary.

Though initially intended to be a self-titled debut, I told Gary that the CD itself should be given a name.

"Do me a favor," I told him. "On the cover, just beneath 'Sections,' I want you to print the words, 'For Now.'"

I realized that "For Now" was as good a name as any, because it was the title of the first track—*and* because it now perfectly defined Perry's involvement with the band.

Unfortunately, I didn't stop there. Just for good measure and because I was feeling particularly spiteful, I had any mention of Matt's name completely deleted.

"Hey man, by the way," Gary said. "Nick just dropped off the masters yesterday and a lot of us really dig you guys. But I've been around the industry for a while now, and uh, well, you know—"

"Spit it out, brother," I said.

"The acknowledgement you wrote for the insert is maybe… a little inflammatory."

"What are you talking about?"

And then he read my very own words back to me:

"'Additional thanks go to the Delancey Street Clinic for convincing me to bypass methadone and remain faithfully addicted to heroin, New York City's Legal Aid Society for keeping us out of jail and in the studio—most of the time, Dr. Wendel for keeping Perry's drug-ravaged heart beating long enough to see the completion of the disc and last, but not least, the former members of Sections for calling it quits so we could get a real band."'

"Craig, I really think you need to tone this down a little," Gary recommended. "I mean, I like some of it. It's very rock & roll and everything, but this kind of stuff is gonna scare away the big labels and eventually, that's who you really wanna get a deal with. And besides, I know that Catherine isn't going to be happy with it either."

Apparently, contrary to popular opinion, record companies *don't* like signing heroin addicts to recording contracts.

"Fine, at this point I don't even care anymore," I said. "Delete what you want but keep as much of it in tact as possible."

"Will do," he said. "As soon as we make the glass master, we'll send the proofs over to you and Catherine for approval."

I disengaged with Gary and later that evening Perry finally appeared. But before I had a chance to berate him for blowing off the session, he informed me of the new milestone.

"Sixty-three hours in the system," he announced. "A new world record."

84

During the first week of June, Catherine packed a few bags of clothes, a box of CD's, and a list of college radio stations to visit before heading out to promote *For Now*. Perry then packed a few bundles of dope, a box of syringes, and a bottle of meth and decided to join her. As a result, I was left alone at the hotel for about four weeks while they trekked westward through college towns en route to their ultimate destination—Pittsburgh. It was there where Catherine determined she could get the biggest bang for her buck, as the city and surrounding area hosted a number of universities and colleges.

While they were on the road trying to generate a buzz, I became engulfed in a cloud of self-medicated complacency. The CD was finally finished and now I could sit back, relax, stay profoundly fucked up and wait for my future to begin. In the meantime, however, safely scoring on the streets of Manhattan had become next to impossible. Angelina's was long gone, Hell's Kitchen was sanitized, The Laundromat had been raided, the area around Beth Israel was barren, the East Village was a police trap, and I couldn't set foot in Harlem without the dealers *thinking* I was a cop and the cops *knowing* I was a junky. As a matter of fact, buying heroin in Manhattan had become so complex that before Perry headed out west, we actually resorted to scoring near the Grand Concourse in the Bronx. Of course, Giuliani was dubbed *Drug Crusader Extraordinaire*, as he dedicated a sizeable chunk of the city's resources to eliminating the scourge. Unfortunately, the trains were now filthy because you never get something for nothing and quite frankly—I felt cheated by the fiscal refiguring.

In any event, once Perry left for Pittsburgh I realized that I lacked testicles large enough to fly solo in the Bronx. As a result, the only remaining spot that wasn't necessarily an arrest waiting to happen was Houston Street, which was still risky and precisely where I was caught swallowing my stash a few months earlier. Even with the unpleasant memory, however, the day after Perry departed I found myself slithering around the area.

For about fifteen minutes I searched for a dope dealer. Then, as I made a right onto Clinton I noticed someone running in my direction. However, he wasn't exactly running, and as he came closer I could tell he was actually skipping along the sidewalk. I soon realized it was Crackhead Jim and that he'd apparently lost his mind, as he continued to bounce down the block while waving to passing strangers—just like a little kid starved for adult attention.

"Hey crackhead!" I blurted out as he almost skipped right by.

"Dude! What's up?" he said.

"I'm trying to score," I told him. "I've been walking around here for fifteen minutes and I can't find a fucking thing."

289

"No shit, dude! It took me an hour but I finally copped a bundle," he said which helped explain his insanely joyful demeanor.

Crackhead Jim was kind enough to sell me a couple of bags from his stash and I immediately got out of the area. After returning to the West Side Inn, I darted into a downstairs bathroom to get off, and while loading the syringe I detected the presence of someone in the adjacent stall.

"Is that downtown shit?" the stranger asked as I caught him peering over the wall. With some anxiety I stopped what I was doing and carefully responded.

"What the fuck are you looking at, dickface?!"

"Don't worry, man. I've been standing here for ten minutes trying to take a piss," he said, which was a subtle way for him to identify himself as a junky because dope usually makes peeing more trouble than it's worth. "You know, you don't have to go downtown to score. There's a spot on 106th and Columbus—and it's not *nearly* as hot."

"That's good to know," I said, not sure what to make of my new acquaintance. He did look familiar, however, and I could only assume that we had frequented some of the same dope spots. Regardless, it was odd to find another junky living at the West Side Inn because of its cost of lodging, which vastly exceeded that of a flophouse or what a typical addict could afford. But Richard Greenberg was hardly typical, and in between fixes he attended Columbia University's prestigious medical school.

While Perry was away, the doctor and I rapidly developed a meaningful friendship as each night we nodded off together in my room. It may not seem like much, but it was about the best a couple of newly acquainted junkies could hope for. Eventually, I would learn that the doctor was failing miserably after only his first semester of medical school. Of course, he knew it was just a matter of time before his doting parents discovered his fall from grace and the jig was up, but in classic junky fashion he decided to look the other way and enjoy the plummet while daddy was still paying the bills. Actually, it was a terribly sad situation.

"I really would've loved to have studied contagious diseases," he once told me in a moment of somber reflection as he mourned the death of his unborn medical career. "It's always been one of my favorite subjects."

"Why don't you study the subject of drug addiction?" I jokingly suggested.

"That wouldn't work out either, I'm afraid."

"Then why not *become* the subject of a study about drug addiction?" I said with a grin while trying to lighten the mood.

The mood didn't lighten, and within a few weeks the doctor disappeared from the hotel.

85

Perry and Catherine returned to New York during the first week of July. Apparently, even though it was summer, the CD was well received and supposedly getting some airplay.

But if a tree falls in a forest and there's no one there to hear it, does it actually make a sound?

Though I was quick to criticize the promotional effort, I was also quick to embrace its positive results as justification to continue along in my opiate-infused version of reality. It seemed I could finally relax and patiently wait for the excitement to unfold. Unfortunately, my complacency with the situation ended the moment I was fired from Bella Luna for being a junky, or at least looking like one. Although I was never provided with a specific reason for the dismissal, I knew that my lifestyle was visibly taking its toll, and the effects were more noticeable on certain days than others.

After getting booted from the restaurant, I skulked back to the hotel and worried about the immediate future. Rent was due within a couple of days and I was almost completely broke. Of course, Perry would support my drug habit until I found another job, but I knew he wasn't making enough money to pay the rent entirely by himself.

When I got back to the room Perry was there, nodding on one of the beds.

*Shit, I don't wanna tell him I got canned. He goes out on the road with Catherine to promote the disc, and then comes right back to work while I get fucked up and fired. What the fuck is wrong with me? Why can't I hang on to a job when he does twice as much dope and still manages to hold it together? I'm such a fucking loser and now I'm down to 20 bucks and two bags of dope. **WHAT THE FUCK AM I***

GONNA DO?!?!

"Hey, Gina's place is empty and we can stay there for free," Perry suddenly blurted out.

IM GONNA TAP A VEIN, STRETCH OUT, AND RELAX!!! THAT'S WHAT I'M GONNA DO!!!

Apparently, Gina had finally found someone willing to impregnate her, and before he had a chance to come to his senses she immediately whisked him away to some desolate, southwestern town. The sudden relocation required Gina to pay for three remaining months on her lease, but she felt the pros vastly outweighed the cons. Now, there would be nothing other than an occasional cactus or a rolling patch of tumbleweed to distract the father of her future offspring from staying on course. So, before the next week's rent was due, Perry and I vacated the West Side Inn and headed to Gina's apartment in Sunnyside.

Although we were forced to sleep on the floor of a virtually barren apartment with no hot water, electricity, or phone service—I felt like I was living the life of a rock star. While each day Perry continued to work at The Boulevard, I remained unemployed and medicated in the dark apartment. There, I spent my days alone in a nodding reverie of self-satisfaction until Perry returned, at which point I booted again as we then sat around and discussed how fabulous we were.

On the morning of July 15th I awoke and realized I was expected to make an appearance in court to address the trumped-up trespassing charge. But to be quite frank, even the *notion* of acknowledging the allegation infuriated me. From my standpoint, police tendencies to play fast and loose with the rules were bolstered by the blind eye of a legal system that encouraged them to do so. As a result, this enabled the cop to send me to jail, rather than issue a summons as he would have under virtually any other trespassing scenario. Most infuriating of all, however, was the fact that my incarceration compromised the quality of the CD as it went to print without ever being completely mixed down.

As far as I was concerned, I held the moral high-ground as the cops and courts were partners in crime, and I refused to dignify the former's behavior by responding to the latter's decree. Since the system had irretrievably wasted my time and effort, I had little difficulty returning the favor by imposing my own version of the Code of Hammurabi, with an eye for an eye and a tooth for a tooth. Consequently, I blew off the scheduled court date and as a result, a warrant would soon be issued for my arrest.

*But you really **were** looking for heroin because you're a junky, and everyone knows it.*

"It doesn't matter, we're gonna be famous."

But your lawyer said you'd beat the charges.

"It doesn't matter, we're gonna be famous."

Douche bag! This isn't like blowing off community service. Failing to appear in court is some serious shit!

"It doesn't matter, we're gonna be famous, and I'll worry about it later."

86

As the summer continued in much the way it began, my life followed suit as each day I awoke in Gina's apartment and tapped a vein. By this point, however, there was a warrant issued for my arrest for failing to appear in court to address the *trespassing* and *intent to purchase* charges that had gotten the whole ball rolling to begin with.

On a more positive note, in August Catherine gleefully informed Perry that we were "number one in Pittsburgh." Though I think she was being deliberately frugal with the details, according to at least one college radio station broadcasting to a summertime audience of approximately zero, "The Wish" was receiving more airplay than any other independently-released single. But regardless of the listenership, as far as I was concerned—number one was number one, and that only better enabled me to look the other way. Unfortunately, however, things would soon be taking a decidedly ominous turn.

By the end of August, Perry's heart was once again turning into vegetable matter. Accordingly, on September 18th he was slated to begin another six-week regimen of antifungal medications at Lenox Hill Hospital. In the meantime I had remained in a fog, unemployed, and determined to ride the gravy train until the last possible second. Then, much to my disappointment, on September 16th Perry took a leave of absence from The Boulevard and by the following day we were completely broke. So, after living off of Perry for months, I finally decided to rise to the occasion and do what anyone else would under such dire circumstances: I gathered up whatever worthless crap Gina left lying around the apartment and had a yard sale.

Most notable among this fine collection of consumer goods were oven mitts, a variety of porcelain figurines, refrigerator magnets, a paperweight, a can opener, a letter opener, 23 stuffed animals, some candles, cutlery and a cutting board, a fancy Zippo, several picture frames and a can of refried beans.

"Why don't you just go out and get a job you lazy fuck?" Perry suggested as I assembled my line of products. "Nobody's gonna buy a bunch of old and abandoned shit anyway."

"A bunch of old and abandoned shit to you—is a treasure trove of new and exciting shit to someone else," I countered. "And I will get a job...*tomorrow.*"

We set up shop right outside the building, and laid out the merchandise on a folding table that Gina had also left behind. Remarkably, within 45 minutes everything was sold, including the beans and the table which left us with about $40 each.

Early the next morning Perry grabbed his Les Paul before departing for the hospital. Mamma didn't raise no fool. He knew full well that the remaining proceeds from the yard sale wouldn't last more than another day, so before arriving for his 8 a.m. appointment at Lenox Hill he would first have to find his guitar a new home. Unfortunately, he failed to realize that the East Village pawn shop on Avenue D, chosen for its proximity to several dope dealers roaming the surrounding streets, wasn't open for business at 7 a.m. *No pawn shop is open for business at 7 a.m.* As a result, he would have no choice but to report to the hospital first, and then manage an escape a little later in the day. Not to be deterred, he took the #6 uptown to the hospital and checked in, and then waited patiently in his room until he felt the coast was clear enough to inconspicuously depart the premises. By 1:30 in the afternoon it was, and after grabbing his guitar and fleeing through a service exit he hopped in a cab heading south. Perry was certain the guitar would fetch at least $700 as it was in stellar condition, and that would be enough to see him through a six-week stint in the hospital. Unfortunately, his estimation was a bit off:

"Three hundred bucks?!?" Perry repeated back to the pawnbroker, flabbergasted by the lowball. "It's worth four times that!"

"That's the best I can do," said the pawnbroker, equally astounded by the haggling junky that stood before him in a hospital gown and with a catheter sticking out of his arm.

"It's a Les Paul, man, a **Les Paul** you filthy cocksucker!"

"Hey man, fuck you! Why don't you just take your business elsewhere?"

Perry probably would have done just that, had a dope dealer not been waiting outside of *this* particular pawnshop.

"Fine," Perry finally said as he collected the money and left the shop, but not before telling the pawnbroker to fuck his mother. He then stepped outside, spent most of the money on two bundles of dope, and then jumped in a cab heading back uptown to Lenox Hill.

As the taxi pulled out, he began fixing his dope in a spoon that was taken from a hospital lunch tray. But just as he was booting, the cabbie made a sharp right turn onto First Avenue causing Perry to drop the loaded syringe on the dirty, taxi-cab floor.

"Take it easy, man!" Perry shouted from the back of the cab, as he picked up the contaminated syringe and plunged it into his arm. "I've got a fucking heart condition."

In the meantime, I had already begun the painful task of finding a job. After two full days of searching, however, I was still jobless and beginning to feel the pressure, as my own $40 had evaporated with only a week-and-a-half left of rent-free living before Gina's lease expired. Although my living conditions had yet to completely bottom out, I was never as impoverished as I was during this period.

As the second day of fruitless job searches came to a close, I curled up on the cold floor of the dark apartment and began to worry. Of course, though I knew it would only be a matter of months before my monetary concerns resolved themselves, my inability to find a job and know exactly where the next bag of dope was coming from made it difficult to look the other way. Without this junky survival tool at my disposal and the onset of withdrawals only a day away, I was forced to come to terms with my sordid condition—but only to a certain extent.

In retrospect, this would have been the perfect opportunity for me to clean up my act and completely get my shit together. After all, *For Now* was getting some attention in Pittsburgh and if the summer was any indication of what was coming in the fall, we were well on our way. However, getting clean wasn't on the itinerary, and rather than eliminating the blight from my life I chose to work around it.

For really the first time during the course of my downward spiral,

I seriously addressed the fact that I looked like complete shit and would've grabbed a flashlight and mirror to confirm it—had I not sold both of them for a dollar. That was stupid. I definitely could've gotten a buck-fifty. Regardless, even without visual aid, I accepted the fact that I looked awful and had to acknowledge it as a continuing factor in relation to my unemployment woes. I realized that the highly sought after jobs in more prestigious restaurants were now off limits to me, and I would have to refine my search for unrefined eateries where lackluster positions were abundant due to the few souls desperate enough to accept them. Now, I had finally become one of those souls and the next few restaurants I worked in would reflect that. To the casual observer, it wasn't so much that I looked specifically like a junky, but I did have a vaguely unhealthy appearance. I was a little underweight, pastier than usual, and had dark circles around sunken eyes that peered-out over protruding cheekbones. Furthermore, my arms were beginning to look bad again. Since I usually tapped only one vein per day, I was able to avoid track marks; however, my arms were always covered in bumps, bruises and scabs. Even so, I felt that as long as they stayed covered, I'd eventually find a dump desperate enough to hire me.

The next day I awoke and mentally prepared a list of appropriate restaurants to investigate. But before commencing the job search, I had other issues to contend with. First and foremost on the list was the small matter of starvation, which supplanted the need to score only because I had several hours before withdrawals were due. Having spent most of the money generated from the yard sale on dope, I hadn't eaten anything substantial now in almost two days. So, with a rumbling belly I picked myself up off the makeshift bed of dirty blankets and sheets, got dressed, jumped the subway turnstiles, and made my way to the hospital. I had a feeling that Perry was somehow getting high while hording his daily dose of meth, and was confident I'd be able to ward of withdrawals *and* fill my gut with hospital fare in a single visit.

After arriving at Lenox Hill, I was directed to Perry's room and when I entered he was in the midst of a drug-related discussion with his roommate, Lawrence. Lawrence was black, in his early thirties, and was the first hospital roommate Perry felt he shared a common bond with. Like Perry, Lawrence had destroyed *his* body as well—but with booze instead of heroin—and after finally admitting himself into the hospital he'd been diagnosed with several, life threatening, alcoholism-related illnesses.

"Hey Craig," Perry said upon my entrance. "This is Lawrence."

"That's nice. Got anything to eat?"

"I've got this delicious chicken sandwich left over from lunch."

It was dry and cold but I didn't care and wolfed it down in seconds. Perry then handed me three methadone pills which confirmed the fact that he'd managed to score. Of course, I too would have preferred dope, but I knew that beggars couldn't be choosers and decided to shut my mouth, especially since I was already beginning to feel sick and a little meth was better than nothing at all.

"You can have this shit too, if you want," Lawrence then said to me as he held out two, darkly coated pills.

"What are they?"

"I don't know. Some bullshit they gave me so I wouldn't drink—but I don't like the buzz."

Apparently, the medically sanctioned remedy of substituting one addictive substance for another was used to treat drunks as well as junkies.

"But aren't you gonna be sick or something?" I asked.

"Na, your boy here got me a 40 when he made a run."

That got me thinking.

"Perry, did you pawn another fucking guitar?!" I decided to ask.

"No."

"Fucking liar."

"Don't worry about it," he said and attempted to change the subject rather than deal with my wrath or even worse, fork over some dope in retribution. "Try one of those pills Lawrence gave you."

I swallowed *both* pills, but if I wasn't so completely broke and thankful for what little charity was being offered I would have had a few words for Perry. Instead, I decided to remain silent, which became easier to do as I began to feel the effects of Lawrence's pills. I wasn't entirely sure what they were, but I grew quite fond of their opiate-like effect that also seemed to eliminate withdrawal symptoms as effectively as methadone. In fact, I was so impressed with the drug that I contemplated the pros and cons of alcoholism, as I clearly preferred the medicinal remedy for this dependency much more than my own.

For five days the routine went uninterrupted, as I showed up at Lenox Hill for Perry's lunch and Lawrence's pills before embarking on an unsuccessful search for employment.

"Why don't you just get on welfare," Lawrence suggested on day five while I rabidly consumed a dry-as-hell turkey sandwich.

"Are you fucking crazy? I would never go on welfare. That's for poor people," I said with a mouthful of free turkey and a poorly timed display of dignity.

"You mean *black* people."

"No, I mean *poor* people."

"Everyday you steal a ride on the subway just to come over here and eat your buddy's lunch meat. You look pretty fuckin' poor to me," Lawrence said. "Just because you're a white boy you don't think you're poor enough to go on welfare."

He was right and without admitting it, that was exactly what I thought. But why should I allow my whiteness to prevent me from getting a little free love from the government?

"You know—I would," I said, "but it'll be weeks before I see any money and I'll be dead by then."

"They'll give you emergency food stamps to get you through until they process the paperwork," Lawrence informed me.

I found out that Lawrence was right about everything. As luck would have it, a government building charged with the distribution of food stamps was located in Queens, not too from Gina's apartment. So, the very next day I completed the necessary paperwork, showed ID, and was provided with public assistance. I then proceeded to a Harlem bodega where I traded a hundred dollars in food stamps for $50 in cash—and purchased four bags of dope, a fresh set of works, two packs of smokes, and a slice of pizza.

87

On September 28th I was seriously beginning to feel the heat. Although thanks to Perry and Lawrence I remained fairly well nourished and avoided withdrawals, I was still unemployed and couldn't help but see the Whitehouse Hotel looming ahead.

"I can't check in to the Whitehouse, Perry."

"Sure you can," he said with a smile as the anti-fungal drip continued to drip.

"No, I can't. **You** don't understand."

"You can stay at Gina's until Friday, and then I'll give you ten bucks to pay for it with."

"Perry, it's not about the ten bucks," I said.

"Oh! Are you a rich, junky, white boy now?" Lawrence suddenly asked me.

"Go fuck yourself," I told him. By this point I'd already heard enough out of Lawrence and besides, he was to be discharged later that day and was of no further use to me. "Perry," I continued. "I have a *really* bad feeling about that place."

"What's wrong, Craig?" Lawrence opened his mouth again. "You don't like hanging out with poor white junkies? Didn't we just have a talk about poor folks the other day?"

"You don't like fucking yourself, Lawrence? Didn't we just have a talk about you fucking yourself?"

"Listen, Craig—I don't know what to tell you," Perry said, ignoring the bad blood that was boiling around him. "Why don't you stay with Jeff until you get a job and I get out of here? Then we'll be able to afford something decent. And Lawrence: There aren't only poor white junkies living at the Whitehouse. There's also crackheads, pedophiles and schizophrenics, and there are almost as many blacks as whites. "

"The last thing in the world Jeff needs right now is for me to be living with him," I told Perry, returning to the matter at hand.

"Well, then I think you might have to deal with the Whitehouse for a few weeks. It'll be temporary, trust me. Here's 40 bucks; go get some dope. They're back in business on 18th Street."

"OK. But the first thing I'm doing is finding a job. Getting high can wait until later."

The first thing I'm doing is finding a job? Getting high can wait until later? Did I actually just say that?

"Fuck that finding a job shit!" Lawrence shouted with just enough fake enthusiasm to really piss me off. "Just wait until those welfare checks start rollin' in. I know how you white people are."

"Perry, I think I'm gonna kill this motherfucker."

"Stay focused, Craig," he told me. "You were doing really well there for a second. Go find a job and then if you want, come back here and we'll celebrate."

Yes. Killing Lawrence would do nothing to improve my plight as there was already a warrant out for my arrest. Now was certainly no time for screwing around. Besides being a fugitive from justice—I was unemployed, addicted to dope, and on the brink of homelessness. I had to find a job and I had to find one fast.

I left the hospital, walked up to 96th Street and then over to Second Avenue before heading south and stepping into every restaurant along the way. I was determined to find something—*anything* before nightfall. If I had to, I would walk all the way to the Village and back until I found someone willing to hire me.

In an amazing stroke of last minute luck, I managed to get hired at the Gotham City Diner which was located on the Upper East Side and not far from the hospital. It was a surprisingly fancy restaurant decked out in silver, and when I entered a woman with blond hair in her early thirties was tending bar and serving customers that were still lingering around from lunch.

"Excuse me," I said to the woman behind the bar. "You guys wouldn't happen to be looking for wait staff, would you?"

"HELL YES!!!!" she said as she held out her hand. "My name's Amanda. I'm the manager. Can you work days?"

"Absolutely," I said, and as the manager was also playing bartender I had a feeling the job was going to be a disaster. However, I also realized it was better than nothing and that regardless of the job, it would be almost impossible to avoid at least a temporary stay at the Whitehouse. Unfortunately, I had a terrible premonition that if I did end up at the Whitehouse—I might never leave.

"What's the uniform?" I asked, though the question made my knees shake.

"Oh," she said with some concern. "It's kind of stuffy: black shoes, black pants and unfortunately a white, long-sleeved dress shirt. Is that gonna be alright?"

"It'll be fine. I happen to love long-sleeved dress shirts."

I agreed to return on the following Monday morning for training. Then, without any money to spare for the subway, I began the three mile trek downtown to score. It took me a little under an hour, and when I arrived I immediately recognized a short and scrawny dope dealer with an associate heading in my direction on 18th Street.

"Hey man, I need four," I said to the dealer as they approached.

"I don't care what you need, junky muthafucka!! Get the fuck outta my face! The police is **everywhere** you fuckin' bitch."

"Alright, man—chill the fuck out!" I told them as they passed.

300

"Fuck you!" he said looking back at me menacingly. "You're lucky if I don't come back there and kick your muthafuckin ass."

Dope dealing is—besides auto towing—perhaps the only business unencumbered by any level of customer service, or even a basic expectation of common courtesy. We'll keep coming back for more no matter what and they know it. Even so, I was somewhat floored by the hostility of this tiny, Hispanic, dope dealer.

"I'll pay you to give-it-a-go you little prick," I told him as he kept walking and I crossed over to the other side of the street. Normally, I wouldn't have been as bold to a drug dealer, let alone *two* drug dealers, but this guy was so nasty, aggressive, and *little* that I almost felt I had to beat him up just to save face. But obviously, his fears were well founded as a police car came cruising by at a speed that suggested its occupants knew exactly what was going on around them. I was then immediately reminded of my own legal issues and kept right on walking. Before leaving the area, however, my curiosity had gotten the better of me as I peered over my right shoulder hoping to catch a glimpse of them busting the little fucker. Then, just as I was turning my head, I noticed the dealer inconspicuously toss a paper bag containing his stash onto the curb next to a parked car.

As soon as the police made a left turn at First Avenue to attempt another pass I spun around, lowered myself, and then crept back across the street toward the parked car using it to shield myself from the dealer, who was by now a little further down the block. I then crawled under the rear bumper and, without revealing anything other than an outstretched arm, grabbed the bag.

Obviously, I expected to find several bundles of dope. However, after taking a peak inside, rather than several bundles of dope I found several bundles of cash. In fact, I would later discover that there was $1,760 to be exact.

As I crawled out from beneath the car and planned a quick escape, I giggled uncontrollably at the sight of the paper bag bursting with the drug dealer's money. Now, I simply needed to get across Second Avenue and out of the area without running into the cops *or* criminals. With that in mind I cautiously stood up, sprinted into the street and unfortunately, although I was able to completely avoid the drug dealers and police *officers*—I was mowed down by the police vehicle. Thankfully, the impact from this collision paled in comparison to the thrashing I took from that taxi on Broadway, and to be quite honest I wasn't even sure if the cops drove into me or I ran into them. All I knew was that for a variety of reasons I needed to get the fuck out of there.

After bouncing off the police car I hit the ground and immediately sprung to my feet. Then, without looking back I sprinted across Second Avenue with a swiftness I didn't think I was capable of. My pace remained constant as I crossed Third Avenue and then Irving Plaza where I was almost struck down again, this time by a truck. Finally, by the time I reached Park I was completely winded and flagged a cab heading north.

"Uptown, please," I told the cabbie in between breaths.

"Who you runnin' from?" he asked.

"I'm not exactly sure. Could be a few people."

As I gradually caught my breath I began to feel the exhilaration of the moment. I managed to fuck up not only the drug dealer, but the police as well by stealing his money and their evidence. In the process, I also evaded what would've been a motherfucker of an arrest, as I not only had an outstanding warrant—but had come dangerously close to getting busted for stealing the dope dealer's cash. Wouldn't that have been a hoot? Instead, I escaped with over $1700. It was like a gift from heaven. There would be no Whitehouse Hotel for me, by God, and as far as the dope dealer was concerned—well *fuck him*. If he gets his ass kicked for losing the money, so be it. He was just another asshole drug dealer and it comes with the territory. Besides, this was just a small, symbolic payback for helping me fuck up my life so badly.

Wait a minute. Did I just admit something I shouldn't?

Fortunately, I had over $1700 to help me look the other way and besides… I was *still* going to be famous.

88

"Hey, I'm coming into the city," I told Perry from a payphone. "You're not gonna believe this shit!!!"

"It's chicken salad or baked ham," he responded. "That's funny. You don't like chicken salad *or* baked ham, do you?"

"I don't need your fucking lunch. Listen to this: Yesterday—"

"There you go again," Perry interrupted. "Just like Lawrence said—acting all uppity and shit."

"Would you shut up for a second?"

"OK, what?"

"I stole over $1700 from the dope dealers yesterday."

"No you didn't."

"I sure as fuck did."

"That was a fucking retarded thing to do and you're gonna be a dead man," said the police informant. "I can't believe you're not dead already."

"It's not like I held them up or anything, stupid! I just swiped it while they weren't looking."

"Do they know it was you who took it?"

"Probably."

"Then you're *probably* gonna be a dead man. But before they find you I need you to go to 125th Street and visit your friend for me. Winston was just here, and he said there's some crazy shit going around that's been killing junkies in Harlem."

"What's it called?"

"911."

"That's almost funny. Did you try any?" I asked.

"I didn't get a chance. A minute after Winston got here my nurse took a look at him and threw him in a wheelchair. But he told me the dealer warned him to cut his dosage in half because two junkies had already OD'd."

"Well, did *he*?"

"No, but you know Winston, he's fearless—*and* stupid. Trust me. He said the shit was so strong he almost drove his cab into the river."

"Winston drove his cab into the river last month," I reminded him.

"Yeah, but this time he said it wouldn't have been his fault."

Ignoring that bit of junky reasoning, I immediately disengaged with Perry and headed directly to 125th Street to investigate the matter. But apparently, all preliminary reports regarding the dope's potency were accurate. The moment Arnold noticed me climbing out of the subway he started jumping up and down, and with his fists held high in the air he triumphantly shouted, **"THE SHIT IS KILLIN' NIGGAS!!!"** I could actually see tears of joy streaming down his face.

Now, for those still unsure about the guiding principles and value system embraced by this particular subset of the drug culture:

There is no product endorsement quite like that of a dead junky.

Within minutes, Arnold was able to locate the source of the incredibly deadly dope. I then jumped in a cab and headed to my little Polish diner to tap a vein.

I must say that 911 lived-up to the hype. However, having the wisdom and forethought acquired by tracing the steps of the *truly* courageous, Ponce De Leon-type junkies, I cut my usual dosage in half so I could live long enough to enjoy the buzz.

After I paid the check and stumbled out of the diner it hit me: that damned, false sense of well being. I suddenly decided that now would be the perfect time to deal with my legal issues. After all, things were going so well. We were getting airplay in Pittsburgh, and I'd found a job and even had some money in my pocket. My worries were clearly behind me. Feeling on top of the world, I headed to the criminal courthouse determined to confront the trespassing charge, as well as the resulting arrest warrant for failing to appear in court. I was impassioned, driven, and on a journey to absolution through accountability that could only be embarked upon by the truly high.

When I arrived at the venerable old building—a bastion of virtue, blind justice, and one overflowing with cops—I ditched my works and hid any remaining dope in a shoe. I then entered and made my way to a reception area. After showing ID, I was provided a copy of the relevant paperwork and directed to a courtroom on the third floor.

Though oblivious at the time, I had created a potentially explosive situation by simply being there in that condition. And, unlike the circumstances surrounding my arrest, I was now actually in possession of heroin and stumbling around a building filled with cops. I definitely should've realized I was in the wrong place at the wrong time.

But I was really, really, high.

I went upstairs to the assigned courtroom and was greeted by a police officer, who, after glancing over the paperwork, said the dockets were jammed and that I should come back at another time. Actually, he said, "We don't have time for this bullshit right now" and to "get the fuck out and come back later."

Later? What the fuck does that mean?

Given the existing arrest warrant, I pointed out that I may have already exhausted the "later" option. He then told me that if I didn't get out of his sight immediately he would arrest me again.

Might it be for trespassing?
I left the building before the irony of it all just killed me.

89

On September 30th I vacated Gina's apartment, and used a portion of the stolen drug money to secure a tiny, one-room studio being rented out of a basement in Jackson Heights for $500 per month. I then went into Manhattan and purchased four long-sleeved dress shirts and four bundles of that deadly dope, one of which I brought to Perry in the hospital.

On the very next day I reported to Gotham City at 10 a.m. to begin training for the lunch shift. Although I was expecting at least another waiter, none were present and I was immediately greeted by Amanda who was apparently managing the restaurant, tending bar, *and* waiting tables.

"Glad you showed up," she said with a strange smile.

"Why wouldn't I show up?"

"I don't know," she said. "But for some reason people just don't show up."

This place might be even worse than I thought.

"I'm not gonna lie to you," she went on. "This isn't the busiest restaurant in the city and the owner's a little bit of a douche, but we try to have fun. And each day you get $25 out of the register to help make up for things."

That was the clincher. Any restaurant willing to enhance the standard shift pay of $2.15 an hour couldn't be generating any significant business else they'd hardly be so generous. Obviously, the little bit extra paid under the table was intended to supplement a shortage of gratuities which are, of course, a waiter's primary source of income. But to be quite frank, this was of little concern to me. I had plenty of cash, the CD was finished, and now it was just a matter of time before my *real* destiny unfurled itself.

By 4 p.m. my training had concluded, and based on the way I handled the restaurant's one and only customer, Amanda was convinced that I was ready to strike out on my own.

"So I'll schedule you for lunches—Tuesday through Friday," she said. "Is that OK?"

"Perfect," I told her. "Are we done?"

"Yep. See you tomorrow."

Then, as I turned to leave she suddenly stopped me.

"Wait a second," she said as she peered out the window. "Here comes Stratis."

"What's *stratis*?"

"He's the owner," she said with veiled disgust. "Let's introduce you and get it over with."

"Now who's this?!?" Stratis bellowed as he entered the restaurant and strutted across the dining room.

"Stratis, this is Craig," Amanda said. "He's gonna be helping us out on days."

"That's great," he said with little interest and without stopping as he passed me on his way to the kitchen.

Stratis Morfogen had a head full of jet-black hair, was dressed in Brooks Brothers, and at around six feet tall I must admit he made a big impression—*which was that of a complete asshole.* I didn't like him from the moment I met him, and that feeling would only intensify with each encounter.

Stratis was about 30 years old, and from a family of successful restaurateurs that had owned and operated several establishments around Manhattan and Queens. And, despite the tired old tales he told of a childhood spent working in his father's restaurant for pennies-per-hour as he learned the value of a dollar, Stratis seemed much more like an overgrown, overindulged, spoiled-rotten brat that had grown up with a silver shovel in his mouth. But even with this I was well contented, and with all the dope and drug money awaiting me in Queens I was able to completely look away from the concerns that had erupted during the previous weeks. Yes, indeed—**everything** was going to be just fine.

I left Gotham and made connections to the #7 bound for Jackson Heights. Within a half-hour I stepped into my humble abode, booted, strapped on a set of headphones and listened to *For Now* as my nod eventually transformed itself into slumber. This would be my routine for the entire month of October while Perry remained attached to an anti-fungal drip at Lenox Hill. Unfortunately, however, though my drug use would go unabated, the earnings from Gotham were so paltry that I was constantly dipping into the stash of stolen money.

After paying rent on the morning of November 1st, I noticed that my vast fortune had suddenly dwindled down to a mere $75. I realized that once again my situation was near desperate, and a vague sense of rage and resentment began to simmer as I clearly saw the Whitehouse on the horizon. Just then, the phone rang.

"Hey, I'm out!!!"

It was Perry.

"Oh!!!" I shouted into the phone as I spotted a target to vent my wrath upon. "What are you out of **THIS TIME,** Perry?!? Drugs, money, *heart valves*? Want me to slaughter another fucking pig for you?! What else, Perry, what else can I possibly do for you?!"

"I'm **OUT OF THE HOSPITAL,** asshole!" he fired back.

"Oh yeah? For how long? A month? Two months? Maybe three?"

"Are you dopesick or something?" he asked.

"NO!!!"

"Are you fucked up?"

"**NO, PERRY—I'M NOT FUCKED UP!!!** I'm just pissed off and sick and tired of all the bullshit!"

"Why don't you boot a bag and relax…and then bring me one because I'm beginning to feel sick."

"Where are you?" I said with a disgusted sigh.

"At the Barnes and Noble on Astor."

"When'd you learn how to read?"

"Fuck you," he said, and then hung up the phone.

I left the apartment and boarded the train to Manhattan. Once there, I transferred to the #6 bound for 125th Street where I copped four bags of dope and two sets of works. Of course, my own personal gratification would wait for no one, so before heading downtown to meet Perry I made a stop at the Polish diner.

Although the dope was fine it did little to improve my disposition, and as I boarded the downtown train my life seemed to be teetering on the brink of disaster. I should have gotten another job the moment I realized Gotham City was a dead end, but with my pockets full of stolen drug money it was too easy to look the other way. Now I was almost completely broke. Even if I were to immediately find another restaurant job it would be at least a week before I'd be making any money and I'd never survive until then.

As I ascended from the subway at Astor Place, Perry was there to greet me.

"Where's my dope?" he immediately asked.

I openly handed him the drugs and a set of works without worrying about the prying eyes of passersby. He then headed into the store and darted into a bathroom while I waited by the magazine racks. Within two minutes he returned.

"The Boulevard fucked me over," he said.

"How?"

"They gave away my job."

"So you're homeless *and* jobless."

"Just jobless," he said. "Oh yeah, that reminds me. I need ten bucks."

"I just gave you two bags of dope!"

"Not for dope—for the hotel."

"Please don't tell me you're staying at the Whitehouse."

"Fuck no! I'm staying at The Sunshine. It's way nicer."

Imagine that, *nicer*—and all for the same ten dollars-a-day. Of course, The Sunshine Hotel was also in the Bowery, and it was about as sunshiny as the Whitehouse was presidential.

Since he wasn't working I gave him $20 which left me with ten.

"Have you heard from Catherine?" I asked.

"Not since I went back into the hospital."

"Well, have you tried to call her?"

"She hasn't been taking my calls," he said.

That set me off again.

"WELL WHAT THE FUCK HAS SHE BEEN DOING?!?"

"I don't know."

"Well then, **FUCK HER!** The CD's recorded and everything else will take care of itself," I said as that false sense of well being reared its ugly head again. "We don't need her anymore."

"Yes we do."

"Maybe you do, asshole, but I sure as fuck don't!" I said, not exactly sure what I meant but trying to sound as convincing as possible.

"Catherine owns the rights to the CD," he informed me.

"So?"

"So?!" he repeated back to me. "Let me explain something to you, Craig. Catherine's totally in control unless *she* decides otherwise. She has all the copies of the disc, and she's the only one with the money or the rights to legally print anymore. Trust me; *you* need her as much as anyone else does. Next time try reading the fucking fine print."

I was absolutely beside myself.

"I DON'T NEED HER! I DON'T NEED YOU! I DON'T NEED ANYONE!!!" I actually screamed out loud.

"Yes, Craig—I know. You are truly a self-sustaining organism and I step back in awe of you. Unfortunately, you signed a contract."

"Wow! How about that, Perry? *A self-sustaining organism*...Nine consecutive syllables and not even a grunt. Very impressive! But let's not forget that *I'm* the hot commodity here, and for giving you a chance at something beyond your own miserable existence you turned me into a worthless fucking junky!" I shouted, noting my own remarkable ability to claim both sides of the spectrum, and all within the span of a single sentence.

Now it was clearly time to go home and I did just that.

On the following morning I left my apartment and headed to Gotham City. When I arrived at 10 a.m. I was confronted by a dark and empty restaurant as Amanda met me at the door.

"Hey Craig," she said with a big smile. "I have some great news for you!"

"What's that?"

"The power's out and you get to have the day off."

"Oh, that's fantastic!" I said with feigned enthusiasm. "So in other words, you're telling me that I'll be spending the day *at home* and not be making any money—as opposed to spending the day *in here* and not be making any money."

"Exactly!" she said with a giggle, apparently misinterpreting the sentiment behind my sarcasm.

"That's fucking great, Amanda," I said and then left the restaurant. Of course, I would've been concerned that the smartass response might garner my immediate dismissal, had I not recognized the extreme unlikelihood of them finding another loser desperate enough to fill the void.

As I wandered toward the subway with four dollars in my pocket, I experienced the sudden, often short-lived realization that most addicts awaken to when they're truly out of options:

I've got to kick. I have no money, no prospect of having any money, no heroin, no meth, and no choice.

Although I wasn't feeling sick just yet, I knew the onset of withdrawals was only hours away and determined that the best course of action was to try to sleep through as much of it as possible. With that in mind I headed back to Jackson Heights, and after exiting the subway station I stepped into the nearest convenience store to buy a newspaper—and to steal a bottle of Tylenol PM.

At just after 11 a.m., as I crossed the threshold of my apartment, I could already begin to feel the sweats erupting. That was enough for me. I popped open the bottle of Tylenol and swallowed ten capsules. As I lay there praying for sleep to overwhelm me, I began to feel my throat swell which I attributed to the massive dose of medication. Then, I passed out…*for almost twelve hours.*

At around 11 p.m., I sat up in bed and vomited in complete darkness. I took a deep breath, tried to clear my head, and then several convulsive heaves followed until my clothes were saturated, and my mattress was nothing short of a sponge soaked in stomach fluid.

"Holy fucking shit," I said panting, as the deluge appeared to have subsided.

Unfortunately, I knew things were just getting underway as another vulgar discharge began to assemble itself within. I immediately jumped up, ran into the little bathroom located just outside my room, and then lowered my head over the toilet bowl. Within seconds I again began heaving uncontrollably, but nothing came forth other than a series of guttural groans. My body was clearly calling the shots now, and the fruitless purge continued until I felt something become unstuck in my bowels. Without a second to spare, I flipped sides and the same sickness began pouring out of my ass. I took another deep breath and tried to collect myself.

"God, it's fucking hot in here," I said aloud as a syrupy perspiration seemed to exude from every pore.

I rose to my feet, ripped off the vomit-laden clothes still clinging to my body, and then stepped into the bedroom to look at the thermostat. It read 68 degrees but my body was on fire. Beyond that my legs had cramps and my skin was becoming super-sensitive, as each time I tried to rub away the soreness it felt like daggers were digging into my flesh.

After swallowing another handful of pills I returned to the bathroom, stepped in the shower, sat down and pulled my knees to my chest as cool water trickled down over my burning body. I then turned on my side and eventually passed out in the fetal position. Sometime later I awoke in much the same way, except for the fact that I was now *freezing*.

With cramps now overwhelming my lower half, I crawled out of the shower and into the bedroom where I wrapped myself in the last vestiges of a laundered wardrobe. Then, without thinking, I returned to my vomit-drenched mattress. It took about ten minutes for a wool sweater to fully absorb the puke and for me to realize what I just did to myself.

I started to cry.

"I'm not gonna make it," I sobbed, overcome by my own degradation. "There's just no way I'm ever gonna make it through this."

As I lay there soaking up vomit and freezing, I tried to calculate how long it would be before the dopesickness ran its course. Since it was just beginning to brighten-up outside, I assumed it was around 6 a.m. which meant there were at least another 24 hours of this to look forward to. I then rose from the bed, undressed, and dragged myself to the laundry basket for a vomit-free ensemble. Unfortunately, before I made the wardrobe change I felt another explosion about to ignite—though I had no idea from which orifice it would come. I ran back into the bathroom and just to be on the safe side, jumped in the shower to eventually vomit. I then sat on the tiled floor, shivering, and watched my fluids disappear down the drain. I wanted to follow them.

I was amazed at the volume of liquid my body had expelled and was exhausted and dehydrated by the effort, but didn't dare take a sip of water for fear of beginning the sequence anew. After some time I rose and then slowly emerged from the shower once more.

I dressed myself in dirty laundry, staked-out a spot on the bedroom floor, and returned to the fetal position while trying to ignore the cramps that were slowly consuming me. At some point I began staring at my old, acoustic beater like it was a bag of dope, and soon decided that I'd had enough of the agony. Who was I trying to kid anyway? Besides, I realized that if I was ever going to quit, I'd have to do it with something other than cold turkey.

I'll go into the city and sell my guitar.

Although I could have mustered up enough strength to jump the subway turnstiles, I doubted my broken body would survive the landing. Furthermore, with the arrest warrant still looming, I realized I couldn't risk an encounter with law enforcement—especially in light of my sad physical shape and inability to flee the scene. Consequently, I gathered up what little change I had for train fare along with my guitar, a dirty needle, and whatever was left of my self respect before heading to the East Village pawn shop on Avenue D.

90

After succumbing to my addiction right there on Avenue D, I returned to Jackson Heights where I got myself dressed for work and then headed back into Manhattan. As I sat on the subway mulling over my options, the notion of getting clean still lingered but only in a vague and unreachable way. Saturday was still three days away and without the possibility of securing methadone, any knee-jerk reaction to quit using was quickly squelched by recollections of the previous night. But regardless, it was clear that I wasn't earning enough money at Gotham to survive—drug addict or not. As soon as I arrived at the restaurant I raised the issue.

"Amanda, I don't think I can afford to work here anymore," I told her, even before she had a chance to greet me.

"Oh no! Please don't leave me," she pleaded. "I really want you to stay."

I was suddenly struck by a profound sincerity in her words. For the first time in a while, I was able to see beyond a cloud of opiated indifference and realize that I had developed a meaningful friendship with someone. Incidentally, Amanda had also become one of *For Now*'s most ardent supporters as she played it continuously in the restaurant.

"I'm really having a hard time getting by," I told her, and her eyes suddenly lit up.

"Do you wanna work Friday nights?!?" she blurted out. "I think they make over three bills on Friday night!"

"Get the fuck outta here!"

"No—I'm serious!" she went on. "Nadia found a better job, so after next Friday the shift is permanently available."

"*Nadia* found a better job?!?!"

"Yeah, I know—hard to believe, right? Anyway, you—"

"Wait a minute," I interrupted her. You're telling me that Nadia—who can barely speak a *word* of English—is leaving this shithole for a better gig?!?"

"Yeah, right," she said. "Listen—it gets a little weird in here on Friday, but I know you'll make a lot of money."

Unfortunately, by now her words were falling on deaf ears, and I needed to narrow the field a bit further to make sure things were really as bad as they seemed.

"You mean to say that **NADIA**, the **ROMANIAN** chick with the **MUSTACHE** and the **FAKE, FUCKING, FOOT** is gonna be making more money than **ME**?!?!"

"Yes!!!" Amanda shouted and then laughed out loud.

Will the indignities ever cease?

"If you want, come in next Friday so she can train you."

No, apparently not.

With little else in terms of choice, I agreed to pick up the shift. Although I couldn't imagine how working at Gotham could result in a $300 windfall, I was in no position to question anything. Besides, I knew Amanda wouldn't deliberately lie to me and was certain the shift would be at least *somewhat* profitable. Until that point, however, I would have to carefully ration my money—and even *more* carefully ration my dope.

My Friday night training shift occurred near the middle of November. That day, I had arrived at the restaurant at 5 p.m. and was confronted by staff members whom I'd only previously seen in passing. I approached the night crew congregating around the bar, but before I even had a chance to introduce myself I was addressed:

"Freee**esssssh meat**!" shouted Maurice Weathers, who was one of the other waiters.

Maurice was also an actor from the Midwest. That night I'd be on the floor with him and Tom Bennington, another aspiring thespian, while an East Hampton model named Melissa Sanford ran the bar. Interestingly enough, Nadia elected not to show up for her final shift, so my training would be administered by Maurice.

"The drawer's almost completely empty and we're out of a ton of shit," Melissa said, shaking her head in semi-disbelief while she counted the change.

"Stratis came in here and hit the register about an hour ago," Tom explained. "He was already looking a little twisted, so he probably just forgot to leave a bank."

"I've got ten bucks," Melissa said. "Anyone else wanna help sponsor the restaurant for a few hours?"

"I've only got five but it's all yours," said Maurice as he reached into his pocket.

"Craig, do you have any cash you can lend us?" Melissa asked.

"I've been working days."

"Enough said."

Given the dimensions of Gotham City and the number of staff members present, there seemed to be some expectation of a significant dinner rush. However, by 7:30 there still wasn't a customer in the restaurant.

"Where the fuck is everyone?" I asked Maurice. "It's Friday night and the place is empty."

"Don't worry," he said with extreme confidence. "They'll be here."

"Late diners?" I asked.

"Actually, this group doesn't do a whole lot of dining. But they'll definitely make an appearance and when they do they won't wanna leave."

"Why's that?"

"There really isn't anywhere else for them to go."

By around 9 p.m. the restaurant was *still* completely empty, with the exception of five teenage boys and girls sitting up front by the windows.

"Hey Craig—you know who that is over there?" Tom asked, gesturing toward one of the girls.

"No."

"That's Mia Tyler."

"Who's Mia Tyler?"

"You call yourself a rocker and you don't know who Mia Tyler is?"

"No," I told him. "Why don't you help spread the word, brother?"

"Mia **TYLER**! Daughter of Stephen, sister of Liv?!?"

For some reason it still wasn't registering, and that must have been apparent from the expression on my face.

"Tyler! That name doesn't ring a bell for you? Stephen Tyler? Aerosmith? The *band?* Ever hear of them?" he continued with profound sarcasm.

Before I had a chance to respond, Melissa called my name.

"Craig—can you run to the store for me? I hate to leave the register completely empty but we really need some juice."

"Sure."

She handed me the fifteen donated dollars and I ran across the street to a Korean grocer, where I stood in line for fifteen minutes with three containers of orange juice and two bottles of cranberry. When I returned, I noticed that two parties of four were now also seated in the restaurant. Unfortunately, however, they were *all* teenagers and

314

everyone knows that *teenagers don't tip*. As Maurice finished taking beverage orders from one of the tables, I approached him to see if I could be of any assistance. Just then, six more teenage girls entered the restaurant.

"Hey Tabitha!" Maurice called out to one of the girls as they walked in.

"Hi Maurice!" Tabitha yelled back. "We're gonna be super-quick tonight."

"OK, I'll be right with you," Maurice said as the girls seated themselves at a large table and Melissa summoned me once more.

"Craig, I need you to run to the store again and grab some pretzels," she said as she handed me five dollars.

"Why didn't you tell me that fifteen minutes ago?"

"We couldn't afford it fifteen minutes ago."

"This place is fucked up," I said, but I was only just beginning to scratch the scandalous surface.

After waiting in line for ten minutes with two bags of pretzels I returned to Gotham and while distributing the snacks, I was summoned by Melissa yet again.

"Craig—I'm sorry, but I need you to get us some chips, and four containers of chocolate and vanilla ice cream," she said. "Two of each."

"Fucking *ice cream*?!?! Are you serious?"

"I'm afraid so. And then go to the liquor store and grab two bottles of rum and three bottles of vodka…the cheap stuff. We're OK for now, but we'll probably need it later."

"What do you want me to pay for all of it with?"

"Here—Tabitha's table just settled the check," she said as she handed me a hundred-dollar bill. "Quick, take it and go before Stratis gets here and empties the register again."

How Maurice collected a hundred dollars from a table of six teenage girls that were there for 15 minutes and ordered nothing beyond beverages was certainly mysterious—but I didn't care. The last thing I wanted to do was waste my time catering to a bunch of unemployed children. I was through with Gotham City and would inform Amanda of my decision as soon as possible.

When I returned with the items at around 10:15 the diner was totally packed with kids, and I'd never before seen a restaurant go from zero to 60 in so little time. It was suddenly like a Chucky Cheese on a Saturday afternoon, except there were no pizzas or parents and the kids were out of control...*really out of control.* Not only were they smoking cigarettes in the restaurant—which was already illegal for adults—but they were shooting spitballs, violently pushing each other around, and at one point a younger boy stood on a table as he bellowed to his buddy in the crowd.

"Ask her out—ask her out you fucking pussy!!!" he shrieked.

Apparently, someone had now finally stepped over the line of what was considered acceptable restaurant behavior.

"Get the fuck off the table you little cocksucker or I'm gonna come over there and beat the fucking shit out of you!!" Maurice roared, while pointing menacingly at the kid from across the dining room.

"Oh...Sorry dude, sorry," the kid yelled back. He then jumped off the table and onto the back of his buddy as the controlled chaos continued.

"This is fucking nuts," I said out loud. Then, with shopping bags full of ice cream and liquor I attempted to weave my way through the crowd and the carnival-like atmosphere.

"Excuse me...excuse me, please...please, excuse me. **HEY! GET THE FUCK OUT OF MY WAY!!!**"

"Oh...Sorry dude, sorry."

Eventually, I made my way behind the bar, and as I unpacked the ice cream I suddenly saw Stratis step into pandemonium.

"Uh-oh," I said to no one in particular.

"What's wrong?" Melissa asked me as she was serving a plate of onion rings to a boy sitting at the bar.

"Here comes Stratis," I told her.

"So?"

"So look at this place," I said. "It's a fucking zoo! Now the shit's gonna hit the fan."

Melissa rolled her eyes, looked at me as if I was crazy and then walked away while her customer attempted to set me straight in between onion rings.

"Well, if Stratis is the shit, and the fan is a big, fat, bag of cocaine well then yeah, that's probably gonna happen," he told me with a ridiculous grin as if he'd just said the funniest goddamn thing ever.

Funny or not, however, he was apparently right. Without a word to anyone Stratis mounted an assault on the register, and as he hastily counted the money he was wiping his nose and looking sweaty.

"Melissa!!! There's only eight hundred dollars in here!" Stratis shouted, and without waiting for a response he bolted out of the restaurant with the money.

Only eight hundred dollars? I was shocked by the figure and didn't understand how that much could suddenly be generated by a kitchen that remained virtually inactive for the entire evening.

"Craig—could you do me a favor and bring this check to table seven?" Maurice asked.

"Yeah, whatever," I said, at this point completely disillusioned by the entire experience.

I grabbed the check and then felt a sudden impact from behind, followed by an embrace. As I turned my head I could see the same, little, bastard—who was earlier scolded for standing on furniture—now behind me with his arms wrapped around my waist.

"Help me! Help me, dude. He's gonna kill me! You gotta help me, dude. Please, you gotta—"

"Get the fuck away from me you little prick!" I said as I peeled him off my back and pushed him onto the floor.

As he lay there resting on his elbows and looking confused, I thought he might be drunk. Then, as his eyes glazed over—out of his mouth came an explosion of punch-colored puke and I was sure of it.

"EEEEWWWWW!!!" squealed a group of girls who were in close proximity to the lad and his liquid.

Completely disgusted, I delivered the check to table seven and decided that I'd had enough of the silliness. Dealing with drunk and puking adults was one thing, because at least *they* were purchasing the alcohol from the restaurant in which they were befouling it with. But this kid had apparently dipped into Daddy's liquor cabinet, and from what I could gather—he wasn't the only one. Inebriated teenagers were on display everywhere, and I didn't want to spend the night babysitting, nor did I see how it could be profitable to do so. I knew Gotham City was a complete waste of time and wanted out of there immediately. Of course, I'd then be jobless, but since tomorrow was Saturday I resigned myself to buying a bottle of methadone along with some time to figure things out. Before walking out of the restaurant, however, I did feel obligated to share my feelings with Maurice, who at the moment was serving drinks to a table of customers.

"Alright you little cocksuckers—that'll be 80 bucks," he said. "Pay the fuck up or get the fuck out."

Then everything suddenly became clearer.

"Maurice!!!! What the fuck are you doing?!?!"

317

"What'd you say?" he shouted back, apparently unable to hear my voice over the roar of juvenile jubilance.

"Aren't their any fucking rules in this place?!?" I asked, and though he now heard the question he was clearly confused by it.

"What do you mean?" he replied, unsure if I was referring to the round of vodkas he'd just served a table of eighth-graders—or the fact that he was charging them $20 a shot.*

* Just prior to publication, in order to more accurately depict the costs and financial burden incurred by underage drinkers at the Gotham City Diner circa 1995, inflationary considerations and adjustments were made with respect to the stated drink price. In reality, Maurice was charging the children $10 each for a shot that would have normally cost about five.

91

A moment after I discovered Gotham City's secret recipe for Friday night success, Maurice casually slipped a $50 bill into my hand. At first, based on my reaction to the evening's events, I assumed his gesture was intended to dissuade me from quitting. But why would *Maurice* care if I quit? I'd spent most of the evening running errands, and though my sudden departure might deprive the tykes he was intoxicating from a few snacks, I'm sure he was unconcerned with the quality of service being provided by an understaffed restaurant. *These* kids weren't going anywhere. After all, it wasn't as if there was a lot of local competition serving booze to brats that couldn't hold their liquor.

Ultimately, I realized that my compensation amounted to hush money. Well beyond Amanda's estimation, Maurice and Tom each made over $400 that night and I'm sure they didn't want me to ruin a good thing. It was all quite brilliant, really. To make ends meet and perhaps support an alleged drug habit, Stratis employed a junky, an immigrant, and a couple of struggling actors to serve liquor to minors in an otherwise failing establishment. *Who the fuck was gonna tell?* By doubling or—in some cases—tripling the price of each drink, waiters pocketed at least 50% of the monies collected, and as the muffled roar of unrestricted adolescence leaked into the street it was usually enough to keep legitimate customers away. Those who did wander in would immediately wander back out, and were either unaware of what was *really* going on—or just didn't want to get involved.

The indifference was demonstrated by not only potential diners, but also police officers charged with patrolling the relatively posh Manhattan neighborhood. In fact, the first time I saw evidence of this I had momentarily forgotten about any underage drinking, and assumed the cop was there to address a certain staff member's inability to comply with court orders.

"Oh Shit!!!" I shouted and then ducked behind the bar during a Friday evening in mid-December, just as one of the boys-in-blue stepped into Gotham.

As the officer was confronted by the brassy illumination of the restaurant his eyes squinted, though that may have been because the sight of what was going on within it was just too much to bear. Then, after scanning the crowd repeatedly and/or shaking his head in disbelief, he seemed reluctant to open Pandora's Box any further than he already had.

"What are you worried about?" Melissa asked me as I cowered in a corner. "He's not gonna do a fucking thing."

Sure enough, the cop left Gotham City almost as quickly as he had entered—clearly shocked by the illicit activity but unable to intervene. I later learned that a large percentage of the teenage revelers came from prestigious and influential families, and as a result the police were extremely reluctant to make waves.

In the meantime, Perry had secured a job at a French restaurant in the East Village called Le Brasserie. Somehow, he managed to impress the owner so completely that he was provided with not only a job, but management-like status and keys to the establishment. Unfortunately, however, though his career in the hospitality industry was blossoming, Catherine remained unreachable.

Rather than hold myself accountable for the stagnation of our music careers, I blamed Perry and in no way did I consider my own drug problem to be a cause. Drugs or not, the CD was completed and though not widely heard, it had already garnered significant praise. Clearly, I had fulfilled my end of the bargain, and whether it was his failure to proceed to the next step or Catherine's—I cared little and resented them both. Still, I held Perry chiefly to blame. It was no longer simply a matter of rolling snake eyes at conception and being dealt a bicuspid valve. Obviously, after open-heart surgery he should have gotten the message, but didn't. Now, after five years of listening to his predictions of fame and fortune it had suddenly dawned on me that I was a 28-year-old dope fiend going nowhere. I obviously couldn't stop using and wasn't even sure that I wanted to. I had fucked up my life by making bad decisions and it was all *Perry's* fault.

By January of 1996 nothing had changed, and like Catherine I stopped taking Perry's calls and began avoiding him completely. He never had anything positive to say, and his presence only reminded me of my own sad existence. I now simply went through the motions like a zombie, getting high after work as I tried to look the other way without acknowledging the darkness that had already consumed me. Gone were the aspirations of old, as well as the steadfast desire to make things work in spite of my poor decision making. Each day I would report to Gotham City to stand around, and then on Friday evening earn anywhere from three to five hundred dollars which was enough for dope *and* rent as life had become absurdly one-dimensional. And fortunately or unfortunately, my tiny apartment provided the perfect backdrop to remain medicated, detached, and indifferent.

"You know, that CD of yours is great!" Melissa told me during a busy, Friday evening shift. "We were listening to it earlier when Amanda told me it was you."

"Oh yeah?" I said. "Well that and a dollar gets me on the fucking subway."

"The subway's a buck-fifty," Maurice pointed out.

"Can I buy one of them?" Melissa asked me.

"Buy what?!?"

"One of your CD's!"

"No!"

"Why the fuck not?!?"

"Because I don't have anymore!" I told her, obviously irritated by the subject.

"So go get some. It is your band, isn't it?"

"Listen: Things haven't turned out quite the way I expected, and you know what? I don't wanna talk about it."

"Well did you think it was gonna be easy, moron?"

"Yes!!!"

After a short pause, the conversation reignited.

"Did you ever consider doing some networking out there?" she asked me.

"Out where?"

"Out there," she repeated while gesturing to the crowd of intoxicated teenagers only a few feet away.

"I'm not gonna ask a bunch of children for help with my music career," I said dismissively. "Besides... *I hate them.*"

"You'd be surprised," she went on. "Some of these kids have close ties to the music industry."

"Yeah, I know—Mia Tyler," I said with complete disinterest.

"Not only Mia."

"Oh really? Well if at any point *Menudo* bellies up to the bar—be sure to let me know."

A little disgusted, I walked away as a commotion near the front of the restaurant caught my attention. One of the taller boys, to whom I'd just served several shots of tequila, was now slapping around a smaller kid at another table.

"HEY!!!" I roared. "Keep your fucking hands to yourself before I shove my foot up your ass!"

"Fuck you!!" he shot back.

Now typically, threats of violence were usually enough to restore order, but this kid had apparently borrowed some courage from Jose Cuervo. Fortunately, Maurice had already impressed me with his zero-tolerance for backtalk and the importance of remaining in control.

"Alright, you've had enough," I told him. "Time to go home."

As Maurice positioned himself by the front door I approached the bully, and while attempting to escort him out of the restaurant he spit in my face.

For a moment I simply stood there in shock. Then, with the bottom of my foot I kicked him in the chest, and as he stumbled backwards Maurice held the door open to ensure a safe landing on the snow-covered sidewalk.

"That was fucking beautiful," Maurice said as a sudden hush fell over the crowd of kiddies. It was as if someone had just been sent to timeout and nobody wanted to be next.

Within a few moments things returned to normal, and as the steady howl of teenage drunkenness resumed I suddenly felt a hand tugging on the back of my shirt.

"Hey mister, hey mister," came a little voice from behind.

I turned and was horrified to see an elementary-school kid standing before me. He wore a plaid shirt and was about four-and-a-half-feet-tall, with bright red hair and a face full of freckles.

"I'll have a Beefeater martini, please—extra dry and straight up with an olive," he said.

"No – fucking – way," I told him.

"Why not?!"

"How old are you?"

"Twelve."

"That's *why not*," I said.

"You just gave my brother a beer and he's only fifteen!"

"Get away from me, Opie—before I call the sheriff."

"If you do he'll take **you** to jail."

"Been there, done that. Now seriously, get the fuck out."

About five minutes later a police officer actually did show up, along with the little prick that spit in my face. The moment the cop walked in, our eyes met and he immediately motioned me over. After I made my way to the front of the restaurant we got right down to business.

"This young gentleman said you assaulted him," the officer told me.

"This young gentleman's a drunk and belligerent asshole," I told *him*.

"Drunk? He's only seventeen. How could he be drunk?"

"I just served him four tequilas in ten minutes. Trust me, *he's fucking toast.*"

Why the cop asked me that question is still a mystery. He knew why the kid was drunk. Most of the neighborhood knew why the kid was drunk. He probably just wanted to see if I'd have the balls to admit it; however, my confession had little to do with courage. Of course, getting arrested was always worth avoiding, but in a very real way I simply didn't care anymore...*about anything*. Go ahead. Call out the cavalry and burn the fucking place to the ground, but just make sure that I'm inside when you do. Good fucking riddance to it. Good riddance to us all.

92

By the beginning of March, I had successfully managed to avoid Perry for almost two months. It seemed I now became irritated by just the sound of his voice, which drove me from the hazy realm of my chemically-concocted complacency, into a wave of depression and self-loathing. Apparently, heroin had become not only the cause of my problem but the solution to it as well, and by remaining in a nod I could sequester my failures and ignore the devastation that was overtaking my life. By avoiding Perry, I could continue to look the other way, indefinitely...*at everything*.

Then on March 5th I accidentally answered the phone at Gotham.

"What's up?"

It was Perry.

"Nothing," I told him.

"I have some news for you," he said. "You wanna meet me outside The Sunshine after work?"

"No."

"Why not?!?"

"Because I *hate* you."

"Get over it and come down here."

"What time?"

"Six o'clock."

"Fine," I said and then hung up the phone.

We ended up meeting at a coffee shop on Avenue A, where he proceeded to fill me in on the situation with Catherine who, until today, he hadn't heard from in months.

"She wants us to meet her tomorrow afternoon," he told me. "Can you get the day off?"

"No," I said even though I already had the day off.

"This is really important, Craig. She wants us to meet with a lawyer."

"Why? Is she suing us?"

"No!" he said firmly. "He's a big *entertainment* lawyer."

"Are you serious?"

"Deadly serious. Actually, he's about as big as they get."

"What's his name?"

"Bob Donnelly," Perry told me. "He represents Dave Matthews and has a shitload of other big clients."

Why exactly the esteemed attorney would be meeting with us I hadn't a clue, but the fact that we'd be in his presence was alone enough for my chemically-dependent ego to awaken from a long winter's nap. Everything was going to be splendid after all, and I would finally be able to make my living as a junky musician. Indeed, I would not only have my cake but eat it too, and be sure to sprinkle the humble crumbs into mouths that said it couldn't be done.

On the following morning, my renewed anticipation for unbridled success overwhelmed me. I woke up at ten, put on my nicest shirt, and though the meeting wasn't until 3 p.m.—I headed into Manhattan at eleven. I then met Perry shortly before noon, and after coming to terms with how great we were we decided to celebrate in the usual way.

After scoring on the corner of 124th Street and Third Avenue, we ducked inside a project to get off in the building's stairwell and as soon as Perry tapped a vein, I offered-up my own. Then, a moment later I tumbled down the staircase. Although I never stopped breathing, it was the first and only time I'd overdosed.

At some point later I regained consciousness on the landing of the 17th floor and was immediately confronted by the smiling faces of an EMT and a firefighter, while a disgusted cop milled about in the background.

"He ain't fuckin' dead!" the firefighter joyfully announced as the EMT sighed with relief. Unfortunately, the sudden prospect of a bust worth making raised the cop's spirits as well. As he eagerly repositioned himself amongst the other municipal employees, I immediately recalled my arrest warrant and pleaded valium to dampen his enthusiasm. Thankfully, before fleeing the scene, Perry had removed any damning evidence from my lifeless body that might have pointed to a heroin overdose as the cause of my condition.

Had Perry not taken the preventive measures he had, I definitely would have been spending some time at Riker's. Instead, I was immediately whisked away to Metropolitan Hospital, while Perry arrived at the all-important meeting without me.

93

To this day, Perry has never fully disclosed the details of the meeting. Therefore, I can only conclude that his silence is part of an ongoing effort to shield me from the consequences of my overdose. It was either that, or he was just too fucked up to remember. Regardless, I eventually realized that being absent from the meeting was likely the straw that broke the back of my musical aspirations. Of course, at the time I was totally oblivious to this. If I was, on some level, conscious of the fact that our fate may have now been detrimentally and irreversibly sealed, that bit of awareness was kept tucked away and heavily sedated.

During the last week of March, a rainy Friday night kept most of the kids away from Gotham City and as a result, I knew I would be unable to pay April's rent. Once again, I suddenly saw the

Whitehouse in my future and became extremely unsettled by it. Egging on my anxiety was the fact that Stratis owed me $200 in shift-pay which had gone unaddressed for over two weeks, along with several unpaid invoices from a variety of vendors who were now refusing to do business with him. That evening, before leaving the restaurant with only $40 in my pocket, I raised the issue with Melissa.

"Well what do you want *me* to do about it?" she asked defensively.

"Pay me out of the register."

She then pulled out the drawer, which had only $135 in it.

"I can't leave the register completely empty or they won't have a bank to work with tomorrow morning," Melissa explained.

"So what? They're not gonna have any customers to work with either."

"I just can't do it, Craig. I'm *really* sorry."

"Don't worry about it," I said. Then, a moment after she stepped away to use the restroom, I took the money out of the register and left Gotham City never to return. On the following evening I packed my bag and checked into the Whitehouse Hotel.

94

I'm not exactly sure when I started pumping cocaine into my arm. I know it happened after moving into the Whitehouse Hotel, and I'm almost certain that Perry was present. Unfortunately, memories of this period are among the haziest of all, and the clouded recollections can only be attributed to my ever-expanding and increasingly reckless drug use.

Initially, I had attempted to join Perry at the Sunshine Hotel, but there were no vacancies and I was forced to check in to the Whitehouse. Though my previous exposure to the infamous flophouse had been sufficient enough to make me fear it, to truly appreciate the degradation within one must venture past the hotel lobby and become a resident. Moments after my own residency was established and I headed up the staircase—like an airborne harbinger of awful things to come—my nose was immediately assaulted by the pungent odor of aseptic cleanser and, as if to justify the sterile noxiousness, the foul stench of forsaken humanity.

I was assigned to stall #38 on the third floor, and would exist within this 8 x 5 foot space for several months. It came without a ceiling and with nothing other than four walls and a cot which claimed roughly half the stall's total area. This left me with just enough floor space for a duffle bag containing all of my worldly possessions—including a walkman, a few articles of clothing, and a couple of bags of dope that were immediately torn into as I came to terms with my new habitat. Of course, my worst fear had now come to fruition and all the dope in the world couldn't change that. But as I sat there tapping a vein, a strange calm had settled over me. A *scary* calm had settled over me. I was tired. I was broken. I didn't even have the desire or energy to rationalize my situation as one last indignity to suffer through before the good times could finally start rolling. Then, at some point, a knock at the door ripped me away from my medicated complacency.

"Yo, man—open up," said a voice on the other side. "They sent me up here with your sheets."

Still seated on my cot, I kicked open the door and was confronted by an older resident whose beard was so dirty that I couldn't tell what color lay beneath.

"It's like a Turkish prison in here," I accidentally slurred while peering at the old man from beneath my nod.

"It's worse," he responded. "At least in prison a man's got some hope."

I would soon learn that the name of the gentleman standing before me was Bill. He had been living at the Whitehouse for several years and was in his mid-fifties, though he looked much older.

"By the way," he mentioned before departing. "I'd get a lock for this door if you wanna keep whatever shit you've got left."

I heeded his advice. I went next door to a bodega that conveniently sold combination locks and by the time I returned—my walkman had already been stolen. If I wasn't so fucked up I would've been completely pissed off. Instead, I decided to wrap myself up in that false sense of well being and eventually fell asleep.

By 9 a.m. I awoke to discussions, arguments, laughter, and a variety of curses emanating from the stalls that surrounded my own. Unfortunately, I was now sober and the reality around me was even more difficult to bear than it had been the previous night. I was jobless, homeless, and officially living at the Whitehouse Hotel. Although my immediate instinct was to score and detach, I knew that I first had to find a job…quickly. With that in mind, I decided it was time to get out of cot and begin the search.

Although I had checked-in over twelve hours ago, the squalor of my new dwelling hadn't fully revealed itself. I was already wasted when I arrived the night before, and without the illumination of sunlight *and* sobriety the surrounding misery had remained largely hidden. Of course, when I opened the door to my stall that first morning—things became infinitely clearer.

The third floor—which was much like every other floor of the hotel—was a gymnasium-sized, rectangular-shaped room. Twenty to thirty stalls lined each wall and within the center of the room was another, smaller, rectangle of stalls. Thus, a hallway separated the rectangles and ran along the perimeter of the entire floor. Everything was dirty and rundown, and the wooden floors were rotting away as the smell of mildew lingered throughout the building.

With my toothbrush and toothpaste in hand, I left my stall and headed into a large bathroom near the main staircase as a hairy old man wearing shit-stained underwear scurried across my path like a frightened rodent. I immediately went about my business and after brushing my teeth, momentarily caught a glimpse of myself in the mirror as a strung-out raccoon stared back. I then exited the bathroom and, without showering or shaving, stumbled out of the Whitehouse to find a job.

I remember getting hired almost immediately at what must've been a very desperate restaurant on Broadway. It was owned and operated by Arabs, and every day Lauren Hutton came in for breakfast. However, beyond that I can only recall the job generated just enough money to pay for ten dollar-a-day accommodations, what would soon become a sixty dollar-a-day drug habit, and a diet consisting exclusively of Little Debbies.

Each day I worked the breakfast/lunch shift and afterwards, would head over to a new spot known as "Bag in a Bag" on Second Street between Avenues B and C. By this point my habit had increased from three booted bags-a-day to four, and after scoring I would immediately retire to the Whitehouse for the evening. My life had become meaningless. Even so, if someone asked—*I still had big plans for the future*. Of course, the answer was purely rote. I had now conditioned myself into believing a false destiny and was just too terrified of the alternate ending to be able to acknowledge it. If for a moment I did, my dysfunction would conveniently rise to the occasion to appease me with a self-serving pep-talk.

By the end of April, Perry had departed the Sunshine Hotel to join me at the Whitehouse. He was assigned to stall #67 which was also located on the third floor, but in the middle rectangle. Although, again, I'm unsure of exactly when I started mainlining cocaine, I know that it happened shortly after Perry's arrival as the notion would've never occurred to me on my own. However, once I was introduced to my very first speedball his presence was never again required.

At first, I stuck to the traditional speedball recipe of mixing heroin with cocaine and realized I quite liked the effect of experiencing both drugs simultaneously. After slipping the concoction into my arm, I could feel the coke pummel my heart and marinate my brain with a skewed, slightly electrified variation of the opiate-induced euphoria. However, I soon also realized I appreciated cocaine for the sake of itself, and actually preferred the intravenously enhanced rush to be unadulterated—even though it made me throw up. As a result, a new routine was established. I would start things off with a needle full of dope, and then periodically administer cocaine throughout the evening and in between purges. Then, after the final coke-rush had run its course, I would mainline the last of my dope to ensure a pleasant end to the evening. It was like jumping out of a plane, *and into a big pile of love.*

Unfortunately, besides puking, the new drug delivery schedule had other drawbacks. Because I was now administering both drugs independently, I began sticking myself six or seven times per evening and in a matter of days my veins had significantly deteriorated. In fact, they usually bled extensively at the slightest penetration. As a result, I soon found myself with little in terms of a viable passageway, and on one evening in particular I decided to skin-pop the last of my stash. Without paying attention to what I was doing or where I was doing it, I plunged the syringe into my right arm—just beneath the shoulder and on the edge of my tricep. It was hardly a fleshy enough area to sustain a skin-pop, and though it hurt like hell I didn't give it much thought at the time. However, within a few days the area around my tricep became swollen and inflamed as an oily orange fluid began to incessantly seep from the puncture wound. Actually, it felt like a gigantic pimple that was about to explode, and though I constantly tried to expel whatever lay hidden within the volcano-like mound of flesh, my efforts yielded only more of the same oily discharge.

On May 1st I finally paid a visit to a downtown clinic where, after shamefully disclosing my dysfunction to the medical staff, I was told that I'd given myself a hematoma which had now abscessed and was clearly infected. To complicate matters, the mass of bacteria was lodged *beneath* my tricep. Consequently, its removal would require a relatively minor surgery which was scheduled for the following week.

As I sat atop an examination table while a doctor finished surveying the self-inflicted damage, I realized I was actually embarrassed by my own condition. No, wait a minute—*I was fucking humiliated.* It was as if for the first time I had officially unveiled my depraved condition to the civilized world.

"I'm *really* sorry about all of this…. I'm gonna quit using," I lied, hoping that for just a moment she could see past the degradation festering before her. "I'm not kidding. I'm definitely gonna quit… I swear it."

I really needed her to say something—*anything* that would help me look the other way. Unfortunately, I hadn't the foggiest notion of what that might be. I wasn't necessarily looking for sympathy, concern, or even medical advice. Maybe, I just needed her to acknowledge the fact that I wasn't like all the others, that I wasn't a hopeless, run-of-the-mill street junky destined for prison or an early grave. I mean—after all—*I was special.* I still had great things to look forward to, *didn't I?* Regardless, she said nothing and continued to finish up her business as if I wasn't even in the room. After a long and awkward silence I finally decided to give it one last-ditch effort.

"I am *so* embarrassed… I can't believe I let this happen to me."

Finally, she responded:

"Oh well, you know—shit happens.*"*

95

I walk fast, but I don't run. I walk like I have an *appointment* to make. A very *important* appointment. The *most* important appointment. Avenue B, Avenue A and then First, Second and Bowery before I'm home at last. In through the front door and up the staircase—three steps at a time—past the second floor and then on up to the third.

Holy shit...my heart's already racing and I haven't even gotten started.

I hang a right, a quick left, and then finally another left. Thirty-three, 34, 35, 36, 37—*stall #38.* This is my home. This is where **I live.** This is where I do things that horrify. This is where I break the law. This is where I hide from the world. This is where I hide from the truth. This is where I hide from...*myself.*

I tear into the dope, empty it into a spoon, cook it up and ram it in.

Ah yes, my old friend...now meet my new friend.

I rip into the cocaine, empty it into a spoon, cook it up and *OOOPS!!!*

*Stop right there. Never cook-up coke unless you're making crack—and everyone knows that **crack is for fucking losers.** Nope, straight from the spoon and into my vein...any vein...please find a vein. Ah yes, there's one! No, it's fucking shot. How about old reliable? Oh—come on, just one more time—just one more. Please baby, please...**YES!!!** There you go...**and again, and again, and again!!!** Ignore the blood—**ignore it!** Now keep looking the other way and **HOLY FUCKING SHIT!!!*** My heart is pounding, sweat is dripping from every pour, and the orange discharge is mingling with blood as I'm ramming a broken needle into a broken vein and thinking, *man—it doesn't get any better than this.*

Sometime in early May, Bill died peacefully in his sleep from unknown causes. Allegedly, however, his body wasn't discovered until a few days later when the aroma of death was finally able to establish itself as the King of All Stenches.

Although I never had any interactions with Bill beyond the first

331

day when he delivered my bed sheets, the distinction he drew between the Whitehouse and prison was more profound than I first realized. In prison, or even jail, one's freedom is stripped away as are, of course, the means to improve one's condition. However, this is usually a temporary situation and in most cases a clean start will eventually be on the horizon. Thus, to the incarcerated psyche, things can *only* get better.

By contrast, a grayish despondency pervaded the Whitehouse Hotel. Everyone and everything in it was hopeless right down to the rotting floorboard, seemingly in a contest to outlive the forlorn souls that traipsed upon it. And whereas most prisoners ultimately have their freedom to look forward to, many Whitehouse residents had already come full circle. For them, there was simply nowhere left to go besides the street, a shelter, back to prison or an early grave. In fact, I've often considered that Bill's sudden death was due to complications brought on by terminal despair. Usually, you could see that despair on the faces of residents—unless they were high, though drug addicts were only one of the many forsaken demographics on the guest list. Of course, my situation was about as bleak as anyone else's and at times I knew it. However, I could quickly neutralize that awareness by coating it in a thick layer of cocaine, followed by a rich finish of heroin just to make sure it didn't know what the fuck was going on.

As my drug consumption continued to fly off the charts, Perry became nothing more than a familiar face. We seldom discussed anything beyond the drugs we were destroying our bodies with, and neither of us ever mentioned Sections, the CD, Catherine or the future. We became two foundering ships that would occasionally pass in the night, though sometimes we were stowaways in a single stall, getting high together but saying nothing. More often than not, however, I found myself alone—sweating profusely and sticking myself for hours.

On the evening before my scheduled surgery, I had suddenly become obsessed with the festering abscess as an orange discharge continued to seep from my arm. Without really thinking about it, I sat on my cot and began prodding and squeezing the area around the puncture wound. As I continued to knead the swollen mound like a man possessed, the oily leakage gradually dissipated until it was replaced by a dark, red, trail of blood that began to seep from the same hole. Several minutes passed before, in terms of discharge, the well had finally begun to run dry. Then, as I ratcheted up the pressure to ensure that all infectious fluids were completely expelled, I felt something burst. Simultaneously, a stream of chunky matter—that looked like orange cottage cheese but smelled like feet—exploded out of my wound and onto the wall. Meanwhile, the puncture hole was now almost large enough to fit the tip of my pinky.

On the following afternoon, I reported to the clinic to have the abscess removed—only to learn that it was now stuck to the wall of the Whitehouse Hotel. Since I had apparently performed my own surgery the night before, any additional procedures would now be unnecessary. Unfortunately, Perry wouldn't be so lucky. Before the end of May and after a terrible bout of night sweats, he headed to Lenox Hill where for the fourth time in two years he was diagnosed with endocarditis. This time, however, the damage to the pig valve was so extensive that Perry would require an immediate replacement, and along with it—another heart surgery.

96

As soon as Perry became aware of his condition, he requested time-off from the owner of Le Brasserie. He was such a highly appreciated and trusted employee, that after disclosing his health problems he was provided with as much time as he needed. Then, in the early morning hours of May 30th—just three days before surgery—Perry broke out of the hospital and into the restaurant with a key that was given to him as some measure of that trust. Although he helped himself to most of what was in the register, he was kind enough to leave behind his co-workers' credit card tips which left little doubt as to who the culprit was.

As far as I was concerned, my life and routine went unchanged. I woke up, went to work, got high, passed out, woke up and started the day anew. With each day I thought about nothing other than making the money I needed to remain exactly the way I was. Beyond that I remember little; then again, I doubt there was much else to recall during those terrible months. Then on July 17th, 1996, TWA Flight 800 en route to Paris exploded off the coast of Long Island—killing all 230 aboard.

As I was heading to work on the morning of July 18th, the Whitehouse lobby was buzzing with news of the awful tragedy. Although it made an impact, it was only temporary and I continued with my day as scheduled. On the *following* day, however, more details emerged, and as my shift at the restaurant concluded I noticed a newspaper resting on an empty table. A picture of Eric and Virginia was plastered to the front page.

For a moment I stood frozen as I felt my throat close and my stomach drop to the floor. I didn't have to read the caption to know that they were among those who'd perished. I then grabbed the newspaper, ran back to the Whitehouse and threw-up in a bathroom on the second floor. My efforts yielded little other than a long series of grueling groans as if I were trying to purge myself of the horror. Unfortunately, it didn't work. I would need something a little stronger—*and a lot less involuntary.*

Clutching a newspaper that I didn't have the courage to read, I descended the staircase and left the Whitehouse to score. As I headed toward my destination, I tried to suspend any thoughts until I was better equipped to come to terms with their content. Unfortunately, the rolled-up paper held tightly in my hand seemed to vibrate with the terrible news, as if it were beckoning me to unfurl it and make it official.

As I passed Avenue B, I ignored a coke spot disguised as a bodega that I normally would have stampeded into. Obviously, this was no job for cocaine. Cocaine only intensified things, sped them up and shoved them in your face. No sir, not today. Today would be exclusively devoted to heroin, as I sought comfort in the arms of my one, true, love.

After returning to my stall, I immediately opened half the stash and got loaded. I then slowly unrolled the newspaper. There they were: Eric and Virginia—smiling, bright-eyed and bushy-tailed. They looked so happy. They were beautiful. The photograph was the very same that I'd carried around for years, though by now my own copy had been lost in the wake of an addiction that, one way or another, ultimately ended up claiming everything.

By this point, all four New York dailies were focusing on the lives of the victims while investigators tried to determine the cause of the accident. With some difficulty I read about how Eric had worked so diligently to establish a thriving dental practice in Manorville, and that Virginia had recently launched a home-based business while battling thyroid cancer. The story then went on to explain how they were flying to Paris to attend Troy's wedding.

Virginia had cancer? Troy was getting married? Where the fuck was I when all of this was going on? Had I become so completely...unavailable?

I began to sob, but then quickly tried to look the other way as I booted what was left of my stash. Unfortunately, my selfish attempt to remove myself from a tragedy that I had no business removing myself from was met with a vengeance on the following day.

On July 20th more intimate details about the victims had surfaced, and it seemed as though the plight of Eric and Virginia Holst took center stage. Once again, I found myself at work surrounded by newspapers with front page pictures and headlines about my dead friends. According to one of the papers, most of the family had departed for Paris on July 16th but due to Eric's busy schedule, the couple decided to leave on the following day which is how they ended up on the ill-fated flight. The story also went on to report that while Eric's body was found almost immediately, Virginia's had yet to be recovered.

"Why the fuck don't they crucify another family?" I asked aloud, not expecting or wanting a response but getting one anyway.

"Because it has all the elements of a great story," said a young woman looking over my shoulder, who happened to have been a photo editor for *Newsday.* "And a great story always sells a lot of newspapers, tragedy or not."

On behalf of my beloved friends, I decided that if I were to allow this commentary to endure for even a moment longer, it would be incumbent upon me to choke the shit out of the photo editor. Troy and Helmer would eventually hear of the incident and know that I loved them, missed them, and felt their pain and now—*so would this fucking bitch.* Instead of resorting to violence, however, I walked away from the woman and out of the restaurant, mid-shift.

Without considering the consequences of essentially quitting my job, I scored and then made my way back to the Whitehouse. As I entered the hotel lobby, my jaw dropped to the floor as I saw Helmer's face on television. He was beseeching the government to intensify recovery efforts as Virginia was still missing. Seeing him there, trying to hold it together while bravely assuming the role of family spokesman, sent me reeling. Of all the media exposure they received, this—by far—hit home the hardest. I should have been there for him. I should have been there for Troy. I should have been *there*. As the news segment concluded, a reporter mentioned that a service would be held at Kennedy Airport for friends and families of the victims on the following day. It all seemed like a grand performance staged to emphasize what a complete piece of shit I was.

That may be so, but you'll still have to attend the service. You grew up with these people.

"Yeah, but I'm a junky."

But Helmer and Troy are your oldest and closest friends!

"Yeah, I know. But I just can't face them right now… I'm a junky."

But what about the big brother bullshit and the surrogate family crap that you used to drone on about you arrogant, unappreciative, hypocrite!!!

"TRUST ME!!! They wouldn't want me there. They didn't even invite me to their wedding because **I'M A FUCKING JUNKY!!!**"

That was about all I could handle. I immediately sprinted upstairs to stall #38.

As I drew half my stash into a syringe, I realized the tragedy was already three days old and it still felt like a bad dream, like it couldn't really be happening. How *could* something like this happen to Eric and Virginia, when such self-absorbed and unappreciative miscreants like Perry and I lived so recklessly, taking everything and everyone around us for granted?

The dope was exceptionally strong, and I thought that with any luck it might kill me. Unfortunately, it only served to banish thoughts of Eric, Virginia, Troy, and Helmer to the area of my brain exclusively reserved for things I didn't want to deal with.

I remained in a vegetative nod for several hours as darkness descended upon the Whitehouse Hotel. At some point I fell asleep and had a dream that I'd died from an overdose. I then awoke with the sheets drenched in sweat before falling back to sleep and being revisited by the same nightmare that had been plaguing me for years. In it, I once again failed to graduate and would be forced to remain at Binghamton for the rest of my life. However, in what was clearly the most perverse rendition of the dream so far, Binghamton had assumed the appearance of the Whitehouse Hotel while Crackhead Jim played the role of my advisor. Then suddenly, at about 3 a.m., I awoke and saw Perry hovering over me.

"Holy shit," I said, unsure if this was yet another nightmare. "How the fuck did you get in here?"

"They never even knew I left," he whispered.

I suddenly realized that Perry had been in the hospital for two months. I couldn't understand how I'd so completely lost track of time, or how I hadn't given him or his surgery a thought in weeks.

"So I suppose the surgery went well," I said.

"Perfectly well...but you don't look so good. We gotta get you outta here."

"No... I think I'll stay a while."

"You don't have a choice. We're going to Florida."

Florida? Fuck that shit! He must be fucking high.

"Are you fucking high?"

"Nope. I quit," he said.

"Yeah, right."

"No, seriously. I've been clean since the surgery."

"That's great, Perry. That's fucking great."

"I'm gonna come back and get you tomorrow."

"Is that a threat?"

"Yes."

"Eric and Virginia are dead," I suddenly blurted out. It was the first time I'd said those words aloud—*and they scared the fucking shit out of me.* I began to weep.

"I know," Perry said.

He then immediately changed the subject but I wasn't really listening, and was too fucked up to understand anyway. He mentioned something about Catherine, something about Bob Donnelly, and something about going to Florida to recover from surgery—before hitting the road to promote the CD.

Oh yeah, there goes that music thing again.

I drew up what was left of my stash.

"Do you really think you need that?" Perry asked as I booted.

"No. I need much, much, more."

"Well when you're finished, you might as well get started on these," he said as he produced two bottles of orange methadone from out of nowhere. "They're each a hundred milligrams, so don't be stupid and drink both at once. I'll pick up some more before we leave."

"Where're we going?"

"To Florida," he reminded me.

337

"I'm not going to fucking Florida," I reminded *him*.

"Yes you are. I'll see you tomorrow."

Tomorrow? There is no tomorrow. There is only here and now, indefinitely. Nothing came before and nothingness will come after, but I won't worry about that. Just cover up and detach, cover up and detach, cover up and detach and then maybe deal with it later…but probably not.

At some point Perry left my stall as the dope eliminated any perceptions beyond that of a sluggish heartbeat. Then, as the sun rose and once again illuminated the gloom and doom around me, I chugged a bottle of meth. It probably should've killed me, especially since a hundred milligrams was about three times as much as my habit warranted, and I was still completely fucked from the dope. A few minutes later I passed out and had another dream that I'd died, only this time at the hands of a murderous Catherine who, like Perry, I hadn't given a thought about in weeks.

At around 11 a.m. I awoke to the sounds of my own sobbing, though I was mentally and physically immobilized by the heroin and methadone cocktail. Somehow, I was aware enough to realize it was July 21st, and that the service at Kennedy Airport was already underway. As I lay there on the dirty cot in my dirty stall, I again made every attempt to rationalize why I shouldn't attend, and that if I did my arrival would be greeted by nothing short of repugnance. Furthermore, I was now being overwhelmed by the effects of two drugs which made it impossible for me to stand—let alone make a dignified appearance at such a somber gathering. If I did manage to somehow get there in one piece, I'd surely humiliate those who I should be there to comfort.

Of course, in reality, the logic behind my rationale was self-serving. I didn't want to go to the service because I didn't have the courage to directly confront what had happened, nor did I have the courage to be confronted. So, instead of heading to the airport like I should have, I selfishly dove into the other bottle of meth. I'd now pushed myself well beyond the brink of consciousness, and according to a few healthcare professionals I probably should've died—though I'm still not entirely sure what they meant by that.

Several hours later, at some point between dusk and dawn of the following day, Perry returned to remove me from my stall. I don't recall much of his arrival besides being drenched in piss at the time, and him calling me a cotwetter. I also have no idea how I made it down the steps, nor do I have any recollection of leaving the Whitehouse Hotel. I wish I could remember but I can't, and I suppose that on some level my unresolved youth still lingers there tainted, toxic, and without closure—like a resentful ghost trapped in a cemetery.

Memories following my departure from the hotel are marked by flashes of disparate scenery: a cab ride in the middle of the night, a grand slip and fall in a public area, Perry, a grassy hill, another public area. By this point, the sum total of my parts amounted to nothing more than a closed pair of eyes that would only occasionally feed information to a brain that didn't know what to do with it.

At some point I became aware of the fact that I was on a moving bus seated next to Perry, but it would be a while before I was able to put things together. When I did, it was like waking up from a nightmare and realizing it wasn't a nightmare. As I opened my eyes, I noticed a newspaper resting on Perry's lap. I don't recall the headline, but the front page featured a picture of Troy's father sitting alone on a folding chair at the memorial. He held himself tightly and wore an expression of pure anguish. As I gazed at the picture I became conspicuous by my absence from it. I should have been there weeping with him. It was photographic evidence of what an asshole I was.

"Where are we?" I groggily whispered, as the overly air-conditioned bus continued on through the darkness.

"I think we're in Virginia," Perry said.

"Why?"

"Places to go and people to see."

"Where are we going, Perry?" I asked, growing somewhat agitated.

"Florida!" he said with a big, bright, smile.

"I don't want to go to Florida."

"Really??? You were all about it last night."

"No I was not fucking all about it!!!"

"It doesn't matter," he said. "Here…drink this."

He then once again pulled a bottle of methadone out of his magic hat and handed it to me.

"Here's to a new start," he said as I opened the seal. "Bottom's up!"

"I don't want a new start."

"That's fine—just drink it anyway," he said with a smile and a twinkle in his eyes. "Just drink it anyway, Craigie."

Needle

340

The Aftermath

Initially, when I completed the first draft of NEEDLE, I intended to take this moment to discuss what became a very surreal recovery, which—like purgatory—is a realm of existence that lingers somewhere between two distinctly different worlds. However, whereas addiction is only one degree of separation removed from the chemically independent, recovery is at least two; therefore, it's impossible to accurately retell the experience in just a few paragraphs. But to be honest, I'm not even sure I ever truly recovered...at least in the clinical sense. In fact, I'm not sure *anyone* can ever truly recover from such a consuming and debilitating affliction—self-imposed or otherwise—and though I've managed to mostly abstain from indulging in any further opiate abuse, in a very specific way I believe I'll miss it for the rest of my life.

When I returned to Manhattan so many years after just barely escaping with my life, I confronted my demons in a borough that had changed dramatically under an elitist mayor with a hidden agenda; and what was once a place that inspired and supported starving artists as passionately as it did the corporate conquerors that invaded it, had somehow become a platform for avarice and arrogance as Manhattan was finally transformed into its own terrible stereotype. This urban metamorphosis inspired my own transformation, and as the self-installed mayor continued to provide safe harbor and fertile ground for the greedy to exploit the most vulnerable among us, I was consumed by an overwhelming passion to help improve the plight of abused and homeless animals which has become, along with my daughter, the focus of my life.

By the winter of 2012-13, a follow-up to NEEDLE will be available at www.NeedleUser.com. It will examine the fallout from a decade of opiate abuse as well as the resulting revelations as I gradually made sense of it all in a city that lost its soul. To be notified of this as well as any other future publications, please visit the website and join on us on Facebook and Twitter, or simply send an email to NeedleNews@yahoo.com. And of course, all profits from NEEDLE as well as any companion pieces will be used to fight animal cruelty and improve the lives of homeless pets, so if you enjoyed the book, please—help spread the word!

16456110R00204

Made in the USA
Lexington, KY
24 July 2012